From Body to Meaning in Culture

From Body to Meaning in Culture

Papers on cognitive semantic studies of Chinese

Ning Yu
University of Oklahoma

John Benjamins Publishing Company

Amsterdam / Philadelphia

^{TM} The paper used in this publication meets the minimum requirements of
American National Standard for Information Sciences – Permanence of
Paper for Printed Library Materials, ANSI z39.48-1984.

Library of Congress Cataloging-in-Publication Data

Yu, Ning, 1954-
    From body to meaning in culture : papers on cognitive semantic studies of Chinese /
        Ning Yu.
        p. cm.
    Includes bibliographical references and index.
    1. Chinese language--Semantics. I. Title. II. Title: Papers on cognitive semantic studies
        of Chinese.
    PL1291.Y85   2009
    495.1'5--dc22   2009007775
    ISBN 978 90 272 3262 5 (HB; alk. paper) ; ISBN 978 90 272 3263 2 (PB; alk. paper)

John Benjamins Publishing Co. · P.O. Box 36224 · 1020 ME Amsterdam · The Netherlands
John Benjamins North America · P.O. Box 27519 · Philadelphia PA 19118-0519 · USA

To my parents

Table of contents

Section 3.   Internal body organs in conceptualization

Preface

The papers collected in this volume were originally published in a period of 12 years, from 1995 to 2007. Their original publication was embedded in a larger academic context in which the notion of "embodiment" attracted a growing interest in Cognitive Linguistics and in cognitive science at large, as is testified by the publication of many monographs and edited volumes, not to mention many more journal articles and book chapters, on this topic (see, e.g., Berdayes, Esposito, and Murphy 2004; Blackman 2008; Csordas 1994; Frank et al. 2008; Gallagher 2005; Gibbs 2006; Johnson 2007; Lakoff and Johnson 1999; Lakoff and Núñez 2000; Sharifian et al. 2008; Strathern 1996; Varela, Thompson, and Rosch 1991; Weiss and Haber 1999; Ziemke, Zlatev, and Frank 2007).

The term *embodiment*, as suggested by the root of the word itself, has to do with the body, which is the existential grounds of the mind. That is, embodiment, as the very essence of human existence, is really about how the body is related to the mind in human experience and cognition. Scholars in cognitive science have already put forward a variety of programmatic theses for the embodiment paradigm including, for instance, the body being mindful, the body being in the mind, the body grounding the mind, the body extending the mind, the body enacting the mind, the body informing the mind, the body schematizing the mind, the body shaping the mind (Yu 2009: 26–27). In a general sense, the term *embodiment* attributes a more active and constructive role to the body in human cognition. As Lakoff and Johnson (1999) have argued, our mind is embodied in the profound sense that the very structure of our thoughts comes from the nature of our body.

While the body is an intimate reality to us, with basic physical structures, functions, and experiences common among all of us, the notion of "body", however, is a multifaceted concept that is culturally constructed, meaning quite different things across cultures, or even within cultures over history (see Yu 2009: 12–28). The meaning of the term *embodiment* has also been "stretched in different directions" (Strathern 1996: 196). There exist different theories of embodiment, often highly divergent from one another, and sometimes having very little in common (Rohrer 2006, 2007a; Violi 2004, 2008). For instance, Rohrer (2007a) lists as many as twelve different "important" senses of *embodiment*, which theorists often use, separately or in a conflated manner, with respect to human cognition (pp. 28–31). In its broadest definition, according to Rohrer (2007b), the embodiment hypothesis is the claim that human physical, cognitive, and social embodiment grounds our conceptual and linguistic systems. In his book titled *Embodiment and Cognitive Science*, Gibbs (2006: 9) outlines the following as the embodiment premise: "People's subjective, felt experiences of their bodies in action provide part of the fundamental grounding for language and thought. Cognition is what occurs when the body engages the physical, cultural world and must be studied in terms of the dynamical interactions between people and the environment". He asserts that human language and thought emerge from recurring patterns of embodied activity and are inextricably shaped by embodied action. He suggests that the key feature for understanding the embodied nature of human cognition is to "look for possible mind-body and language-body connections" (p. 9).

The chapters in this collection all attempt to demonstrate, from different angles, the language-body connections that may reflect, to some extent, the mind-body connections as manifested in the interaction between the body and the physical and cultural world. Although focusing on the linguistic evidence from Chinese language and culture, the chapters analyze within the cognitive semantic framework the conceptual and experiential basis of linguistic categories, which is of primary importance within Cognitive Linguistics in general (see Geeraerts and Cuyckens 2007). Collectively, they emphasize the primacy of semantics in linguistic analysis and reveal the encyclopedic and perspectival nature of linguistic meaning, which, according to Geeraerts and Cuyckens (2007), are fundamental characteristics of Cognitive Linguistics.

In this collection, some chapters have also taken up a cross-linguistic and cross-cultural perspective comparing Chinese with English. Exploring the bodily basis and cultural dynamics of language and thought, all the chapters, in one way or another, demonstrate how human meaning, which is often metonymic and metaphoric in nature, arises from the interaction between body and culture. While the body is a potentially universal source for metonymies and metaphors that structure abstract concepts and thoughts, cultural models also set up specific perspectives from which certain aspects of bodily experience or certain parts of the body are viewed as especially salient and meaningful in the understanding of those abstract concepts and thoughts and in different cultural values attached to them (see Gibbs 1999). The exploration of the bodily basis and cultural dynamics of language and thought can shed light on the universal and culture-specific aspects of cultural models that shape the dimensions of cognition (see, also, Dirven, Wolf, and Polzenhagen 2007).

The twelve chapters collected in this volume all deal with instances of cultural conceptualization, which is distributed, though unevenly, across the minds in a cultural group (Sharifian 2003, 2008). They are divided into three sections. The first section, consisting of four chapters, has the heading "Bodily experience in feeling and thinking". The chapters in this section together show how feeling and thinking are conceptualized and described in terms of bodily based metaphors in Chinese culture. In the light of Cognitive Linguistics' claim for the ubiquity of metaphor in everyday and literal language, these chapters also demonstrate the prominence of metaphor in the realms of abstract thought and emotional and aesthetic experiences as it emerges from the interplay of body and culture (Gibbs 2008; Kövecses 2005). Specifically, Chapters 1 and 2 study how the role of the body in emotional experiences and the impact of emotions on the body is conceptualized metaphorically in Chinese culture and manifested in the Chinese language. Chapter 3 is a semantic analysis of instances of synesthetic metaphors in literature, by which one sense modality is perceived and described in terms of another. It shows that human meaning and understanding are embodied, fundamentally constrained by the function of our body in the environment, and by the constitution of our sense organs. Chapter 4 takes up the study of Chinese metaphors of thinking. An analysis of the Chinese data manifesting two conceptual metaphors suggests that thinking is in part conceptualized in terms of our common bodily experience of spatial movement and vision. It also notes a case in which different cultural models interpret the functioning of the mind and the body differently.

The second section, with the heading "External Body Parts in Conceptualization", consists of five chapters. They focus on some terms of external body parts – "hand" and its subparts "finger" and "palm", "face" and its subparts "eye" and "mouth" – which contribute to the understanding of many abstract concepts. In all these cases, meaning derives from semantic extension of some basic bodily experiences through human imagination structured by metonymy and metaphor. They illustrate how our living body has served as a semantic template in the evolution of our language and thought.

The third section, "Internal Body Organs in Conceptualization", consists of three chapters, i.e. Chapters 10 to 12. They shift the focus to two internal body organs – "gallbladder" and "heart" – which are exceptionally significant in Chinese culture. In his recent book studying the deepest sources of human understanding, Johnson (2007: ix) argues that "meaning grows from our visceral connections to life and the bodily conditions of life". These chapters provide evidence supporting this claim. In Chinese culture, the gallbladder is traditionally conceptualized as the container of courage and as having the function of making judgments and decisions in mental processes and activities. Along this tradition, the heart is conceptualized as the central faculty of cognition and as the seat of both thoughts and feelings (see, also, Yu 2009).

All the chapters (except Chapter 9) in this collection are reprinted with permissions from the original publishers and in their original form. Chapter 9 has not been published previously and an earlier version of it was presented at the

10th International Cognitive Linguistics Conference held at Jagiellonian University, Krakow, Poland, July 2007.

I want to take this opportunity to thank many people who have vitally influenced my intellectual life in the past dozen of years during which these chapters were originally published. These are too many to list here, but they include Eugene H. Casad, Marcelo Dascal, René Dirven, Charles Forceville, Roslyn Frank, Raymond Gibbs, Mark Johnson, Zoltán Kövecses, George Lakoff, Ronald Langacker, Susanne Niemeier, Jan Nuyts, Gary Palmer, Günter Radden, and Farzad Sharifian. My thanks also go to the original publishers, who have generously granted me the permissions to reprint the original publications. I am gratefully indebted to Jan Reijer Groesbeek and Hanneke Bruintjes at John Bejamins Publishing Company for their editorial guidance and assistance in the preparation of this collection for publication.

References

Berdayes, Vicente, Luigi Esposito, and John W. Murphy (eds.). 2004. *The Body in Human Inquiry: Interdisciplinary Explorations of Embodiment*. Cresskill, NJ: Hampton Press.

Blackman, Lisa. 2008. *The Body*. Oxford/New York: Berg.

Csordas, Thomas J. (ed.). 1994. *Embodiment and Experience: The Existential Ground of Culture and Self*. Cambridge/New York: Cambridge University Press.

Dirven, René, Hans-Georg Wolf, and Frank Polzenhagen. 2007. Cognitive Linguistics and cultural studies. In *The Oxford Handbook of Cognitive Linguistics*, Dirk Geeraerts and Hubert Cuyckens (eds.), 1203–1221. Oxford/New York: Oxford University Press.

Frank, Roslyn M., René Dirven, Tom Ziemke, and Enrique Bernárdez (eds.). 2008. *Body, Language, and Mind (Vol. 2): Sociocultural Situatedness*. Berlin/New York: Mouton de Gruyter.

Gallagher, Shaun. 2005. *How the Body Shapes the Mind*. Oxford/New York: Oxford University Press.

Geeraerts, Dirk, and Hubert Cuyckens. 2007. Introducing Cognitive Linguistics. In *The Oxford Handbook of Cognitive Linguistics*, Dirk Geeraerts and Hubert Cuyckens (eds.), 3–21. Oxford/New York: Oxford University Press.

Gibbs, Raymond W. 1999. Taking metaphor out of our heads and putting it into the cultural world. In *Metaphor in Cognitive Linguistics*, Raymond W. Gibbs and Gerard J. Steen (eds.), 145–166. Amsterdam/Philadelphia: John Benjamins.

Gibbs, Raymond W. 2006. *Embodiment and Cognitive Science*. Cambridge/New York: Cambridge University Press.

Gibbs, Raymond W. (ed.). 2008. *The Cambridge Handbook of Metaphor and Thought*. Cambridge: Cambridge University Press.

Johnson, Mark. 2007. *The Meaning of the Body: Aesthetics of Human Understanding*. Chicago: University of Chicago Press.

Kövecses, Zoltán. 2005. *Metaphor in Culture: Universality and Variation*. Cambridge: Cambridge University Press.

Lakoff, George, and Mark Johnson. 1999. *Philosophy in the Flesh: The Embodied Mind and Its Challenge to Western Thought*. New York: Basic Books.

Lakoff, George, and Rafael Núñez. 2000. *Where Mathematics Comes From: How the Embodied Mind Brings Mathematics into Being*. New York: Basic Books.

Rohrer, Tim. 2006. Three dogmas of embodiment: Cognitive linguistics as a cognitive science. In *Cognitive Linguistics: Current Applications and Future Perspectives*, Gitte Kristiansen, Michel Achard, René Dirven, and Francisco J. Ruiz de Mendoza Ibáñez (eds.), 119–146. Berlin/New York: Mouton de Gruyter.

Rohrer, Tim. 2007a. The body in space: Dimensions of embodiment. In *Body, Language and Mind (Vol. 1): Embodiment*, Tom Ziemke, Jordan Zlatev, and Roslyn M. Frank (eds.), 339–377. Berlin/New York: Mouton de Gruyter.

Rohrer, Tim. 2007b. Embodiment and experientialism. In *The Oxford Handbook of Cognitive Linguistics*, Dirk Geeraerts and Hubert Cuyckens (eds.), 25–47. Oxford/New York: Oxford University Press.

Sharifian, Farzad. 2003. On cultural conceptualizations. *Journal of Cognition and Culture* 3: 187–207.

Sharifian, Farzad. 2008. Distributed, emergent cultural cognition, conceptualization and language. In *Body, Language, and Mind (Vol. 2): Sociocultural Situatedness*, Roslyn M. Frank, René Dirven, Tom Ziemke, and Enrique Bernárdez (eds.), 109–136. Berlin/New York: Mouton de Gruyter.

Sharifian, Farzad, René Dirven, Ning Yu, and Susanne Niemeier (eds.). 2008. *Culture, Body, and Language: Conceptualizations of Internal Body Organs across Cutlures and Languages*. Berlin/New York: Mouton de Gruyter.

Strathern, Andrew. 1996. *Body Thoughts*. Ann Arbor, MI: University of Michigan Press.

Varela, Francisco J., Evan Thompson, and Eleanor Rosch. 1991. *The Embodied Mind: Cognitive Science and Human Experience*. Cambridge, MA: The MIT Press.

Violi, Patrizia. 2004. Embodiment at the crossroads between cognition and semiosis. *Recherches en Communication* 19: 199–217.

Violi, Patrizia. 2008. Beyond the body: Towards a full embodied semiosis. In *Body, Language, and Mind (Vol. 2): Sociocultural Situatedness*, Roslyn M. Frank, René Dirven, Tom Ziemke, and Enrique Bernárdez (eds.), 53–76. Berlin/New York: Mouton de Gruyter.

Weiss, Gail, and Honi F. Haber (eds.). 1999. *Perspectives on Embodiment: The Intersections of Nature and Culture*. New York: Routledge.

Yu, Ning. 2009. *The Chinese HEART in a Cognitive Perspective: Culture, Body, and Language*. Berlin/New York: Mouton de Gruyter.

Ziemke, Tom, Jordan Zlatev, and Roslyn M. Frank (eds.). 2007. *Body, Language and Mind (Vol. 1): Embodiment*. Berlin/New York: Mouton de Gruyter.

Publication sources

Chapter 1 – Yu, Ning. 1995. Metaphorical expressions of anger and happiness in English and Chinese. *Metaphor and Symbolic Activity* 10(2), 59–92. (www.informaworld.com)

Chapter 2 – Yu, Ning. 2002. Body and emotion: Body parts in Chinese expression of emotion. In Nick Enfield and Anna Wierzbicka (eds.), special issue "The Body in Description of Emotion: Cross-Linguistic Studies". *Pragmatics and Cognition* 10(1/2), 341–367. (John Benjamins)

Chapter 3 – Yu, Ning. 2003. Synesthetic metaphor: A cognitive perspective. *Journal of Literary Semantics* 32(1), 19–34. (Mouton de Gruyter)

Chapter 4 – Yu, Ning. 2003. Chinese metaphors of thinking. In Gary B. Palmer, Cliff Goddard, and Penny Lee (eds.), special issue "Talking about Thinking across Languages". *Cognitive Linguistics* 14(2/3), 141–165. (Mouton de Gruyter)

Chapter 5 – Yu, Ning. 2003. The bodily dimension of meaning in Chinese: What do we do and mean with "hands"? In Eugene H. Casad and Gary B. Palmer (eds.), *Cognitive Linguistics and Non-Indo-European Languages*, 337–362. Berlin/New York: Mouton de Gruyter.

Chapter 6 – Yu, Ning. 2000. Figurative uses of *finger* and *palm* in Chinese and English. *Metaphor and Symbol* 15(3), 159–175. (www.informaworld.com)

Chapter 7 – Yu, Ning. 2001. What does our face mean to us? *Pragmatics and Cognition* 9(1), 1–36. (John Benjamins)

Chapter 8 – Yu, Ning. 2004. The eyes for sight and mind. *Journal of Pragmatics* 36(4), 663–686. (Elsevier Limited)

Chapter 9 – Yu, Ning. 2007. Speech organs and linguistic activity and function. Paper presented at the 10th International Cognitive Linguistics Conference held at Jagiellonian University, Krakow, Poland, July 2007.

Chapter 10 – Yu, Ning. 2003. Metaphor, body, and culture: The Chinese understanding of *gallbladder* and *courage*. *Metaphor and Symbol* 18(1), 13–31. (www.informaworld. com)

Chapter 11 – Yu, Ning. 2007. Heart and cognition in ancient Chinese philosophy. *Journal of Cognition and Culture* 7(1/2): 27–47. (Koninklijke Brill N. V.)

Chapter 12 – Yu, Ning. 2007. The Chinese conceptualization of the heart and its cultural context: Implications for second language learning. In Farzad Sharifian and Gary B. Palmer (eds.), *Applied Cultural Linguistics: Implications for Second Language Learning and Intercultural Communication*, 65–85. Amsterdam/Philadelphia: John Benjamins.

Bodily experience in feeling and thinking

CHAPTER 1

Metaphorical expressions of anger and happiness in English and Chinese

This article presents a comparative study of metaphorical expressions of anger and happiness in English and Chinese. It demonstrates that English and Chinese share the same central conceptual metaphor ANGER IS HEAT, which then breaks into two subversions in both languages. Whereas English has selected FIRE and FLUID metaphors, Chinese uses FIRE and GAS for the same purpose. Similarly, both English and Chinese share the UP, LIGHT, and CONTAINER metaphors in their conceptualizations of happiness, although they differ in some other cases. These two languages also follow the same metonymic principle in talking about anger and happiness by describing the physiological effects of these emotions. A descriptive difference observed throughout the study, however, is that Chinese tends to utilize more body parts, especially internal organs, than English in its metaphors of anger, happiness, and other emotional states. A principled explanation of the difference observed throughout the study, however, is that Chinese tends to utilize more body parts, especially internal organs, than English in its metaphors of anger, happiness, and other emotional states. A principled explanation of the differences between the two languages is then made on the basis of referring to the theories of yin-yang and of the five elements of Chinese medicine. These theories form a cognitive or cultural model underlying the metaphorical conceptualization in Chinese. This study shows that metaphors of anger and happiness are primarily based on common bodily experience, with surface differences across languages explainable from cultural perspectives. It also provides empirical evidence, from a language other than English, to support the claim that metaphor is essential in human understanding, meaning, and reasoning.

1. Introduction

The study of metaphor has a very long history. Traditionally, metaphor is viewed as a matter of special or extraordinary language – a set of deviant linguistic expressions whose meaning is reducible to some set of literal propositions. Viewed as such, it is called "a figure of *speech*," and its study was confined mostly to rhetoric. This view can be traced back as early as Aristotle, who believed metaphor to be primarily decorative and ornamental in nature. According to this view, metaphors are not necessary; they are just nice. The more popular current approach, however, views metaphor as pervasive and essential in language and thought (e.g., Johnson, 1987; Lakoff, 1987, 1990, 1993; Lakoff & Johnson, 1980, 1980). It is, as Lakoff (1986) argued, not just a way of naming, but also a way of thinking; it is a figure of *thought* as well as a figure of speech. On this view, a metaphor "is a process by which we understand and structure one domain of experience in terms of another domain *of a different kind*" (Johnson, 1987, p. 15). Hence, the study of metaphor is central not only to rhetoric but also to the study of language and cognition in general.

Language is part of culture. Metaphor is one of the most important features in language that reflects cognitive vision and epitomizes cultural context. The cross-language study of metaphor, therefore, should shed much light on cross-cultural similarities and dissimilarities in ways of thinking and speaking. However, this area of study has remained almost uncultivated and this article represents an initial effort in the area.

Extensive studies have been made on the function of metaphor in the conceptualization of emotions in English (Fesmire, 1994; Kövecses, 1986, 1988, 1990, 1991; Lakoff, 1987; Lakoff & Johnson, 1980; Lakoff & Kövecses, 1987). A central claim of these studies is that human emotions, which are abstract in nature, are largely understood and expressed in metaphorical terms. Although this claim is meant to be universal, the evidence supporting it is mainly derived from English. The question remains as to whether, and to what extent, the claim could hold up in other languages. This article intends to provide an answer from Chinese. To do this, I make a cross-language study of metaphor to see how English and Chinese are similar and different in metaphorical expressions of anger and happiness. My comparative study is based mainly on Lakoff and Johnson (1980), Lakoff and Kövecses (1987), and Kövecses (1991), from which the English examples are taken. I also demonstrate an underlying model in Chinese culture that can offer a principled explanation of the differences between English and Chinese.

2.   Metaphorical conceptualization of anger

In English, according to Lakoff and Kövecses (1987), "The cultural model of physiological effects, especially the part that emphasizes HEAT, forms the basis of the most general metaphor for anger: ANGER IS HEAT" (p. 197). As Lakoff and Kövecses suggest, however, this central metaphor has two versions in English: one in which heat is applied to solids and the other in which it is applied to fluids. When ANGER IS HEAT is applied to solids, the version of metaphor is ANGER IS FIRE. Under this metaphorical concept, there is a large group of metaphorical expressions that encode and elaborate the general concept in one way or another. For instance:

(1) a. Those are inflammatory remarks.
    b. She was doing a slow burn.
    c. He was breathing fire.
    d. Your insincere apology just added fuel to the fire.
    e. After the argument, Dave was smoldering for days.
    f. Boy, am I burned up!
    g. Smoke was pouring out of his ears.

This kind of systematic conceptualization of emotion in metaphorical terms is not specific to English. It is also true in Chinese. I have found that the general metaphorical concept that ANGER IS HEAT is exactly applicable in Chinese and that it also yields two subversions. When ANGER IS HEAT is applied to solids in Chinese, we get exactly the same metaphorical concept as ANGER IS FIRE, of which the metaphorical expressions are all quite conventionalized.[1]

(2) a. 别惹我发火。
    Bie re   wo fa-huo.
    don't provoke me shoot-fire
    'Don't set me on fire (i.e. Don't cause me to lose my temper).'

    b. 他正在火头上。
    Ta zheng-zai huo tou shang.
    he right-at fire head on
    'He's at the height of flare (i.e. on the top of his anger).'

    c. 你在火上加油。
    Ni zai huo shang jia you.
    you PRT fire on   add oil
    'You're pouring oil on the fire.'

    d. 那家伙怎么这么大火?
    Nei jiahuo zenme zheme da huo?
    that guy how so   big fire
    'How come that guy's got such a big fire (i.e. so hot-tempered)?'

---

1.   In this article, the Chinese examples are provided with a word-for-word gloss and an English translation. In the gloss, the following abbreviations are used: ASP = aspect marker, PRT = particle, MOD = modifier marker, COM = complement marker, CL = classifier, and BA = preposition *ba* in the so-called *ba*-sentences. In the English translation, two versions are given where possible or necessary, the first being more literal and the second, more idiomatic.

e. 他肝火很旺。
    Ta gan-huo hen wang.
    he liver-fire very roaring
    'He's got a roaring fire in his liver (i.e. He's hot-tempered).'

f. 他大动肝火。
    Ta da   dong gan-hou.
    he greatly move liver-fire
    'He got flamed up in liver (i.e. flew into a rage).'

g. 他心火正旺。
    Ta xin-huo   zheng wang.
    he heart-fire PRT   roaring
    'He's having a roaring fire in his heart (i.e. He's very angry).'

h. 他心头火起。
    Ta xin-tou   huo qi.
    he heart-head fire flare-up
    'Fire started to flare up in his heart (i.e. He flared up with anger).'

i. 他压不住心头怒火。
    Ta ya-buzhu   xin-tou   nu-huo.
    ta press-unable heart-head angry-fire
    'He was unable to control the angry fire in his heart (i.e. unable to control his anger).'

j. 他满腔怒火。
    Ta man qiang nu-huo.
    he full cavity angry-fire
    'His thoracic cavity is full of angry fire (i.e. He's filled with anger).'

k. 他气得七窍生烟。
    Ta qi   de   qi-qiao   sheng yan.
    he get-angry COM seven-aperture emit smoke
    'He was so angry that smoke was shooting out of his eyes, ears, nose and mouth (i.e. He was fuming with anger).'

l. 他窝了一肚子火。
    Ta wo   le yi duzi huo.
    she hold-in PRT one belly fire
    'She held in a belly of fire (i.e. She was simmering with rage).'

m. 他怒火中烧。
    Ta nu-huo   zhong shao.
    he angry-fire middle burn
    'He has angry fire burning inside him (i.e. He's burning with anger).'

n. 他火冒三丈。

Ta huo mao san   zhang.

he fire rise three zhang

'His fire (i.e. anger) is flaming up as high as ten meters.'

o. 他怒火万丈。

Ta nu-huo   wan   zhang.

he angry-fire ten-thousand *zhang*

'His angry fire is over thirty-three thousand meters high.'

Although English and Chinese share exactly the same conceptual metaphor AN-GER IS FIRE, the actual linguistic expressions they use for the conceptualization may be similar or different. In both languages, the emotion of anger is conceptualized as a destructive force that may be harmful not only to the angry people but also to people around them.

Descriptively, a difference between English and Chinese is that Chinese tends to use more body-part words in its conventionalized phrases of anger, as is illustrated by (2e–l). In these examples, the internal organs – heart and liver, as well as thoracic cavity and belly – are specified as places where "fire burns" when one gets angry. Also, the seven apertures in the head are conceptualized, in (2k), as the outlets of anger when it gets intense. Intuitively or medically, excessive anger will hurt one's body, especially certain parts of the body. For now, I would suggest that the use of body parts for the conceptualization of anger in Chinese provides a piece of evidence supporting the claim that metaphor of emotions cross-linguistically is grounded in bodily or physiological experience. Later I show how this is true.

The second version of ANGER IS HEAT in English, according to Lakoff and Kövecses (1987), is ANGER IS THE HEAT OF A FLUID IN A CONTAINER, as the following linguistic metaphors show:

(3) a. You make my blood boil.
     b. Simmer down.
     c. I had reached the boiling point.
     d. Let me stew.
     e. She was seething with rage.
     f. She got all steamed up.
     g. Billy's just blowing off steam.
     h. He flipped his lid.
     i. He blew his top.

In contrast to the second English version where ANGER IS HEAT is applied to fluids, the Chinese alternative version is applied to gases, and the conceptual metaphor thus derived is ANGER IS THE HOT GAS IN A CONTAINER. This metaphorical concept is actually based on our commonsense knowledge of the physical world: When gas closed up in a container is *heated*, it will expand and cause increasing *internal pressure* to the container, with an ultimate consequence of explosion. This process of physical reaction is exemplified in the following conventionalized expressions grouped under the GAS metaphor:

(4)   a.   我可受不了这份窝囊气。
     Wo   ke   shou   bu-liao   zhe-fen   wo-nang   qi.
     I   PRT receive   unable   this-kind   hold-in-bag   gas
     'I really can't bear this kind of bagged gas (i.e. bear being subjected to this kind of annoyances).'

   b.   你又在气我了。
     Ni   you   zai   qi   wo   le.
     you   again   PRT   gas   me   PRT
     'You're again gassing /pumping me up (i.e. getting me angry again).'

   c.   他脾气很大。
     Ta   pi-qi   hen   da.
     he   spleen-gas   very   big
     'He's got big gas in spleen (i.e. is hot-tempered).'

   d.   你又发脾气了。
     Ni   you   fa   pi-qi   le.
     you   again   expand   spleen-gas   PRT
     'You again expanded the gas in spleen (i.e. got angry).'

   e.   我心气不顺。
     Wo   xin-qi   bu   shun.
     I   heart-gas   not   smooth
     'I'm feeling the gas in heart is impeded (i.e. feeling unhappy).'

   f.   他心中有气。
     Ta   xin-zhong   you   qi.
     he   heart-inside   have   gas
     'He has gas (anger) in his heart.'

   g.   他最近肝气郁结。
     Ta   zuijin   gan-qi   yujie.
     he   recently   liver-gas   pent-up
     'He's been irritable recently.'

h. 他憋了一肚子气。

Ta bie   le yi duzi qi.

he hold-back PRT one belly gas

'He held back a belly of gas (i.e. was filled with pent-up anger).'

i. 他在生闷气。

Ta zai sheng-men-qi.

he PRT produce-contained-gas

'He's producing contained gas (i.e. sulky).'

j. 他气鼓鼓的。

Ta qi-gugu   de.

he gas-inflate PRT

'He's ballooned with gas (i.e. inflated with anger).'

k. 他气乎乎的。

Ta qi-huhu   de.

he gas-puff-and-blow PRT

'He's puffing and blowing with gas (i.e. gasping with anger).'

l. 他气势汹汹。

Ta qi-shi   xiongxiong.

he gas-force surge-surge

'His fierce air is surging higher and higher (i.e. He's blustering with rage).'

m. 他怒气冲冲。

Ta nu-qi   chongchong.

he angry-gas soar-soar

'His angry gas is soaring and soaring (i.e. He's in a state of fury).'

n. 他拿我出气。

Ta na   wo chu-qi.

he take me vent-gas

'He took his gas out on me (i.e. vented his anger on me).'

o. 他怒气冲天。

Ta nu-qi   chong-tian.

he angry-gas soar-sky

'His angry gas is gushing into the sky (i.e. He's in a towering rage).'

Here, gas is mapped onto the emotion of anger. Therefore, it can be "received" or "pumped" into a container in (4a–b). It has its volume, "big" in (4c), and can be 'expanded' in (4d). This will increase the internal pressure to the container, as in (4e–j). The force of the contained gas can be very strong, as in (4k–m), 'surging' upward as hot gas always does. When increasing the internal pressure, the gas has to exhaust through some outlet, as in (4n), or it may lead to explosion, as in (4o).

Although FLUID and GAS are very different source domains, they share some basic metaphorical entailments which, according to Lakoff and Kövecses (1987), are details of knowledge carried over from the source domain to the target domain. It is the identity of these entailments, which include HEAT, INTERNAL PRESSURE, and POTENTIAL AND DANGER OF EXPLOSION, that makes it possible for them to be carried over from different source domains (FLUID and GAS) to the same target domain (ANGER). Although only INTERNAL PRESSURE is highlighted in the GAS metaphors, as in (4), HEAT is understood from the common sense: The internal pressure of gas to its container is increased by the increasing heat.

Again, as (4c–h) show, Chinese seems to use more body-part nouns than does English in the conceptualization of anger in terms of gas. Also, it is interesting to note that, when the GAS metaphor is used, the associated internal organs are liver, heart, and spleen, as shown in (4c–g).[2] Of these three, liver and heart also appear in the FIRE metaphors, but spleen never does.

In addition to the general metaphorical concept ANGER IS HEAT, Lakoff and Kövecses (1987) suggested that, governed by the common cultural model, English also makes use of a general metonymic principle: THE PHYSIOLOGICAL EFFECTS OF AN EMOTION STAND FOR THE EMOTION.

With this principle, the cultural model yields a system of metonymies for anger:

(5)   BODY HEAT
    a. Don't get hot under the collar.
    b. Billy's a hothead.
    c. They were having a heated argument.
    d. When the cop gave her a ticket, she got all hot and bothered and started cursing.

    INTERNAL PRESSURE
    e. When I found out, I almost burst a blood vessel.
    f. He almost had a hemorrhage.

    REDNESS IN FACE AND NECK AREA
    g. She was scarlet with rage.
    h. She got red with anger.
    i. He was flushed with anger.

---

2.   I am aware of the interesting fact that spleen is also used in the metaphorical expression of anger in English. The examples are: *He was in a fit of spleen* and *He vented his spleen on me.* However, these are no longer common expressions, and hence not comparable to the Chinese SPLEEN metaphors, which are indispensable in everyday use.

AGITATION

j.   She was shaking with anger.

k.   I was hopping mad.

l.   He was quivering with rage.

INTERFERENCE WITH ACCURATE PERCEPTION

m.   She was blind with rage.

n.   I was beginning to see red.

o.   I was so mad I couldn't see straight.

Apparently, Chinese observes the same metonymic principle, and similar metonymic expressions are found common in everyday use. For instance:

(6)   BODY HEAT

a.   我气得脸上火辣辣的。
     Wo qi   de   lian-shang huo-lala de.
     I   gas COM face-on   fire-hot PRT
     'I got so angry that my face was peppery hot.'

     INTERNAL PRESSURE

b.   别把肺给气炸了。
     Bie   ba   fei   gei   qi   zha   le.
     don't PRT lung PRT gas explode PRT
     'Don't burst your lungs with gas (rage).'

c.   别气破了肚皮。
     Bie   qi   po   le   du-pi.
     don't gas break PRT belly-skin
     'Don't break your belly skin with gas (rage).'

d.   他额角上暴起了青筋。
     Ta   ejiao   shang baoqi le   qing jin
     he   temple on   bulge PRT blue vein
     'Blue veins stood out on his temples.'

     REDNESS IN FACE AND NECK AREA

e.   他们争得个个面红耳赤。
     Tamen zheng de   gege   mian-hong-er-chi.
     they   argue COM everyone face-red-ear-red
     'They argued until everyone became red in the face and ears.'

f. 他们争得面红脖子粗。

    Tamen zheng de   lian-hong-bozi-cu.

    they   argue COM face-red-neck-thick

    'They argued until their faces turned red and their necks became thicker.'

g. 他气得脸上红一阵，白一阵，青一阵，紫一阵。

    Ta qi de   lian-shang hong-yi-zhen, bai-yi-zhen,

    he gas COM face-on   red-a-while   white-a-while

    qing-yi-zhen, zi-yi-zhen.

    blue-a-while purple-a-while

    'He was so angry that her face turned red, pale, blue, and purple.'

AGITATION

h. 他怒发冲冠。

    Ta nu   fa   chong   guan.

    he angry hair push-up hat

    'His angry hair is pushing up his hat (i.e. He is extremely angry).'

i. 他气得两眼瞪得溜圆。

    Ta qi de   liang yan deng de   liuyuan.

    he gas COM two eye glare COM very-round

    'He was so angry that his eyes glared until they became very round (or his eyes were round with anger).'

j. 他气得竖眉瞪眼。

    Ta qi de   shu-mei   deng-yan.

    she gas COM upright-brow glare-eye

    'She was angry with upright brows and glaring eyes.'

k. 他气得吹胡子瞪眼睛。

    Ta qi de   chui-huzi   deng-yanjing.

    he gas COM blow-moustache glare-eye

    'He was so angry that he was blowing his mustache and opening his eyes wide.'

l. 他气得浑身发抖。

    Ta qi de   hun-shen   fadou.

    she gas COM whole-body tremble

    'Her body was shaking all over with rage."

m. 他气得双手颤抖。

    Ta qi de   shuang-shou chandou.

    he gas COM both-hands quiver

    'His hands were quivering with anger.'

n. 他气得直跺脚。

Ta qi de zhi duo-jiao.

he gas COM constantly stamp-foot

'He kept stamping his feet with rage.'

o. 他气得咬牙切齿。

Ta qi de yao-ya-qie-chi.

he gas COM gnash-teeth

'He was gnashing her teeth with anger.'

INTERFERENCE WITH ACCURATE PERCEPTION

p. 我气得两眼发黑。

Wo qi de liang yan fa hei.

I gas COM two eye become black

'I was so angry that my eyes turned blind.'

q. 我气得头昏眼花。

Wo qi de tou-hun yan-hua.

I gas COM head-giddy eye-blurred

'I was so angry that my head became giddy and my vision blurred.'

From these English and Chinese examples, we can see that the metonymic expressions for the emotion of anger are very similar between the two languages. This is expected because, as is assumed, these expressions are primarily based on bodily experience that should be universal among all human beings. As some examples show, however, cultural models do enter and influence the selection of linguistic expressions for a particular physical experience. This is well illustrated by the contrast between (5n) and (6p), which both express the interference of anger with visual perception. The English example selects "*see red*" but the Chinese one selects "*see black*." However, the physiological effects of anger they refer to should be the same among speakers of both languages.

A most remarkable descriptive difference between English and Chinese, as manifested in (5) and (6), is again that Chinese tends to specify more body parts in its conventionalized linguistic expressions of anger than English does. In (5), only "head" and "vessel" are specified in two of the 15 English examples. In contrast, all 17 Chinese examples in (6) specify one or two body parts, which include "face" (four times), "eyes" (five times), "lungs," "belly skin," "temples," "veins," "ears," "neck," "hair," "brows," "mustache," "hands," "feet," "teeth," "head," and the whole "body." In short, both English and Chinese make use of body parts in their conventionalized expressions of anger; the difference between them seems to be that body parts tend to be implied in English, whereas they are expressed in Chinese.

In summary, both English and Chinese use the central conceptual metaphor ANGER IS HEAT, as (1), (2), (3), and (4) have shown. For English, its two subversions are (a) ANGER IS FIRE and (b) ANGER IS THE HEAT OF A FLUID IN A CONTAINER. For Chinese, however, they are (a) ANGER IS FIRE and (b) ANGER IS THE HOT GAS IN A CONTAINER. Also, as (5) and (6) show, both languages observe the same metonymic principle, describing the emotion of anger by referring to its related physiological effects.

It needs to be noted, however, that there is a very important difference between Chinese and English in the use of the HEAT metaphor. The difference can be described as follows in Figure 1. In Figure 1, the capitalized words refer to abstract concepts, whereas the italicized words are lexical items. In English, FIRE and FLUID, the source domains, are mapped onto ANGER, the target domain, with the arrowbeads of the lines indicating the direction of the mapping. At the lexical level, however, there exists a difference between the word *fire* and the word *fluid*. The word *fire* has acquired its metaphorical meaning of "anger." Different from *fire*, the word *fluid* itself does not have such a metaphorical sense (hence "?"), whereas the conceptual matching between FLUID and ANGER is realized by those lexical items associated with FLUID (*boil, simmer, stew, seething, steamed,* etc.). In either case, however, the word *anger* is a more basic lexical item that names the ANGER concept literally. On the other hand, in Chinese, the two source domains that are mapped onto the target domain ANGER are FIRE and GAS. At the lexical level, both words *huo* 'fire' and *qi* 'gas' refer metaphorically to the ANGER concept, but they seem to have no literal counterpart that is more basic and equivalent to the English word *anger*.

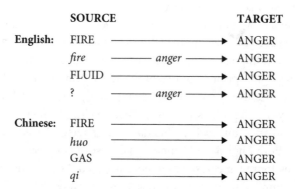

Figure 1. An important difference between English and Chinese in the conceptualization of anger

It also needs to be noted that, although the Chinese words *fen* and *nu* (both meaning 'indignation', 'rage', 'fury', and 'anger') are literal lexical items for the emotion of anger, they are different from *huo* 'fire' and *qi* 'gas' in shades of sense and style and are, by far, less common words which cannot substitute for *huo* 'fire' and *qi* 'gas' most of the time. In fact, *huo* 'fire' and *qi* 'gas' are the most basic words referring to the emotion of anger in Chinese. This seems to suggest that to a greater extent the emotion of anger is understood and expressed metaphorically in Chinese. For this reason, *huo* 'fire' and *qi* 'gas' are so conventionalized metaphors for anger in Chinese that they appear more literal than metaphorical to native speakers of Chinese. It is worth mentioning that the words *huo* 'fire' and *qi* 'gas' are highly derivational, and they form compounds with other words. In Chinese, for instance, *fa-huo* 'shoot-fire', *nao-huo* 'irritate-fire', *dong-huo* 'move-fire', *mao-huo* 'emit-fire', *guang-huo* 'light-fire', *shang-huo* 'raise-fire', *gua-huo* 'hang-fire', *sheng-qi* 'produce-gas', *dong-qi* 'move-gas', *gua-qi* 'hang-gas', and so forth all mean "get angry" in daily use.

Based on the examples collected in Chinese, it may be assumed that the selection of internal organs in the conventionalized metaphors of anger is not random. Specifically, only liver and heart are found in the FIRE metaphors, whereas liver, heart, and spleen appear in the GAS metaphors. In a later section, I try to answer some basic questions as to why in Chinese the GAS rather than FLUID metaphor is selected, why Chinese tends to use more internal organs, and why certain internal organs are chosen over others in the anger metaphors.

3.   Metaphorical conceptualization of happiness

According to Lakoff and Johnson (1980) and Kövecses (1991), a major conceptual metaphor for the notion of happiness in English is orientational: HAPPY IS UP. Under this metaphorical concept some of the metaphorical expressions are:

(7) a. I'm feeling up.
    b. That boosted my spirits.
    c. My spirits rose.
    d. Thinking about her always gives me a lift.
    e. We had to cheer him up.
    f. They were in high spirits.

Chinese shares exactly the same metaphorical concept and has a number of conventionalized lexical expressions that express happiness in terms of an upward orientation. Again, most of them are so conventionalized that they are no longer taken as metaphorical.

(8) a.   他很高兴。
          Ta hen gao-xing.
          he very high-spirit
          'He is very high-spirited (happy).'

     b.   他很兴奋。
          Ta hen xing-fen.
          he very spirit-lift
          'He is very spirit-lifted (excited).'

     c.   他处于亢奋状态之中。
          Ta chu-yu   kang-fen zhuangtai zhizhong.
          he situate-in high-lift state   inside
          'He is in the state of high liftedness (i.e. extreme excitement).'

     d.   他们情绪高涨。
          Tamen qingxu gao-zhang.
          they   mood   high-rise
          'Their spirits are running high.'

     e.   他们个个情绪高扬。
          Tamen gege   qingxu gao-yang.
          they   everyone mood   high-raise
          'They're all in high-raised spirits (i.e. high in spirits).'

     f.   他们个个兴高采烈。
          Tamen gege   xing-gao cai-lie.
          they   everyone spirit-high color-strong
          'They're all in high spirits and with a strong glow (in great delight).'

     g.   他兴冲冲的。
          Ta xing chongchong de.
          he spirit rise-rise   PRT
          'His spirits are rising and rising (i.e. He's pleased and excited).'

     h.   他兴头很高。
          Ta xing-tou   hen gao.
          he spirit-head very high
          'The head of his spirits is very high (i.e. He's in high spirits).'

     i.   他正在兴头上。
          Ta zheng zai xing-tou   shang.
          he PRT   at spirit-head on
          'He is at the head (height) of his spirits.'

j. 这下提起了我的兴致。
   Zhe-xia   tiqi   le   wo-de xingzhi.
   this-moment raise ASP my   mood
   'This time it lifted my mood (or interest).'

k. 他得意扬扬。
   Ta deyi   yangyang.
   he complacency raise-raise
   'He looked triumphant."

l. 他扬扬自得。
   Ta yangyang zi-de
   he raise-raise self-pride
   'He looked immensely proud of himself.'

Obviously, the data from Chinese support the claim that metaphorical orientations are not arbitrary, but have a basis in the physical and cultural experience (Lakoff & Johnson, 1980). It is apparent that English and Chinese are very similar in this aspect, that is, the concept HAPPY is oriented UP while SAD or UNHAPPY is oriented DOWN.[3]

However, there cannot always be a one-to-one relationship between English and Chinese due to cultural differences. In English, according to Kövecses (1991),

---

3. In English the SAD/UNHAPPY IS DOWN metaphors include:

(i) a. I'm feeling down.
    b. He's really low these days.
    c. I fell into a depression.
    d. My spirits sank.

In Chinese, however, the concept SAD/UNHAPPY IS DOWN has a twin version: SAD/UNHAPPY IS HEAVY. These two can be used separately, or in combination, as the following examples show:

(ii) a. 他情绪低落。
     Ta qingxu di-luo.
     he   mood   low-sink
     'He's feeling low and down.'

   b. 他心情沉重。
     Ta xin-qing   chen-zhong.
     he heart-state weighty-heavy
     'He is in a heavy state of mind (i.e. has a heavy heart).'

   c. 他情绪低沉。
     Ta qingxu di-chen.
     he   mood low-weighty
     'He's feeling down and heavy.'

The coherence of the DOWN and HEAVY metaphors is intuitively supported by our physical experience: What is heavy tends to be down, and vice versa.

closely related to the HAPPY IS UP metaphor is another conceptual metaphor of upward orientation: BEING HAPPY IS BEING OFF THE GROUND. Instances of this type include:

(9)   a.   I was flying high.
      b.   She was on cloud nine.
      c.   I'm six feet off the ground.
      d.   We were in the clouds.
      e.   I was just soaring with happiness.
      f.   After the exam, I was walking on air for days.
      g.   They were riding high.
      h.   I was floating.

However, the metaphorical concept BEING HAPPY IS BEING OFF THE GROUND does not seem to be applicable in Chinese. I think the reason for the difference is that in Chinese, although BEING HAPPY IS BEING UP, this upward orientation has its upper limit. It is desirable only when it reaches as high, and stays in the air as long, as one can "jump" or "leap," as shown in (17a–c) below; that is, being momentarily off the ground. It follows that being sustainedly off the ground is undesirable: It is not mapped positively onto happiness but negatively onto complacency and pride. Thus, when the Chinese say 他飘飘然 *Ta piaopiaoran* 'He's floating,' or 他又在云里雾里了 *Ta you zai yunli-wuli le* "He is again in clouds and fog," it means that the person is so smug that he has lost his senses. This is contrary to the accepted virtues of modesty and steadiness. The Chinese believe in the saying 得意不能忘形 *Deyi buneng wangxing* 'When complacent, one should not forget one's manner (Don't let complacency turns one's head)' and 脚踏实地 *jiao ta shi di* 'One should have one's feet planted on solid ground (Be earnest and down-to-earth).' Being sustainedly off the ground is seen, in this culture, as being out of self-control and, therefore, is not good. Although happiness should be oriented upward, it should also be 'well-grounded.'

The following lexical examples, which form a complimentary-derogatory contrast, should provide some indirect linguistic evidence in support of the claim that being sustainedly off the ground is not so desirable in Chinese:

(10)   Complimentary compounds meaning "steady and firm":
      a.   稳重   *wen-zhong* 'stable and heavy'
      b.   持重   *chi-zhong* 'steady and heavy
      c.   沉稳   *chen-wen* 'weighty and stable'

Derogatory compounds meaning "frivolous and superficial":
- d. 轻浮   *qing-fu* 'light and floating'
- e. 轻飘   *qing-piao* 'light and drifting'
- f. 飘浮   *piao-fu* 'drifting and floating'

Here the words in (10a–c) all have semantic features of [+ downward] and [+ on-the-ground], whereas those in (10d–f) are featured by [+ upward] and [+ off-the-ground]. The complimentary-derogatory contrast, as I tend to believe, reflects the established values in Chinese culture.

Although some English metaphorical concepts such as BEING HAPPY IS BEING OFF THE GROUND are not applicable in Chinese, Chinese also has some that are not applicable in English. An example is HAPPINESS IS FLOWERS IN THE HEART. For instance:

(11)   a.   他心里乐开了花。
         Ta xin-li   *le*   *kai*   *le*   *hua.*
         he   heart-inside   happy   bloom   PRT   flower
         'He's so happy that flowers are blooming in her heart.'

      b.   他心花怒放。
         Ta xin-hua   *nu-fang.*
         he   heart-flower   wildly-bloom
         'Flowers are blossoming wildly in his heart.'

In these two examples, flowers are mapped onto happiness, with "blooming" or "blossoming" suggesting its increasing intensity. This metaphorical concept, though a minor one, is rooted in Chinese culture in which flowers, particularly "big red flowers" (大红花 *da hong hua*), are traditionally symbols of happiness. From a cultural perspective, this FLOWER metaphor reflects the more introverted character of the Chinese: Reactions to happiness in the heart are highlighted. This serves as a contrast to the English BEING HAPPY IS BEING OFF THE GROUND metaphor that characterizes a more extroverted character.

According to Kövecses (1991), another major metaphorical concept of happiness in English is HAPPINESS IS LIGHT, under which the metaphorical expressions are, for instance:

(12)   a.   When she heard the news, she lit up.
      b.   Nothing to worry about, brighten up.
      c.   He radiates joy.
      d.   She has a sunny smile.
      e.   You are the sunshine in my life.
      f.   He was gleaming.
      g.   She was shining with joy.

HAPPINESS IS LIGHT is also applicable in Chinese, as illustrated by the following examples, in which (13a) is a repetition of (8f) cited in the group of the UP metaphors earlier:

(13) a. 他们个个兴高采烈。
> *Tamen gege   xing-gao   cai-lie.*
> they   everyone spirit-high glow-strong
> 'They're all in high spirits and with a strong glow (i.e. in great delight).'

 b. 他容光焕发，喜气洋洋。
> *Ta rong-guang huanfa, xi-qi   yangyang.*
> he face-light   glow   happy-air vast-vast
> 'He has a glowing face, and a strong air of happiness.'

 c. 他喜形于色。
> *Ta xi   xing yu se.*
> he happiness show in color
> 'His happiness showed in his (facial) color.'

 d. 他笑逐颜开。
> *Ta xiao zhu yan   kai.*
> he smile drive color beam
> 'He smiled, which caused his face to beam (i.e. beamed with a smile).'

 e. 他喜笑颜开。
> *Ta xi-xiao   yan-kai.*
> he happy-smile color-beam
> 'He smiled happily, her face beaming (i.e. beamed with a happy smile).'

It is worth mentioning here that the word *yan* in (13d–e) means both "color" and "face," or rather, "happy glowing face" in Chinese. A relevant and important fact is that *yan*, when it means "face," is always used, asymmetrically, in a happy but never unhappy sense. Thus, one can say *xiao yan* 'smiling face,' but not *ku yan* 'crying face.' In contrast, with *lian*, another word meaning 'face,' the asymmetry in usage is not existent. So one can say, for instance, both *xiao lian* 'smiling face' and *ku lian* 'crying face.'

From (12) and (13), it is apparent that both English and Chinese depict happiness in terms of LIGHT. It is predictable that they both also conceptualize unhappiness or sadness in terms of DARK.[4]

A third major metaphor conceptualizing happiness is the CONTAINER type, namely HAPPINESS/JOY IS A FLUID IN A CONTAINER. The conventionalized linguistic expressions encoding this conceptual metaphor in English include:

(14) a. We were full of joy.
　　　b. The sight filled them with joy.
　　　c. I brimmed over with joy when I saw her.
　　　d. She couldn't contain her joy any longer.
　　　e. Joy welled up inside her.
　　　f. He was overflowing with joy.
　　　g. My heart is filled with joy.

In a similar vein, Chinese also applied the CONTAINER metaphor in its expression of happy feeling, which is mapped onto FLUID in the CONTAINER:

(15) a. 他心中充满喜悦。
　　　　　Ta xin-zhong　chongman xiyue.
　　　　　he heart-inside fill　　　happiness
　　　　　'His heart is filled with happiness.'
　　　b. 他满心欢喜。
　　　　　Ta man-xin huanxi.
　　　　　he full-heart joy
　　　　　'His heart is full of joy.'

4.　For SADNESS/UNHAPPINESS IS DARK, examples in English and Chinese include:
　　(i)　a.　He's feeling overcast.
　　　　b.　He's feeling gloomy.
　　　　c.　He's in a dark temper.
　　(ii)　a.　他情绪阴郁。
　　　　　　Ta　qingxu　yinyu.
　　　　　　he　mood　gloomy
　　　　　　'He's feeling gloomy.'
　　　　b.　她黯然泪下。
　　　　　　Ta　anran　lei　xia.
　　　　　　she　dim/faint　tears　down
　　　　　　'She felt gloomy/dim and burst into tears.'

   c. 她再也按捺不住心中的喜悦。

     Ta zai-ye   anna-buzhu xin-zhong   de   xiyue.

     she no-longer press-unable heart-inside MOD happiness

     'She could no longer contain the joy in her heart.'

   d. 喜悦之情如泉水流入她的心里。

     Xiyue zhi   qing   ru quan-shui   liu   ru

     joy   MOD feeling like spring-water flow into

     tade xin-li.

     her   heart-inside

     'The feeling of joy flowed into her heart like spring water (welled into her heart).'

   e. 他满怀喜悦。

     Ta man-huai   xiyue.

     he full-bosom   happiness

     'His bosom is filled with happiness.'

Although it is obvious that English and Chinese share the CONTAINER metaphor in expressing happiness, there is a descriptive difference between English and Chinese within the limited scope of examples given. That is, in English the container is largely the body, whereas in Chinese it is mainly the heart inside the body. Given the fact that in English the heart can also be the container of happiness, as in (14g), and in Chinese such a container can also be a larger body part – bosom or thoracic cavity, as in (15e) – the difference between Chinese and English on this point can be put like this: Chinese places more emphasis on the heart as the container than does English. In English, examples without using "heart" are very common. On the other hand, in Chinese such examples are rarely, if ever, seen. Generally, heart, and sometimes bosom or chest, are specified as the container of happiness.

    Although the difference here seems to be one of degree, it does contribute to the more general difference between the two languages, namely, Chinese tends to use more body parts than does English and that the difference in the relative prominence given to the heart as the container of happiness nicely coincides with the difference in national character (between extroversion and introversion) mentioned earlier. When the body is the container, the fluid of happiness that overflows is more readily seen than if the heart is the container, because the heart is but an internal organ and whatever overflows it is still inside the body.

    According to Kövecses (1991), some behavioral reactions to happiness are associated with the emotion of happiness and, therefore, the expressions of such response are metonymic of the emotion. For instance, JUMPING, DANCING, SMIL-ING, and BRIGHT EYES are associated with happiness. Thus, in English there are:

(16) JUMPING
    a. He jumped for joy.
    b. He was leaping with joy.

    DANCING
    c. We were dancing with joy.
    d. They kicked up their heels.
    e. She had a ball.

    SMILING
    f. She was smiling with happiness.
    g. They were all smiles.
    h. He grinned from ear to ear.
    i. He was all teeth.

    REACTIONS IN EYES
    j. Amusement gleamed in his eyes.
    k. His eyes glinted when he saw the money.
    l. His eyes were shining.
    m. Her eyes were sparkling like diamonds.

In Chinese, similar expressions are also common:

(17) JUMPING
    a. 孩子们高兴得活蹦乱跳。
       Haizimen gao-xing   de   huo-beng   luan-tiao.
       kids   high-spirit COM energetically-skip wildly-jump
       'The kids were jumping and skipping for joy.'

    b. 他们欢呼雀跃。
       Tamen huan-hu   que-yue.
       they   merrily-hail bird-leap
       'They were hailing merrily and jumping like birds.'

    DANCING
    c. 他们喜跃忭舞。
       Tamen xi-yue   bian-wu.
       they   happily-leap gladly-dance
       'They were jumping and dancing for joy.'

d. 他们兴奋得手舞足蹈。

Tamen xing-fen de   shou-wu   zu-dao.

they   spirit-lift COM hands-dance foot-dance

'They were dancing for joy (lit. They were so happy, their hands and feet dancing).'

SMILING

e. 他高兴得嘴巴都合不拢。

Ta gao-xing   de   zuiba   dou   he   bu   long.

he high-spirit COM mouth even shut not close

'He was so happy that he could not close his mouth.'

f. 他笑容满面。

Ta xiao-rong   man-mian.

he smile-expression all-over-face

'He had a broad smile on her face (was all smiles).'

REACTIONS IN EYES AND BROWS

g. 他眉开眼笑。

Ta mei-kai   yan-xiao.

he brow-open eye-smile

'He was all smiles (lit. His brows were open and eyes smiling).'

h. 他喜眉笑眼。

Ta xi-mei   xiao-yan.

he happy-brow smile-eye

'He was all smiles (lit. His brows were happy and eyes smiling).'

i. 他舒眉展眼。

Ta shu-mei   zhan-yan.

he smooth-brow stretch-eye

'He had a happy face (lit. His brows smoothed and his eyes stretched).'

j. 他喜上眉梢。

Ta xi-shang   mei-shao.

he happiness-climb brow-tip

'Happiness crawled up to the tips of his brows.'

Note that in expressing the emotion of happiness in terms of the facial features, Chinese highlights not only eyes, as English does, but also brows. Brows are regarded as one of the most obvious indicators of internal feelings. This can be further illustrated by some four-character set phrases metonymic for unhappiness: 眉头紧锁 *meitou-jinsuo* 'brows are tightly locked or knitted,' 愁眉锁眼 *choumei-suoyan* 'worried brows and knitted eyes,' and 愁眉苦脸 *choumei-kulian* 'worried brows and bitter face.' Although both English and Chinese use eyes as indicators of happy feeling, a difference seems to be apparent with regard to the focus of emphasis. English emphasizes the increase of brightness of eyes, as (16j–m) show, whereas Chinese focuses on the change in the physical shape of eyes, as illustrated by (17g–i). It is arguable that the eye expressions in both English and Chinese are rooted in common bodily experience, whereas the choice of one aspect over the other for emphasis is largely a matter of cultural convention.

From the examples given in this section, we can see that Chinese does match English in the use of a number of major conceptual metaphors of happiness. These include: HAPPY IS UP, HAPPINESS IS LIGHT, and HAPPINESS IS A FLUID IN A CONTAINER. In addition, Chinese is also similar to English in describing one's happiness by referring to some common behavioral reactions to the emotion, such as jumping, dancing, smiling, and response in eyes and/or brows. That is, both languages observe the same metonymic principle. However, English and Chinese do not share some other conceptual metaphors, as illustrated by (9) from English and (11) from Chinese. The examples concerning happiness in this section reinforce the observation made in the previous section that Chinese tends to use more body-part nouns in the expression of emotions.

4.   The underlying model of the metaphors

In this section, I try to answer two questions that arose in the previous sections. First, as I have shown, both English and Chinese utilize exactly the same central conceptual metaphor for anger: ANGER IS HEAT. However, although they both share one subversion of the HEAT metaphor ANGER IS FIRE, they differ in the use of the other one: In English, ANGER IS A HOT FLUID IN A CONTAINER; in Chinese, ANGER IS THE HOT GAS IN A CONTAINER. Although similarities between the languages are due to the common human bodily experience, this question remains to be answered: Why does Chinese differ from English in using the GAS rather than FLUID metaphor?

Second, as I have suggested, Chinese tends to utilize more body parts than English in conceptualizing anger and happiness, and it seems that the selection of certain body parts over others is not all random. The question here is then: Why should this be so? However, I limit myself to the internal organs because I believe the reason for selecting external body parts is 'visible', and hence relatively apparent. For instance, the reason why Chinese selects eyebrows, in addition to eyes, for the conceptualization of happiness or anger is visible there on the face: Even children can interpret facial expressions and know how to draw the simplest happy and angry faces.

In trying to answer the above two questions, I offer an underlying model of the conceptual metaphors discussed in the previous sections by referring to some fundamental theories of Chinese philosophy and medicine. These include the theory of *yin-yang* and the theory of five elements. Chinese medicine applies these theories to account for the relations between humans and nature, between the internal organs inside the human body, and between the internal organs and the external body parts.

To answer the first question, I first give the dictionary meanings of the Chinese word *qi* as follows (from Wu et al., 1981, pp. 535–536):

(18) a. gas (as opposed to fluid and solid: 毒气 *du-qi* 'poison gas')
  b. air (打开窗户透一透气 *dakai chuanghu touyitou qi* 'open the window to let in some fresh air')
  c. breath (停下来歇口气 *tingxialai xie kou qi* 'stop to catch one's breath'; 气功 *qi gong* 'breathing exercises')
  d. smell, odor (香气 *xiang qi* 'a sweet smell'; 臭气 *chou qi* 'a bad odor')
  e. weather (秋高气爽 *qiu gao qi shuang* 'fine autumn weather')
  f. airs, manner (官气 *guan qi* 'bureaucratic airs')
  g. spirit, morale (打气 *da qi* 'pump air, i.e. boost the morale or cheer on')
  h. make angry, enrage (我故意气他一下 *Wo guyi qi ta yixia* 'I got him angry on purpose')
  i. get angry, be enraged (他气得直哆嗦 *Ta qi de zhi duosuo* 'He trembled with rage'; 他说的是气话 *Ta shuo de shi qi hua* 'He just said it to vent his anger')
  j. bully, insult (挨打受气 *ai da shou qi* 'be beaten and bullied')
  k. (in Chinese medicine) vital energy, energy of life

Apparently, the (18h–j) senses are directly related to the discussion of the GAS metaphor. However, (18k), the term in Chinese medicine is also very relevant, as we will see shortly. What is that "vital energy or energy of life"? According to Chinese medicine (Chen, 1989b), the human body is composed of three basic kinds of substance: *qi* 'gas,' *xue* 'blood,' and *jinye* 'fluids other than blood,' which serve as the basis upon which the organs, tissues, and so forth function. The so-called *qi* is "the moving but invisible, nutritive substance which functions as the motive power for the physiological movement of internal organs" (Chen, 1989b, p. 1010). Also, *qi* and blood are mixed together, and circulate through *jingluo*, which is defined in Chinese medicine as "main and collateral channels, regarded as a network of passages, through which vital energy circulates and along which the acupuncture points are distributed" (Wu et al., 1981, p. 359). However, it is *qi* that pushes blood forward rather than vice versa. Wherever *qi* is locally impeded, it will affect the circulation of blood and local pain may occur as a result of increased internal pressure in that area. This is where acupuncture can come in to stimulate the circulation of *qi,* and hence, of blood. If the impediment is sustained, illness will occur in that area and related areas. The causes for the impediment of circulation of *qi* are various, but negative emotions, especially anger, are most significant. This may point to the reason why *qi* is one of the basic words for the emotion of anger.

Furthermore, the theory of *yin-yang* also accounts for the reason why Chinese has chosen the GAS metaphor over the FLUID one under the central conceptual metaphor ANGER IS HEAT. According to this theory, all things in the universe are governed by the law of the unity of opposites, which can be summarized by two Chinese words: *yin* 'feminine; negative' and *yang* 'masculine; positive.' Some examples are listed in Table 1 (from Chen, 1989a, p. 997). The opposites of *yin* and *yang* have a set of binary properties as are given in Table 2 (from Chen, 1989a, p. 997).

Considering Tables 1 and 2, it should be obvious why Chinese has chosen the FIRE and GAS, instead of FIRE and FLUID as in English, for the conceptual metaphor ANGER IS HEAT. The fundamental contrast between *yin* and *yang* has cast fire and gas on one hand, and water and all other fluids on the other, into two opposing categories. The former is naturally related to heat, whereas the latter is closely associated with cold. It should be noted, however, that the theory of *yin-yang* contrast also states that *yin* and *yang* are not only opposed to each other, but also dependent on each other, and can even turn into one another under certain conditions. A simple example is that, in nature, water and other fluids *(yin)* evaporate into vapor or gas *(yang)* when being heated and that vapor or gas *(yang)* liquefies *(yin)* when cold. This dialectical nature of *yin-yang* makes the HOT FLUID metaphor easily understandable to Chinese-speaking people, although they themselves have made little or no use of this metaphorical mapping.

Table 1. Some opposites of yin and yang

Yin	Moon	Land	Night	Cold	Water	Winter
Yang	Sun	Heaven	Day	Heat	Fire	Summer

Table 2. Some binary properties of yin and yang

Yin	Stative	Controlled	Dim	Cold	Soft	Weak
Yang	Dynamic	Excited	Bright	Hot	Hard	Strong
Yin	Passive	Covert	Internal	Lower	Downward	Fluidic
Yang	Active	Overt	External	Upper	Upward	Gaseous

It is notable that, although the GAS metaphor highlights the property of internal pressure to the container, the internal pressure cannot be separated from heat, and heat is actually the cause of the increasing internal pressure, which is the effect. Although heat itself is not highlighted in the GAS metaphors, it is understood from commonsense knowledge that the gas in a closed-up container expands and causes increasing internal pressure until explosion, with increasing heat. Therefore, both HEAT and INTERNAL PRESSURE are present in both FLUID (of English) and GAS (of Chinese) metaphors, although one property is more highlighted in one metaphor than in the other. This difference is also consistent with our commonsense knowledge that the difference between fluid and gas is temperature (i.e. fluid will turn into gas when heated, whereas gas will turn into fluid when cold). Therefore, a FLUID metaphor cannot be an anger metaphor unless HEAT is emphasized, whereas a GAS one can be an anger metaphor without HEAT being highlighted because HEAT is already a necessary condition of GAS. This difference between fluid and gas is obvious in the theory of *yin-yang*, in which gas is categorized with heat and fluid with cold. It is interesting to note that, in expressing anger in Chinese, the GAS metaphor, with its less emphasis on HEAT, generally indicates less intensity than does the FIRE metaphor, which emphasizes HEAT. This difference suggests that the intensity of anger expressed relates directly to the intensity of HEAT in the metaphor.

I now turn to the second question: Why does Chinese make use of more internal organs than English, and why is their specific selection not random? To answer this question, I refer to the five-element theory of Chinese medicine. According to this theory, the universe is composed of five basic elements – wood, fire, earth, metal, and water – which are in a relation of mutual promotion and restraint, as shown in Figure 2 (from Chen, 1989a, p. 1000).

In Figure 2, the lines forming the outer pentagon indicate the relation of promotion, and the lines forming the inner five-pointed star indicate the relation of restraint, with arrowheads indicating directions of promotion or restraint. Specifically, wood promotes fire as its fuel, fire promotes earth because whatever is burned turns into earth, earth promotes metal because the latter comes from the former, metal promotes water because the former is melted into fluid when being heated, and water promotes wood as its indispensable nutrient. On the other hand, wood restrains earth since trees can 'hurt' the soil by absorbing its nutrients, earth restrains water because floods can be contained by earth banks or dams, water restrains fire with its potential to put fire out, fire restrains metal because all kinds of metal will be melted by fire, and metal restrains wood because metal tools are used to cut wood. It is with this relation of mutual promotion and restraint among the five elements that the balance of the universe is achieved.

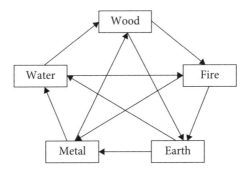

Figure 2. Relation of mutual promotion and restraint between the five elements

In Chinese medicine, the theory of the five elements is applied to define nature and the human body as well as the potential relations between them. Natural phenomena, human organs, and human emotions are classified, according to their properties, into five categories headed by the five elements. Some of the relevant examples are given in Table 3 (from Chen, 1989a, p. 1001).

In Chinese medicine, the internal organs of primary importance, which are called *zang*, include liver, heart, spleen, lungs and kidneys. Each of these are closely related to an internal organ of secondary importance called *fu*, respectively gallbladder, small intestines, stomach, large intestines and bladder. Similarly, the five *zang* organs are also each related closely to a sense organ, accordingly eyes, tongue, lips, nose and ears. Therefore, liver and gallbladder are complementary to each other in function, and liver disease will usually affect the gallbladder (and vice versa), and its clinical symptoms will show in the eyes. Also, the emotion of anger is regarded as one of the major internal factors that causes liver diseases. It is believed that there exists a correlation between the emotion of anger and liver

Table 3. Five categories under the five elements

Elements	Wood	Fire	Earth	Metal	Water
Locations	East	South	Center	West	North
Seasons	Spring	Summer	Late summer	Autumn	Winter
Climates	Windy	Hot	Wet	Dry	Cold
Organs					
Zang	Liver	Heart	Spleen	Lung	Kidney
Fu	Gallbladder	Small intestine	Stomach	Large intestine	Bladder
Sense	Eyes	Tongue	Lips	Nose	Ears
Emotions	Anger	Happiness	Anxiety	Grief	Fright

disease: Those who are quick to anger are especially vulnerable to liver disease; conversely, those with liver disease are symptomatically quick to anger (Shen, 1989). It is also believed that the liver diseases with excessive heat usually start in spring when the weather is windy and when woods are luxuriant. This is how the theory of five elements is applied in Chinese medicine. What is particularly relevant here, however, is that the categorization and conceptualization based on the five-element theory, as is illustrated in Table 3, have actually influenced the usages of the Chinese language. This influence is manifested in the metaphorical use of internal organ names to refer to such abstract concepts as emotions.

It should now be apparent why Chinese uses more internal organ terms in its expression of emotion. The underlying cultural model based on the fundamental theories of Chinese medicine has led to a cultural emphasis in China of sensitivity to the physiological effects of emotions on the internal organs. This, in turn, has influenced the way Chinese people talk about emotions. In the following, I limit my discussion mainly to the emotions of anger and happiness, in keeping with the theme of this article, but I also make references to other abstract concepts metaphorically expressed by the names of the internal organs.

Let us first consider the only positive emotion of happiness in Table 3. As is shown, the internal organs categorized with it are the heart and small intestine. Probably because the former is viewed as the actual container for the emotion of happiness, only the heart, but not the small intestine, is used to refer to happiness metaphorically, as is illustrated in (15). However, it should be noted that the heart and small intestine do occur in other metaphorical expressions; (19) shows some examples:

(19) a. 他心肠很软。
     Ta xin-chang   hen ruan.
     he heart-intestine very soft
     'He has a very soft heart (lit. His heart and intestines are very soft).'

    b. 他真是一个好心肠的人。
     Ta zhen shi yige hao xin-chang   de   ren.
     he really is a   good heart-intestine MOD man
     'He is really a kindhearted man (lit. He is really a man with a good heart and intestines).'

    c. 他真是一个热心肠。
     Ta zhen shi yige re   xin-chang.
     he really is a   hot heart-intestine
     'He is really a warmhearted person (lit. He is really a person with a warm heart and intestines).'

> d. 他的心肠真硬。
>
> *Tade xin-chang   zhen ying.*
>
> his   heart-intestine really hard
>
> 'He is really hardhearted (lit. His heart and intestines are really hard).'
>
> e. 他真是一个铁心肠。
>
> *Ta zhen shi yige tie   xin-chang.*
>
> he really is a   iron heart-intestine
>
> 'He is really an iron-hearted person (lit. He is really a person with an iron heart and intestines).'
>
> f. 他真是一个黑心肠。
>
> *Ta zhen shi yige hei   xin-chang.*
>
> he really is a   black heart-intestine
>
> 'He is really a black-hearted person (lit. He is really a person with a black heart and intestines).'"

Here *xin* 'heart' and *chang* '(small) intestine' are used metaphorically to characterize a person. A descriptive distinction between the Chinese originals and their idiomatic English translations is that, although English uses heart only in the depiction, Chinese uses both heart and (small) intestine for exactly the same purpose. This surface difference across the languages may be explained by the underlying model illustrated in Table 3. It is worth mentioning that in the Chinese examples, although only the more general term of 'intestine' is used – instead of the more specific "small intestine" which should be categorized with "heart" – we could assume that "small intestines" were originally meant. "Small" is left out because metaphorical language use does not need to be as accurate as medical science. More importantly, it would violate the language-internal principle of balance and parallelism should "small" be added.

Next, let us turn to the emotion of anger. As shown in Table 3, the internal organs categorized with this emotion are the *zang* and *fu* organs liver and gallbladder. A difference between the two, which is parallel to the difference between heart and (small) intestines in the preceding case, is that the *zang* organ liver is the one selected in the metaphorical conceptualization of anger, as exemplified in (2). However, gallbladder, the *fu* organ, is also used metaphorically in some other expressions, together with liver, as in (20):

(20) a. 他气得肝胆具裂。

Ta qi de gan-dan   ju   lie.

he gas COM liver-gallbladder both split

'He was so angry that his liver and gallbladder both split.'

b. 他们个个肝胆相照。

Tamen gege gan-dan   xiang   zhao.
they   all   liver-gallbladder mutually treat
'They all have utter devotion (to friends).'

c. 他肝胆过人。

Ta gan-dan   guo   ren.
he liver-gallbladder surpass people
'He is unsurpassed in valor.'

In (20a) "liver" and "gallbladder" are containers, and split as the GAS inside them, that is, anger, expands with heat. In (20b–c), however, "liver" and "gallbladder" are used together to refer to devotion and courage respectively. Given Table 3, it is understandable why liver and gallbladder should go together in the Chinese metaphors. It is interesting to note that, when "gallbladder" is chosen alone in Chinese, it stands for courage rather than anger. In Chinese, for instance, 胆量 *dan-liang* (gallbladder-capacity) means "courage"; 胆大 *dan-da* (gallbladder-big) means "bold; brave," whereas 胆小 *dan-xiao* (gallbladder-small) means "timid; cowardly," and a coward is called a 胆小鬼 *dan-xiao gui* (gallbladder-small devil), who is likely to "lose the gallbladder upon hearing wind blow" (闻风丧胆 *wen feng sang dan*), or to "have a broken gallbladder due to fear or fright (吓破了胆 *xia po le dan*). The reason behind the conceptual metaphor GALLBLADDER IS (THE CONTAINER FOR) COURAGE is that, according to the theory of internal organs in Chinese medicine, the gallbladder also has the function of influencing thinking activities and determining personality (Chen, 1989b).

Although liver and gallbladder are categorized with the emotion of anger in Table 3, it does not mean that the other internal organs are not related to, or affected by, the emotion of anger in the five-element schema. For instance, the liver, as the 'storeroom' of blood, promotes the heart, the "pump" of blood, in the same way wood promotes fire. This kind of "metaphorical" relationship is shown in Table 3, in which the heart is categorized under fire. In addition, according to the theory of internal organs in Chinese medicine (Chen, 1989b), the heart governs the whole human body, including all the other internal organs, and it also commands mental or psychological activities, including all the emotions. Therefore, although the heart seems to be the only internal organ used in the happiness metaphors, it is also one of the major internal organs that appear in the anger metaphors, the others being liver and spleen.

The spleen, as in Table 3, is categorized together with the stomach because both of them are responsible for digestion and absorption. The spleen is an internal organ of primary importance, that is, *zang,* in the sense that it digests and absorbs nutrition only and transports it to the whole body. It is closely related to the liver and heart in the same way earth is related to wood and fire. Although the emotion with which it is categorized is anxiety, it is also related to anger, a more intense kind of emotion. As noted earlier, in the anger metaphors, spleen collocates only with gas (*qi*), but not fire (*huo*). An interesting parallelism to be noted here is that doctors of Chinese medicine only talk about 脾气 *pi qi* 'spleen qi', but not 脾火 *pi huo* 'spleen fire'. On the other hand, when it comes to liver and heart, they talk about both 肝火 *gan huo* 'liver fire' and 肝气 *gan qi* 'liver qi', and 心火 *xin huo* 'heart fire' and 心气 *xin qi* 'heart qi'. This use in the medical language is paralleled in the use of everyday language, as Table 4 illustrates.

As Table 4 shows, 脾火 *pi huo* 'spleen fire' is not used in either medical or everyday language. Contrastively, the others are used in both. This example illustrates how Chinese everyday language is influenced by, or correlated to, Chinese medical language.

Incidentally, when the *zang* organ spleen is paired with its *fu* partner stomach, that is, *pi-wei* (spleen and stomach), they together mean "taste" or "liking" metaphorically, as the following examples show:

(31)   a.   这不合他的脾胃。
              Zhe bu he   tade pi-wei.
              this not suit his   spleen-stomach
              'This does not suit his taste (or This is not to his liking)'.

        b.   他们俩脾胃相投。
              Tamen lia   pi-wei   xiang   tou.
              they   two spleen-stomach each-other cater-to
              'They two have similar likes and dislikes'.

One fact to be noted here is that whenever *zang* and *fu* organs are paired in metaphorical expressions, their order is fixed, that is, the *zang* always comes before the *fu* organ: 肝胆 *gan-dan* 'liver and gall', 心肠 *xin-chang* 'heart and intestines', and 脾胃 *pi-wei* 'spleen and stomach'. This takes place, as mentioned earlier, because the *zang* organs are taken as more important than the *fu* organs in Chinese medicine.

Table 4. Parallelism between medical and everyday uses

	Medical Language	**Daily Language**
Gan huo "liver fire"	Liver heat	Irascibility
Gan qi "liver gas"	Liver gas	Irritability
Xin huo "heart fire"	Heart heat	Pent-up fury
Xin qi "heart gas"	Heart gas	Mood
Pi huo "spleen fire"	–	–
Pi qi "spleen gas"	Spleen gas	Temperament, bad temper

5.   Conclusion

In this article, I have made a comparative study of metaphorical expression of anger and happiness in English and Chinese. With regard to anger, English and Chinese share exactly the same central conceptual metaphor ANGER IS HEAT. This central metaphor has two subversions for both languages. As for the first one, English and Chinese both have ANGER IS FIRE. However, they differ in their use of the second HEAT metaphor: It is FIRE IS A HOT FLUID IN A CONTAINER for English, and ANGER IS THE HOT GAS IN A CONTAINER for Chinese. In conceptualizing happiness, English and Chinese have these metaphors in common: HAPPY IS UP, HAPPINESS IS LIGHT, and HAPPINESS IS A FLUID IN A CONTAINER. However, they do not share some others, such as the OFF THE GROUND metaphor in English versus the FLOWER metaphor in Chinese. In addition, both English and Chinese follow the same metonymic principle: They talk about anger and happiness by describing the physiological effects of the emotions. A descriptive difference between English and Chinese that is apparent is that Chinese tends to utilize more body parts, especially internal organs, than English does in depicting anger and happiness.

I have accounted for some main differences between English and Chinese by referring to the theories of *yin-yang* and of the five elements of Chinese medicine. It is suggested that these theories underlie the metaphorical conceptualization of emotions such as anger and happiness in Chinese. It is also found that there exists a strong parallelism in Chinese between everyday language and medical language. The two possible kinds of relationship between these languages and their underlying theories of *yin-yang* and the five elements are expressed in Figures 3 and 4.

In Figure 3, the underlying theories first influence the medical language, which in turn passes on the influence to the everyday language. In Figure 4, the underlying theories simultaneously influence the everyday and medical languages, which also influence each other. It is not clear to me, now, as to which one provides a better description. But in either case, the theories of *yin-yang* and of the five elements serve as an underlying model that exerts a strong impact on the use of Chinese language.

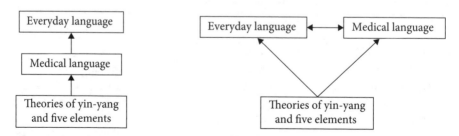

Figure 3. One-directional relation   **Figure 4.** Two-directional relation

I believe that the results of this study have some important implications. Lakoff (1993) claims that, although there is an extensive range of nonmetaphorical concepts, "as soon as one gets away from concrete physical experience and starts talking about abstractions or emotions, metaphorical understanding is the norm" (p. 205). Lakoff (1990) proposed that the question "as to whether all abstract human reasoning is a metaphorical version of imagistic reasoning" be "a major question for future research in cognitive linguistics" (p. 39). My study is a response to this proposal, and it shows that evidence from Chinese empirically supports his claim from the point of view of emotions. Metaphor is so pervasive and irreducible in the expression of such abstract emotion concepts as anger and happiness that it appears to play an essential or indispensable role in our understanding and speaking. In short, "metaphor is not merely a linguistic mode of expression"; rather, "it is a pervasive mode of understanding by which we project patterns from one domain of experience in order to structure another domain of a different kind," and "it is one of the chief cognitive structures by which we are able to have coherent, ordered experiences that we can reason about and make sense of" (Johnson, 1987, pp. xiv–xv). For further evidence from Chinese supporting the claim, see Yu (1992), in which I showed that synesthetic metaphor is pervasive in Chinese as well as in English in referring to various sensory categories.

Second, results of this study also strongly support the argument about the embodiment of metaphorical understanding:

> Metaphorical understanding is not merely a matter of arbitrary fanciful projection from anything to anything with no constraints. Concrete bodily experience not only constrains the 'input' to the metaphorical projections but also the nature of the projections themselves, that is, the kinds of mappings that can occur across domains. (Johnson, 1987, p. xv)

Specifically, these results support Lakoff and Kövecses's (1987) prediction that metaphors for anger should not be randomly distributed in the languages of the world, and that the emotion of anger should be basically understood in terms of heat and internal pressure. Although English and Chinese differ in their selection of one of the two major conceptual metaphors: ANGER IS A HOT FLUID IN A CONTAINER versus ANGER IS THE HOT GAS IN A CONTAINER, it is obvious that both metaphors involve heat and internal pressure. This serves as evidence supporting Lakoff and Kövecses's (1987) suggestion that emotional concepts are embodied; that is, they have a basis in bodily experience. But why should English select the FLUID metaphor and Chinese select the GAS one? As I showed, the selection of one over the other is determined by the underlying cognitive or cultural model. In the case of emotion of anger, its physiological effects are various, and which one is actually chosen in a conventionalized expression to instantiate a particular conceptual metaphor is largely affected by cultural preference. That is, metaphor here is primarily grounded in physical experience but is also constrained by cultural models.

Acknowledgments

An earlier version of this article was presented at the spring 1993 Southeastern Conference on Linguistics in Auburn, AL. I would like to express my sincere thanks to Jane H. Hill, Donna M. Johnson, LuMing Mao, Howard R. Pollio, Muriel Saville-Troike, and Rudolph C. Troike, who have read various versions of this article and made valuable comments. I am also heartily grateful to Mark Johnson and Zoltán Kövecses for their incisive and constructive comments and suggestions. However, I am solely responsible for the content.

References

Chen, Z. (1989a). Yin yang wu xing [Theories of yin and yang, and of the fiv elements]. In W. Jin, C. Meng, J. Zhu, S. Xu, H. Chen, S. Chen, Z. Shen, X. Wu, X. Li, S. Li, S. Yu, J. Zhang, S. Hu, J. Xu, Z. Xu, D. Sheng, & X. Ji (Eds.), *Jiating yixue quanshu* (pp. 997–1002). Shanghai, China: Shanghai Science and Technology Press.

Chen, Z. (1989b). Zang xiang [Theory of internal organs]. In W. Jin, C. Meng, J. Zhu, S. Xu, H. Chen, S. Chen, Z. Shen, X. Wu, X. Li, S. Li, S. Yu, J. Zhang, S. Hu, J. Xu, Z. Xu, D. Sheng, & X. Ji (Eds.), *Jiating yixue quanshu* (pp. 1003–1012). Shanghai, China: Shanghai Science and Technology Press.

Fesmire, S. A. (1994). Aerating the mind: The metaphor of mental functioning as bodily functioning. *Metaphor and Symbolic Activity, 9,* 31–44.

Johnson, M. (1987). *The body in the mind: The bodily basis of meaning, imagination, and reason.* Chicago: University of Chicago Press.

Kövecses, Z. (1986). *Metaphors of anger, pride, and love: A lexical approach to the structure concepts.* Philadelphia: Benjamins.

Kövecses, Z. (1988). *The language of love: The semantics of passion in conversational English.* Lewisburg, PA: Bucknell University Press.

Kövecses, Z. (1990). *Emotion concepts.* New York: Springer-Verlag.

Kövecses, Z. (1991). Happiness: A definitional effort. *Metaphor and Symbolic Activity, 6,* 29–46.

Lakoff, G. (1986). A figure of thought. *Metaphor and Symbolic Activity, 1,* 215–225.

Lakoff, G. (1987). *Women, fire, and dangerous things: What categories reveal about the mind.* Chicago: University of Chicago Press.

Lakoff, G. (1990). The invariance hypothesis: Is abstract reason based on image-schemas? *Cognitive Linguistics, 1,* 39–74.

Lakoff, G. (1993). The contemporary theory of metaphor. In A. Ortony (Ed.), *Metaphor and thought* (2nd ed., pp. 202–251). Cambridge: Cambridge University Press.

Lakoff, G., & Johnson, M. (1980). *Metaphors we live by.* Chicago: University of Chicago Press.

Lakoff, G., & Kövecses, Z. (1987). The cognitive mdoel of anger inherent in American English. In D. Holland & N. Quinn (Eds.), *Cultural models in language and thought* (pp. 195–221). Cambridge: Cambridge University Press.

Shen, Z. (1989). Bianzheng [Dialectical principles in Chinese medicine]. In W. Jin, C. Meng, J. Zhu, S. Xu, H. Chen, S. Chen, Z. Shen, X. Wu, X. Li, S. Li, S. Yu, J. Zhang, S. Hu, J. Xu, Z. Xu, D. Sheng, & X. Ji (Eds.), *Jiating yixue quanshu* (pp. 1024–1033). Shanghai, China: Shanghai Science and Technology Press.

Wu, J., Wang, Z., Liu, S., Wei, D., Wang, B., Ying, M., Wang, J., Gao, H., Zheng, R., Wu, Q., Zhuang, Y., Zhao, M., Lin, Y., Lin, X., & Wang, G. (Eds.). (1981). *Han Ying cidian* [A Chinese-English dictionary]. Beijing, China: Commercial Press.

Yu, N. (1992). A possible semantic law in synesthestic transfer: Evidence from Chinese. *The SECOL Review, 16,* 20–40.

CHAPTER 2

Body and emotion

Body parts in Chinese expression of emotion

This study presents a semantic analysis of how emotions and emotional experiences are described in Chinese. It focuses on conventionalized expressions in Chinese, namely compounds and idioms, which contain body-part terms. The body-part terms are divided into two classes: those denoting external body parts and those denoting internal body parts or organs. It is found that, with a few exceptions, the expressions involving external body parts are originally metonymic, describing emotions in terms of their externally observable bodily events and processes. However, once conventionalized, these expressions are also used metaphorically regardless of emotional symptoms or gestures. The expressions involving internal organs evoke imaginary bodily images that are primarily metaphorical. It is found that the metaphors, though imaginary in nature, are not really all arbitrary. They seem to have a bodily or psychological basis, although they are inevitably influenced by cultural models.

1. Introduction

During the last decade, the study of human emotion from a linguistic perspective has achieved remarkable results (see, e.g., Athanasiadou and Tabakowska 1998; Kövecses 1990, 2000; Niemeier and Dirven 1997; Palmer and Occhi 1999; Russell et al. 1995; Wierzbicka 1990, 1992, 1999). A question that emerges from this intensive study is how the role of the body in emotion and the impact of emotion on the body is conceptualized in different cultures and manifested in different languages. To answer this question obviously calls for cross-cultural and cross-linguistic collaboration.

In this study, which is part of my effort to investigate the role of the body in human meaning and understanding (see Yu 2000, 2001, 2003), I concentrate on the body-part terms used in Chinese expression of emotion. I do this because I believe that the explicit use of body-part terminology in emotion expressions is the tip of the iceberg, which is a good place for landing if we want to know more about the whole submerged under the sea. In particular, I study expressions that are conventionalized in usage. They usually take either of the two forms in Chinese: compounds and idioms. In this sense, my study belongs basically to the field of lexical semantics. Again, I believe, such studies are a good starting point, paving the way for broader and more integrated studies at higher levels such as grammar and discourse (see Wierzbicka 1997).

Generally, Chinese compounds consist of two elements (represented by two characters). In this study one of the two elements is a body-part term, which can take the first or second position. When it takes the first position, it is subject-like, with the element following it, either verbal or adjectival, functioning as its predicate (S-P). When it takes the second position, it can be preceded by a verbal or adjectival element, the internal relationship between the two being, respectively, Verbal-Object (V-O) or Adjectival-Noun (A-N). Sometimes, however, the verb-noun collocation could be Predicate-Subject (P-S) in relation, that is, the two elements are in a reversed order. Chinese idioms, by which I refer to 成语 *chengyu* 'set phrases', are usually composed of four elements (i.e., four characters in writing). Quite often they are two compounds in juxtaposition. In this case, they often involve two body-part terms.

The body-part terms under my study can be divided into two subcategories: the external and the internal. In Sections 2 and 3, separately, I present data to show what external and internal body parts are involved in conventionalized expressions of emotion in Chinese. In the discussion of Section 4, I attempt a preliminary semantic analysis of the data and suggest the implications of the analysis. Section 5 is a brief conclusion.

2. External body parts

In this section I show what external body parts are involved in Chinese expressions of emotions. I start with the head, the top of our body. There are two terms referring to the head in Chinese: 头 *tou* and 首 *shou*. In the idioms below, head and neck are combined with face, forehead, brows, feet, heels, as well as a kind of gaseous vital energy in the body, known as *qi* in Chinese.[1]

---

1.   In collecting Chinese data I used the following popular dictionaries: Lü and Ding (1980, 1989, 1996), Wang (1992), Wei (1995), and Wu (1993). In the lexical examples, the parentheses contain glosses and single quotes contain translations (where PRT stands for "particle" in a broad sense). It must be pointed out that the English emotion words I use in the glosses and translations, though based on the Chinese-English dictionaries, are used in a loose sense. This is because categorizations and lexicons of emotion as well as others can be different to varying degrees across languages and cultures, and that is the primary motivation behind the Natural Semantic Metalanguage (NSM) for cross-linguistic analysis (see, e.g., Wierzbicka 1992, 1999). So, when I use an English emotion word X in the glosses, translations, or main text, it should be interpreted as "X is in some sense equivalent or similar to the Chinese original".

(1) a. 垂头丧气 *chui-tou sang-qi* (hang down-head lose-gas[energy]) 'become dejected and despondent; hang one's head in dismay'

b. 灰头土脸 *hui-tou tu-lian* (gray/dusty-head earthy-face) '(*dial.*) dejected; despondent; depressed'

c. 疾首蹙额 *ji-shou cu-e* (aching-head knitted-forehead) 'with aching head and knitted brows – frowning in disgust; with abhorrence'

d. 仰首伸眉 *yang-shou shen-mei* (raise-head stretch-brows) 'hold one's head high; feeling proud and elated'

e. 翘首企足 *qiao-shou qi-zu* (raise-head lift-feet) 'raise one's head and stand on tiptoe expecting; crane one's neck and stand on tiptoe in pleasurable expectation; eagerly look forward to'

f. 延颈企踵 *yan-jing qi-zhong* (extend-neck lift-heels) 'crane one's neck and stand on tiptoe; eagerly look forward to; anxiously expect'

When people are dejected and despondent, in frustration or dismay, their heads will droop and they look "deflated" (1a). They also have "dirty" heads and faces that may otherwise be bright and shining (1b). As in (1c), the emotions of disgust and abhorrence cause both a bodily sensation (headache) and a facial gesture (frown). Example (1d) presents a contrast to (1a), as the person feeling proud and elated "raises his head" and "stretches his brows". He seems to be "pumped up". The contrast between these two examples with regard to the posture of the head exemplifies the conceptual metaphors HAPPY IS UP and UNHAPPY/SAD IS DOWN (see, e.g., Kövecses 1991, 2000; Lakoff and Johnson 1980, 1999; Yu 1995). Both (1e) and (1f) are about anxiety of expectation: people will "crane their neck and stand on tiptoe" while "looking forward to" the expected. It is noteworthy that these examples, originally metonymic in character, are often used metaphorically when no bodily movements mentioned accompany the eager or anxious expectation.

It goes without saying that the face, the front side of the head, is the most expressive of emotion. Therefore, those who are interested in emotions study facial expressions to see how they are related (e.g., Ekman and Rosenberg 1997; Russell and Fernández-Dols 1997; Wierzbicka 1993, 1999, 2000).[2] The close relationship

---

2. Of course, the interest in human face is by no means limited to how it reveals emotions. As Stevenage (2000) points out in her introduction to the recent *Pragmatics and Cognition* special issue on facial information processing, research on the face has been conducted in multidisciplinary science including psychology, clinical case studies, neuroscience, and computer science. In social and behavioral sciences, as pointed out by Tracy (1990), the conceptions of face have for

between emotion and face is richly reflected in the Chinese language. There is a large number of expressions describing emotions in terms of their facial reactions. Given below are some examples.

(2) a. 脸堆笑容   *lian-dui-xiao-rong* (face-pile up smiling-expression) 'one's face wreathed with smiles; be all smiles with happiness'

    b. 面红耳赤   *mian-hong er-chi* (face-red ears-red) 'become red in the face; flush with anger, shame or shyness'

    c. 脸涨绯红   *lian-zhang-fei-hong* (face-swell-red-red) 'flush with embarrassment'

    d. 脸红脖子粗 *lian-hong bozi-cu* (face-red neck-thick) 'get red in the face from anger or excitement; flush with agitation'

    e. 脸如黄蜡   *lian-ru-huang-la* (face-like-yellow-wax) 'one's face turned waxen with fright; become waxen yellow in the face with fright'

    f. 面如土色   *mian-ru-tu-se* (face-like-earth-color) 'turn pale with fright'

    g. 脸色阴沉   *lian-se yin-chen* (face-color overcast-heavy) 'look sullen; look unhappy'

    h. 面带喜色   *mian-dai-xi-se* (face-bring-happy-color) 'a happy expression on one's face'

    i. 面带愁容   *mian-dai-chou-rong* (face-bring-worried-expression) 'with a sad air; wearing a worried look; with a troubled countenance'

    j. 面有愠色   *mian-you-yun-se* (face-has-irritated-color) 'look irritated, disgruntled, or angry'

Again, there are two basic terms, 脸 *lian* and 面 *mian*, in Chinese that refer to the face. Examples (2a-g) do not include any emotion words, but their usage is conventionalized with certain emotions. On the other hand, Examples (2h-j) contain emotion words as they specify the emotions expressed on the face. In (3) are some compounds with *lian* 'face' indicating people's emotional states.

(3) a. 脸热   *lian-re* (face-hot) 'feel ashamed'

    b. 脸红   *lian-hong* (face-red) 'blush with shame or embarrassment'

---

long attracted research interests in diverse disciplines such as sociology, anthropology, linguistics, communication as well as psychology (see, e.g., Brown and Levinson 1987; Giles and Robinson 1990; Goffman 1959, 1967, 1974; Ho 1976; Hu 1944; Hwang 1987; Ting-Toomey 1988, 1994; Yu 2001)

c. 红脸 *hong-lian* (redden-face) 'blush for being shy; blush with anger; get angry'

d. 绷脸 *beng-lian* (stretch-face) 'pull a long face; look serious or displeased'

e. 板脸 *ban-lian* (harden-face) 'straighten one's face; put on a stern expression'

f. 上脸 *shang-lian* (up to-face) 'blush for drinking wine; grow dizzy with success or praise'

People's face will "feel hot" (3a), burning with shame. Their face will also "turn red" (3b), blushing with shame or embarrassment. However, *hong-lian* (redden-face) in (3c) means "blush for being shy or with anger". Unhappy or displeased, people have muscles on their face tight, resulting in a "stretched face" (3d). In (3e) *ban* is originally a noun meaning "board (e.g., of metal)". In this case it is a verb meaning "harden (the face like a board)". Originally meaning "blushing for drinking wine", (3f) has come to mean, by extension, "being too complacent with success or praise". Being over complacent is similar to being intoxicated with alcohol.

That the face is the body part most expressive of emotions because it has some features most affected by, and communicative of, emotions. These are eyebrows, eyes, mouth, and so forth. As I already pointed out elsewhere (Yu 1995 or 1998), eyebrows are perceived in Chinese as one of the most obvious indicators of emotional states.

(4) a. 愁眉不展 *chou-mei bu-zhan* (worried-brows not-spread.out) 'brows contracted without relaxation; knitting one's brows in anxiety; with knitted brows in worry'

b. 愁眉苦脸 *chou-mei ku-lian* (worried-brows bitter-face) 'wear a worried look'

c. 扬眉吐气 *yang-mei tu-qi* (raise-brows exhale-air) 'feel elated after unburdening oneself of resentment; feel elated and exultant; feel proud and elated'

d. 眉飞色舞 *mei-fei se-wu* (brows-fly color-dance) 'with dancing eyebrows and radiant face – enraptured; exultant; a look of delight'

Usually, knitted brows are associated with negative emotions and vice versa. So "worried brows" are contracted to a frown (4a and 4b) whereas "raised" or even "flying" eyebrows indicate an elated mood (4c and 4d). Very often brows are combined with eyes in idioms expressing emotions, as illustrated by (5). Once again, there are more than one term in Chinese referring to the eyes, and 眼 *yan* and 目 *mu* are two basic ones.

(5) a. 愁眉锁眼 *chou-mei suo-yan* (worried-brows locked-eyes) 'knit one's brows in anxiety or despair; look extremely worried'

b. 冷眉冷眼 *leng-mei leng-yan* (cold-brows cold-eyes) 'contemptuous; indifferent'

c. 横眉怒目 *heng-mei nu-mu* (horizontal-brows angry-eyes) 'with frowning brows and angry eyes; darting fierce looks of hate'

d. 横眉竖眼 *heng-mei shu-yan* (horizontal-brows vertical-eyes) 'glare in anger'

e. 直眉瞪眼 *zhi-mei deng-yan* (upright-brows glaring-eyes) 'stare in anger; fume'

f. 舒眉展眼 *shu-mei zhan-yan* (smooth-brows stretch-eyes) 'relax the brows and stretch the eyes to show pleasure; smiling eyes; a beaming face'

g. 眉开眼笑 *mei-kai yan-xiao* (brows-open eyes-smile) 'be all smiles; beam with joy'

h. 喜眉笑眼 *xi-mei xiao-yan* (happy-brows smiling-eyes) 'be all smiles; be smiling all over'

As these examples show, words of various semantic categories are used to describe brows and eyes: emotion words, tactile adjectives, verbs denoting emotional reactions or facial movements, and orientation adjectives. Especially interesting is the contrast between (5d) and (5e), for instance, in which both "horizontal" and "upright" brows express anger. Assumably, however, the inconsistent expressions refer to similar eyebrow displays. Their function is to describe the strong emotion metonymically or metaphorically, but not to describe the brows realistically. In (5) above eyes are juxtaposed with brows, while in the compounds below they appear alone highlighting some negative emotions.

(6) a. 急眼 *ji-yan* (impatient/anxious-eyes) '(*dial.*) become angry; feel anxious'

b. 傻眼 *sha-yan* (stupid-eyes) 'be dumbfounded; be stunned'

c. 白眼 *bai-yan* (white-eyes) 'supercilious look; contemptuous look'

d. 红眼 *hong-yan* (red-eyes) 'see red; become infuriated; be jealous; be green-eyed'

e. 眼红 *yan-hong* (eyes-red) 'covet; be envious; be jealous; be furious'

f. 眼热 *yan-re* (eyes-hot) 'covet; be envious'

g. 眼馋 *yan-chan* (eye-greedy) 'cast covetous eyes at; covet; be envious'

In (6c) "white eyes" actually refer to the whites of the eyes, as supercilious or contemptuous eyes display much of their whites. In Chinese angry or jealous people are said to have "red eyes" (6d) although, more often than not, their eyes are not really bloodshot. Those who tend to be envious and jealous are said, humorously, to have "red-eye disease" (红眼病 *hong-yan bing*), which is a popular name for conjunctivitis. Covetousness is after all considered a disease. It is interesting to note that in English envious and jealous people are "green-eyed" rather than "red-eyed". Example (6e) is a synonym to (6d) in the sense of envy or jealousy. So is (6f), in which the adjective makes reference to temperature, though, instead of color. But red is after all a "hot" color. In (6g), which is again synonymous to the previous three, the epithet focuses on a standing-out part (the eyes) of the whole (the person). In the following are some idioms involving eyes and some other body parts.

(7) a. 翻白眼 *fan-bai-yan* (turn-white-eyes) 'show the whites of one's eyes (as from emotion or illness); feel angry, or disappointed'

b. 白眼看人 *bai-yan kan-ren* (white-eyes see-people) 'look upon others with contempt or disdain; treat people superciliously)

c. 眼竖目横 *yan-shu mu-heng* (eyes-vertical eyes-horizontal) 'stare in anger or contempt'

d. 目瞪口呆 *mu-deng kou-dai* (eyes-stare mouth-dumb) 'be struck dumb with astonishment or fear; stare in bewilderment or mute amazement'

e. 瞠目结舌 *cheng-mu jie-she* (staring-eyes knotted-tongue) 'be wide-eyed and tongue-tied with fear or surprise; stare dumbfounded'

f. 触目惊心 *chu-mu jing-xin* (strike-eyes shock-heart) 'startling; shocking'

g. 眼跳心惊 *yan-tiao xin-jing* (eyes-jump heart-startle) 'eyes twitching and heart shocked – nervous apprehension'

In (7d) and (7e) the physical reactions to the emotions are very similar: one's eyes widely open and mouth or tongue unable to move. So are those in (7f) and (7g), which describe the impact of emotion on the eyes and the heart. The compounds in (8) below contain the mouth, and the tongue and teeth inside it. All of them describe observable symptoms of the emotions, except for (8g) where "cold" is metaphorically related to the emotion of scorn. It suggests attitude rather than temperature.

(8) a. 咂嘴 *za-zui* (click-mouth) 'make clicks of admiration, praise, surprise, etc.'

b. 撇嘴 *pie-zui* (curl-mouth) 'curl one's lips in contempt, disbelief, disappointment, or displeasure; twitch one's mouth'

c. 撅嘴 *jue-zui* (pout-mouth) 'pout one's lips in displeasure'

d. 咋舌 *ze/zha-she* (bite-tongue) 'be left speechless or breathless with wonder, fear or shock'

e. 咬牙 *yao-ya* (grit-teeth) 'grit one's teeth in anger or hatred'

f. 切齿 *qie-chi* (gnash-teeth) 'gnash one's teeth in anger or hatred'

g. 齿冷 *chi-leng* (teeth-cold) 'laugh sb. to scorn'

Of the features on or around the face, the ears and nose seem to be less expressive of emotions than brows, eyes, and mouth. In the examples below (9a) and (9c) refer to bodily acts responsive to or expressive of certain emotions while (9b) describes a sensation that we feel in the nose on the verge of crying. Note that to wrinkle one's nose is a common bodily reaction to disgust, for instance, but it does not seem to have entered into the ranks of conventionalized compounds and idioms in Chinese.

(9) a. 抓耳挠腮 *zhua-er nao-sai* (tweak-ears scratch-cheeks) 'tweak one's ears and scratch one's cheeks (as a sign of anxiety or delight)'

b. 令人酸鼻 *ling-ren-suan-bi* (make-one-sour-nose) 'make one feel like crying (for sadness)'

c. 嗤之以鼻 *chi-zhi-yi-bi* (sneer.at-it-with-nose) 'give a snort of contempt; sneer at with contempt'

The examples below involve hair, moustache, and fine hair. In Chinese, notably, the hair standing on end is associated with anger or rage, as in (10a) and (10b). In contrast, the fine hair standing on end is related to fear or fright, as in (10d).

(10) a. 令人发指 *ling-ren-fa-zhi* (make-one's-hair-point) 'make one's hair stand on end – extremely angry'

b. 怒发冲冠 *nu-fa-chong-guan* (angry-hair-push-hat) 'bristle with anger; be in a towering rage'

c. 吹胡子瞪眼 *chui-huzi deng-yan* (blow-moustache stare-eyes) 'puff and glare; foam with rage; snort and stare in anger'

d. 寒毛直竖 *han-mao zhi-shu* (fine-hair upright-stand) 'hair standing on end with fright'

Leaving the head, I now turn to hands and feet, located at the ends of our four limbs. In Chinese, again, there are two terms referring to the feet: 脚 *jiao* and 足 *zu*.

Of the examples below the reference to the hand in (11c) and (11d) is implicit. All the examples describe the bodily acts or gestures expressive of certain emotions.

(11) a. 手舞足蹈   *shou-wu zu-dao* (hands-wave feet-dance) 'dance for joy'
      b. 搓手顿脚   *cuo-shou dun-jiao* (rub-hands stamp-feet) 'wring one's hands and stamp one's feet – get anxious and impatient'
      c. 捶胸顿足   *chui-xiong dun-zu* (pound-chest stamp-feet) 'thump one's chest and stamp one's feet in anguish, grief or deep sorrow'
      d. 扼腕   *e-wan* (grip-wrist) 'hold one's own wrist in excitement, disappointment, sorrow or despair'
      e. 跳脚   *tiao-jiao* (jump-feet) 'stamp one's foot with anxiety or rage'

Example (11c) above involves the chest, which with a cavity inside is conceived of as a container of emotions. Similar to the chest is the belly, which is also conceptualized as a container of emotions. The chest, or chest cavity, and the belly are thus different from other external body parts in that they are affected by emotions from within, as illustrated by the following expressions.

(12) a. 开怀大笑   *kai-huai da-xiao* (open-bosom big-laugh) 'laugh heartily (with great joy)'
      b. 放怀大笑   *fang-huai da-xiao* (open-bosom big-laugh) 'laugh to one's heart content'
      c. 满怀喜悦   *man-huai xiyue* (full-bosom joy) 'full of gladness; brimming with joy'
      d. 满腔怒火   *man-qiang nu-huo* (full-chest.cavity angry-fire) 'be filled with flaring anger'
      e. 一腔冤仇   *yi-qiang yuanchou* (one-chest.cavity enmity) 'be full of grievances'
      f. 满腹忧愁   *man-fu you-chou* (full-belly sorrow-anxiety) 'be full of sorrow and anxiety'
      g. 令人捧腹   *ling-ren-peng-fu* (make-one-hold-belly) 'make one hold one's belly with laughing; split one's sides with laughter'

Since emotions are contained inside the chest, people would "open their bosom" (12a and 12b), that is, to "release emotions from their chest", to laugh to their heart's content. As (12c–e) show, when people are filled with a certain emotion, they "have their chest cavity full of that emotion". Such is also the case with (12f), where the container is the belly. As in (12g), "hold one's belly" is a metonymy for laughing, especially in a convulsive manner. A convulsion of emotion will usually cause human body to shake, and that is what (13a) and (13b) are about. In these examples, people's "flesh is quivering" as their heart is shaken with fear. Example (13c) describes an uneasy sensation "flesh-numb" when one finds something disgusting or nauseating.

(13) a. 肉跳心惊   *rou-tiao xin-jing* (flesh-jump heart-startle) 'shudder with fear'

b. 肉颤心惊   *rou-chan xin-jing* (flesh-quiver heart-startle) 'feel nervous and creepy; tremble with fear'

c. 令人肉麻   *ling-ren-rou-ma* (make-one's-flesh-numb) 'making one's flesh creep; disgusting; nauseating; sickening'

In this section, I have presented the Chinese emotion expressions involving external body parts. The bodily events, symptoms, and processes of emotions discussed here are supposedly visible. In the next section I turn to emotion expressions containing internal body parts, namely, the inner organs that are not observable from outside the body.

3. Internal body parts

I have found seven terms for inner organs in the conventionalized emotion expressions in Chinese. The inner organs are spleen, liver, intestines, stomach, gallbladder, lungs, and heart. As will be seen, the frequency of occurrence of these inner organs is very unevenly distributed. First, look at (14).

(14) a. 发脾气   *fa pi-qi* (expand spleen-gas) 'lose one's temper; get angry; flare up'

b. 动肝火   *dong gan-huo* (move liver-fire) 'get angry; flare up; fly into a rage'

c. 肝肠欲裂   *gan-chang yu-lie* (liver-intestines about.to-split) 'be heartbroken; be deeply grieved'

d. 肝肠寸断   *gan-chang cun-duan* (liver-intestines inch-cut) 'be heartbroken; be deeply grieved; overwhelmed by grief; sorrow-stricken'

e. 愁肠百结   *chou-chang bai-jie* (worried-intestines hundred-knots) 'with anxiety gnawing at one's heart; weighed down with pent-up feelings of anxiety or sadness'

f. 回肠九转   *huichang jiu-zhuan* (intestines[ileum] nine-twists) 'with anxiety gnawing at one's heart; weighed down with grief'

g. 牵肠挂肚   *qian-chang gua-du* (pull-intestines hang-stomach) 'feel deep anxiety; be very worried; be deeply concerned'

h. 悬肠挂肚   *xuan-chang gua-du* (suspend-intestines hang-stomach)
'cause extreme worry and distress'

In (14a) and (14b), anger is referred to as "the gas in the spleen" and "the fire in the liver". These two expressions represent the two Chinese versions of the metaphor ANGER IS HEAT that I have discussed in detail in my earlier study (Yu 1995). The Chinese versions are ANGER IS FIRE and ANGER IS HOT GAS IN A CONTAINER, whereas for English they are ANGER IS FIRE and ANGER IS HOT FLUID IN A CONTAINER (Kövecses 2000; Lakoff and Kövecses 1987). Examples (14c) and (14d) refer to the liver and intestines as they are "damaged" by the intense emotion of deep grief. In (14e) and (14f) intestines are no longer as they should be because anxiety has caused them to be "knotted" or "twisted". In (14g) and (14h) *du*, generally known as "belly", is also an informal term for "stomach", of which a formal name in Chinese is 胃 *wei*. The deep concern and worry for others will "pull" or "suspend" people's intestines and "hang up" their stomach.

According to the theory of internal organs in Chinese medicine, the gallbladder has the function of influencing thinking activities and determining personality. In the Chinese language, however, the gallbladder is fundamentally related to courage, and the conceptual metaphor in this regard is GALLBLADDER IS (THE CONTAINER FOR) COURAGE (see Yu 1995). This is illustrated by the following expressions.

(15)   a. 胆量   *dan-liang* (gallbladder-capacity) 'courage'
       b. 胆大   *dan-da* (gallbladder-big) 'bold; brave; courageous'
       c. 胆小   *dan-xiao* (gallbladder-small) 'timid; cowardly'
       d. 胆小鬼   *dan-xiao gui* (gallbladder-small devil) 'coward'
       e. 肝胆   *gan-dan* (liver-gallbladder) 'sincerity; heroic spirit; courage'
       f. 肝胆过人   *gan-dan guo-ren* (liver-gallbladder surpass-people) 'far surpass others in daring'

The amount of courage you have is the "capacity of your gallbladder" (15a). This capacity, "big" or "small", determines whether you are a courageous or cowardly person (15b and 15c). A coward is simply a "gallbladder-small devil" (15d). The compound in (15e) and the idiom in (15f) show that the liver and the gallbladder in combination can also refer to courage.

(16)   a. 胆怯   *dan-qie* (gallbladder-timid) 'nervous'
       b. 胆怵   *dan-chu* (gallbladder-frightened) 'frightened'
       c. 胆虚   *dan-xu* (gallbladder-void) 'afraid; scared'
       d. 胆寒   *dan-han* (gallbladder-frigid) 'be struck with terror; be overcome by fear'
       e. 落胆   *luo-dan* (fall-gallbladder) 'extremely scared'

Given in (16) are compounds about fear. If you are nervous or frightened, it is because your gallbladder is "timid" or "frightened" in the first place (16a and 16b). Also, the reason for your fear is that your gallbladder is "void" of its content – courage (16c). Any terror that strikes or overcomes you makes your gallbladder "frigid" and out of function (16d). If your gallbladder has "fallen" with fright, you no longer possess any courage at all (16e). The idioms below, which also involve soul and heart, provide further illustration. As these examples show, fear becomes overwhelming as the gallbladder is "damaged" (17a and 17e), "lost" (17b and 17c), or "trembling" (17d).

(17) a. 胆裂魂飞   *dan-lie hun-fei* (gallbladder-split soul-fly) 'be frightened out of one's wits'

b. 亡魂丧胆   *wang-hun sang-dan* (dead-soul lost-gallbladder) 'be scared out of one's wits; be half dead with fright'

c. 闻风丧胆   *wen-feng sang-dan* (hear-wind lose-gallbladder) become terror-stricken, panic-stricken, or terrified at the news'

d. 胆战心惊   *dan-zhan xin-jing* (gallbladder-tremble heart-startle) 'tremble with fear; be terror-stricken'

e. 胆破心惊   *dan-po xin-jing* (gallbladder-break heart-startle) 'be scared to death'

In (17d) and (17e) above the heart is affected by the emotion of fear, and so is it in (7f), (7g), (13a) and (13b), where it is combined with eyes and flesh. But the heart is by no means only related to fear. In fact, it is conceptualized as the seat or container for emotion in general. In one way, emotion is conceptualized in Chinese as fluid in the container. The following expressions, for instance, refer to emotions and their impact as "tide" in the heart.

(18) a. 心潮   *xin-chao* (heart-tide) 'a tidal surge of emotion; surging thoughts and emotions'

b. 心潮起伏   *xin-chao qi-fu* (heart-tide rising-falling) 'a tidal surge of emotions'

c. 心潮翻滚   *xin-chao fan-gun* (heart-tide turning-rolling) 'emotions tumbling like a tide'

d. 心潮澎湃   *xin-chao pengpai* (heart-tide surging) 'feel an upsurge of emotion'

In Chinese the metaphor HEART IS THE SEAT/CONTAINER FOR EMOTIONS is manifested linguistically in an extremely rich fashion, as the evidence below will demonstrate. First, look at (19). These are expressions of happiness. People who are happy have an "open heart" (19a). An "open" heart is "bright" (19b) and "vast" (19c) inside, and may have "flowers wildly bloom" (19d) inside.

(19) a. 开心   *kai-xin* (open-heart) 'happy; joyous; elated'
      b. 爽心   *shuang-xin* (bright-heart) 'happy; feel good'
      c. 心旷神怡   *xin-kuang shen-yi* (heart-vast spirit-joyful) 'relaxed and joyful; carefree and happy'
      d. 心花怒放   *xin-hua nu-fang* (heart-flower wildly-bloom) 'burst with joy; be wild with joy'

In (20) below two different emotional states, namely relief and admiration, are expressed in terms of heart. One interesting conceptualization of heart is that it will be lifted by such emotions as fright and anxiety, ready to "jump" through one's throat and into one's mouth. Conversely, it will come back down to its normal position when relieved from those emotions. Examples (20a) and (20b) describe the process of relief as the heart being "laid" or "falling" back down. Also, the heart moves violently when shaken by intense emotions. It will come down to a good "rest" (20c and 20d) when the emotions that shake it calm down. In (20e) feeling relieved is, literally, having a "broad heart" or "broadening the heart", since the heart is supposed to contract with certain intense emotions, leaving a narrow space inside. Examples (20f) and (20g) pertain to different emotions. Admiration or love literally means "topple one's heart" (20f) so that it tilts and falls toward the object of admiration or love. In (20g) being charmed, enchanted, and overcome with admiration is having one's "heart drunk" with the "alcohol" of those emotions.

(20) a. 放心   *fang-xin* (lay down-heart) 'set one's mind at rest; rest assured; feel relieved'
      b. 落心   *luo-xin* (fall-heart) '(*dial.*) feel relieved; be relaxed'
      c. 落心   *xie-xin* (rest-heart) 'in a relaxed mood; free from worries'
      d. 息心   *xi-xin* (rest-heart) '(*dial.*) be at ease; rest assured; feel relieved'
      e. 宽心   *kuan-xin* (broad-heart) 'feel relieved; be relaxed; feel free from anxiety'
      f. 倾心   *qing-xin* (topple-heart) 'be overcome with admiration; fall in love with; lose one's heart to'
      g. 心醉   *xin-zui* (heart-drunk) 'be charmed; be enchanted; be overcome with admiration'

The heart in (21) is affected by such negative emotions as vexation, oppression, annoyance, distress, disappointment, and disgust. Examples (21a) and (21b) evoke the image of the heart-container being "closed up", as opposed to that of "openness" in (19). Examples (21c–h) refer to the negative emotions as the heart being in disorder, pain, or trouble. In the last four, the heart is described respectively in tactile, visual, and sensational terms, as affected by the negative emotions.

(21) a. 窝心   *wo-xin* (nested-heart) '(*dial.*) feel irritated; feel vexed'
      b. 堵心   *du-xin* (block-heart) 'feel oppressed; having a load on one's mind'
      c. 糟心   *zao-xin* (messed-heart) 'vexed; annoyed; dejected'
      d. 痛心   *tong-xin* (paining-heart) 'feel pained, distressed, or grieved'
      e. 心痛   *xin-tong* (heart-paining) 'feel pained, distressed, or grieved'
      f. 心疼   *xin-teng* (heart-aching) 'love deeply; feel sorry; be distressed'
      g. 心烦   *xin-fan* (heart-troubled) 'be vexed; be perturbed'
      h. 烦心   *fan-xin* (trouble-heart) 'annoying; vexatious; troublesome'
      i. 心寒   *xin-han* (heart-frigid) 'be bitterly disappointed and pained'
      j. 寒心   *han-xin* (frigid-heart) 'be bitterly disappointed; be afraid'
      k. 灰心   *hui-xin* (gray/dusty-heart) 'lose heart; be discouraged'
      l. 恶心   *e-xin* (sicken-heart) 'feel like vomiting; feel nauseated; feel sick; disgusted/disgusting'

The heart is the container of emotions and, for good or ill, it will be affected by its contents. As in (22a) anger is a destructive force (fire) in the heart. The force, as it gets intensive, can "hurt" (22b) or even "destroy" (22c) the container. Even if the force of emotion is not so intensive, as in (22d) and (22e), it still can change the "look" or "quality" of the container.

(22) a. 心头火起   *xin-tou huo-qi* (heart-head fire-flare.up) 'flare up with anger'
      b. 痛心疾首   *tong-xin ji-shou* (paining-heart aching-head) 'with bitter hatred'
      c. 腐心切齿   *fu-xin qie-chi* (rotten-heart gnashing-teeth) 'with deep hatred'
      d. 心灰意懒   *xin-hui yi-lan* (heart-gray/dusty will-lazy) 'be disheartened; be downhearted'
      e. 心灰意冷   *xin-hui yi-leng* (heart-gray/dusty will-cold) 'be downhearted; be dispirited'

In the expressions in (23) the heart is related to two emotions, guilt and grief. As shown by the first three examples, guilty people really feel "guilty in the heart" (23a), and they have their "heart hollow" (23b) or have "lost their heart" (23c). In Chinese *suan* is originally a taste word meaning "tart" or "sour". It has come to mean "sore" or "pain" in the body. In this way "tart heart" (23d) and "heart sour" (23e) refer to grief in the sense that it causes "heartache". In the same sense, grief as a sharp force can "wound the heart" (23f), "twist the heart" (23g), and "fragment the heart" (23h). The idioms in (23i–k) further illustrate the destructive nature of grief. It can "pierce the heart like ten thousand arrows", and it can "tear the heart and split the lungs". In a fit of grief people will "thump their heart and shed tears of blood".

(23) a. 心疚   *xin-jiu* (heart-guilty) 'feel sorry and anxious'
      b. 心虚   *xin-xu* (heart-void) 'with a guilty conscience; diffident'
      c. 亏心   *kui-xin* (lose-heart) 'have a guilty conscience; go against conscience'
      d. 酸心   *suan-xin* (tart-heart) 'be grieved; feel sad'
      e. 心酸   *xin-suan* (heart-sour) 'be grieved; feel sad'
      f. 伤心   *shang-xin* (wound-heart) 'sad; grieved; brokenhearted'
      g. 绞心   *jiao-xin* (twist-heart) 'sorrow-stricken; grief-stricken'
      h. 心碎   *xin-sui* (heart-fragmented) 'be heartbroken'
      i. 万箭穿心   *wan-jian-chuan-xin* (ten.thousand-arrows-pierce-heart) 'in extreme grief'
      j. 撕心裂肺   *si-xin lie-fei* (tear-heart split-lungs) 'be extremely grieved'
      k. 椎心泣血   *chui-xin qi-xue* (thump-heart sob-blood) 'beat one's heart and shed tears of blood – be heartbroken'

The examples in (24) show how the heart will react to fear. It will become "timid" (24a) and be "throbbing" (24b). The heart will become "frigid" and fine hair will "stand on end" (24c). Juxtaposed in (24d–f) are the heart and the gallbladder. Fear can "lift the heart and hang up the gallbladder" (24d), "shock the heart and drop the gallbladder" (24e), or strike them so hard as to make "both split" (24f).

(24) a. 心怯   *xin-qie* (heart-timid) 'be scared'
      b. 心悸   *xin-ji* (heart-throb) 'be scared'
      c. 心寒毛竖   *xin-han mao-shu* (heart-frigid fine.hair-standing) 'shudder with fright'
      d. 提心吊胆   *ti-xin diao-dan* (lift-heart hang-gallbladder) 'have one's heart in one's mouth'
      e. 惊心掉胆   *jing-xin diao-dan* (shock-heart drop-gallbladder) 'be frightened out of one's wits'
      f. 心胆俱裂   *xin-dan ju-lie* (heart-gallbladder both-split) 'be frightened out of one's wits; be terror-stricken'

Finally, (25) gathers the expressions of anxiety related to the heart. The heart feels "anxious" (25a) or "flurried" (25b) in anxiety. Anxiety, as a force, can "hang" (25c) and "lift" (25d) the heart, that is, "suspend it in the air" (25e). It can also cause pain to the heart by "pinching it" (25f). Even worse, as a destructive force like fire, anxiety can "scorch" (25g) and "fry" (25h) the heart. The idioms (25i–k) also demonstrate different degrees of anxiety. In (25i) it stirs up feelings of uneasiness and restlessness in the heart. In (25j) and (25k) it is "burning" the heart like fire.

(25) a. 心切   *xin-qie* (heart-anxious) 'eager; impatient; anxious'
    b. 心慌   *xin-huang* (heart-flurried) 'be flustered; be nervous; get alarmed'
    c. 挂心   *gua-xin* (hang-heart) 'be concerned about; be anxious for'
    d. 提心   *ti-xin* (lift-heart) 'worry; feel anxious'
    e. 悬心   *xuan-xin* (suspend-heart) 'be on tenterhooks'
    f. 揪心   *jiu-xin* (pinch-heart) 'anxious; worried; heartrending; agonizing; gnawing'
    g. 焦心   *jiao-xin* (scorch-heart) 'feel terribly worried'
    h. 煎心   *jian-xin* (fry-heart) 'feel extremely anxious'
    i. 忧心如焚   *xin-shen bu-an* (heart-soul not-peaceful) 'feel uneasy or restless; be disturbed'
    j. 心急火燎   *you-xin ru-fen* (worried-heart like-burning) 'burning with anxiety'
    k. 心神不安   *xin-ji huo-liao* (heart-anxious fire-flaming) 'burning with impatience; in a nervous state'

In this section I have presented the Chinese expressions of emotion involving internal body parts. Most of them are what Wierzbicka (1999: 297–302) calls "internal bodily images", which are primarily metaphorical in nature since they refer to imaginary events and processes taking place inside the body.

4. Discussion

In the previous two sections I laid out the Chinese data consisting of conventionalized emotion expressions containing body-part terms. As far as my data covers, 22 external and 7 internal body parts are involved. The external body parts are head, face, forehead, eyebrows, eyes, nose, mouth, teeth, tongue, cheeks, ears, hair, moustache, fine hair, neck, chest (including chest cavity), belly, flesh, hands, wrist, feet, and heels. The seven internal body parts, or internal organs, are heart, lungs, liver, stomach, gallbladder, spleen, and intestines. Besides, blood, the gaseous vital energy of *qi,* color or complexion of face, soul, will, and spirit are also found in some of the idioms.

Notably, the occurrence of the body-part terms is very unevenly distributed. Most of them have very limited roles in expressing specific emotions, and only a few of them play diverse parts in expressing a broad range of emotions. As manifested in the linguistic evidence, the face is the most expressive of emotions among the external body parts. The next two are eyes and eyebrows. While the face, as a whole, is the barometer of emotions (see Yu 2001), its focus seems to be located around the eyes and brows. The eyes and brows are paired together not only physically but also conceptually in Chinese, as the following compounds and idioms demonstrate.

(26) a. 眉眼   *mei-yan* (brows-eyes) 'appearance; looks; features'
     b. 眉目   *mei-mu* (brows-eyes) 'features; looks; sign of a positive outcome'

(27) a. 小姑娘眉眼长得很俊。
        Xiao guniang mei-yan   zhang de   hen jun.
        little girl   brows-eyes grow COM very pretty
        'The little girl is very pretty.'
     b. 计划有了眉目。
        Jihua you   le   mei-mu.
        plan have PRT brows-eyes
        'The plan is beginning to take shape.'

Apparently, as in (26), brows and eyes are such important features that they together actually stand for the whole face or looks. Furthermore, (26b) is also mapped into an abstract domain to refer to the "face" of abstract things. (27) gives two sentential examples. If people's brows and eyes are pretty, they are "good-looking" as a whole (27a). If things, concrete or abstract, start to show their "brows and eyes", then they have already gained a "face" and taken "shape" (27b). But for my purpose here, the point is that in Chinese brows and eyes are really important twins in the domain of emotions. Look at the following idioms.

(28) a. 眉高眼低   *mei-gao yan-di* (brows-high eyes-low) 'an expression on the face'
     b. 眉眼高低   *mei-yan gao-di* (brows-eyes high-low) 'an expression on the face'
     c. 眉目含情   *mei-mu han-qing* (brows-eyes contain-emotion) 'one's eyes wear an expression of coquetry; with an expression of coquetry in one's eyes'
     d. 眉目传情   *mei-mu chuan-qing* (brows-eyes pass-emotion) 'flash amorous glances; make eyes at sb.; cast glances of love; cast flirting glances between sexes'
     e. 眉来眼去   *mei-lai yan-qu* (brows-come eyes-go) 'make eyes at each other; exchange love glances with sb.'
     f. 眉语目传   *mei-yu mu-chuan* (brows-speak eyes-communicate) 'speaking or communicating with one's brows and eyes'

As shown in (28a) and (28b), one's emotions are manifested in the spatial "layouts" of brows and eyes. This is because brows and eyes actually "contain" (28c) and "pass" (28d) emotions, especially in "exchange of glances" (28e) between sexes. In short, brows and eyes are capable of "speaking and communicating" (28f). It is worth mentioning that in all the above examples, where brows and eyes are juxtaposed, the order is brows first and eyes second but not vice versa. All the evidence cited here, as well as that shown in (4) and (5), seems to point to the fact that brows take a very prominent position in conceptualization and expression of emotions and looks in Chinese, certainly more so than in English.

As the data have shown, Chinese emotion expressions involving terms of external body parts are generally composed of body-part terms in collocation with other words that modify, predicate, or govern them. The words in collocation belong to a variety of semantic domains, as listed below:

i.   emotion (e.g., worried brows; angry hair)
ii. color (e.g., red face [shyness, anger]; white eyes [contempt])
iii. temperature (e.g., face hot [shame]; eyes hot [jealousy])
iv. orientation/dimension (e.g., vertical eyes [anger]; neck thick [anger])
v.   bodily sensation (e.g., stiff tongue [fear, surprise]; flesh creepy [disgust])
vi. bodily movement (e.g., gritting teeth [anger, hatred]; snorting nose [contempt])

As listed above, category (i) makes explicit use of emotion words, attaching them to the body parts that reveal the specified emotions. In category (ii), certain color terms are applied to characterize certain emotions. The choice of color words seems to reflect, to some extent, the physiological symptoms of certain emotions on certain body parts. The motivation behind the choice seems to be reinforced by the related category of temperature (iii). When viewed together, there seems to be some consistency parallel between both categories, namely, "hot colors" tend to go with certain emotions while "cold colors" tend to go with a different set of emotions. For instance, "white eyes" (from the whites of eyes) goes with contempt, and so do "cold brows", "cold eyes", and "teeth cold" (probably from a "cold grin"). The similar parallel is also found between "red face" and "red eyes" on the one hand, and "hot face" and "hot eyes" on the other. As noted earlier, however, there is a difference between Chinese and English in the color associated with jealousy: it is "red eyes" in Chinese and "green eyes" in English. It will be interesting to make cross-linguistic and cross-cultural studies on what color and temperature words are used to describe what emotions.

Apparently, the choice of orientation words in category (iv) is less predictable. There, both "horizontal" and "vertical" brows denote anger, and so is the case with eyes. The effect here seems to be more cartoon-like, that is, to "catch" something real, physically or psychologically, in an artistically exaggerated manner. In category (v), the expressions describe emotions in terms of bodily sensations caused by the emotions. Thus, grief will cause a "tingling nose" and disgust will make the "flesh creepy". Category (vi) is by far the largest category. It contains expressions that describe emotions by referring to the bodily movements in reaction to those emotions. As a broad category, bodily movements can be convulsive to varying degrees, from "eyes twitching" and "fine hair standing on end" with fear, to "stamping feet" and "pounding chest" with grief, for instance.

Viewed as a whole, the conventionalized expressions involving external body parts are metonymic in nature. They follow the metonymic principle THE PHYSIOLOGICAL EFFECTS OF AN EMOTION STAND FOR THE EMOTION (Lakoff and Kövecses 1987). They refer to emotions by describing their externally observable bodily events and processes. It seems that there are only a few exceptions, like "bosom opened (to release emotions)", which is metaphorical in the first place.

In sharp contrast to the expressions with external body-part terms, those expressions containing terms of internal body parts are primarily metaphorical. They evoke internal bodily images that are imaginary in character (Wierzbicka 1999). For an overview, the following is a list of all seven internal organs and the emotions with which they are linked. Given in the parentheses are the images evoked in the expressions.

i.   spleen: anger (gaseous energy of *qi* expanding)
ii. liver: anger (fire burning)
                    sadness (split, ripped into pieces)
iii. intestines: anxiety (knotted, twisted, hanged)
                    sadness (knotted, twisted, split, ripped into pieces)
iv. stomach: anxiety (hanged)
v.   lungs: sadness (split)
vi. gallbladder: fear (void, frigid, hanged, dropped, lost, trembling, split)
vii. heart: anger (fire burning)
                    anxiety (troubled, hanged, lifted, suspended, pinched, scorched, fried, being burned by fire)
                    sadness (pain, frigid, wounded, twisted, fragmented, pierced, torn apart, pounded)
                    fear (shocked, throbbing, frigid, lifted, split)
                    happiness (open, vast, bright, blooming)
                    relief (laid down, settled down, calm down, broad)
                    admiration (toppled, drunk)
                    vexation (closed up, blocked, messed up, troubled, pain)
                    disappointment (frigid, gray)

disgust (vomiting)
hatred (pain, rotten)
guilt (void, lost)

Note that the list is based on my data that consist of conventionalized expressions found in dictionaries. In daily language, for instance, we can say something to the effect "Don't explode your lungs with gas (i.e. anger)" (see Yu 1995). While this saying is very idiomatic, it is not a compound or idiom listed in the dictionaries. Therefore, the link between lungs and anger is not listed here. As shown in the list, the heart is linked to various emotions while the rest are linked to one or two only. In my data, the heart is the most recurrent of all body parts in conventionalized emotion expressions. The linguistic evidence certainly reflects the conceptualization of heart as the container of all emotions.

Obviously, the expressions involving internal body parts also contain words from such semantic domains as emotion (e.g., worried intestines, heart anxious), color (e.g., gray heart), temperature (e.g., gallbladder frigid), dimension (e.g., heart vast, broad heart), bodily sensation (e.g., heart aching, heart tingling), and bodily movement (e.g., heart throbbing, gallbladder trembling). But there is a difference in quantity. For instance, bodily movement is the largest category with the external body parts, but it is very small here. The two examples given above are the only two, and "heart throbbing" is the only bodily movement we can really feel. In contrast, we cannot really tell how "gallbladder trembling" feels. The gallbladder example is certainly not on a par with "eyes twitching" or "flesh quivering" that has real physiological basis. Other examples that demonstrate the difference include "worried brows" versus "worried intestines", "gray head" versus "gray heart", and "neck thick" versus "broad heart". In short, the difference under discussion is not just quantitative, but also qualitative. To summarize, the expressions involving external body parts are primarily metonymic, whereas those involving internal body parts are fundamentally metaphorical.

Now I turn to the major kinds of metaphorical images found in the expressions involving internal organs. The previous list has already provided an overview. Here I want to focus on the emotions that involve at least two internal organs. Notably, they are the four negative emotions listed below. In the list I use more general words where possible. For instance, "break" includes "split", "rip into pieces", "wound", "fragment", "pierce", and "tear apart".

i.	anger:	gas expanding spleen	Pain
		fire burning liver, heart	Damage
ii.	anxiety:	blocking (knot, twist) intestines	Pain
		lifting (pull, hang, suspend, lift) intestines, stomach, heart	Pain

	hurting (pinch) heart	Pain
	fire burning (scorch, fry, flame) heart	Damage
iii. sadness:	blocking (knot, twist) intestines	Pain
	breaking (split, rip into pieces, wound, fragment, pierce, tear apart) liver, intestines, lungs, heart	Damage
	hurting (twist, pound) heart	Pain
	freezing (frigid) heart	Pain
iv. fear:	lifting (hang, lift) gallbladder, heart	Pain
	breaking (split) gallbladder, heart	Damage
	freezing (frigid, trembling) gallbladder, heart	Pain
	losing (void, dropped, lost) gallbladder	Damage

As this list shows, anger is linked to spleen, liver, and heart; anxiety to intestines, stomach, and heart; sadness to intestines, liver, lungs, and heart; fear to gallbladder and heart. The heart is the only organ linked to all emotions. Note that on the right column, I use "Pain" and "Damage" to characterize the physical impact of the negative emotions on the internal organs as dramatized by the metaphorical images. It should be pointed out that there is no cutting line between physical pain and physical damage. As the condition intensifies, pain can certainly change to damage. Thus, for instance, as the gas expands increasingly in the spleen, it will cause damage to the container (see Yu 1995). No matter what organs are involved, sustained hanging or a freezing temperature will convert pain to damage, too.

Although the negative emotions listed above inflict either pain or damage on the internal organs, we can see some interesting similarities and differences in how they do it. With anger, gas (*qi*) expands in the spleen and fire burns in the liver and heart. Both processes are related to heat, namely, heat causes gas to expand and fire produces heat. They both converge on the metaphor ANGER IS HEAT (see Lakoff and Kövecses 1987; Yu 1995). Another emotion that is heat related is anxiety: it "scorches", "fries", and "flames" the heart. The similarity here seems to suggest that anxiety and anger overlap each other.

In contrast to anger and anxiety, which are heat related to different degrees, fear and sadness are cold related. Fear makes the gallbladder "frigid" and "trembling" and the heart "frigid" and "throbbing". Similarly, sadness, as well as (bitter) disappointment, causes the heart to be frigid. Fear and sadness also have another commonality, namely, as their intensity increases, they both "break" the internal organs involved. These organs are gallbladder and heart for fear, and liver, intestines, lungs, and heart for sadness. Besides, fear also does some unique "damage" to the gallbladder. In "shaking" it, fear can "void" its content, or "snap its base" making it "drop off its stem" in a complete "loss".

Noticeably, both anxiety and sadness "block" the "pipes" of intestines by "knotting" and "twisting" them. They also "hurt" the heart, though in somewhat different ways. The former "pinches" it while the latter "twists" and "pounds" it. From the images here we can "feel" some similarities and differences between anxiety and grief.

Moreover, there is another interesting point about anxiety and fear. As pointed out earlier, these two emotions contrast each other in the aspect of temperature. Anxiety is related to heat, and fear to cold. On the other hand, however, the two emotions also have a commonality: they both "lift into the air" the organs they affect. Thus, anxiety will "raise" intestines, stomach, and heart and keep them "suspended in the air", while fear will "lift" gallbladder and heart and "hang them up there". It is worth mentioning that the feeling of relief, linked to the heart in the overall list, poses an interesting contrast to anxiety and fear. While anxiety and fear "lift" the heart and "hang it up in the air", relief "lays it back down" and lets it "rest on solid ground".

The data analysis presented above offers two implications. First, the similarities and differences between the four emotion concepts, namely anger, anxiety, sadness, and fear, suggest that they have more than one facade and they relate to one another in a complex network. Emotion concepts do not have clear-cut boundaries, and there may be overlaps between them. The multi-images cast in metaphorical mode mirror the multi-facades of the concepts and the multi-links in their relations. The finding here supports the script hypothesis that categories of emotions are fuzzy, with the borders between categories vague, the status of membership within a category varying, and different categories overlapping one another (Russell 1991).

Second, those metaphorical images, viewed as a whole, reflect the "Chinese way" of understanding emotions. In this particular way, for instance, anger is conceptualized as "hot gas" as well as "fire", the gallbladder as linked to courage, the heart as "commander" of all mental or psychological activities including emotions, and so forth. All these, and many more, seem to be modeled on the theory of internal organs of Chinese medicine (see Yu 1995). The underlying folk theory, or cultural model, has influenced how Chinese people talk about emotions in a specific way. On the other hand, viewed at a more abstract level, the metaphorical images seem to conform, in general, to a universal tendency expressed in the form of a conceptual metaphor EMOTION IS FORCE (Kövecses 2000). That is, they dramatize emotions as physical forces and emotional experiences as impact of those forces. The metaphor maps physical forces we experience around us onto cognitively based feelings we experience inside us. The mapping is imaginary, but not arbitrary. Thus, at a more specific level, we see a division of labor among metaphorical images. For example, "heat" is linked to anger and anxiety, but "cold" to fear and sadness (as well as disappointment). "Lifting up" is linked to anxiety and fear, but "letting down" to relief. "Hurting" is linked to anxiety and sadness, and "breaking" to sadness and fear. The images of "blocking" and "closing up" are found with sadness and anxiety (and vexation), but that of "opening up" and "broadening" with happiness and relief. It seems that these metaphorical images in Chinese have a bodily or psychological basis, although they are inevitably affected by cultural models.[3] It will be enlightening to know how other languages are different or similar regarding internal bodily images in their emotion expressions. That is why the study of emotion language should be a cross-linguistic enterprise.

5. Conclusion

It seems to be appropriate to say, at this time, that there are two important factors that interact and affect emotion language, or human language in general. These are culture and body. The question is not whether or not culture and body both play their roles at all, but how big a role they each play, in the evolution of human language. I believe that it is wrong to take an "either or" approach to the cultural and the bodily bases of language and cognition, that is, the claim for one naturally means the denial of the other. Only an integrated and balanced approach can draw a complete picture. The impact of culture on language is a prominent and fruitful subject in the existing literature, but the role of the body in human meaning and understanding has not received due attention. It cries for extensive empirical studies on a cross-linguistic and cross-cultural basis. Systematic study of linguistic evidence can open a window into the enculturated and embodied nature of human cognition.

References

Athanasiadou, A. and Tabakowska, E. (eds). 1998. *Speaking of Emotions: Conceptualization and Expression.* Berlin: Mouton de Gruyter.

Brown, P. and Levinson, S.C. 1987. *Politeness: Some Universals in Language Usage.* Cambridge: Cambridge University Press.

Ekman, P. and Rosenberg, E.L. (eds). 1997. *What the Face Reveals.* New York: Oxford University Press.

Giles, H. and Robinson, W.P. (eds). 1990. *Handbook of Language and Social Psychology.* Chichester, England: John Wiley & Sons.

---

3.   For a discussion of the relationship between language, culture, body, and cognition, readers are referred to Yu (2001). There I propose a hypothetical generalized "Triangle Model" that is attempted to describe the relationship between language, culture, and body, and the way in which culture and body interact and affect language.

Goffman, E. 1959. *The Presentation of Self in Everyday Life*. Garden City, NY: Doubleday.

Goffman, E. 1967. *Interaction Ritual: Essays on Face-to-Face Behavior*. Garden City, NY: Doubleday.

Goffman, E. 1974. *Frame Analysis: An Essay on the Organization of Experience*. Cambridge, MA: Harvard University Press.

Ho, D.Y. 1976. "On the concept of face". *American Journal of Sociology* 81(4): 867–884.

Hu, H.C. 1944. "The Chinese concepts of 'face'". *American Anthropologist* 46: 45–64.

Hwang, K. 1987. "Face and favor: The Chinese power game". *American Journal of Sociology* 92(4): 944–974.

Kövecses, Z. 1990. *Emotion Concepts*. New York: Springer-Verlag.

Kövecses, Z. 1991. "Happiness: A definitional effort". *Metaphor and Symbolic Activity* 6(1): 29–46.

Kövecses, Z. 2000. *Metaphor and Emotion: Language, Culture, and Body in Human Feeling*. Cambridge: Cambridge University Press.

Lakoff, G. and Johnson, M. 1980. *Metaphors We Live By*. Chicago: University of Chicago Press.

Lakoff, G. and Johnson, M. 1999. *Philosophy in the Flesh: The Embodied Mind and Its Challenge to Western Thought*. Chicago: University of Chicago Press.

Lakoff, G. and Kövecses, Z. 1987. "The cognitive model of anger inherent in American English". In D. Holland and N. Quinn (eds), *Cultural Models in Language and Thought*. Cambridge: Cambridge University Press, 195–221.

Lü, S. and Ding, S. (eds). 1980. *Xiandai Hanyu Cidian* [Modern Chinese Dictionary]. Beijing: The Commercial Press.

Lü, S. and Ding, S. (eds). 1989. *Xiandai Hanyu Cidian Bubian* [Modern Chinese Dictionary Supplement]. Beijing: The Commercial Press.

Lü, S. and Ding, S. (eds). 1996. *Xiandai Hanyu Cidian* [Modern Chinese Dictionary] (revised ed.). Beijing: The Commercial Press.

Niemeier, S. and Dirven, R. (eds). 1997. *The Language of Emotions: Conceptualization, Expression, and Theoretical Foundation*. Amsterdam: John Benjamins.

Palmer, G.B. and Occhi, D.J. (eds). 1999. *Languages of Sentiment: Cultural Constructions of Emotional Substrates*. Amsterdam: John Benjamins.

Russell, J.A. 1991. "Culture and the categorization of emotions". *Psychological Bulletin* 110(3): 426–450.

Russell, J.A. and Fernández-Dols, J.M. (eds). 1997. *The Psychology of Facial Expression*. Cambridge: Cambridge University Press.

Russell, J.A., Fernández-Dols, J., Manstead, A.S.R., and Wellenkamp, J.C. (eds). 1995. *Everyday Conceptions of Emotion: An Introduction to the Psychology, Anthropology and Linguistics of Emotion*. Dordrecht: Kluwer.

Stevenage, S.V. 2000. "Giving each other a helping hand: Introduction to the special issue on facial information processing". *Pragmatics and Cognition* 8(1): 1–7.

Ting-Toomey, S. 1988. "Intercultural conflict styles: A face-negotiation theory". In Y.Y. Kim and W.B. Gudykunst (eds), *Theories in Intercultural Communication*. Newbury Park, CA: Sage, 213–235.

Ting-Toomey, S. (ed.). 1994. *The Challenge of Facework: Cross-Cultural and Interpersonal Issues*. Albany: State University of New York Press.

Tracy, K. 1990. "The many faces of facework". In H. Giles and W.P. Robinson (eds), 209–226.

Wang, T. (ed.). 1992. *Xin Xiandai Hanyu Cidian* [A New Dictionary of Modern Chinese Language]. Haikou, China: Hainan Press.

Wei, D. (ed.). 1995. *Han Ying Cidian* [A Chinese-English Dictionary] (revised ed.). Beijing: Foreign Language Teaching and Research Press.

Wierzbicka, A. (ed.). 1990. *Australian Journal of Linguistics* 10(2) (Special issue on the semantics of emotions).

Wierzbicka, A. 1992. *Semantics, Culture, and Cognition: Universal Human Concepts in Culture-Specific Configurations*. New York: Oxford University Press.

Wierzbicka, A. 1993. "Reading human faces: Emotion components and universal semantics". *Pragmatics and Cognition* 1(1): 1–23.

Wierzbicka, A. 1997. "A response to Michael Bamberg". In S. Niemeier and R. Dirven (eds), 227–229.

Wierzbicka, A. 1999. *Emotions across Languages and Cultures: Diversity and Universals*. Cambridge: Cambridge University Press.

Wierzbicka, A. 2000. "The semantics of human facial expressions". *Pragmatics and Cognition* 8(1): 147–183.

Wu, G. (ed.). 1993. *Han Ying Da Cidian* [Chinese-English Dictionary] *Vols. 1 & 2*. Shanghai: Shanghai Jiao Tong University Press.

Yu, N. 1995. "Metaphorical expressions of anger and happiness in English and Chinese". *Metaphor and Symbolic Activity* 10(2): 59–92.

Yu, N. 1998. *The Contemporary Theory of Metaphor: A Perspective from Chinese*. Amsterdam: John Benjamins.

Yu, N. 2000. "Figurative uses of *finger* and *palm* in Chinese and English". *Metaphor and Symbol* 15(3): 159–175.

Yu, N. 2001. "What does our face mean to us?" *Pragmatics and Cognition* 9(1): 1–37.

Yu, N. 2003. "The bodily dimension of meaning in Chinese: What do we do and mean with 'hands'?". In E. Casad and G.B. Palmer (eds), *Cognitive Linguistics and Non-Indo-European Languages*. Berlin: Mouton de Gruyter, 337–362.

CHAPTER 3

Synesthetic metaphor

A cognitive perspective

The theory of conceptual metaphor claims that poetic metaphor basically uses the same cognitive mechanisms as everyday metaphor; and what makes poetic metaphor look different, however, is its extension, elaboration, and combination of those mechanisms in ways that go beyond the ordinary. In light of this claim, the present study focuses on a particular kind of metaphor, synesthetic metaphor, with data extracted from the novels and short stories by Mo Yan, a preeminent contemporary Chinese novelist highly acclaimed for his innovation with language. An analysis shows that his use of synesthetic metaphors (as well as other metaphors and figures), although very novel and unusual, largely conforms to some general tendencies found in both ordinary and poetic language by previous empirical studies. The finding supports the claim that human meaning and understanding are embodied, constrained by the body we have and how it functions.

1. Introduction

The past few decades have witnessed an intellectual movement leading to the recognition that metaphor is not only a figure of speech, but also "a figure of thought" (Lakoff 1986). The study of metaphor has expanded its traditional territory from literary criticism and rhetoric to various fields that overlap, to various degrees, on the common ground of cognitive science, including linguistics, psychology, anthropology, and philosophy. Leading in this movement for the last two decades is a cognitive theory of metaphor known as "the theory of conceptual metaphor", associated with cognitive linguistics. This theory holds that metaphor is pervasive and ubiquitous in everyday language and thought, rather than just a rhetorical device of poetic imagination (e.g., Gibbs 1994; Johnson 1987; Lakoff 1987a, 1993; Lakoff and Johnson 1980, 1999; Lakoff and Turner 1989; Sweetser 1990; Turner 1991).

According to the theory of conceptual metaphor (Lakoff 1993), metaphor is not merely a matter of words, but also a matter of thoughts. It is primarily conceptual in nature, with surface manifestation in language. It is the main mechanism through which abstract concepts are comprehended and abstract reasoning is performed. One cannot think abstractly without thinking metaphorically. As a basic cognitive structure, metaphor allows us to understand a relatively abstract concept in terms of a more concrete or more structured concept. Structurally, metaphors are mappings across conceptual domains, involving projections from a source domain to a target domain. Such mappings are asymmetric in that they are unidirectional, that is, from the more concrete to the more abstract. They are partial in that only part of the structure of the source domain is projected to the target domain. A concept in a particular target domain can receive metaphorical mappings from different source domains, seemingly inconsistent with each other. Metaphorical mappings are not arbitrary, but grounded in the body and bodily experience in the physical and cultural world (see, also, Yu 1995, 1998, 2000, 2001, 2002, 2003).

One of the central claims of the theory of conceptual metaphor, as summarized by Lakoff and Turner (1989), is that metaphor in poetry is not an essentially different phenomenon from metaphor in ordinary language; poetic metaphor basically uses the same cognitive mechanisms as everyday metaphor; and what makes poetic metaphor look different, however, is its extension, elaboration, and combination of those mechanisms in ways that go beyond the ordinary. Taking the approach of cognitive poetics,[1] Freeman (2000) argues that metaphors are not just strategies for enlivening otherwise prosaic language, but also markers of poets' ways of thinking about the world, and signs of their conceptual universe. Since literary language shares much with ordinary language, and artistic usage with everyday usage, discoveries about one usually bear on the other (Lakoff 1987b). "There are thus strong arguments in favor of approaching artistic metaphor together with everyday metaphor, even via everyday metaphor" (Sweetser 1992: 722).

In light of this central claim of the theory of conceptual metaphor, in this paper I study a particular kind of metaphor, synesthetic metaphor, namely, metaphor that maps across various sensory domains. My data is drawn from Chinese literature, but my analysis, I believe, will shed light on intersense metaphors in general. I will show that synesthetic transfers generally go in parallel directions in both everyday and literary language in Chinese. It is hoped that this study of Chinese

---

1.   As Tsur defines it, cognitive poetics "is an interdisciplinary approach to the study of literature employing the tools offered by cognitive science", and "it attempts to find out how poetic language and form, or critic's decisions, are constrained and shaped by human information processing" (Tsur 1992: 1). Shen suggests that cognitive poetics focuses on poets' "selective use, or 'preference' for certain structures over others, beyond a specific context" such as text, poet, school or period (Shen 1997: 64). With this focus, it can provide "a reasonable explanation for the observation that, despite the creativity and novelty manifested in poetic language…some semantic aspects of poetic language are rather systematic and constrained" (Shen 1997: 65). Freeman, who emphasizes the contributions of cognitive linguistics to cognitive poetics, argues that "The kind of analysis cognitive poetics provides opens up the cognitive layers upon which a literary text is built and, in doing so, provides a reading that reveals the frame and structure of meaning that is endemic and central to the text itself" (Freeman 2000: 277).

synesthetic metaphor will reinforce the claim that literary metaphors use the same mechanisms as conventional metaphors but extend, elaborate, and compose them in extraordinary ways. In Section 2, I review previous studies on synesthetic metaphors that are particularly relevant to the present study. In Section 3, I look closely at the Chinese data to show how literary synesthesia conforms to the same constraints as synesthesia in everyday language. Section 4 is the conclusion.

2. Studies of synesthetic metaphors

Synesthesia is "a term denoting the perception, or description of the perception, of one sense modality in terms of another" (Preminger 1974: 839). As is indicated by this definition, it is primarily a perceptual phenomenon, upon which linguistic description is based.[2] As Tsur points out, literary synesthesia "is the exploitation of verbal synaesthesia for specific literary effects", and "is typically concerned with verbal constructs and not with 'dual perceptions'" (Tsur 1992: 245). But empirical studies have proved that even literary synesthesia is constrained: it does not map randomly from any sensory domain to any other one. Human sense modalities traditionally fall into five categories: touch, taste, smell, sound, and sight, hierarchically from the lowest to the highest. It is apparent that there should be twenty theoretically possible kinds of cross-modal transfers, with four destinations from each of the five sources. However, empirical studies in various languages and literatures (e.g., Shen 1997; Ullmann 1959/1951; Williams 1976; Yu 1992) have shown that synesthetic metaphors are quite selective in terms of directionality of their transfers.

Investigating poets writing in English, French, and Hungarian, Ullmann (1959) is the first to discuss the "panchronistic" nature in synesthetic transfers, namely, that despite such factors as individual temperament, imagination, and modes of vision, and fashionable trends of literary expression and aesthetic doctrine, there exist some correspondences which authors of different generations, nationalities and temperaments had in common. Specifically, Ullmann discovered three overall tendencies (1959: 276–284). The first tendency, which he calls "hierarchical distribution", is that synesthetic transfers tend to go from the "lower" to

---

2.   During the past decades, psychologists have conducted fruitful research on synesthesia as a perceptual phenomenon (e.g., Baron-Cohen and Harrison 1997; Cytowic 1989; Harrison 2001; Marks 1978; Marks et al. 1987). Many studies have also focused on synesthesia as a descriptive phenomenon, that is, synesthetic metaphor, in literature (e.g., Bogumil 1988; Downey 1912; Engstrom 1946; Marks 1982; Nelson 1968; O'Malley 1957; Shen 1997; Tsur 1992; Ullmann 1959; Yu 1992) and in everyday language (e.g., Barcelona 2000; Dirven 1985; Osgood 1980; Taylor 1995; Williams 1976; Yu 1992).

the "higher" sensory modes, namely, touch → taste → smell → sound → sight.[3] The second tendency, in keeping with the first one, is that touch, the lowest level of sensation, is the predominant source of transfers. The third tendency is that sound, rather than sight, is the predominant destination for synesthetic transfers, which is somewhat unexpected from the hierarchical point of view. According to Ullmann's interpretation, this is because visual terminology is incomparably richer than its audio counterpart.

While Ullmann's (1959) study is limited to synesthetic metaphors in poetry, Williams' (1976) study, in contrast, is restricted to synesthetic adjectives in daily English (also with some evidence from other Indo-European languages and Japanese) that have resulted from diachronic semantic change. He summarizes his findings as diagramed in Figure 1, in which he very justifiably breaks the sense of sight into two subcategories: color and dimension. Specifically, touch words, if they transfer at all, tend to transfer to taste, color, and sound. Taste words tend to transfer to smell or sound. Dimension words may transfer to color or sound while color and sound words trade metaphors. If certain sense transfers depart from these tendencies, they tend to disappear from language use. In short, Williams' (1976) study of synesthetic metaphor in ordinary language reinforces Ullmann's (1959) findings about poetic synesthesia: synesthetic transfers tend to move upward, that is, from the lower senses to higher senses.

Based on their findings, both Ullmann (1959) and Williams (1976) have proposed possible universal principles in the process of synesthetic transfer. However, they have also expressed the need for wider investigation of more languages before these hypotheses can be established as universal principles. To test their hypotheses, I have applied their approaches to the study of data collected from Chinese literary and ordinary language (Yu 1992). Regarding literary synesthetic metaphors, I have found that Ullmann's first two tendencies (i.e., the hierarchical distribution and touch as the predominant source) have their parallel tendencies in Chinese. His third tendency, sound as the predominant destination, is not so clear in Chinese because my data, by chance or not, shows no evidence of sight as being a less frequent destination than sound. With regard to synesthetic metaphors in ordinary language, I have found that Williams' generalization about the routes for synesthetic transfers stands strong and is basically testable in Chinese except that Chinese dimension words transfer, in a regular fashion, not only to color and sound, but also to taste and smell. The results of my study show that, despite those features peculiar to Chinese, synesthetic metaphor in Chinese does conform to the general tendencies observed by Ullmann (1959) and Williams (1976) in English and some other languages.

---

3.   Note that Ullmann (1959) actually divides the sense of touch into two categories, that is, he distinguishes heat from touch. I combine the two into one here to follow the tradition.

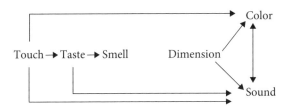

Figure 1. Routes for synesthetic transfers (from Williams 1976)

From the perspective of cognitive poetics, Shen (1997) studies cognitive constraints on three poetic figures including synesthetic metaphor. He argues that cognitive constraints provide an explanatory mechanism that accounts for regularities characterizing poetic language over and above context (e.g., a specific text, poet, school, or period). Those regularities found in poetic language, he concludes, "conform to *cognitive* rather than linguistic or contextual constraints, i.e., constraints which are derived from our cognitive system and its organizing principles" (Shen 1997: 35). In particular, Shen (1997) addresses the issue that poetic metaphors seem to be highly selective with respect to their directionality of mapping, that is, mapping tends to be one-directional rather than both ways. He has analyzed synesthetic metaphors drawn from modern Hebrew poetry and found that the Hebrew corpus "conforms fully" (Shen 1997: 49) to Ullmann's observation regarding directionality of mapping in synesthetic metaphors, namely, they tend to map lower terms onto higher ones in the hierarchy. He proposes that the "low to high" mapping follows from the general cognitive constraint which states that "a mapping from more 'accessible' or 'basic' concepts onto 'less accessible' or 'less basic' ones seems more natural, and is preferred over the opposite mapping" (Shen 1997: 51). He conducted an experiment to solicit judgments from the subjects and found that they indeed prefer the "low to high mapping" as "more natural" than its inverted counterpart.

The researches reviewed above show that synesthetic metaphors in both poetic and everyday language share the same directionality of mapping. What is especially significant is the fact that the findings are cross-linguistic and cross-cultural so that they may as well reflect some general mechanisms in human language and cognition that are rooted in embodied experience. It is worth noting that these findings fit well with the the theory of conceptual metaphor outlined in Section 1 above.

3.   Analysis of synesthetic metaphors in Chinese

Having laid out the backdrop of my study, in this section I intent to lend further support to the claim of the theory of conceptual metaphor that poetic (or literary in general) metaphors basically use the same cognitive mechanisms as everyday metaphors and what makes them look different is their extension, elaboration, and combination of those mechanisms in ways that go beyond the ordinary. To do this, I will look closely at some synesthetic metaphors extracted from the literary works by a contemporary Chinese novelist, Mo Yan, whose representative works include *Red Sorghum, The Garlic Ballads, The Republic of Wine, Big Breasts and Full Hips*, and so on.[4]

In commenting on the writing style of Mo Yan as "China's preeminent novelist", Wang says, "Whatever the subject matter, a torrential flow of rich, unpredictable, often lacerating words remains his trademark" (Wang 2000: 487). For my purpose in this study, I pick out Mo Yan because his novels, sometimes labeled as "avant-garde" by critics for their originality and creativity, are especially well known for their "bold and unrestrained erotic imagery" (Wang 2000: 487). As a master of words, Mo Yan's creative use of language warrants close scrutiny from purely aesthetic and stylistic points of view.

In what follows, I will analyze some examples of synesthetic metaphors from Mo Yan's novels and short stories. For the purpose of convenience, I will provide English translations, which are my own, below their Chinese originals. In translating these examples, I try to be faithful to the originals, paying special attention to retaining their metaphorical structure and capturing their overall imagery. The italics for emphasis are mine.

Following Williams (1976), I will divide the sense of sight into two subclasses: color and dimension. The first synesthetic metaphor in (1) has touch as its source domain, and smell as its target domain.

(1)   屋子里充满热嘟嘟的腥气,好象刚用开水烫过死鸡死鸭。《球状闪电》
       The house was full of *bubbling-hot stench*, like a dead chicken or duck being scalded by boiling water. (*Ball-Shaped Lightning*)

In this sentence, the "stench", a bad smell, is as "hot" as boiling water that is "bubbling". This compressed intersense metaphorical image is then followed by the simile that furnishes another grotesque image of "a dead chicken or duck being scalded by boiling water", which actually echoes and reinforces the preceding

---

4.   Quite a number of Mo Yan's novels or stories are now available in English translations. Interested readers are referred to *World Literature Today* Vol. 74, No. 3 for several critical essays on Mo Yan and his literary works.

synesthetic metaphor. This extraordinary image, however, is grounded in the basic synesthetic transfer TOUCH → SMELL that conforms to the "low to high" mapping direction. It is worth pointing out that the Chinese counterpart for the English word "bubbling" is 嘟嘟 *dudu,* which is an onomatopoeia that can suggest the sound of bubbles rising in water, namely "bubbling". Then, "bubbling-hot" (热嘟嘟), the modifier for the "stench", is itself a synesthetic metaphor mapping sound to touch. If this observation is correct, it constitutes a downward mapping from sound to touch (SOUND → TOUCH). But as mentioned above, "bubbling-hot" is likely compressed from "hot as boiling water that is bubbling", with the overt link "boiling water" left out (which occurs in the following simile). If that is the case, the compression also makes "bubbling-hot" a case of transferred epithet that is metonymic in nature.

The two examples in (2) below are synesthetic metaphors mapping from touch to sound.

(2) a. …… 曲子轻松明丽，细腻多情，仿佛春暖花开的三月里柔媚的轻风吹拂着人们的脸庞。《民间音乐》

… the *music* was light and *bright,* exquisite and emotive, *stroking* people's faces like a gentle breeze in warm and flowery March. (*Folk Music*)

   b. 瘦老头的叫声弹性丰富，尖上拔尖，起初还有间隔，后来竟连成一片。《球状闪电》

The *screams* of that thin old man possessed *a high elasticity,* getting more and more *sharp-pointed,* with *gaps* in between at first, but extending to a constant *stretch* after a while. (*Ball-Shaped Lightning*)

In (2a), the word of sound "music" is predicated by words of color "bright" and touch "stroking", resulting in a composite synesthetic metaphor COLOR + TOUCH → SOUND. Both mappings conform to Williams' routes for synesthetic transfers in Figure 1 (Williams 1976). Again, the simile, in which the "breeze" (that can be felt) is mapped onto "music" (that can be heard), helps to condense the image evoked by the cross-modal metaphor. In (2b), the target domain is again sound, while the source domains are touch and dimension. The "screams" have the quality of "elasticity", a quality of material objects. The objects with this quality have a shape. They will change their shape under external pressure, but will bounce back into their original shape when relieved of such pressure, like, for instance, a piece of sponge. Since the "screams" have the properties of objects, they of course have a tangible "shape", which is "changing" in the process. They are getting more and more "sharp-pointed" on the front side as they are "hurled" out of the old man's mouth. Initially, they are "discrete objects", but gradually they are forming into one of a long "stretch" in shape. The image, with all its graphic nature, derives from a composite synesthetic metaphor mapping from touch and dimension to sound: TOUCH + DIMENSION → SOUND.

The next three examples in (3) contain synesthetic transfers from touch to color.

(3)   a.   鸦鹊飞掠而过的阴影象绒毛一样扫着他的脸。《枯河》
            The *shadows* of the crows and magpies skimming over were *brushing* his face like *fine feathers*. (*Dry River*)

      b.   房子里灰暗了一分钟，潮湿的、浅黄色的阳光就从门缝里挤进来。《球状闪电》
            For a minute it was murky in the house, and then a *damp*, light yellow *sunlight* squeezed itself inside through the crack of the door. (*Ball-Shaped Lightning*)

      c.   也许是因为生理补偿或是因为努力劳作而变得极大的左眼里突然射出了冷冰的光线，刺得我浑身不自在。《白狗秋千架》
            Her left *eye,* which had become monstrously large, perhaps as a result of physiological compensation or hard work, suddenly shot out *an ice-cold beam, pricking* me with overwhelming annoyance. (*White Dogs and the Swings*)

In (3a), the "shadows" of the birds flying over, which appeals to the sense of sight, is said to be "brushing" the person's face, thus evoking one's sensation in touch (TOUCH → COLOR). The sensation is intensified by the simile that compares the "shadows" to "fine feathers", which echoes the fact that those were "shadows" of birds. The skilful use of language really catches the harmony of the senses in this instance. In (3b), the vivid image of a "sunlight squeezing through the crack of the door, and into the house" is modified by an adjective of touch "damp", thus giving rise to the synesthetic metaphor TOUCH → COLOR. This synesthetic metaphor creates a mixed sensation amid the seemingly semantic conflict between "dampness" and "sunlight". Therefore, it can be interpreted as an example of synesthesia and oxymoron in one. Viewed in a larger context, the synesthetic and oxymoronic collocation "damp sunlight" is also open to an interpretation of a use of transferred epithet. That is, it is the hot and humid air inside the house that is "damp" (cf. Example 1 above), whereas the ray of "sunlight squeezing in through the crack of the door" simply puts the "dampness of the air" into the "spotlight". The condensed image is open to imagination and interpretation, but it comes down to a synesthetic metaphor involving a simple upward mapping (TOUCH → COLOR). It is the unusual extension and compression of this ordinary mapping that have charged the image with extraordinary aesthetic power. In (3c), the female character has lost her right eye while her left eye appears to be unnatural and unusual. In this particular instance, it "shoots out" an "ice-cold beam" that is "pricking" the narrator's body. Considering that one's eyes do have a certain quality of light but cannot "shoot out a beam" that is "ice-cold" and "pricking", we may say that this sensational depiction of the character's eye is derived from a composite synesthetic metaphor: DIMENSION + TOUCH → COLOR.

The synesthesia in (4) consists in a double transfer from taste and dimension to sound:

(4) 她笑得比蜜还甜，声音曲曲折折，如同唱歌。《球状闪电》
She laughed, a *laugh sweeter* than *honey*, with a *sound curving* and *zigzagging*, as if singing. (*Ball-Shaped Lightning*)

On the one hand, the sound of the laugh is "sweeter than honey", and on the other hand, it travels in space, leaving behind it a "curving and zigzagging line". The simultaneous mappings from two source domains to one target domain give rise to another composite synesthetic metaphor: TASTE + DIMENSION → SOUND.

The examples in (5) below contain synesthetic transfers from sound to color:

(5) a. ……   一道残缺的杏黄色阳光，从浓云中，嘶叫着射向道路。《红高粱》
… a broken ray of apricot *sunlight* was *neighing* and jetting, out of the dark thick clouds, toward the road. (*Red Sorghum*)

b. 汽车的尾部拖着一条长长的焦黄的尾巴，车头上噼噼叭叭地晃动着白炽的光芒。《红高粱》
Trailing behind the vehicle was a long brown tail, and in its front white *lights* kept swaying, *crackling and spluttering*. (*Red Sorghum*)

(5a) creates a dynamic image: the "apricot sunlight", having penetrated the "dark thick clouds", is "screaming" as a horse does while "jetting" toward the road. Although the sunlight is dashing down from the sky, with all its strength, it is interfered by the "clouds", which cause the ray of sunlight to be "broken" rather than as a solid whole. This powerful image is rooted in, among other things, a synesthetic metaphor: SOUND → COLOR. In (5b), a truck is bumping along a dirt road, stirring up a "tail" of dust behind it, and its front lights sending out white beams that keep swaying in a "crackling and spluttering" manner. In this image, however, the "noises" of the white swaying lights also echo the noises of the vehicle bumping on a rough dirt road. That is, this SOUND → COLOR synesthetic metaphor may be said to be based on a transferred epithet.

The next two examples are transfers that move downward from sight to smell:

(6) a. 风吹来，把香气吹成带状。《金发婴儿》
        The wind blew over, *turning* the *fragrance* into the *shape of a belt*.
        (*Golden-Hair Baby*)

    b. 清冽的空气里，游荡着一股股暗红色的血腥味。《红高粱》
        In the chilly air were floating strands of *dark red smell* of blood. (*Red Sorghum*)

The image in (6a), although very simple, is exceptional in that the wind can "shape" the scent, which is basically invisible and diffuse in nature, into a "belt", which then becomes tangible. This synesthetic metaphor, which maps dimension to smell, goes against the tendencies formulated by both Ullmann (1959) and Williams (1976) because it involves a "high to low" mapping: DIMENSION → SMELL. In (6b), the motivation for the intersense metaphor COLOR → SMELL is more obvious if we view it as being based on a transferred epithet, since it is the smell of blood that is "dark red". As I have noticed in my earlier study (Yu 1992), some dimension and color adjectives have also transferred to taste or smell categories in everyday Chinese. For instance, 薄酒 *bo-jiu* (thin-wine) 'weak or light wine', 厚味 *hou-wei* (thick-taste) 'savory; rich or greasy food', 味不正 *wei bu-zheng* (taste not-straight) 'not the right flavor', and 清香 *qing-xiang* (clear-fragrance) 'delicate fragrance; faint scent'. In English, as Williams (1976) points out, the dimension adjectives *flat* and *thin* are regularly used to modify words of taste as well (e.g. *flat drink, flat cooking, thin beer*).

Finally, the examples in (7) describe sound in terms of sight. This is a more common type of synesthetic metaphor.

(7) a. 高粱的茎叶在雾中滋滋乱叫，雾中缓慢地流淌着在这块低洼平
        原上穿行的墨河水明亮的喧哗，一阵强一阵弱，一阵远一阵
        近。《红高粱》
        The stalks and leaves of the sorghums were squeaking noisily in the fog, through which *flowing* slowly was the *brightly shining hubbub* of the Ink River crossing this low plain, sometimes strong, and sometimes weak, sometimes far, and sometimes near. (*Red Sorghum*)

    b. 河上传来的水声越加明亮起来，似乎它既有形状又有颜色，不
        但可闻，而且可见。《透明的红萝卜》
        The *sound* of the water coming from the river was getting *brighter and brighter*, as if it had *shape* as well as *color*, and not only audible but also *visible*. (*The Crystal Carrot*)

    c. 刘大号对着天空吹喇叭，暗红色的声音碰得高粱棵子索索打
       抖。《红高粱》
       Big Trumpet Liu was blowing the trumpet toward the sky, its *dark red*
       sounds hitting the sorghum stalks, making them tremble with rustles.
       (*Red Sorghum*)

    d. 笛声低沉压抑，颤抖不止，如缓缓爬来的黑色巨蟒 …… 《球状
       闪电》
       The sound of the bamboo flute was *low* and *heavy,* and kept *quivering,*
       like *a monstrous black boa* crawling over … (*Ball-Shaped Lightning*)

In (7a), the "hubbub" of the river is "brightly shining", and "flowing" slowly through the fog. Apparently, the writer has intentionally transferred the epithets describing the river itself to the noise it makes, so that the sound of the surging river has acquired the properties of the river itself. The composite synesthetic metaphor DIMENSION + COLOR → SOUND makes the sound of the river "a mirror image" for the river itself. It becomes the "shining shadow" of the river. The cross-modal image creates extra space for the reader's imagination. A similar example is found in (7b) from a different story, where the sound of the river is again described in terms of color and dimension. In (7c), the "sounds" of the trumpet, making a strong physical impact on the sorghum stalks around, are "dark red", a color that is a reflection of the blood scattered on the battlefield in depiction. The synesthetic metaphor, COLOR → SOUND, has evoked a stirring tragic image as forceful as the sounds of the trumpet under discussion. The sound described in (7d) is produced by a bamboo flute, which is a traditional Chinese folk musical instrument, typically played to produce high-pitch and fast-tempo music. In this particular instance, however, it is "low" and "heavy", "quivering" its way through space, "like a monstrous black boa crawling over". What is unique in this image is that multiple cross-modal transfers are combined and compressed into one composite synesthetic metaphor DIMENSION + TOUCH + COLOR → SOUND, which transcends the division of sense organs. The metaphor has also compressed into itself a simile in which the music produced by the bamboo flute is compared to a "monstrous black boa" that is "crawling over". It is this unusual combination and compression of various rhetorical elements that make the image so powerful and striking.

    To sum up, I have analyzed examples of synesthetic metaphors extracted from the novels and short stories by Mo Yan, showing how he experiments with the resources of language. The images he has shaped with words are graphic and powerful, and constitute the "literariness" and "poeticality" by which his novels and short stories are distinguished. What is most significant for our purpose here, however, is the fact that, despite all their novelty and originality, Mo Yan's synesthetic metaphors, by

and large, conform with the general tendencies described in the previous section. I
have found 11 kinds of cross-modal mapping in all, as listed in (8) below:

(8) a. TOUCH → SMELL
     b. TOUCH → SOUND
     c. TOUCH → COLOR
     d. TASTE → SOUND
     e. DIMENSION → SOUND
     f. DIMENSION → COLOR
     g. COLOR → SOUND
     h. SOUND → COLOR
     i. DIMENSION → SMELL
     j. COLOR → SMELL
     k. SOUND → TOUCH

Of these 11 kinds only last three (8i–k) are downward transfers. The eight upward
transfers (8a–h) all follow the routes that Williams has specified for synesthetic
transfers in ordinary language, as in Figure 1. It is worth mentioning here that this
analysis and description still do not reflect the fact that, in the corpus of my data,
those downward transfers really represent isolated occurrences whereas those upward transfers, and especially some of them (i.e., 8b, c, e, f, g, h), are recurring with
high frequency (see Yu 1992 for discussion).

The question is: What makes Mo Yan's intersense images so "poetic" if they
have basically used the same synesthetic transfers as in ordinary language? The
answer to this question lies in a claim of the theory of conceptual metaphor (Lakoff and Turn 1989) that poetic metaphors extend, elaborate, and combine the
same cognitive mechanisms as ordinary metaphors use in ways that go beyond the
ordinary. Thus, we see the following combinations of sources that are mapped to a
single target in a composite fashion.

(9) a. (SOUND → TOUCH) → SMELL
     b. COLOR + TOUCH → SOUND
     c. TOUCH + DIMENSION → SOUND
     d. DIMENSION + TOUCH → COLOR
     e. TASTE + DIMENSION → SOUND
     f. DIMENSION + COLOR → SOUND
     g. DIMENSION + TOUCH + COLOR → SOUND

With double or triple mappings, the synesthetic metaphors are extended, elaborated, and compressed in ways that go beyond the ordinary. Furthermore, this
creative use of synesthetic metaphors is also combined with novel use of other
figures such as simile, oxymoron, transferred epithet, as well as other kinds of

metaphors. In such a way, those images are packed with stimuli that simultaneously appeal to multiple sensations and evoke multiple experiences. It is in this extraordinary way that Mo Yan demonstrates himself as a master of, and innovator with, words.

4. Conclusion

The theory of conceptual metaphor prefers to treat poetic metaphor as a special case of ordinary metaphor, the former being constrained by the same basic cognitive mechanisms as the latter. In this study, I have lent further support to this claim by analyzing examples of synesthetic metaphor extracted from the novels and stories by Mo Yan, who is highly acclaimed by literary critics for his striking innovation with language. I have shown that his use of synesthetic metaphors (as well as other metaphors and figures), although very novel and unusual, largely conforms to some general tendencies found in both ordinary and poetic language by previous empirical studies (e.g., Ullmann 1959; Williams 1976).

Those general tendencies, in fact, fall into the paradigm of the conceptual metaphor theory, which "characterizes meaning in terms of *embodiment*, that is, in terms of our collective biological capacities and our physical and social experiences as beings functioning in our environment" (Lakoff 1987a: 267). On this view, meaning is based on experience, bodily as well as socio-cultural. Our bodily experience in and with the world sets out the contours of what is meaningful to us and determines the ways of our understanding (Johnson 1987; Lakoff 1987a; Lakoff and Johnson 1980, 1999). When we talk about our bodily being functioning in the physical world, the notion of space stands out. The conceptual domain of space occupies a special place in cognitive linguistics, which rests on "an essentially visuo-spatial conception of meaning and conceptualization, in which symbolic structures are derived from embodied constraints upon human perception and agency in a spatial field" (Sinha 1995: 7). The spatial domain is especially important because it is also commonly mapped onto other more abstract domains, giving rise to spatial conceptualization of more abstract concepts in a metaphorical fashion, which Lakoff (1987a: 283–284) calls "The Spatialization of Form hypothesis". This hypothesis "requires a metaphorical mapping from physical space into a 'conceptual space'", under which "spatial structure is mapped into conceptual structure" (p. 283). In general, there are two special cases in spatial conceptualization of abstract concepts: the location-dual, and the object-dual (Lakoff 1993; see, also, Yu 1998). For instance, "trouble" as an abstract state or concept is understood in terms of location (e.g., "I'm in trouble") or object (e.g., "I have trouble"). Thus, in cognitive linguistics, spatialization of abstract concepts is a general

cognitive principle: to view abstract concepts as three-dimensional locations, entities or substances that exist in space. This is what conceptual metaphor theory calls
metaphorical mapping from the more concrete to the more abstract, or from the
more structured to the less structured.

Relevant to the present study is the fact that the theory of conceptual metaphor provides a theoretical framework that can account for the general tendencies
in synesthetic metaphors discovered by Ullmann (1959) and Williams (1976) in
their empirical studies. For instance, according to Williams' routes for synesthetic
transfers in Figure 1, touch and dimension, the two categories that fundamentally
correspond to objects and locations in space, basically function as source domains
but not as target domains. Also, as Ullmann (1959) has noted, sound, rather than
sight, is the predominant target domain, which is unexpected from the hierarchical (i.e., the "low to high" mapping) point of view. However, this "unexpectedness"
indeed follows from the theory of conceptual metaphor. Sound is more abstract
than sight in the sense that it has no spatial existence. So, its understanding and
description are expected to undergo metaphorical mapping in terms of entities
and substances that do have spatial existence. Therefore, according to Williams'
routes for synesthetic transfers in Figure 1, sound receives cross-modal transfers
from four (which is the most) source domains: touch, taste (which is based on
touch), dimension, and color. Thus, a voice can be "firm" or "soft" (touch), "sweet"
or "bitter" (taste), "deep" or "high" (dimension), and "darkening" or "silvery"
(color). As a source domain for sight, sound only provides transfers to color, but
not to dimension. Thus, a color can be "loud" or "quiet", but a dimension, say,
height or depth, cannot. This is because color is a quality that is visible only when
existing with spatial dimensions. For the same reason, a color can be "thick" or
"deep", but a dimension, say, height or depth, cannot be "red" or "black" in the
same synesthetic sense. Finally, let me turn to smell, the sensory domain that is
closely tied with taste, but similar to sound in that it exists in the air and has no
visible existence in space. As such, it does not regularly transfer to other sensory
domains, as is obvious from Williams' (1976) diagram in Figure 1. Again, this in-
activity is predicted by conceptual metaphor theory, but unexpected from Ullmann's (1959) hierarchical point of view. According to Ullmann's hierarchical distribution, smell, which is at the middle of the hierarchy of the senses, is expected
to transfer to sound and sight, the "higher" sensory domains. As a target domain,
smell receives transfers from taste (a "sweet" or "spicy" smell) and, via taste, from
touch (a "sharp" or "heavy" smell), which is expected by Ullmann's hierarchical
distribution and shown in Williams' diagram. However, my earlier study in Chinese (Yu 1992) shows that some Chinese dimension words have transferred to
taste and smell, constituting "downward" mappings. There, I suggest that the transfer of this kind seems too strong to be categorized as irregular in Chinese. This

kind of transfer does not exist in Chinese only. As Williams (1976) points out, six English dimension words (*acute, fat, flat, high, small,* and *thin*) have also transferred to taste, although only *flat* and *thin* still remain active and natural in modern usage. From the perspective of conceptual metaphor theory, however, transfers from dimension to taste and smell do not constitute irregular mappings, for the reason explained above. The fact that there are more transfers to taste and smell from touch than from dimension may be explained from a physiological point of view: touch, but not dimension, is physiologically wired to taste and smell.

As this study has demonstrated, synesthetic metaphors in literature, which "appear eccentric and arbitrary" as a "recherché stylistic device" (O'Malley 1957: 396), actually conform to the same cognitive constraints as they do in ordinary language. Both poetic and non-poetic uses of synesthetic metaphors largely share the same pattern, although this pattern may appear stronger in ordinary than poetic language. This is because metaphors, whether conventional or novel, are grounded in our bodily experiences in the world. More generally, as cognitive linguistics claims, human meaning and understanding are embodied, fundamentally constrained by the function of our body in the environment, and by the constitution of our sense organs.

References

Barcelona, Antonio (2000). On the plausibility of claiming a metonymic motivation for conceptual metaphor. In *Metaphor and Metonymy at the Crossroads: A Cognitive Perspective,* Antonio Barcelona (ed.), 31–58. Berlin: Mouton de Gruyter.

Baron-Cohen, Simon, and John E. Harrison (eds). (1997). *Synaesthesia: Classic and Contemporary Readings.* Oxford: Blackwell.

Bogumil, Mary L. (1988). *Joyce's Use of Synaesthsia: The Intra- and Inter-episodic Recurrence of Sensory Impressions in* Ulysses. Ph.D. Dissertation at the University of South Florida.

Cytowic, Richard E. (1989). *Synesthesia: A Union of the Senses.* New York: Springer-Verlag.

Dirven, René (1985). Metaphor as a basic means for extending the lexicon. In *The Ubiquity of Metaphor: Metaphor in Language and Thought,* Wolf Paprotté and René Dirven (eds.), 85–119. Amsterdam: John Benjamins.

Downey, June E. (1912). Literary synesthesia. *Journal of Philosophy* 9: 490–498.

Engstrom, A.G. (1946). In defense of synesthesia in literature. *Philological Quarterly* 35: 1–19.

Freeman, Margaret H. (2000). Poetry and the scope of metaphor: Toward a cognitive theory of literature. In *Metaphor and Metonymy at the Crossroads: A Cognitive Perspective,* Antonio Barcelona (ed.), 253–281. Berlin: Mouton de Gruyter.

Gibbs, Raymond W. (1994). *The Poetics of Mind: Figurative Thought, Language, and Understanding.* Cambridge: Cambridge University Press.

Harrison, John (2001). *Synaesthesia: The Strangest Thing.* Oxford: Oxford University Press.

Johnson, Mark (1987). *The Body in the Mind: The Bodily Basis of Meaning, Imagination, and Reason.* Chicago: University of Chicago Press.

Lakoff, George (1986). A figure of thought. *Metaphor and Symbolic Activity* 1: 215–225.

Lakoff, George (1987a). *Women, Fire, and Dangerous Things: What Categories Reveal about the Mind.* Chicago: University of Chicago Press.

Lakoff, George (1987b). Foreword. In *Death is the Mother of Beauty,* Mark Turner. Chicago: University of Chicago Press.

Lakoff, George (1993). The contemporary theory of metaphor. In *Metaphor and Thought* (2nd ed.), Andrew Ortony (ed.), 202–251. Cambridge: Cambridge University Press.

Lakoff, George, and Mark Johnson (1980). *Metaphors We Live By.* Chicago: University of Chicago Press.

Lakoff, George, and Mark Johnson (1999). *Philosophy in the Flesh: The Embodied Mind and Its Challenge to Western Thought.* New York: Basic Books.

Lakoff, George, and Mark Turner (1989). *More than Cool Reason: A Field Guide to Poetic Metaphor.* Chicago: University of Chicago Press.

Marks, Lawrence E. (1978). *The Unity of the Senses.* New York: Academic Press.

Marks, Lawrence E. (1982). Synesthetic perception and poetic metaphor. *Journal of Experimental Psychology: Human Perception and Performance* 8: 15–23.

Marks, Lawrence E., Robin J. Hammeal, and Marc H. Bornstein (1987). *Perceiving Similarity and Comprehending Metaphor.* Chicago: University of Chicago Press.

Nelson, Osea C. (1968). *Literary Synesthesia and the Twentieth-Century Anglo-American Poetic Consciousness.* M.A. Thesis at the University of Wyoming.

O'Malley, Glenn (1957). Literary synesthesia. *The Journal of Aesthetics and Art Criticism* 15: 391–411.

Osgood, Charles E. (1980). The cognitive dynamics of synaesthesia and metaphor. *Cognition and Figurative Language,* Richard P. Honeck and Robert R. Hoffman (eds.), 203–238. Hillsdale, NJ: Lawrence Erlbaum.

Preminger, Alex (1974). *Princeton Encyclopedia of Poetry and Poetics.* Princeton, NJ: Princeton University Press.

Shen, Yeshayahu (1997). Cognitive constraints on poetic figures. *Cognitive Linguistics* 8: 33–71.

Sinha, Chris (1995). Introduction to the special issue on "Spatial Language and Cognition". *Cognitive Linguistics* 6: 7–9.

Sweetser, Eve E. (1990). *From Etymology to Pragmatics: Metaphorical and Cultural Aspects of Semantic Structure.* Cambridge: Cambridge University Press.

Sweetser, Eve E. (1992). English metaphors for language: Motivations, conventions, and creativity. *Poetics Today* 13: 705–724.

Taylor, John (1995). *Linguistic Categorization: Prototypes in Linguistic Theory* (2nd ed.). Oxford: Clarendon.

Turner, Mark (1991). *Reading Minds: The Study of English in the Age of Cognitive Science.* Princeton, NJ: Princeton University Press.

Tzur, Reuven (1992). *Toward a Theory of Cognitive Poetics.* Amsterdam: North Holland.

Ullmann, Stephen (1959/1951). *The Principle of Semantics* (2nd ed.). Glasgow: Jackson.

Wang, David Der-Wei (2000). The literary world of Mo Yan. *World Literature Today* 74: 487–494.

Williams, Joseph M. (1976). Synesthetic adjectives: A possible law of semantic change. *Language* 52: 461–478.

Yu, Ning (1992). A possible semantic law in synesthetic transfer: Evidence from Chinese. *The SECOL Review* 16: 20–40.

Yu, Ning (1995). Metaphorical expressions of anger and happiness in English and Chinese. *Metaphor and Symbolic Activity* 10: 59–92.

Yu, Ning (1998). *The Contemporary Theory of Metaphor: A Perspective from Chinese.* Amsterdam: John Benjamins.

Yu, Ning (2000). Figurative uses of *Finger* and *Palm* in Chinese and English. *Metaphor and Symbol* 15: 159–175.

Yu, Ning (2001). What does our face mean to us? *Pragmatics and Cognition* 9: 1–36.

Yu, Ning (2002). Body and emotion: Body parts in Chinese expression of emotion. In the special issue on "The body in description of emotion: Cross-linguistic studies", Nick Enfield and Anna Wierzbicka (eds.). *Pragmatics and Cognition* 10: 341–367.

Yu, Ning (2003). The bodily dimension of meaning in Chinese: What do we do and mean with "hands"? In *Cognitive Linguistics and Non-Indo-European Languages,* Eugene H. Casad and Gary B. Palmer (eds.), 337–362. Berlin: Mouton de Gruyter.

CHAPTER 4

Chinese metaphors of thinking

This article studies two of the four special cases, namely THINKING IS MOVING and THINKING IS SEEING, that constitute the metaphor system THE MIND IS A BODY, in Chinese. An analysis of linguistic data suggests that these two conceptual metaphors are grounded in our common bodily experiences of spatial movement and vision. It shows that the conceptualization of mind and mental activities is fundamentally structured by metaphors consisting of mappings from the domain of body and bodily experiences. It is found that, while the Chinese expressions under analysis largely conform to the conceptual mappings originally derived from linguistic evidence in English (Lakoff and Johnson 1999), there exists a difference between these two languages that reflects a significant difference between the related cultures. That is, Western cultures' binary contrast between the heart, the seat of emotions, and the mind, the locus of thoughts, does not exist in traditional Chinese culture, where the heart is conceptualized as housing both emotions and thoughts. It is a case in which different cultural models interpret the functioning of the mind and the body differently.

1. Introduction

During the past two decades, cognitive science has seriously challenged the fundamental assumption that most of our thinking about the world is literal, directly corresponding to an external reality. The results of cognitive linguistic studies show that human minds are embodied and thinking and reasoning are largely metaphorical and imaginative, shaped by the human body (e.g., Gibbs 1994; Johnson 1987; Lakoff 1987; Lakoff and Johnson 1980, 1999). As has been demonstrated in English and other Indo-European languages, the central metaphor about the mind and thinking is THE MIND IS A BODY (Sweetser 1990; see, also, Jäkel 1995; Radden 1996; Turner 1991; etc.), which is a metaphor system with four special cases: (1) THINKING IS MOVING, (2) THINKING IS PERCEIVING, (3) THINKING IS OBJECT MANIPULATION, and (4) ACQUIRING IDEAS IS EATING (Lakoff and Johnson

1999).[1] The MIND AS BODY metaphor consists of some general mappings shared by its four special cases (Lakoff and Johnson 1999: 235–236):

THINKING IS PHYSICAL FUNCTIONING

IDEAS ARE ENTITIES (LOCATIONS, OBJECTS, AND FOOD) WITH AN INDE-PENDENT EXISTENCE

THINKING OF AN IDEA IS FUNCTIONING PHYSICALLY WITH RESPECT TO AN INDEPENDENTLY EXISTING ENTITY

A preliminary analysis of data suggests that the central MIND AS BODY metaphor and its special cases are also found in Chinese. In this paper, I will focus on the first two of the special cases, namely thinking as moving and thinking as perceiving (more specifically, as seeing), which I have studied more thoroughly. But before I proceed, I would like to emphasize the fact that the other two special cases, i.e., thinking as object manipulation and acquiring ideas as eating, do exist in Chinese as well. Here are a few examples that reflect certain facets of their existence.[2]

(1) THINKING IS OBJECT MANIPULATION.

    a. 思想交流   *sixiang jiaoliu* (thought exchange) 'exchange of thoughts/ideas'

    b. 思想火花   *sixiang huohua* (thought sparks) 'sparks of thoughts/ideas'

    c. 抛在脑后   *pao zai nao hou* (toss at brain back) 'ignore/neglect (thoughts/ideas)'

    d. 挖空心思   *wa-kong xinsi* (dig-empty thoughts/ideas) 'rack one's brains'

    e. 思想包袱   *sixiang baofu* (thought bundle) 'load weighing on one's mind'

---

1.   In this article I use the word *thinking* in a broad sense to refer to mental activities including "thinking", "knowing", "understanding", "remembering", and so on, which are all interrelated in one way or another (see, e.g., Fortescue 2001: 17). In Chinese, various words can mean roughly "think" and "thought". For instance, both 思*si* and 想*xiang* mean "think" together with some related senses, but the former can also be used as a noun to mean "thought" and "thinking" whereas the latter cannot. The compounding of these two, 思想*sixiang*, is a noun meaning roughly "thought", "thinking", "idea", and "ideology".

2.   The data cited in this study is collected from the dictionaries (Lü and Ding 1989, 1996, Wei 1995, Wu 1993) and actual discourse. For those lexical examples, morpheme-by-morpheme or word-by-word glosses, which reflect the original metaphorical structure or imagery, are provided in the parentheses after them, followed by more idiomatic translations in the single quotes. The more idiomatic translations are taken from Wei (1995) and Wu (1993) wherever possible. In the glossing of sentential examples, CL = classifier, MOD = modifier marker, and PRT = particle.

> f. 思想疙瘩   *sixiang geda* (thought knot) 'a knot or hang-up on one's mind'
>
> g. 旧思想的束缚   *jiu sixiang-de shufu* (old idea's binding) 'the binding of old ideas'

Thoughts and ideas can be "exchanged" and when they are in contact they can produce "sparks", as in (1a) and (1b). When purposefully ignoring some thoughts or ideas, one "tosses them to the back of one's brain" (1c). Sometimes thinking is mining, as in (1d), in which one tries to "dig out" all the thoughts or ideas. The "bundle of thought" in (1e) is the load weighing on one's mind and, as such, one can continue to carry it or throw it away. One's thoughts and ideas, like strings, can get entangled into one or more "knots", which will bother the mind and inhibit one's thinking if not disentangled. What is even worse is that old ideas and concepts can "tie up" one's mind and restrict its function.

(2)   ACQUIRING IDEAS IS EATING.

> a. 精神食粮   *jingshen shiliang* (spiritual grain) 'nourishment for the mind; spiritual food'
>
> b. 陈腐观念   *chen-fu guannian* (stale-rotten idea/concept) 'an outworn idea/concept'
>
> c. 陈糠烂谷子   *chen-kang lan-guzi* (stale-chaff rotten-millet/unhusked rice) 'old ideas or stale topics'
>
> d. 馊主意   *sou zhuyi* (spoiled ideas/suggestions) 'a lousy idea; a stupid suggestion'
>
> e. 如饥似渴   *ru-ji si-ke* (like-hungry like thirsty) '(acquiring ideas) with great eagerness'
>
> f. 囫囵吞枣   *hulun tun zao* (whole swallow dates) 'swallow a date whole – lap up information without digesting it; read without understanding'
>
> g. 搜肠刮肚   *sou-chang gua-du* (search-intestines scrape-stomach) 'search intently for an idea; rack one's brains'

The "spiritual grain" in (2a) usually refers to new thoughts or ideas that will nourish one's mind. Old ideas, concepts, and topics are "stale and rotten grains" that are not edible, as in (2b) and (2c). The word *sou* in (2d) specifically describes cooked food that has spoiled and turned sour, for instance, in the heat. A lousy idea or stupid suggestion is such "spoiled and sour food" that will make you sick if you "eat" it. In (2e) and (2f), acquiring ideas is eating and drinking. For that reason, one has to "search the intestines and scrape the stomach" in order to discover any good ideas that one may have, as in (2g).

Having shown some examples of thinking as object manipulation and acquiring ideas as eating, I will analyze the metaphors of thinking as moving and seeing in the next two sections. It is hoped that my analysis will reveal the Chinese way of talking about thinking in particular, and contribute to the understanding of the embodied mind in general.

2.   Thinking as moving

Under the metaphor THINKING IS MOVING, the mental activity of thinking is conceived of as physical action of moving in space. As Lakoff and Johnson (1999) point out, the basis of this metaphor is the fact that in real life we often get information by moving around in the world. They (1999: 236) list the following mappings for this metaphor:

> THINKING IS MOVING
>
> IDEAS ARE LOCATIONS
>
> REASON IS A FORCE
>
> RATIONAL THOUGHT IS MOTION THAT IS DIRECT, DELIBERATE, STEP-BY-STEP, AND IN ACCORD WITH THE FORCE OF REASON
>
> BEING UNABLE TO THINK IS BEING UNABLE TO MOVE
>
> A LINE OF THOUGHT IS A PATH
>
> THINKING ABOUT X IS MOVING IN THE AREA AROUND X
>
> RETHINKING IS GOING OVER THE PATH AGAIN

These conceptual mappings underlie many English expressions, such as, *My mind was racing, My mind wandered for a moment, How did you reach that conclusion? I'm stuck! I can't go any farther along this line of reasoning, I can't follow you, Where are you going with this? Can you go over that again?* (Lakoff and Johnson 1999: 236–237)

On analogy with spatial movement, the metaphor THINKING IS MOVING involves a starting point, a path, and an end point. Successful thinking, therefore, moves from the starting point, along the right path, and to a desired end point. It is worth noting that, grammatically speaking, the agent of movement can be either the thinking person or his/her thoughts/mind, depending on the context. For example, when I say "I'm stuck! I can't go any farther along this line of reasoning", I am talking about my "mind" rather than "me" the person.

Now, let us examine the THINKING AS MOVING metaphor in Chinese. First, it is reflected in the compound words given in (3) and illustrated in (4).

(3) a. 思路 *si-lu* (thinking-route/path) 'train of thought; thinking'
     b. 想到 *xiang-dao* (think-reach) 'think of; call to mind; expect sth. to happen'
     c. 想通 *xiang-tong* (think-through) 'straighten out one's thinking; become convinced'
     d. 想出 *xiang-chu* (think-out) 'think out; think up'
     e. 想开 *xiang-kai* (think-open) 'accept a situation; not take it to heart'

(4) a. 门外一阵喧哗打断了她的思路。
         Men-wai   yi-zhen xuanhua daduan le   tade si-lu.
         door-outside one-CL hubbub break   PRT her thinking-route
         'A hubbub outside the door interrupted her train of thought (lit. broke the way her thought was going).'
     b. 她忽然想到一件重要的事情。
         Ta huran   xiang-dao yi-jian zhongyao de   shiqing.
         she suddenly think-reach a-CL   important MOD matter
         'She suddenly thought of something important.'
     c. 只要想通了，他就会积极地去干。
         Zhiyao   xiang-tong   le, ta jiu   hui jiji   de   qu gan.
         as-long-as think-through PRT he then   will active MOD go do
         'Once he's straightened out his thinking (lit. thought it through), he'll go all out on the job.'
     d. 她想出一条妙计。
         Ta xiang-chu yi-tiao miao   ji.
         she think-out a-CL   wonderful scheme
         'She thought out (or thought up) a brilliant scheme.'
     e. 想开点儿，别生气了。
         Xiang-kai   dianr, bie   shengqi   le.
         think-open a-bit   don't be-angry PRT
         'Calm down (lit. Think it open a bit). Don't take it to heart.'
     f. 她遭人遗弃，一时想不开就自杀了。
         Ta zao   ren yiqi,   yi-shi xiang-bu-kai   jiu   zi-sha   le.
         she was   sb. deserted a-time think-not-open then self-kill PRT
         'She was deserted by someone, and in despair (lit. unable to think it open for a while) she took her own life.'

Thinking, especially careful thinking, takes a special "route", as in (3a). This route can be "broken" or "cut off" (4a), resulting in interruption of thinking. In (3b), and illustrated by (4b), the word which means "think of" and "expect" in Chinese literally means "think and reach". That is, when you think of or expect something, you "reach" it physically. Of course, in this case, as in many others, *dao* 'reach (spatially)' has been functionalized to suggest attainment of more abstract kinds like "think of or expect something", but viewed in a larger context this is an example of motivated grammaticalization. As is very common, there are obstacles along one's "thinking route", which will hinder one's "thinking movement". When this happens, one has to "think through" (3c) these obstacles in order to reach the desired location. As illustrated in (4c), the person has to "think through" his mental barriers (i.e., to straighten out his thinking) first before he can commit himself to action. Note that while REASON IS A FORCE, REASONING IS MOVING WITH A FORCE. That is why one can "go through" one's mental barriers with reasoning.

In (4d), thoughts and ideas are understood as being in a container. They are ready for use only after they are removed from the container. People have to "think them out". This is also an example of thinking as object manipulation (cf. 1d). Sometimes, people can be confined by their own thoughts on something bad, and they need to "think and open" (3e) the container to get out of it. In (4e), the person is advised to "get out of" the angry thought that may have "trapped" him. The example in (4f) illustrates the usage of (3e) in negation. The word *bu* 'not' occurs between *xiang* 'think' and *kai* 'open' and means "unable" in this case. So the expression as a whole literally means "think but unable to open". After being struck by the tragedy of her lover's desertion, the woman was unable to "think her way out of despair", so she committed suicide.

As mentioned above, successful thinking takes a correct direction to a desired destination, as the following examples illustrate. The sentences in (6) respectively exemplify the expressions in (5).

(5)　a.　晕头转向　　*yun-tou zhuan-xiang* (dizzy-head revolving/losing-direction) 'confused and disoriented'

　　　b.　拐弯　　　　*guai-wan* (make-turn) 'turn a corner; make a turn; change one's opinion to another point of view; pursue a new course'

(6)　a.　这道算题真难，把我搞得晕头转向。
　　　　 Zhe-dao suan-ti　　 zhen　nan,　　ba-wo-gao-de yun-tou
　　　　 this-CL　 math-problem really difficult got-me　　 dizzy-head
　　　　 zhuan-xiang.
　　　　 losing-direction
　　　　 'This mathematical problem is really difficult; it's got me confused.'

b. 他思想一时还拐不过弯来。

   Ta sixiang   yi-shi   hai guai-bu-guo-wan-lai.

   he thinking a-time still unable-to-make-a-turn

   'For the time being, he hasn't straightened out his thoughts yet (lit. his thinking still can't make the turn back [to the right path]).'

When people are confused, they have "lost their direction", i.e., they are "disoriented" and unable to think clearly, as in (5a) and (6a). Since successful thinking requires "right routes", it is possible for people to "go astray" and "head in the wrong direction". They then need to "make a turn" in their thinking in order to "get back on the right track" (5b and 6b). The compounds in (7) provide more examples of a similar kind.

(7) a. 反思 *fan-si* (reverse-think) 'engage in self-examination or introspection; rethink profoundly'
     b. 反省 *fan-xing* (reverse-examine oneself critically) '(engage in) introspection, self-examination, or soul-searching'

Once people have pursued a wrong course, they need to engage in self-examination, introspection, rethinking, or soul-searching. As suggested by *fan* 'reverse' in (7a) and (7b), they need to "go back" and "retrace" the distance covered to find out what has gone wrong and where it has gone wrong.

The need to "go back" is also reflected in the compounds in (8), which all refer to "thinking of something in the past".

(8) a. 追思 *zhui-si* (chase-think) 'recall; reminisce'
     b. 追想 *zhui-xiang* (chase-think) 'recall; reminisce'
     c. 追溯 *zhui-su* (chase-trace) 'trace back to; date from'
     d. 追怀 *zhui-huai* (chase-cherish) 'call to mind; recall; reminisce'
     e. 追念 *zhui-nian* (chase-miss) 'think back; recall; reminisce'
     f. 追忆 *zhui-yi* (chase-recall) 'recall; recollect; look back'
     g. 追悔 *zhui-hui* (chase-regret) 'repent; regret'

As these compounds show, to recall, recollect, reminisce, or regret something in the past involves "chasing" it. This is because, in Chinese as much as in English, the past is conceptualized as being behind us and – where time as moving objects – as moving farther and farther away from us (Yu 1998, 1999; see also Lakoff 1993a). So when we want to think of something in the past, which is retreating farther away with time, we have to "turn around" and "chase" it in order to "catch up with it" and "get hold of it". Note that the English morpheme *re-* in *recall, recollect, reminisce, regret, reflect, retrospect, rethink,* etc., also means "back" and "again" and has a basic spatial sense that can be found, for instance, in *return, retreat, retrace, retract,* and so forth.

Sometimes, one's thinking can "travel" or "wander" very far and deep, as the examples in (9) and (10) demonstrate.

(9) a. 深谋远虑   *shen-mou yuan-lü* (deep-contemplate far-consider) 'think deeply and plan carefully; be circumspect and far-sighted'

  b. 思深虑远   *si-shen lü-yuan* (think-deep consider-far) 'think deep and consider far; be thoughtful and farseeing'

  c. 遐想/遐思   *xia-xiang/xia-si* (far-thinking) 'reverie; daydream'

(10) 满天的繁星会引起人们无边无际的遐想。
   Man-tian de   fan-xing   hui yinqi renmen wu-bian-wu-ji
   whole-sky MOD manifold-stars will cause people no-bound-no-edge
   de   xia-xiang.
   MOD far-thinking
   'A star-studded sky induces fantastic (lit. boundless and edgeless) reveries.'

When people are thinking carefully, to set up a long-term plan, for instance, they will try to make their thinking "go as deep and far as possible", as in (9a) and (9b). That is, they should be as thoughtful and farsighted as possible. In a reverie, a person's thoughts "wander far" without limit or restriction (9c), as is illustrated in (10).

While "easy thinking" involves "a smooth journey" to a desired location, "hard thinking" entails "movement" that does not lead to the destination straightforwardly, as suggested by idioms in (11), of which (11a) and (11b) are exemplified in (12).

(11) a. 想来想去   *xiang-lai xiang-qu* (think-coming think-going) 'turn over and over in one's mind'

  b. 左思右想   *zuo-si you-xiang* (left-think right-think) 'think over from different angles; turn something over in one's mind'

  c. 前思后想   *qian-si hou-xiang* (ahead-think behind-think) 'turn over in one's mind; reflect and muse; think over again and again'

(12) a. 我想来想去，还是认为自己没有错。
   Wo xiang-lai   xiang-qu,   haishi renwei ziji meiyou cuo.
   I   think-coming think-going still believe self haven't erred
   'I've thought it over and over, and still think I'm right.'

b. 她躺在床上左思右想，一夜没合眼。

Ta   tang zai-chuang-shang zuo-si   you-xiang, yi-ye
she lie   on-bed   left-think right-think whole-night
mei   he   yan.
hasn't closed eyes
'She lay awake all night, thinking the matter over and over again.'

All three idiomatic expressions in (11) refer to "thinking hard over something". When thinking something over and over in their mind, people think in a "coming and going" fashion, "around" the topic they are thinking about, as in (11a). The "back-and-forth movement" suggests a futility of effort: they are returning to where they set off. This expression also reminds of the iterative movement many people tend to make, i.e., pacing up and down, while pondering hard upon something. In (11b) and (11c), thinking over is said to be "thinking left and right or ahead and behind" in one's mind. Apparently, "turning back and forth or left and right" entails changing one's "angles of looking", namely, the shifting of one's "viewpoint". In this sense, the metaphor THINKING IS MOVING is related to the one to be addressed in the next section, THINKING IS SEEING.

Related to (11) are the two idioms in (13), which describe people in a dilemma.

(13) a. 进退两难   *jin-tui liang-nan* (advance-retreat both-difficult) 'find it difficult to advance or to retreat – be in a dilemma'
b. 左右为难   *zuo-you wei-nan* (left-right feel-difficult) 'in a dilemma; in an awkward predicament'

(14) 我想去看看她，可是不是时候。不去吧，又不放心。真是左右为难。
Wo xiang qu kankan ta, keshi bu shi shihou. Bu qu ba, you bu
I   want go see   her but not is time   not go PRT then not
fangxin.   Zhen shi zuo-you   wei-nan.
feel-relieved really is left-right feel-difficult
'I'd like to go and see her myself, though it isn't an appropriate time. But I'll never stop worrying if I don't go. It really is difficult to decide what to do for the best (lit. really difficult to turn either left or right).'

In (13), one's indecisiveness to make up one's mind is finding it difficult to move forward or backward (13a), or to turn left or right, as in (13b), illustrated in (14). The conflicts in thought are expressed in spatial terms.

In sum, the Chinese expressions discussed in this section exhibit numerous aspects of the THINKING AS MOVING metaphor. We see that thinking is moving along a correct path to a desired location. The manner of thinking is the manner of moving. There may be barriers or containments that block or confine thinking or the thinking person, and successful thinking requires going through or getting out of them. Thinking may hit upon a wrong path and, in that case, it needs to make a turn back to the right path. In self-examination or retrospection, thinking needs to reverse the course it has taken, while in recollection or regret, it needs to go back and chase the things in the past. When working hard on something, thinking tends to go back and forth or turn left and right. Facing a dilemma, it tends to be hesitant, going forward or backward, or turning left or right. These points largely conform to Lakoff and Johnson's (1999) list of mappings based on data from English.

3.   Thinking as seeing

Under the metaphor THINKING IS SEEING, the mental activity of thinking is conceptualized as the physical activity of seeing. Since we win most of our knowledge through vision, we "take an important part of our logic of knowledge from our logic of vision", and "conceptualize knowing as seeing" (Lakoff and Johnson 1999: 238). While THINKING IS MOVING emphasizes the process of thinking, THINKING IS SEEING focuses on the result of thinking. People think in order to understand, and they know after they understand. Therefore, closely related to this metaphor are its twin versions UNDERSTANDING IS SEEING and KNOWING IS SEEING. Here is the list of mappings of the THINKING AS PERCEIVING metaphor relevant to its "seeing" portion (from Lakoff and Johnson 1999: 238):

> THINKING IS PERCEIVING/SEEING
>
> IDEAS ARE THINGS PERCEIVED/SEEN
>
> COMMUNICATING IS SHOWING
>
> ATTEMPTING TO GAIN KNOWLEDGE IS SEARCHING
>
> BECOMING AWARE IS NOTICING
>
> AN AID TO KNOWING IS A LIGHT SOURCE
>
> BEING ABLE TO KNOW IS BEING ABLE TO SEE
>
> BEING IGNORANT IS BEING UNABLE TO SEE
>
> IMPEDIMENTS TO KNOWLEDGE ARE IMPEDIMENTS TO VISION
>
> DECEPTION IS PURPOSEFULLY IMPEDING VISION
>
> KNOWING FROM A "PERSPECTIVE" IS SEEING FROM A POINT OF VIEW
>
> EXPLAINING IN DETAIL IS DRAWING A PICTURE
>
> DIRECTING ATTENTION IS POINTING
>
> PAYING ATTENTION IS LOOKING AT

These metaphorical mappings again underlie many English expressions, e.g., *I see what you're saying, I don't see the point, Do I have to draw you a picture? I get the picture.* Besides, what enables you to know is "enlightening", and enabling people to know something is "shedding light on" it, making it "come to light", or "pointting it out", so that they can "see" it. On the other hand, if you don't want someone to know something, you either keep the person "in the dark" or "cover the thing up" (see Lakoff and Johnson 1999: 238–239).

The THINKING AS SEEING metaphor is also richly manifested in the Chinese lexicon and discourse. In Chinese the most basic and common word for "see", "look at", or "watch" is *kan,* which also has the extended meaning of "think" and some other related ones, as shown in (15a), illustrated by sentential examples in (15c–h).

(15) a. 看   *kan* (see) 'see; look at; watch; think; consider; look upon; regard; judge'

  b. 看法 *kan-fa* (see-method) 'a way of looking at a thing; perspective; view; opinion'

  c. 我看他是个可靠的人。
      Wo kan ta shi ge kekao de   ren.
      I   see he is   a reliable MOD person
      'I think he is (or I see him as) a reliable person.'

  d. 你对这件事怎么看？
      Ni dui   zhe-jian shi   zenme kan?
      you with-respect-to this-CL matter how   see
      'What's your view on this matter? (lit. How do you see this matter?)'

  e. 我们应该全面地看问题。
      Women yinggai quan-mian de   kan wenti.
      we   should all-sides   MOD see problems
      'We should approach (lit. see) problems from all angles.'

  f. 你们应该看清形势。
      Nimen yinggai kan qing   xingshi.
      you   should see clearly situation
      'You should make a correct appraisal of (lit. see clearly) the situation.'

  g. 你们必须从实质上看。
      Nimen bixu cong shizhi   shang kan.
      you   must from essence on   see
      'You must judge (lit. see) by essentials.'

  h. 他把人民的利益看得高于一切。
      Ta ba renmin-de liyi   kan de gao   yu   yiqie.
      he PRT people's   interests see as higher than all-else
      'He considers (lit. sees) the interests of the people as above everything else.'

Obviously, the THINKING IS SEEING metaphor is based on our visual and spatial experiences. For instance, located in a particular point in space, people will have a particular "view" of an object. This particular "view" will shape their "impression" or "opinion" of the object. The compound noun in (15b), which has the literal meaning of "method or way of seeing", means "view", "perspective", or "opinion" in Chinese. In (15c) what the speaker enunciates is his or her "view" of a person. This "view" may be partial and biased because it is based on a particular "viewpoint" or "standpoint" in space that the speaker takes. That is why different people often have different "views" on the same object. It is, therefore, wise to ask other people for their "views" on issues, as does the speaker of (15d). It is also important that we try to "see" an object "from all angles", as suggested by (15e), in order to avoid "one-sided views". If we want to have a good and thorough understanding of something, even something as abstract as a situation, we need to "see it clearly" (15f). "Seeing clearly" sometimes entails more than "seeing the appearance or surface clearly", i.e., "seeing the essence or true nature clearly" (15g), and that is why things like the X-ray have been invented. If we "see" something as "higher" than others, we consider it as more important than them (15h), since what is more important is "higher" up in our conceptual hierarchy.

The metaphor THINKING IS SEEING is further illustrated by the compounds in (16), which all contain the verb *kan* 'see'. The sentential examples in (17) illustrate (16a), (16b) and (16d).

(16)   a.   看穿   *kan-chuan* (see-penetrate) 'see through'
      b.   看透   *kan-tou* (see-pass through) 'understand thoroughly; gain an insight into; see through; know clearly'
      c.   看破   *kan-po* (see-break) 'see through'
      d.   看开   *kan-kai* (see-open) 'accept or resign oneself to an unpleasant fact or situation'

(17)   a.   小张一眼就看穿了他的诡计。
        Xiao Zhang yi-yan   jiu   kan-chuan   le   ta-de guiji.
        Xiao Zhang one-glance then see-penetrate PRT his   trick
        'Xiao Zhang saw through his trick right off (i.e. at one glance).'
      b.   这一招棋我看不透。
        Zhe yi-zhao qi   wo kan-bu-tou.
        this one-CL chess-move I   see-not-pass through
        'I don't quite understand (lit. can't see through) this move.'
      c.   我看透了她的心思。
        Wo kan-tou   le   ta-de xinsi.
        I   see-pass through PRT her   state-of-mind
        'I gained an insight into her mind.'

d. 伯母去世，你要看开些，不要过分悲伤。

Bomu qushi,   ni   yao   kan-kai xie, bu-yao guofen
auntie passed-away you should see-open a-bit don't   too-much
beishang.
grieve

'Auntie has passed away. Try to resign yourself to that fact (or to see beyond that a bit) and don't grieve too much.'

As part of our visual experience, we know that we cannot see through something unless it is transparent like glass. Under the metaphor of THINKING IS SEEING, however, our "thinking-seeing" has the power to "penetrate" whatever "barriers are in our way". Note that, to a certain degree, the metaphors of thinking as moving and seeing are similar to each other. This is because seeing itself is understood as a special kind of moving, i.e., the "eye light" moving from the eyes to the target (cf. thinking as moving to a desired location).[3] So in "seeing", the "eye light", like laser, can "penetrate", "pass through", "break", or "open" those "barriers". Once your "eye light" reaches what is beyond, you gain a good understanding of it. Note that (16d) *kan-kai* (see-open) is parallel to (3e) *xiang-kai* (think-open). Both of them apply to a negative situation in which someone needs to "open" the containment in which they are "trapped". In (17a), a trick is something bad "wrapped up" in something good. If people can "see through" the nice wrapping, then they understand how bad it is inside. In (17b), if one is "unable to see through" a move in a chess game, or metaphorically beyond it, then one fails to understand the purpose of the move. In (17c) the speaker "gained an insight into the mind" of someone else by "seeing through" it. In (17d) the person is "trapped" in a grief situation and needs to "see it open" and "get out of it".

When people see something from a particular "viewpoint", they obtain merely a "one-sided" view that may lead to an inaccurate impression. This is the experiential basis for the compounds in (18), with (18a) and (18c) illustrated by the sentential examples in (19).

(18) a. 看扁 *kan-bian* (see-flat) 'underestimate (a person)'
      b. 看低 *kan-di* (see-low) 'look down on; belittle'
      c. 小看 *xiao-kan* (small-see) 'look down upon; underestimate; belittle'

(19) a. 别把人看扁了。
      Bie ba ren   kan-bian le.
      don't PRT people see-flat   PRT
      'Don't underestimate people (lit. see people as being flat).'

3. See Lakoff (1993b) for discussion of the metaphor SEEING IS TOUCHING, i.e., seeing is the eye reaching out and touching the target.

b. 你可别小看了这件事。

Ni ke bie xiao-kan le zhe-jian shi.

you ever don't small-see PRT this-CL matter

'Don't ever underestimate the importance of this matter (lit. see this matter as being small).'

All three compounds have similar meanings. If one is "seen" as being "flat", he or she is of course not "outstanding". The compounds in (18b) and (18c) both literally mean "to see an object as lower or smaller than it actually is". In these examples, ability or importance is described spatially. For example, in (19b), what is more important is "bigger" whereas what is less important is "smaller" (cf. Matisoff 1986: 18–19).

In the foregoing compounds, the verb *kan* 'see' combines with a word (or a morpheme) that denotes spatial dimensions or actions that have spatial consequences. But this is not always the case, as illustrated by (20) and (21).

(20) a. 看轻 *kan-qing* (see-light) 'underestimate; look down upon; treat lightly'

   b. 看重 *kan-zhong* (see-heavy) 'think highly of; regard as important; value; overestimate'

(21) a. 你太看轻这件事了。

   Ni tai kan-qing zhe-jian shi le.

   you too-much see-light this-CL matter PRT

   'You treat the matter too lightly (lit. see the matter as being too light).'

   b. 不要只看重书本知识，还要在实践中学习。

   Bu-yao zhi kan-zhong shuben zhishi, hai yao

   don't only see-heavy book knowledge also should

   zai-shijian-zhong xuexi.

   in-practice learn

   'We must not consider that book knowledge alone is important (lit. only see book knowledge as being heavy); we should also learn through practice.'

In these examples, things "seen as light or heavy" are regarded as unimportant or important, respectively. There seems to be a conceptual parallel between weight and importance: what is heavy "carries more weight" and, therefore, is more important than what is light.[4] *Qing* 'light' and *zhong* 'heavy', as words indicating

---

4.   Of course, the parameter of weight, as any other parameter, is relative to context and situation. In a different context, what is "heavy" may not be as good or desirable as what is "light", e.g., *heavy-hearted* vs. *light-hearted* (see, e.g., Matisoff 1986: 27–28).

weight, are related to spatial dimensions as well. Materials being equal, what is bigger is heavier and vice versa.

All the foregoing examples illustrate the mental use of the visual verb *kan* 'see', the most common verb of sight in Chinese. There are other visual verbs commonly used in a mental sense. Of the three visual verbs in (22), the first two have developed nominal, and the last one verbal, senses of mental activity.

(22) a. 见   *jian* 'see; catch sight of' → 'view; opinion; idea'
     b. 观   *guan* 'look at; watch; observe' → 'outlook; view; concept; notion; idea'
     c. 视   *shi* 'look at' → 'regard; look upon'

All these visual verbs combine with other words to form compounds in the mental domain. To illustrate, let us start with *jian* 'see'.

(23) a. 见解   *jian-jie* (see-interpret/understand) 'view; opinion; understanding'
     b. 短见   *duan-jian* (short-view) 'shortsighted view/opinion'
     c. 高见   *gao-jian* (high-view) 'your brilliant idea; your opinion'
     d. 管见   *guan-jian* (pipe-view) 'my humble opinion; my limited understanding'
     e. 偏见   *pian-jian* (tilted-view) 'prejudice; biased opinion'
     f. 浅见   *qian-jian* (shallow-view) 'superficial view; my humble opinion'
     g. 远见   *yuan-jian* (far-view) 'foresight; vision'
     h. 灼见   *zhuo-jian* (bright/luminous-view) 'profound view; penetrating view'
     i. 卓见   *zhuo-jian* (tall and erect-view) 'excellent opinion; brilliant idea'

In (23a), the way one sees something and how one interprets or understands it constitutes one's view, opinion, or understanding. Similarly, in the rest of the compounds, *jian* 'see' has become nominal, meaning "view", "opinion", or "idea". Those words (or morphemes) that modify it are spatial and/or visual. Thus, a "short view" is a shortsighted opinion (23b), while a "high view" is a brilliant idea (23c). A "piped view" offers a narrow or limited understanding, as viewed through a pipe (23d). A "tilted view" is prejudice or a biased opinion (23e), whereas a "shallow view" is a superficial understanding (23f). A "far view" is foresighted and visionary (23g), while a "bright or luminous view" refers to profound or penetrating understanding (23h) and a "tall and erect view" indicates an excellent opinion or a brilliant idea (23i). These compounds containing *jian* 'see; opinion' further illustrate the cross-domain transfer from the visual to the mental.

Now let us look at the compounds containing *guan* 'look at' in (24).

(24) a. 观点 *guan-dian* (view-point) 'point of view; viewpoint; stand-point'

   b. 观念 *guan-nian* (view-think of/thought) 'sense; idea; concept'

   c. 悲观 *bei-gaun* (sad-view) 'pessimistic'

   d. 乐观 *le-guan* (happy-view) 'optimistic; hopeful'

   e. 客观 *ke-guan* (guest-view) 'objective'

   f. 主观 *zhu-guan* (host-view) 'subjective'

   g. 人生观 *rensheng-guan* (life-view) 'outlook on life'

   h. 世界观 *shijie-guan* (world-view) 'world view; world outlook'

Again, we can see how people "see", i.e., what "viewpoint" or "standpoint" they take, shapes how they think. For instance, they may have a "sad view" (24c) or a "happy view" (24d) and therefore develop a pessimistic or optimistic outlook. When they take a "guest view" (24e) or "host view" (24f), they tend to become more objective or subjective in their mental judgment respectively. In short, the way people "see" life or the world determines how they think about life or the world, as in (24g) and (24h).

The compounds in (25) contain *shi* 'look at'. They describe, literally, the way people "see" and, metaphorically, the way they "think". Remember that *shi* 'look at' has extended to mean "look upon" or "regard" as shown in (22c).

(25) a. 傲视 *ao-shi* (haughty-look at) 'turn up one's nose at; regard with disdain'

   b. 鄙视 *bi-shi* (scorn-look at) 'despise; disdain; look down upon'

   c. 歧视 *qi-shi* (different-look at) 'discriminate against'

   d. 忽视 *hu-shi* (overlook-look at) 'ignore; overlook; neglect'

   e. 正视 *zheng-shi* (straight-look at) 'face squarely; deal with seriously and carefully'

   f. 轻视 *qing-shi* (light-look at) 'belittle; look down on; underrate'

   g. 重视 *zhong-shi* (heavy-look at) 'attach importance to; pay attention to; think highly of; take sth. seriously; value'

   h. 珍视 *zhen-shi* (precious-look at) 'value; prize; cherish; treasure'

In all these cases, we say "look at", but mean "think of". Thus, "look at with scorn" means "despise or disdain" (25b). "Look at differently" means "discriminate against" (25c). "Look over or not look at" means "ignore or neglect" (25d). "Look straight at" means "face up to or deal with seriously and carefully" (25e). Examples (25f) and (25g) parallel (20a) and (20b). As in (25h), if people "see something as precious", they "value and cherish" it. All these compounds actually refer to mental activities, which may or may not be accompanied by the physical action of "looking" denoted literally by the verb.

In Chinese, still other visual verbs have developed senses of mental activity, as shown in (26) and illustrated in (27).

(26) a. 望 *wang* 'gaze into the distance; look far into the distance' → 'hope; expect; look forward to'

      b. 瞻 *zhan* 'look forward/ahead' → 'look forward to; look to'

      c. 顾 *gu* 'turn round and look at; look back; look at' → 'take into consideration; think of'

(27) a. 望你速归。
        Wang ni su   gui.
        gaze you immediately return
        'Hope you'll return as soon as possible.'

      b. 他瞻望未来。
        Ta zhan-wang   weilai.
        he look ahead-look far future
        'He looked forward to/thought of the future.'

      c. 她回顾过去。
        Ta hui-gu   guoqu.
        she turn round-look back past
        'She looked back at/thought about the past.'

      d. 你别只顾自己。
        Ni bie zhi gu   ziji.
        you don't only look-at self
        'Don't just think of yourself.'

      e. 不要瞻前顾后！
        Bu-yao zhan-qian   gu-hou!
        don't   look ahead-front look behind-back
        'Don't be overcautious and indecisive!'

When you hope that something will happen or somebody will come, you "gaze into the distance for the thing or person to come into sight" (27a). This is the same image that the English idiomatic phrase *look forward to*, meaning "expect eagerly", evokes. In (27b), the verb is in fact a compound of (26b) and (26a). In Chinese, as well as in English, the future is conceptualized as ahead of us (Yu 1998, 1999). Therefore, when you think of the future, you "look forward to" it. The person in (27c) "turned around and looked back" as she recalled the past. This is because the past is conceptualized as behind us. In (27d), the verb *gu* 'look back/look at' really means "think of", and selfish people always think of themselves. The idiom in (27e) contains both (26b) and (26c). An overly cautious and indecisive person, with too many worries and fears on the mind, is someone who "keeps looking ahead and behind" but does not "make a move" (cf. 13 and 14).

As shown, in both Chinese and English the future is "ahead of" us whereas the past lies "behind us". This conceptualization combines with the metaphor THINK-ING IS SEEING to produce interesting examples such as (27b) and (27c). That is, when thinking of the future, people simply "look ahead". When thinking of the past, however, they need to "turn around and look back". The compounds in (28) further illustrate that one has to "turn around and look back" when recalling the past (Yu 1998, 1999).

(28) a. 回首   *hui-shou* (turn around-head) 'look back; recollect'
      b. 回眸   *hui-mou* (turn around-eye) 'look back; recollect; recall'
      c. 回溯   *hui-su* (turn around-trace back) 'recall; look back upon'
      d. 回忆   *hui-yi* (turn around-recall/recollect) 'call to mind; recollect; recall'
      e. 回想   *hui-xiang* (turn around-think) 'think back; recollect; recall'
      f. 回念   *hui-nian* (turn around-miss) 'think back; recollect; recall'
      g. 回思   *hui-si* (turn around-think of/long for) "think back; recollect; recall'

All these verbs exclusively related to the past contain a morpheme *hui* meaning "turn around" or "turn back" (cf. 8). Note, again, that the Chinese morpheme *hui* is comparable to the English morpheme *re-*, meaning "back" or "again", which also has a basic spatial sense. Since the past is behind us, we cannot "see" it if we do not "turn around" first.

In Chinese, as explained, seeing is conceptualized as the "eye light" traveling from the eyes to the target. One's eyesight depends on how far the "eye light" can travel. Let us look at the idiomatic expressions in (29).

(29) a. 目光短浅   *mu-guang duan-qian* (eye-light short-shallow) 'shortsighted'
      b. 目光远大   *mu-guang yuan-da* (eye-light far-large) 'farsight-ed; farseeing'
      c. 目光如炬   *mu-guang ru-ju* (eye-light like-torch) 'farsighted; looking ahead with wisdom'
      d. 高瞻远瞩   *gao-zhan yuan-zhu* (high-look ahead far-gaze) 'stand high and see far; show great foresight'
      e. 站得高，看得远   *zhan-de-gao,   kan-de-yuan* (stand-COM-high, see-COM-far) 'stand high and see far; have vi-sion; be farsighted'

If one's "eye light" is "short and not deep", one is shortsighted (29a). Conversely, if a person's "eye light" is "far and large", then this person is farsighted or farseeing (29b). Note that we are here talking about mental, rather than physical, "short-sightedness" or "far-sightedness". The simile in (29c) makes the metaphor clearer. If an individual's "eye light" is like a torch, then this person is one of vision and wisdom. Similarly, a 明眼人 *ming-yan ren* (bright-eyed person) is a person of good sense. The expressions in (29d) and (29e) have the same meaning. Those people who stand higher can see farther. So the people of great vision and wisdom are often said to be standing high, say, on a mountaintop and seeing far.

   It is commonsense that seeing depends on light from the sun or electricity. This commonsense dictum also applies to the domain of thinking. Look at (30) and (31).

(30) a. 明白   *ming-bai* (bright-white) 'clear; obvious; plain; understand; re-alize; know'
      b. 明亮   *ming-liang* (bright-light) 'well-lit; bright; shining; become clear'
      c. 模糊   *mohu* 'blurred; indistinct; dim; vague'
      d. 朦胧   *menglong* '(of moonlight, etc.) dim; hazy; obscure'

(31) a. 这个问题很明白。
          Zhe-ge wenti hen ming-bai.
          this-CL matter very bright-white
          'This matter is quite clear.'

      b. 听了她这番解释，老张心里明亮了。
          Ting le   ta   zhe-fan jieshi,   Lao Zhang xin   li
          hear PRT her this-CL explanation Lao Zhang heart in
          ming-liang le.
          bright-light PRT
          'Her explanation helped Lao Zhang straighten out his thinking (lit. After Lao Zhang heard this explanation of hers, it became bright and light inside his heart).'

      c. 她对这个问题还有一些模糊的认识。
          Ta dui   zhe-ge wenti   hai you yixie mohu   de   renshi.
          she about this-CL question still have some blurred MOD ideas
          'She still has some confused ideas about the question.'

      d. 他年轻时有过朦胧的人道主义思想。
          Ta nianqing shi   you-guo   menglong de   rendaozhuyi
          he young   time used-to-have dim   MOD humanitarian

sixiang.

thought

'When he was young, he had hazy notions of humanitarianism.'

Example (31a) shows that what is "bright and white" is easy to understand. In such circumstances, one understands well as one's thinking is "enlightened" (31b). The person in (31c) has some "blurred or dim" ideas about the question, so she is still confused about it, while the person in (31d) did not understand humanitarianism well as he only had some "dim or hazy" notions about it. In short, light helps people see whereas lack of light hinders people from seeing. Given the THINKING IS SEEING metaphor, this is also the case with thinking.

To conclude, we can summarize some facets of the THINKING AS SEEING metaphor as reflected in this section. First of all, thinking in this case is determined by its "starting point", i.e., its "viewpoint" or "standpoint". It is facilitated by light and hindered by a lack of it. The manner of thought is the manner of sight, where the "eye light" moves from the eyes to the target. As the moving "eye light", thought has force, and is capable of penetrating barriers or containers. Thinking of the future is looking ahead and thinking of the past is looking back. Indecisive thinking is continuing to look ahead and behind. The higher the viewpoint is, the further thinking as seeing can reach. Again, these points largely fall into the pattern outlined in Lakoff and Johnson's (1999) list of mappings of the THINKING AS SEEING metaphor based on English data.

4.   Thinking in heart or mind

While Chinese and English share the central conceptual metaphor THE MIND IS A BODY and its special cases, their actual linguistic manifestation should display both similarities and differences. For instance, I discussed the Chinese Examples (8) and (28) in which *hui* 'turn around; go back' and *zhui* 'chase; run after' occur in the compounds denoting "thinking of the past". In English, one also "looks back" when thinking of the past. Besides, as I pointed out, *re-* in English, which has a spatial sense of "going back" as in *return, retreat, retrace, retract*, also occurs in words denoting "thinking of the past", such as *recall, recollect, regret, reflect, review, retrospect*. These examples serve as linguistic evidence showing that Chinese and English share at least four conceptual metaphors: THINKING IS MOVING, THINKING IS SEEING, TIME PASSING IS MOTION OF OBJECTS OR PEOPLE, and THE PAST IS BEHIND US. That is, in both languages, thinking of the past entails that the thinker "turns around" before "looking at it" (seeing) or "going for it" (moving). At the linguistic level, however, it seems that the conceptual metaphors and the bodily experiences in which the metaphors are grounded are more clearly and richly manifested in Chinese than in English in this particular case.[5]

At this point, I want to discuss a more important difference between Chinese and English that may reflect an important difference across cultures. That is, in English, thinking is regarded as taking place in one's mind associated with one's brain, whereas in Chinese it is traditionally conceptualized as taking place in one's heart. First look at the Chinese examples in (32).

(32) a. 我们要有冷静的头脑。
          Women yao   you lengjing de   tou-nao.
          we   should have cool   MOD head-brain
          'We should have a cool head (or, be sober-minded).'

      b. 我们应该把头脑里的错误思想清除出去。
          Women yinggai ba tou-nao   li de   cuowu sixiang qingchu
          we   should PRT head-brain in MOD wrong ideas   clear
          chuqu.
          out
          'We should rid our minds of erroneous ideas.'

      c. 僵化思想束缚着一些人的头脑。
          Jianghua sixiang shufu zhe yixie ren-de   tou-nao.
          stiffened ideas   bind PRT some people's head-brain
          'An ossified way of thinking shackles some people's minds (lit. Stiffened ideas are binding some people's minds).'

In these examples, *tounao,* literally "head and brain", means "mind" in modern Chinese. It is where one's thoughts and ideas are stored and one's thinking takes place. However, the examples below show that the heart is the "thinking organ" and the locus of the mind.

(33) a. 心事   *xin-shi* (heart-thing) 'sth. weighing on one's mind; a load on one's mind; worry'
      b. 心思   *xin-si* (heart-thought) 'thought; idea; thinking; state of mind'
      c. 心想   *xin-xiang* (heart-think) 'think; think to oneself'
      d. 心算   *xin-suan* (heart-calculate) 'mental arithmetic; doing sums in one's head'

Here, things weighing on our mind are "things weighing on our heart" (33a). Thoughts and ideas are "in our heart" (33b). When we think, our "heart thinks"

---

5. Readers are referred to my earlier studies (Yu 1995, 1998, 2000, 2001) for examples of more detailed comparisons between Chinese and English.

(33c). When we do mental arithmetic, our "heart calculates" (33d). Now, look at the idioms in (34).

(34) a. 心口如一 *xin-kou ru-yi* (heart-mouth like-one) 'say what one thinks; frank and forth-right'

b. 心想事成 *xin-xiang shi-cheng* (heart-think things-accomplished) 'goals accomplished as one hopes or wishes'

c. 眼不见，心不烦 *yan-bu-jian, xin-bu-fan* (eyes-not-see, heart-not-worry) 'what the eye doesn't see the heart doesn't worry about – out of sight, out of mind'

d. 劳心者治人，劳力者治于人。
Lao-xin   zhe   zhi   ren,   lao-li
work with-heart persons rule people work with-physical strength
zhe   zhi   yu ren.
persons ruled by people
'Those who work with their minds (lit. hearts) rule and those who work with their hands (lit. physical strength) are ruled.'

If people say what they think, their "heart and mouth are like one" (34a). The idiom in (34b) is often used by people who want to express good wishes to others: "I hope things will happen (or be accomplished) as you think they will in your heart". Example (34c) is roughly equivalent to the English proverb, *Out of sight, out of mind*, and (34d) is a well-known saying in Confucianism about the difference between mental and manual labor. An important difference between (32) and (34), which is worth emphasizing, is that (34) contains conventionalized expressions, namely idioms, and idiomatic sayings but (32) does not.

The linguistic phenomenon observed here seems to mirror an important difference in the related cultures. In Western cultures, there is a binary contrast between the heart and the mind. The mind is the location of thought whereas the heart is the seat of emotions. On the other hand, this distinction between the heart and the mind does not exist in traditional Chinese culture (Lin 2001). In ancient Chinese philosophy, they are conceptualized as being one (Lin 2001), housing thoughts and feelings, ideas and emotions, and rendered by a single Chinese character 心 *xin,* which is sometimes glossed as "heart-mind" in English (Hansen 1992). According to traditional Chinese medicine, the heart "governs the spirit light" (Wiseman and Feng 1998: 264). That is, it controls all mental activities and psychological states: carrying out thinking, storing memory, producing emotions, commanding will, governing perception, and evolving dreams (Wang et al. 1997: 181). In the Ming and Qing dynasties, however, the functions of the brain as the organ for mental activities came to be recognized. Today, the relationship between the heart and the brain is still under debate in Chinese medicine (see Wang et al. 1997: 180–182, 929–931). One view sees the brain as the house for mental activities, but the heart ultimately controls it by transporting blood to it. A different view argues that the notion of "heart" in the theories of Chinese medicine cannot be equated to the bodily organ. Instead, it is a combination of heart and brain.

The general conception of the heart in Chinese culture is reflected in the senses attached to the word *xin* 'heart' in the Chinese language. Given in (35) is the translation (my own) of the first two senses listed under *xin* 'heart' in one of the most popular Chinese dictionaries (Lü and Ding 1996: 1397).

(35)   a.   The organ inside the body of human beings and other higher animals that gives impetus to the circulation of blood. The heart of a human being is in the center, a little to the left side, of the thoracic cavity, with the shape of a circular cone and the size of one's own fist. Inside the heart there are four cavities, of which the upper two are called atriums and the lower two called ventricles. The diastoles and systoles of the atriums and ventricles circulate blood to all parts of the body. The heart is also called "the heart organ".

       b.   Usually also refers to the organ for thinking, and to thoughts, emotions, etc.

Obviously, (35a) is more of a scientific definition of the "physical heart" while (35b) represents more of a cultural conception of the "mental heart". According to a popular Chinese-English dictionary (Wei 1995), two English senses, supposedly equivalent to (35a) and (35b) are given for the word *xin* 'heart': (a) "the heart"; and (b) "heart; mind". That is, the Chinese word *xin* 'heart' also includes the meaning of "mind" in English. This is a good example of differences in categorization and lexicon across languages and cultures that should be dealt with carefully (see, e.g., Wierzbicka 1992; Goddard and Wierzbicka 1994; Goddard 2003).

5.   Conclusion

In this article I have analyzed the first two of the four special cases of the central metaphor THE MIND IS A BODY in Chinese, namely thinking as moving and seeing. These two metaphors are interrelated and share some similarities, because seeing is sometimes understood in terms of moving, i.e., the "eye light" moving from the eyes to the target. For this reason, both metaphors share the image schemas in Figure 1. Here, (1) is the ordinary SOURCE-PATH-GOAL schema, in which the trajector moves from A to B. In (2), the trajector has to go through an obstacle in order to get to B. (3) and (4) present two special cases of (2), where the obstacle is the container of either A or B.

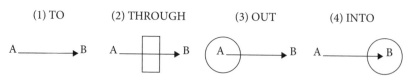

Figure 1.   Image schemas in the metaphors of thinking as moving and seeing

As shown in the data, there are two major differences between thinking as moving and thinking as seeing. Light is an important factor in the latter but not in the former. Then, lexically, the verbs for seeing have developed senses of thinking, so that one verb that primarily means "see" also means "think". On the other hand, in thinking as moving, it is usually words of thinking in collocation with words of moving or spatial words (e.g., "think-coming think-going" meaning "think over and over") that constitute the metaphor.

It has been noted that, in Chinese, thinking is conceptualized as taking place in the heart as well as in the brain. This may reflect the Chinese cultural model in which the heart commands all mental and psychological activities and controls the brain. The Chinese word *xin* refers to both the physical heart, the internal organ, and the "mental heart", or the "mind" as is called in English. That is, in Chinese, *xin* is the heart and the mind in one. The Chinese conception of *xin* can be distinguished from the predominant Western belief that the heart, the seat of emotions, contrasts with the mind, the locus of thoughts.

In this article then, I claim that Chinese shares with English the central conceptual metaphor THE MIND IS A BODY and its four special cases. I should emphasize, however, that the commonality exists at the conceptual level. At the linguistic level, the specific expressions that manifest the underlying conceptual metaphors may or may not be similar. What is significant is the finding that both Chinese and English transfer the overall logic of both spatial movement and vision into the abstract domain of mind and mental activities. In both languages, the two domains are linked via conceptual mappings from the source to the target, whereas their difference seems to be a matter of degrees to which, and manners in which, the conceptual mappings are actually manifested linguistically in each language. As Neumann (2001: 125) suggests, cross-linguistic studies of metaphor can "furnish methodologically sound evidence for the cognitive status of metaphor, as cannot be derived from a monolingual perspective". The fact that distant languages share metaphors in a systematic way supports the cognitive status of these metaphors as primarily conceptual, rooted in common human experiences.

References

Fortescue, Michael
    2001   Thoughts about thought. *Cognitive Linguistics* 12, 15–45.
Gibbs, Raymond W.
    1994   *The Poetics of Mind: Figurative Thought, Language, and Understanding*. New York: Cambridge University Press.
Goddard, Cliff
    2003   Thinking across languages and cultures: Six dimensions of variation. *Cognitive Linguistics* 14(2/3): 109–140.
Goddard, Cliff, and Anna Wierzbicka (eds.)
    1994   *Semantic and Lexical Universals: Theory and Empirical Findings*. Amsterdam: John Benjamins.
Hansen, Chad
    1992   *A Daoist Theory of Chinese Thought: A Philosophical Interpretation*. New York: Oxford University Press.
Jäkel, Olaf
    1995   The metaphorical conception of mind: "Mental activity is manipulation". In Taylor, J. R. and R. E. MacLaury (eds.), *Language and the Cognitive Construal of the World*. Berlin: Mouton de Gruyter, 197–229.
Johnson, Mark
    1987   *The Body in the Mind: The Bodily Basis of Meaning, Imagination, and Reason*. Chicago: University of Chicago Press.
Lakoff, George
    1987   *Women, Fire, and Dangerous Things: What Categories Reveal about the Mind*. Chicago: University of Chicago Press.
    1993a   The contemporary theory of metaphor. In Ortony, A. (ed.), *Metaphor and Thought* (2nd ed.). Cambridge: Cambridge University Press, 202–251.
    1993b.   The metaphor system and its role in grammar. In Beals, K., G. Cooke, D. Kathman, S. Kita, K. McCullough and D. Testen, (eds.), *Papers from the parasession on the correspondence of conceptual, semantic and grammatical representations*. Chicago: Chicago Linguistic Society, 217–241.
Lakoff, George, and Mark Johnson
    1980   *Metaphors We Live By*. Chicago: University of Chicago Press.
    1999   *Philosophy in the Flesh: The Embodied Mind and Its Challenge to Western Thought*. New York: Basic Books.
Lin, Min
    2001   *Certainty as a Social Metaphor: The Social and Historical Production of Certainty in China and West*. Westport, CT: Greenwood.
Lü, Shuxiang, and Ding, Shengshu (eds.)
    1989   *Xiandai Hanyu Cidian Bubian* [Modern Chinese Dictionary Supplement]. Beijing: The Commercial Press.
    1996   *Xiandai Hanyu Cidian* [Modern Chinese Dictionary] (revised ed.). Beijing: The Commercial Press.
Matisoff, James A.

1986   Hearts and minds in Southeast Asian languages and English. *Cahiers de Linguistique: Asie Orientale* 15, 5–57.

Neumann, Christoph
2001   Is metaphor universal? Cross-language evidence from German and Japanese. *Metaphor and Symbol* 16, 123–142.

Radden, Günter
1996   Motion metaphorized: The case of *coming* and *going*. In Casad, E. H. (ed.), *Cognitive Linguistics in the Redwoods: The Expansion of a New Paradigm in Linguistics*. Berlin: Mouton de Gruyter, 423–458.

Sweetser, Eve E.
1990   *From Etymology to Pragmatics: Metaphorical and Cultural Aspects of Semantic Structure*. Cambridge: Cambridge University Press.

Turner, Mark
1991   *Reading Minds: The Study of English in the Age of Cognitive Science*. Princeton, NJ: Princeton University Press.

Wang, Qi, Luo Xijia, Li Yun, and Liu Yanjiao
1997   *Zhongyi Zangxiang Xue* [Theory of Internal Organs in Chinese Medicine]. Beijing: People's Health Press.

Wei, Dongya (ed.)
1995   *Han Ying Cidian* [A Chinese-English Dictionary] (revised ed.). Beijing: Foreign Language Teaching and Research Press.

Wierzbicka, Anna
1992   *Semantics, Culture and Cognition: Universal Human Concepts in Culture-Specific Configurations*. New York: Oxford University Press.

Wiseman, Nigel, and Feng Ye
1998   *A Practical Dictionary of Chinese Medicine*. Brookline, MA: Paradigm Publications.

Wu, Guanghua (ed.)
1993   *Han Ying Da Cidian* [Chinese-English Dictionary] (vols. 1 & 2). Shanghai: Shanghai Jiao Tong University Press.

Yu, Ning
1995   Metaphorical expressions of anger and happiness in English and Chinese. *Metaphor and Symbolic Activity* 10, 59–92.

1998   *The Contemporary Theory of Metaphor: A Perspective from Chinese*. Amsterdam: John Benjamins.

1999   Spatial conceptualization of time in Chinese. In Hiraga, M. K., C. Sinha and S. Wilcox (eds.), *Cultural, Psychological and Typological Issues in Cogntive Linguistics*. Amsterdam: John Benjamins, 69–84.

2000   Figurative uses of *finger* and *palm* in Chinese and English. *Metaphor and Symbol* 15, 159–175.

2001   What does our face mean to us? *Pragmatics and Cognition* 9, 1–36.

2002   Body and emotion: Body parts in Chinese expression of emotion. In Enfield, N. J. and A. Wierzbicka (eds.), the special issue on "The Body in Description of Emotion: Cross-Linguistic Studies". *Pragmatics and Cognition* 10, 341–367.

2003   The bodily dimension of meaning in Chinese: What do we do and mean with "hands"? In Casad, E. H. and G. B. Palmer (eds.), *Cognitive Linguistics and Non-Indo-European Languages*. Berlin: Mouton de Gruyter, 337–362.

External body parts in conceptualization

CHAPTER 5

The bodily dimension of meaning in Chinese

What do we do and mean with "hands"?

This paper presents evidence from Chinese in support of the claim that our bodily experience plays a prominent role in the emergence of linguistic meaning. It focuses on one particular body-part term for "hand" as it is used in Chinese to denote more abstract concepts via metaphor and metonymy. It also looks at some English data for the purpose of comparison. The study demonstrates that the Chinese linguistic expressions discussed are formed via metaphor and metonymy grounded in our immediate bodily experiences with hands, and that linguistic meaning can be said to be the extension of bodily experiences through human imagination structured by metaphor and metonymy. This study, therefore, supports the claim that our living body has served as a semantic template in the evolution of our language and thought.

1. Introduction

In this study I explore the bodily dimension of meaning in Chinese from the theoretical perspective of cognitive semantics (Lakoff and Johnson 1980, 1999; Johnson 1987; Lakoff 1987; Langacker 1987; Sweetser 1990; Turner 1991; Gibbs 1994). I present evidence taken from the Chinese lexicon in support of the claim that our bodily experience plays a prominent role in the emergence of linguistic meaning. In particular I attempt to demonstrate that much of meaning originates in bodily experience and that the body and its behavior in environment are bearers of meaning.

As humans, our bodily experience provides the experiential basis of our cognition. This bodily basis of human meaning is reflected in the language we use. For instance, it has been widely documented that body-part terms are used to describe or characterize object parts and locative relationships across languages (e.g., Brugman 1983; Brugman and Macaulay 1986; MacLaury 1989; Levinson 1994; Svorou 1994; Walsh 1994; Allan 1995; Heine 1995; Matsumoto 1999). Body-part terms are also found to denote temporal and logical relationships (e.g., Hollenbach 1995) and linguistic actions (e.g., Goossens 1995; Pauwels and Simon-Vandenbergen 1995). All this provides evidence for linguistic manifestation of embodied cognition.

The present study also aims to uncover such embodied cognition via a systematic linguistic analysis. I focus on a particular body-part term in Chinese, 手 *shou* 'hand', as it is used in the Chinese lexicon to denote abstract concepts via metaphor and metonymy. I will cite some English idioms, where relevant, for the purpose of comparison.[1]

It goes without saying that our hands are one of our most important external body parts with which we deal with the external world. As humans, with bipedal and upright posture, we eat, work, and play with our hands. Different from four-legged animals, we humans walk and run with our two legs, but we still need to swing our hands to keep our body in balance. Our everyday bodily experiences with hands establish the cognitive schemas upon which we build more abstract and complex concepts. This is a process of metaphoric and metonymic conceptu-alization and categorization. It is then manifested in our language. To illustrate the embodied nature of abstraction, let me cite a few examples. Given in (1) is a set phrase containing *shou* 'hand', as well as *yan* 'eyes'. This aphorism describes the psycho-social inconsistencies of people whose ability does not match their wishes, or who are too critical of others' ability while they themselves are not capable at all. However, the abstraction is grounded in our bodily experience. Our eyes set goals, and our hands act to achieve those goals. While we can "aim high" with our eyes, our aim may be too high for us to "reach" with our hands.

(1)　眼高手低
　　　yan-gao　shou-di
　　　eyes-high hands-low
　　　'have high standards but little ability; have great ambition but little talent; have sharp eyes in criticizing others but clumsy hands in doing things oneself'

(2)　有些领导嘴硬手软。
　　　Youxie lingdao zui-ying　　shou-ruan.
　　　some   leaders mouth-tough hands-soft
　　　'Some leaders talk tough but act soft.'

(3)　两手抓，两手都要硬。
　　　Liang-shou zhua, liang-shou dou   yao　　ying.
　　　two-hands grab, two-hands both must-be tough
　　　'To grab with both hands, with both hands tough.'

In (2), which contains *shou* 'hand' and *zui* 'mouth', "hands-soft" refers metaphori-cally to some leaders' inability or unwillingness to back up in deeds their tough talk

---

1.　The English examples cited are taken either from English dictionaries or from Kövecses and Szabó (1996), which contains a section devoted to the English idioms involving the body-part term *hand*. Some of the conceptual metonymies and metaphors discussed in this paper are also taken from there.

in words ("mouth-tough"). In particular, the sentence may refer to those leaders who are unable or unwilling to carry out the well-known political slogan in China, once strongly advocated by the late leader Deng Xiaoping, as in (3). The slogan is known as "the two-hand strategy". In Chinese the verb *zhua* literally means "grab". In a more abstract sense, it also means "take charge of something (especially, a task)". More specifically, "to grab with both hands" refers to a balanced effort to promote construction of both "material civilization" and "spiritual civilization", which are also synonymous expressions for "economic reform" and "political control". That is, *on the one hand,* China should open up economically to increase the growth, and *on the other hand,* it also needs to tighten up politically to maintain social stability. A leader should work equally hard on both fronts, namely, "to grab with both hands tough, rather than one hand tough and the other soft".

Again, such abstract concepts of "balanced effort" and "hard work" are grounded in our bodily experiences with hands. Or, to put it differently, our concrete bodily experiences have worked their way up to help us make sense of more abstract concepts and enable us to reason about them. Note that one of the preceding sentences contains the English expression *on the one hand...on the other hand.* This expression also shows the contrast between two aspects that balance each other off. Often used to refer to a contrast of abstract concepts, it has clearly been derived from our experience of a body that is basically symmetrical along its primary axis.

In the following I will demonstrate the distribution of *shou* 'hand' in the Chinese lexicon, illustrating with sentences where necessary.[2] In the Chinese lexicon, a large number of compounds contain *shou* 'hand' as a constituent. I will not include, however, compounds referring to concrete objects, such as 扳手 *ban-shou* (pull/turn-hand) 'spanner; wrench' and 扶手 *fu-shou* (support-hand) 'handrail; banisters'. The compounds to be discussed can be roughly divided into nominals and verbals,[3] which are separately dealt with in the two sections below.

2. Nominals

In nominal compounds, the morpheme *shou* 'hand' can be either the modified or modifying constituent. When it is a modified constituent, it is preceded by a modifier, which can be adjectival, verbal, or nominal. When it is a modifier, it precedes the head nominal.

---

2. In collecting the Chinese data I used the following dictionaries in China: Lü and Ding (1980, 1989), Wei (1995), and Wu (1993). In the lexical examples, the parentheses contain glosses. Some examples are marked as "dialectal" (*dial.*) in the dictionaries.

3. Verbals here include adjectivals, also referred to as stative verbals in Chinese.

2.1.   Hands and persons

In the Chinese lexicon *shou* 'hand' is used very often in a metonymic (synecdochic) mold to refer to the whole person, as represented by the conceptual metonymy THE HAND STANDS FOR THE PERSON.[4] Many compounds of this kind focus on the ability, competence, expertise, experience of a person in general or in a particular trade, profession, or skill. Typically, these are adjective-noun compounds, as in (4).

(4)   a.   高手   *gao-shou* (high-hand) 'past master; master-hand'
       b.   低手   *di-shou* (low-hand) 'incompetent person'
       c.   硬手   *ying-shou* (hard/tough-hand) 'skilled hand; able person'
       d.   好手   *hao-shou* (good-hand) 'good hand; past master'
       e.   能手   *neng-shou* (able-hand) 'dab; expert; crackerjack; good hand'
       f.   妙手   *miao-shou* (marvelous-hand) 'highly skilled man'
       g.   里手   *li-shou* (inside-hand) 'expert; old hand'

Since hands are the external body parts with which people work, those who are good or bad at doing some thing are then said to have good or bad hands for carrying it out. In (4a) and (4b) the quality of being good or bad is conceptualized metaphorically in spatial terms: a "high" hand is better than a "low" hand. It is interesting to note that in Chinese a brilliant disciple or student of a good master or teacher is called a 高足 *gao-zu* (high-foot). In the human body schema, a "high foot" is still lower than a "high hand".

(5)   a.   对手   *dui-shou* (opposing/opposite-hand) 'opponent; rival'
       b.   敌手   *di-shou* (enemy-hand) '(of an opponent) match; adversary'
       c.   国手   *guo-shou* (nation/national-hand) 'athlete or player on the national team'

The term *shou* 'hand' is also used metonymically to refer to people who compete, in sports and otherwise, as in (5). Terms such as (5a, b) probably originate in physical fights, like Chinese martial arts, in which opponents often fight with their hands. Here are some related compounds: 交手 *jiao-shou* (cross-hand) means either "a fight/battle" or "to fight (with sb.)"; 出手 *chu-shou* (deal out-hand) means "the opening moves (in a fight); start to fight"; 还手 *huan-shou* (return-hand) means "to strike/hit back". Besides, in a fight, a draw or tie is called 平手 *ping-shou* (even-hand). It is apparently a spatial metaphor in which neither of the two opponents "gets the

---

4.   Another metonymy of this kind very common in Chinese, as well as in English, is THE FACE STANDS FOR THE PERSON, which I have discussed in detail elsewhere (Yu 2001). The bodily basis for this metonymy is that the face, with eyes, nose and mouth on its front and ears to its sides, is the most distinctive part of a person. See, also, Ukosakul (2003) for a discussion of its manifestation in Thai.

upper hand" (cf. 4a, b). These compounds have been mapped onto various kinds of physical and abstract competition, bringing with them the inference pattern of the source domain of physical fights with hands. In contrast to (5c), a player on the national soccer team is called a 国脚 *guo-jiao* (nation/national-foot).

Since hands are usually applied directly to tasks, those who work as assistants to their superiors are called "hands", as in (6). It is interesting to note that, as in (6d), "second hand" in Chinese can refer to an assistant, in the sense that the person is "second" to the "first hand", the person in charge, whereas in English it only means "used" or "unoriginal". In (6e) a "under hand" is the person who works "under the hand of" (i.e., assists) another person (cf. 11b below). (6f) shows a difference between Chinese and English. In English a capable assistant is called *a right hand* or *a right-hand man*, whereas *left-handed* is associated with some derogatory senses, such as "unskillful", "awkward", or "unsuccessful" (e.g., *Longman Dictionary of Contemporary English*). This asymmetry does not exist in Chinese.

(6) a. 助手   *zhu-shou* (assistant-hand) 'aide; assistant; helper'
     b. 帮手   *bang-shou* (help-hand) 'helper; assistant'
     c. 副手   *fu-shou* (vice/deputy-hand) 'assistant; helper'
     d. 二手   *er-shou* (second-hand) 'assistant; secondhand'
     e. 下手   *xia-shou* (under-hand) 'assistant; helper'
     f. 左右手   *zuo-you-shou* (left-right-hand) 'right hand; right-hand man'

(7) a. 黑手   *hei-shou* (black-hand) 'a vicious person manipulating sb. or sth. from behind the scene; evil backstage manipulator'
     b. 打手   *da-shou* (beat-hand) 'hired roughneck; hired thug'
     c. 扒手   *pa-shou* (pick-hand) 'pickpocket; shoplifter'
     d. 旗手   *qi-shou* (flag-hand) 'flag holder; forerunner; leader'
     e. 舵手   *duo-shou* (helm-hand) 'helmsman; steersman; leader'

The words in (7) are often used in metaphorical senses. For instance, (7c) can refer to people in politics who make illegitimate political profits. (7d) literally refers to the person who holds the flag in front of a troop in a marching parade. But by metaphor it has come to mean "leader" or "forerunner" of a movement. (7e), literally referring to the person who steers the helm on a ship, has often been used as a metaphor for the leader of a nation who navigates the nation as a ship. The examples in (4–7) reflect the conceptual metonymy THE HAND STANDS FOR THE PERSON, which is also found in English. People are physical living things in the world, but the synecdochic process involved here, like close-ups in visual arts, characterizes them in a way that highlights their certain abstract qualities.

2.2.   Hands and means

Now, I turn to compounds that are abstract nouns. In these, the term *shou* 'hand' is usually the modifying constituent of a noun-noun compound. Means, measures, skills, techniques, tactics, tricks, and artifices are all associated with "hands", but their meaning has extended from the physical domain of bodily activities into abstract domains of mental activities. The metonymy at work is THE HAND STANDS FOR THE SKILL/MEANS.

(8) a. 手段 *shou-duan* (hand-part) 'means; measure; method; artifice'
   b. 手法 *shou-fa* (hand-method) 'skill; technique; trick; gimmick'
   c 手腕 *shou-wan* (hand-wrist) 'trick; artifice; skill; finesse; tactics'
   d. 手笔 *shou-bi* (hand-pen) 'literary skill; (manner of handling things or spending money) ostentation and extravagance'

(8a) can be modified by 铁腕 *tie-wan* (iron-wrist) to form an idiomatic phrase 铁腕手段 *tie-wan shou-duan* (iron-wrist means), which simply means "strong and firm means". A strong hand should be supported by a strong "wrist". The strength of hands is associated with the concepts of power and control. I will return to this connection shortly. When people are doing manual work (e.g., handicrafts), the skills or techniques of doing the job is the way (i.e., the method) their hands move, hence "hand method" for skill and technique in general, as in (8b). Skilful movements of hands, to some extent, depend on the function of the wrist, and that is how "hand wrist" is related to tricks, artifices, and so forth, originally played by hands (8c). Writers' literary skills are manifested in their literary works originally written out with a pen held in the hand (of course, before the typewriter and computer eras). Therefore, the former is associated with how the pen is used by the hand in writing (8d).

(9) a. 手头 *shou-tou* (hand-end) 'at/on hand; one's financial condition at the moment'
   b. 手面 *shou-mian* (hand-surface/size) '(*dial.*) the extent of one's spending'

The two examples in (9) are related to financial means and the manner of spending money. Both are usually understood in spatial terms, as in (10). People use their hands to give out money when they spend it. Therefore, hands are associated with the manner of spending and the financial condition, so (10a) and (10b) have a metonymic basis. But in reality one's financial situation has nothing to do with "the end of one's hands", nor does one's manner of spending have anything to do with "the surface/size of one's hands". They involve mapping from the concrete to the abstract, so they are also metaphorical.

(10) a. 他手头比过去宽多了。

 Ta shou-tou bi   guoqu kuan duo le.

 he hand-end compared-with past   wider a-lot PRT

 'He's much better off than before.'

  b. 你手面太阔了，要节约一点才好。

 Ni shou-mian tai kuo le, yao jieyue

 you hand-surface too broad PRT need be-thrifty

 yidian   cai   hao.

 a-little-more then better

 'You spend too freely, and you should be more thrifty.'

As mentioned earlier, the hand is associated with power and control, which always involve skills, means, tactics, etc. Kövecses and Szabó (1996) defined the relevant metonymy and metaphor as THE HAND STANDS FOR CONTROL and CONTROL IS HOLDING IN THE HAND. Also at work is the orientational metaphor CONTROL IS UP. These are represented by the compounds in (11). "Hand-heart" literally refers to the center of the palm, which metaphorically refers to control (see Yu 2000). If you are "at the center of my palm" (11a), you are "in my grip" or under my control. If you are "under my hands" (11b), you are under my leadership, guidance, direction, or control (cf. 6e).

(11) a. 手心 shou-xin (hand-heart/center) '(the extent of) control'
  b. 手下 shou-xia (hand-underneath/below) 'under the leadership (or guidance, direction) of; under; at the hands of sb.'

Apparently, the association of hands with power and control is parallel in Chinese and English. In English, one can say: *His life was in my hand, I suffered at his hands, The meeting is getting out of hand, I'll give you a free hand, The cabinet approved last week strengthened his hand for the difficult tasks ahead.* Pertinent idiomatic phrases include: *rule with an iron hand, keep a strict hand upon a person*, etc. The metonymic and metaphoric conceptualizations behind these expressions are very similar to the Chinese expressions.

3. Verbals

Now I turn to a discussion of the class of verbal compounds. Although other forms are possible, most verbal compounds containing *shou* 'hand' are subject-predicate or verb-object constructions. In the former, *shou* 'hand' is the "subject", predicated by a verb (including adjective) that follows it. In the latter, *shou* 'hand' is the "object" following a verb.[5]

3.1.   Hands and traits

The first group of verbals, in (12), contains subject-predicate compounds. The morpheme *shou* 'hand' takes the first position, followed by an adjectival predicate that describes a particular characteristic of the hand. The *shou* constituent here is no longer used synecdochically to stand for the whole person, as in (4–7) above, but the compounds still characterize the people they describe.

(12) a. 手痒   *shou-yang* (hand-itch) 'one's fingers itch; have an itch to do sth.; be anxious to do sth.'

   b. 手黏   *shou-nian* (hand-sticky) 'sticky-fingered; thievish'

   c. 手长   *shou-chang* (hand-long) 'be greedy; grasping'

   d. 手短   *shou-duan* (hand-short) 'feel in the wrong for taking bribes'

   e. 手软   *shou-ruan* (hand-soft) 'be irresolute; be softhearted'

   f. 手黑   *shou-hei* (hand-black) '(*dial.*) cruel'

   g. 手辣   *shou-la* (hand-peppery) 'vicious; ruthless'

   h. 手松   *shou-song* (hand-loose) 'free with one's money; free-handed; open-handed'

   i. 手紧   *shou-jin* (hand-tight) 'closefisted; tightfisted; be hard up'

   j. 手大   *shou-da* (hand-big) 'spend money freely'

When anxious to do something, people feel "an itch in their hands" (12a). The feeling of "itch" is connected to the concept of anxiety to do something in both Chinese and English, but this bodily feeling is "located" in hands in Chinese and in fingers in English (See Yu 2000). In (12b) thieves are said to have "sticky hands" that will have things stuck onto them. In English, *He is sticky-fingered* or *He has sticky fingers* makes use of similar conceptualization. (12c) says that greedy people have exceptionally "long hands" that can reach out farther than ordinary hands. It resembles the English word *grasping* in the sense of "eager for more". Example (12d) refers to people who have taken bribes and therefore cannot act with justice as if they had "shorter hands" now. (13) is a popular aphorism in Chinese: "mouth-soft" is the opposite of "mouth-tough" in (2). After you have eaten others' treats, you are unable even to "talk tough" any more.

---

5.   Here I use the term "object" in a loose sense, because the verbs may not always be transitive, but may include some that are unaccusative in nature. That is to say, the nouns following these verbs may not necessarily be their direct objects.

(13) 拿了人家的手短，吃了人家的嘴软。

　　　Na le renjia-de shou-duan, chi le renjia-de zui-ruan.

　　　take PRT others' hand-short eat PRT others' mouth-soft

　　　'If you have taken others' bribes, your hands are short; if you have eaten others' treats, your mouth is soft (i.e., One cannot act with justice after taking bribes; one cannot speak uprightly after eating others' treats).'

In (12e) "hands soft" is again the same as in (2). With "soft hands", one cannot handle things that are "tough". (12f, g) have similar meanings, both describing people who are cruel, vicious, and ruthless, and often used in idioms like 心狠手黑 *xin-hen shou-hei* (heart-cruel hand-black) 'cruel and vicious' and 心毒手辣 *xin-du shou-la* (heart-poison hand-peppery) 'wicked and malignant'. Note that *shou-hei* (hand-black) and *hei-shou* (black-hand) in (7a) are different. The former is a verb meaning "to be cruel"; the latter is a noun referring to "an evil backstage manipulator". (12h-j) denote the attitudes or manners with which people spend money (cf. 9a, b). If their "hands are loose", money will "flow" out fast through their fingers. If, on the other hand, "their hands are tight", they can hold the money and save it. People with "big hands" tend to spend money in "big" ways. Those who are wasteful and extravagant are said to have "big hands and big feet" (大手大脚 *da-shou da-jiao*). To some extent, English usage parallels Chinese usage in this domain. For instance, people unwilling to spend money are said to be "closefisted" or "tightfisted"; people happy to spend are said to be "open-handed" or "free-handed". The difference, of course, is that the feet do not enter into the English usage.

Now the question remains as to the cognitive processes involved in forming the compounds of (12). They all seem to characterize people's psychological states in terms of the physical states of their hands. However, (12a) *shou-yang* 'hand-itch' may be distinguished from the rest of the group. It arguably involves a metonymic process in which the physical reaction in the hands (they "itch") is linked to a person's mental state of anxiety and stands for that mental state. But the remaining ones in (12) should be taken as instances of a metaphor THE PSYCHOLOGICAL CHARACTERISTIC OF A PERSON IS THE PHYSICAL CHARACTERISTIC OF HIS/HER HAND. It is upon this metaphoric basis that the metonymy THE HAND STANDS FOR THE PERSON has also operated. Of course, other metaphors may motivate particular cases. For instance, (12f) *shou-hei* (hand-black) 'cruel', as well as (7a) *hei-shou* (black-hand) 'evil backstage manipulator', involves the metaphor THE MORAL/ETHICAL IS CLEAN or THE IMMORAL/UNETHICAL IS DIRTY, which also accounts for such English phrases as *have clean hands, get one's hands dirty*, and *catch someone red-handed*.

Examples (12b–j) are metaphorical in that there is no real connection between the psychological characteristics of people and the physical characteristics of their hands. Thus, a greedy person does not necessarily have "long hands" (or rather "long arms") as (12c) suggests. However, these metaphorical compounds really have their grounding in our daily tactile-kinesthetic experiences with our bodies. For instance, other factors being equal, a basketball player with longer arms has a better chance of grabbing rebounds.

3.2.   Hands and moves

As mentioned earlier, hands are external body parts with which physical work is done. When we start to do something physically, we use our hands. Hands then have come to be associated with the idea of "starting something" in general, including mental work that entails the use of the brains rather than the hands. The metonymy THE HAND STANDS FOR THE ACTIVITY and the metaphor THE MIND IS THE BODY seem to be operative here. (14) contains the Chinese words that mean "start" or "begin", all containing *shou* 'hand'. In terms of internal structure they are verb-object compounds.

(14) a. 动手   *dong-shou* (move-hand) 'start work; get to work'
      b. 着手   *zhuo-shou* (put.to-hand) 'put one's hand to; set about'
      c. 入手   *ru-shou* (put.into-hand) 'start with; begin with'
      d. 下手   *xia-shou* (lower-hand) 'put one's hand to; start doing sth.'
      e. 上手   *shang-shou* (get.up.into-hand) 'get started'
      f. 开手   *kai-shou* (open-hand) '(*dial.*) start; begin'

Obviously, the meaning here has derived from our bodily experiences with our hands as we deal with the physical world. When we start to do something, we "move our hands" (14a) and "put them to the thing" (14b) we do. Or we "put our hands into the thing" (14c) in order to "handle" it. Sometimes we "lower our hands to the thing" we do as we start to "bend over" it (14d). Or, the thing gets started when it "gets up into our hands" (14e). Usually, we cannot "handle" things with our hands closed, so it is necessary for us to "open our hands" first as we start to do something (14f). (15) provides three sentential examples.

(15) a. 我们应立即着手制定计划。早点儿动手，早点儿完成。
      Women ying   liji   zhuo-shou   zhiding   jihua,
      we   should immediately put-hand-to work-out plan
      zaodianr   dong-shou, zaodianr   wancheng.
      a-little-early move-hand a-little-early finish
      'We should immediately start working out a plan. The sooner we start, the sooner we finish.'

b. 我完全不了解情况，无从下手。

Wo wanquan bu liaojie qingkuang, wucong xia-shou.

I completely not know situation no-way lower-hand

'I'm entirely in the dark about this matter, so I have no idea how to handle it (i.e., how to start).'

c. 解决问题要从调查研究入手。

Jiejue wenti yao cong diaocha yanjiu ru-shou.

solve problem should at investigation study put-hand-into

'To solve a problem, one has to start with investigation (i.e., first put our hand to investigation).'

The examples in (15) show that we "use our hands" even if we start to deal with abstract things. That is, the more abstract concept is expressed in terms of those physical actions of our hands. The English expressions *put one's hand to something* and *turn one's hand to something* reflect similar metonymic and metaphoric extensions.

(16) a. 插手 *cha-shou* (stick/plant.into-hand) 'take part; lend a hand; have a hand in; poke one's nose in; meddle in'

b. 沾手 *zhan-shou* (touch-hand) 'have a hand in'

c. 搭手 *da-shou* (join/add-hand) 'give a hand; help'

d. 累手 *lei-shou* (tire-hand) '(*dial.*) participate in'

The compounds in (16) all roughly express the meaning of "participating in something". When you have taken part in something, you have either "stuck your hands into" it (16a), or "made your hands touch" it (16b), or "joined or added your hands to" it (16c), or "made your hands tired by causing them to work on the thing" (16d). It is noteworthy that in English, in addition to the idiom *have a hand in something*, there are still other idiomatic phrases involving the body part of fingers that have similar or related meanings. For instance, *have/get a finger in something, get one's fingers into something, keep fingers on something, keep fingers on one's own affairs, have/stick a/one's finger in the/every pie* (See Yu 2000 for further discussions).

(17) a. 住手 *zhu-shou* (stop-hand) 'stay one's hand; stop; hands off'

b. 歇手 *xie-shou* (rest-hand) 'stop (work, etc.); stop doing sth.'

c. 罢手 *ba-shou* (cease-hand) 'give up; stop'

d. 丢手 *diu-shou* (toss-hand) 'wash one's hands of; give up'

e. 撂手 *liao-shou* (put/throw.down-hand) 'lay aside what one is doing; quit; throw up (one's job)'

f. 撒手 *sa-shou* (cast-hand) 'refuse to have anything more to do …'

g. 甩手 *shuai-shou* (swing-hand) 'refuse to do; wash one's hands of'

h. 抖手 *dou-shou* (jerk-hand) 'wash one's hands of'

    i.   洗手   *xi-shou* (wash-hand) 'stop doing wrong and reform oneself'
    j.   了手   *liao-shou* (finished-hand) '(*dial.*) be over and done with'
    k.   收手   *shou-shou* (take.back/put.away-hand) '(*dial.*) stop working; call it a day'

In contrast to the examples in (14), the words in (17) all have the meaning of "stop (doing sth.)". When we cease the activity, we "stop and remove our hands from" it (14a–c). Sometimes we stop the work by "tossing or throwing or casting it away" (14d–f). The physical action of our hands metonymically or metaphorically suggests our anxiety to quit the work. Sometimes we stop doing something by "swinging or jerking our hand(s)" to show our contempt to or frustration with the work, as in (14g, h). In (14i) one quits by "washing one's hands clean". Typically, this word refers to those who are determined to stop doing wrong things: they would "wash their dirty hands" and "keep them clean" forever. As in (14j), when one thing is over, it is finished or done with our hands, i.e., it should get out of our hands. It is worth noting that (14k) is not listed in the dictionaries, but I personally learned it from the speakers of a dialect in Hubei Province of China. It seems to make good sense that whenever we quit, we "take our hands back and put them away".

    English also uses the noun *hand* in phrases such as *stay one's hand, hands off, wash one's hands of, throw one's hands up*. Besides, in phrases such as *give up, throw up*, or *lay aside (what one is doing)*, the use of hands is implied even though it is not lexicalized.

3.3.   Hands and transactions

As can be seen from (14–17), based on our bodily experience, we conceptualize "starting, doing, and stopping something" in terms of physical contact between our hands and some object. This section discusses examples that refer to managing one's business affairs. In a broader sense, business handling is related to the concept of control. If you are in charge of a certain business, you control it. If you fail to handle the business, you lose control of it. Besides, the conceptualization of business as an object motivates the metonymy THE HAND STANDS FOR CONTROL and the metaphor CONTROL IS HOLDING IN THE HAND.

  (18) a. 接手 *jie-shou* (take.over-hand) 'take over (a job, responsibilities)'
        b. 经手 *jing-shou* (pass-hand) 'handle; deal with'
        c. 过手 *guo-shou* (pass/cross-hand) 'handle'

In (18a), as people take over a job, the job and the duties associated with it are "handed over" to them. They then have the job and everything going with it in their hands. If they have too many things to do at a time, they "have their hands full". The English phrase *take over* also suggests an action by hands. (18b, c) show that if people have handled or dealt with something, it should have "passed through their hands". The English verb *handle* obviously has *hand* as its root. Another English example is a commercial printed on the stationery of an insurance company: "Allstate – You're in good hands". In both languages, the physical reasoning has mapped into an abstract domain.

This type of reasoning is also reflected in goods and property transaction, ownership, etc. The metaphor in operation is POSSESSION IS HOLDING IN THE HAND. See (19) below.

(19) a. 倒手 *dao-shou* (shift-hand) 'change hands'
  b. 转手 *zhuan-shou* (turn-hand) 'sell what one has bought'
  c. 易手 *yi-shou* (change-hand) '(of properties) change hands'
  d. 到手 *dao-shou* (reach-hand) 'come to one's hands'
  e. 脱手 *tuo-shou* (get.off-hand) 'sell; dispose of'
  f. 出手 *chu-shou* (get.off-hand) 'get off one's hands; sell'
  g. 抢手 *qiang-shou* (snatch-hand) '(of goods) in great demand'

(19a, b) both refer to "making profits by selling what one has bought". The imagery is that one takes in goods from another person's hands, and then passes them off to the hands of a different person. (19c) denotes the change of ownership of properties. In (19d) buying or obtaining is conceptualized as "getting things into one's hands", whereas in (19e, f) the idea of selling is said to be "getting things off one's hands". Additionally, the phrase 出手大 *chu-shou da* (get off-hand big) means "spend money freely" (cf. 12j). (19g) describes the great demand on particular goods. Goods that enjoy very good sale are called 抢手货 *qiang-shou huo* 'goods in great demand', i.e., they are "goods at which people all snatch with their hands". Given the above examples, it is not difficult to see why used goods are called 二手货 *er-shou huo* 'second-hand goods'. There is no doubt that more abstract kinds of transactions are modeled on physical transactions expressed by these compounds literally. For the same reason, English has such expressions as *change hands, pass through many hands, come to one's hands,* and *lay one's hand on something*. When *dispose of* means "sell", it suggests the physical actions of using hands.

3.4. Hands and manners

This section discusses examples that literally describe various kinds of physical movements or actions of hands whereas, metonymically and metaphorically, they express abstract states. The conceptual metonymies are THE HAND STANDS FOR THE MANNER and THE HAND STANDS FOR THE ATTITUDE.

(20) a. 伸手   *shen-shou* (extend-hand) 'ask for (money, honor, gifts, etc.);
       reach out for (official post, power, etc.)'
   b. 缩手   *suo-shou* (draw.back-hand) 'shrink from doing sth.; be over
       cautious'
   c. 袖手   *xiu-shou* (tuck.in.sleeve-hand) 'look on with folded arms'
   d. 垂手   *chui-shou* (droop-hand) 'obtain sth. with hands down'
   e. 反手   *fan-shou* (turn.over-hand) 'turn one's hand over□a most easy
       thing to do'
   f. 拱手   *gong-shou* (cup-hand [in solution]) 'submissively'
   g. 抬手   *tai-shou* (raise-hand) 'be magnanimous; not be too hard on
       sb.; make an exception in sb's favor'
   h. 放手   *fang-shou* (release-hand) 'have a free hand; go all out; release
       one's control; give up'

When we want something, we reach out our hands to grab it. If we are anxious to get it, we may reach out "with both hands". This tactile-kinesthetic reasoning is metaphorically extended to the abstract concept of obtaining honor or power (20a). So, there are phrases such as 伸手要官 *shen-shou yao guan* 'reach out one's hands for an official post', and伸手要权 *shen-shou yao quan* 'reach out one's hands for power'. The instances are related to the metaphor POSSESSION IS HOLDING IN THE HAND. (20b) refers to a hand movement opposite to (20a) in direction. When we want to shrink from doing something, we "draw our hands back" from it. This physical action provides a bodily basis for understanding the abstract concept of withdrawing. (20b) is often combined with 缩脚 *suo-jiao* (draw back-foot) to re-sult in the idiom 缩手缩脚 *suo-shou suo-jiao* 'to be over cautious'. When people are nervous, they are likely to "shrink up" with tight muscles. Accordingly, they cannot move their hands and feet freely. Only when they are in a more relaxed state can they be more productive. That is why it is important to "have a free hand" when one does one's work.

   In (20c) *xiu* is primarily a noun meaning "sleeve(s)", and is used as a verb here meaning "tuck...in sleeves". Literally, (20c) describes an old-fashioned habitual act in Chinese culture: when people are not doing anything, especially in cold weath-er, they tend to tuck their hands in the sleeves. It is used, metonymically and met-aphorically, in an idiom 袖手旁观 *xiu-shou pang-guan* (look on with one's hands tucked in the sleeves) 'look on/stand by with folded arms'. Usually, when we are not doing anything, our hands are down by our sides, in a drooping position, which is their canonical neutral or idle position in accordance to our upright pos-ture. If we can acquire something, e.g., a goal, a success, a win, with our hands down, it means that is a very easy thing to do (20d). We can acquire it "without lifting a finger". Chinese idioms such as 垂手可得 *chui-shou ke de* 'win something with hands down; get something without lifting a finger' and 垂手可成 *chui-shou ke cheng* 'success would be easy and sure' make use of this bodily reasoning. Similarly, (20e) is used to denote that something is very easy to do or to get, as easy as to turn one's hand over, as in the idiom 反手可得 *fan-shou ke de* 'get something as easily as turning one's hand over'. (20f) usually refers to one's manner or attitude of submissiveness, as in the phrase 拱手让人 *gong-shou rang ren* 'surrender something submissively; hand something over with a bow'. In Chinese culture, *gong-shou* is a traditional type of solution, in which one cups one hand in the other before the chest. (20g) evokes the image of a person standing in the way of another, with both arms extending sideward, blocking the latter's pass. If the former "raises one hand", then the latter can get by spatially, or get off in an abstract sense. When asking for mercy, one would usually use the phrase 高抬贵手 *gao tai gui shou* (high raise noble hand) 'be lenient; be magnanimous'. (20h) has two meanings, as exemplified by (21a, b). In (21a) *fang-shou* means "have a free hand" or "go all out" while (21b) is what a professional figure skater says about her unwillingness to give up and end her figure skating career.

(21) a. 我们信得过你，你就放手干吧。
      Women xindeguo ni, ni jiu fang-shou   gan ba.
      we   trust   you you just release-hand do PRT
      'We trust you. Just do your work with a free hand (i.e., go boldly ahead with your work).'

   b. 我不愿就此放手，离开我喜爱的滑冰。
      Wo bu yuan   jiuci   fang-shou,   likai wo xi'ai de
      I   not willing like-this release-hand leave I   love MOD
      huabing.
      skating
      'I'm unwilling to give up like this and leave skating that I love so much.'

In the Chinese lexicon there are more compounds relating to doing or handling things that contain *shou* 'hand', as given below.

(22) a. 拿手 *na-shou* (take-hand) 'adept; expert; good at'
   b. 得手 *de-shou* (obtain-hand) 'succeed; be accomplished'
   c. 应手 *ying-shou* (respond-hand) 'convenient; handy'
   d. 顺手 *shun-shou* (convenient-hand) 'at one's convenience'
   e. 随手 *sui-shou* (come.along-hand) 'without extra trouble'
   f. 碍手 *ai-shou* (hinder-hand) 'be in the way; be a hindrance'
   g. 束手 *shu-shou* (tie-hand) 'have one's hands tied; be helpless'

When we can "take a firm grasp" of the thing, we are very good at handling it
(22a). In Chinese one's specialty or forte is called 拿手好戏 *na-shou hao xi* (take-
hand good play), a drama metaphor meaning "the play that an actor or actress
does best". When the matter being dealt with "gets into our hands" or "provides a
good hang for us to hold", we can then handle it with success (22b). When the
thing being dealt with is "responsive to our hand movements", then we can handle
it with ease (22c). When the things we do "go along with our hands", we can do
them conveniently, as in (22d, e). In (22f), on the other hand, we cannot do anything well when our hands are hindered by something. Very often, the idiom 碍手
碍脚 *ai-shou ai-jiao* (hinder-hand hinder-foot) is used in the same sense. It can
also denote in an abstract sense people's lack of freedom to act as they want. The
implied metaphor is FREEDOM (TO ACT) IS HAVING THE HANDS FREE (FOR AC-
TION). (22g) is a related instance, as in the idioms 束手束脚 *shu-shou shu-jiao*
(tie-hand tie-foot) 'be bound hands and feet; be over-cautious' and 束手无策 *shu-
shou wu-ce* (tie-hand no-resources) 'be at a loss what to do; be at one's wit's end'.
Now I turn to a group that comprises diverse examples. Some are adjective-noun
compounds, and the others are verb-object ones.

(23) a. 赤手 *chi-shou* (bare-hand) 'unarmed'
      b. 空手 *kong-shou* (empty-hand) 'empty-handed'
      c. 白手 *bai-shou* (empty-hand) 'empty-handed; with no possessions'
      d. 信手 *xin-shou* (at.will-hand) 'do sth. spontaneously, without much
          thought or effort'
      e. 一手 *yi-shou* (one-hand) 'skill; trick; single-handed; all alone'
      f. 双手 *shuang-shou* (both-hands) 'with both hands'
      g. 假手 *jia-shou* (borrow-hand) 'do sth. through sb. else'

(23a–c) all mean "empty-handed" literally, but (22a) refers to people who are unarmed whereas (23b, c) refer to people who have no possessions. They often appear in idioms 赤手空拳 *chi-shou kong-quan* (bare-hand empty-fist) 'unarmed',
空手而归 *kong-shou er gui* (empty-hand return) 'return empty-handed', and 白手
起家 *bai-shou qi jia* (empty-hand build-up home) 'start empty-handed; build up
one's fortune from scratch'. In (23d) people who do something spontaneously are
said to have their hands act "at their own will", as in the idiom 信手挥霍 *xin-shou
huihuo* (at will-hand spend freely) 'spend money at will'. In one sense, (23e) means
"single-handed", as in the idioms 一手包办 *yi-shou bao ban* (one-hand all-do) 'do
everything single-handed; keep everything in one's own hands' and 一手遮天 *yi-
shou zhe tian* (one-hand cover sky) 'shut out the heavens with one hand'. In a different sense, (23e) means "proficiency" or "skill", i.e., THE HAND STANDS FOR THE
SKILL. Thus, 有一手 *you yi-shou* (have one-hand) means "have proficiency or skill
in something", 露一手 *lou yi-shou* (show one-hand) means "show off one's skill",

and 留一手 *liu yi-shou* (save one-hand) means "hold back a trick or two in teaching a trade or skill". (23f) often occurs in the phrases 双手捧上*shuang-shou peng-shang* (both-hand hand over) 'offer on a silver platter' (cf. 20f) and 双手赞成 *shuang-shou zancheng* (both-hand agree) 'raise both hands in approval; be all for it'. In (23g) to get someone to do what you want to be done is said to "borrow a hand". A common idiom is 假手于人 *jia-shou yu ren* (borrow-hand from a person) 'achieve one's end through the instrumentality of someone else; use the hand of someone else'.

The examples discussed in this section can be seen as linguistically manifesting the metonymy THE HAND STANDS FOR THE ACTIVITY and the metaphor THE MIND IS THE BODY. English has similar examples (Kövecses and Szabó 1996). If people want to wait and see, they would "hold their hand". If they do not want to do anything, they will "sit on their hands" or "put their hands in their pockets" (cf. 20c). If people can do something very easily, they are said to "do it with one hand behind their back" (cf. 20d, e). If they are authorized to act as they see fit, they are "given a free hand" (cf. 20h). On the other hand, if they are said to "have their hands tied behind their back", it means that they cannot act as they want. These English examples are grounded in the common bodily experiences with hands, too.

3.5. Hands and links

In this section, the compounds that I discuss refer to the abstract notions of unity and disunity, and cooperation and separation, in bodily terms. The conceptual metaphor at work here is UNITY/COOPERATION IS JOINING HANDS or DISUNITY/SEPARATION IS PARTING HANDS.

(24) a. 携手   *xie-shou* (join-hand) 'join hands; hand in hand'
   b. 连手   *lian-shou* (link-hand) '(*dial.*) take concerted action'
   c. 联手   *lian-shou* (connect-hand) 'be united with; jointly; cooperatively'
   d. 合手   *he-shou* (combine-hand) '(*dial.*) be cooperative'
   e. 勾手   *gou-shou* (hook-hand) '(*dial.*) collude with; gang up with'
   f. 分手   *fen-shou* (separate-hand) 'part company with; go separate ways'

As shown in (24a–d), the meanings of unity, cooperation, and collaboration have been derived from the bodily action of joining hands. (24a, b) are often used in these idioms: 携手并进 *xie-shou bing jin* (join-hand side-by-side advance) 'advance together hand in hand' and 联手合作 *lian-shou hezuo* (connect-hand cooperate) 'take concerted action in cooperation'. (24c) has exactly the same sound and more or less the same meaning as (24b). (24d) is a dialectal usage. (24e) expresses unity or cooperation in a derogatory sense, i.e., between two bad guys, with their "hands hooked up together" for evil purposes. (24f), which evokes the image of two hands separating from each other, refers to cutting off relationship with someone, as well as physical separation.

Obviously, the compounds in (24) originally refer to humans with hands. But they have come to denote relationship between institutions, organizations or countries that do not have hands in a physical sense. This metaphorical mapping is manifested in English too. So *join hands with someone* or *be hand in hand with someone* can mean "cooperate with someone" as well as convey their original physical senses.

3.6. Hands and problems

This section discusses the compounds that describe problems that are difficult to handle, as in (25). For (25a–f) the metaphor is PROBLEMS ARE OBJECTS, while the objects vary in kind, shape, etc. The related metaphor is SOLVING PROBLEMS IS MANIPULATING OBJECTS WITH HANDS. For (25g) the metaphor is PROBLEMS ARE ANIMATE THINGS. Here animate things can be as big as animals or as small as insects.

(25) a. 缠手 *chan-shou* (twine-hand) 'troublesome; hard to deal with; (of an illness) hard to cure'
　　 b. 绕手 *rao-shou* (wind-hand) '(*dial.*) troublesome; thorny'
　　 c. 烫手 *tang-shou* (scald-hand) 'troublesome; knotty'
　　 d. 棘手 *ji-shou* (thorn-hand) 'thorny; troublesome; knotty'
　　 e. 扎手 *zha-shou* (prick-hand) 'difficult to handle; thorny'
　　 f. 辣手 *la-shou* (sting-hand) 'thorny; troublesome; knotty'
　　 g. 咬手 *yao-shou* (bite-hand) '(*dial.*) difficult to handle; thorny'

The bodily experiences underlying these compounds are really familiar ones. If the matter or problem we are dealing with tends to "twine or wind our hands", then it must be troublesome (25a, b). If something is "scalding hot", like a pot of boiling water, it is then potentially dangerous to deal with (25c). Similarly, things or problems that "thorn, prick, or sting our hands" must be tough or hard to handle (25d-f). If we are not careful with the things that can "bite our hands", the consequence for that will not be difficult to imagine (25g). Given below are two sentential examples of (25g).

(26) a. 这件事以前没干过，刚接触有点咬手。
　　　 Zhe-jian shi　yiqian mei　　gan guo, gang
　　　 this-CL　thing　before　have-not done PRT　just
　　　 jiechu　youdian yao-shou.
　　　 contact　a-little　bite-hand
　　　 'I hadn't done this thing before. When I first contacted (i.e., did) it, it was a little hard to handle (hand-biting).'

b. 这种东西成套地买价钱太咬手，还是零买吧。

Zhe zhong dongxi cheng-tao de   mai jiaqian tai
this kind stuff   whole-set MOD buy price   too
yao-shou,   hai-shi ling   mai ba.
hand-biting just   by-piece buy PRT
'If we buy this stuff by the set, the price is too high (hand-biting). Let's just purchase by the piece.'

As in (26a), the job is conceptualized as something concrete: your hands can actually "contact" and "handle" it. In this case, however, the job is like an untamed animal that would bite your hands when you contact it. (26b) leads us back to the examples in (19) about business transactions. In business transactions, such as purchasing, the norm is 一手交钱一手交货 *yi-shou jiao qian yi-shou jiao huo* (one-hand hand-over money, one-hand hand-over goods). This idiom evokes the image where the buyer and seller simultaneously hand over the money and goods into each other's hands. That is the "fair play" in the business transaction; it is accomplished by hands. You pay money with your hands. If the price of the goods you want to buy is too high, it "bites" your hands. There is no doubt that the abstract reasoning via metaphor reflected in (25) and (26) is based on our tactile-kinesthetic experiences with our hands. When, in English, problems are said to be "thorny" or "knotty", it entails the same metaphorical conceptualization that problems are solved by hands rather than brains.

4. Conclusion

In this study I have demonstrated that the Chinese compounds discussed are formed via metaphor and metonymy grounded in our immediate bodily experiences with hands. In this sense, meaning can be said to be the extension of bodily experiences through human imagination structured by metaphor and metonymy, as Vico ([1744] 1968) argued over 200 years ago (see also Danesi 1993). This study supports the claim that our living body has served as a semantic template in the evolution of our language and thought (Sheets-Johnstone 1990).

Some examples in this study involve metonymy only, while others involve only metaphor. But in most examples metonymy and metaphor interact and interplay in intricate ways for which Goossens (1995) coined the term "metaphtonymy". In many cases, metonymy may be the initial process through which the compounds are formed. However, these compounds have subsequently undergone metaphorical transformations that extend far beyond the prototypical meanings denoting various actions of hands. The metaphorical extension is a process of abstraction, but abstraction is embodied in the sense that it can be traced back to its root meaning of bodily activities with hands.

The commonalities between Chinese and English by far outweigh their differences. They share several conceptual metaphors and metonymies pertaining to the hand. Differences arise at the surface linguistic level. The use of the hand may be explicit in one language but implicit in the other. For instance, "to release one's hand(s)" in Chinese is "to give up" in English. One language may use a different but related body part to express a concept. An example is the use of the hand in Chinese versus the finger, a subpart of the hand, in English. A thief has "sticky hands" in Chinese and "sticky fingers" in English. The two languages use the hand in somewhat different contexts to express the same or similar concepts. Thus, "tuck one's hands in sleeves" in Chinese and "put one's hands in pockets" in English both have the meaning "purposefully avoid getting involved". The similar expressions in these two languages may have slightly different senses. For instance, the Chinese equivalent to the English idiom "wash one's hands of..." has the sense of disengagement, but it primarily means "stop doing wrong or evil and reform oneself". These differences can be attributed to different "cultural preferences" (Kövecses and Radden 1998; Yu 1995, 1998). The commonalities, on the other hand, are rooted in the common knowledge about and bodily experiences with hands.

Finally, there is no doubt that much of language rests in the hands. According to gestural theories, the use of the body, and especially of the hands, to refer to objects, beings and events in the immediate environment, and furthermore, to refer to abstract notions, ideas and affective states, was the protoform of communication and language (Danesi 1993). Gestures are an integral part of language, presenting thought in action and revealing a new dimension of the mind (McNeill 1992). More generally, it has been argued in various fields that the mind itself is the extension of the body and that meaning and thinking are modeled on the body (e.g., Danesi 1993; Johnson 1987; Shapiro 1985; Sheets-Johnstone 1990). It is time to give the body its due (Sheets-Johnstone 1992) and to put the body back in the mind (Johnson 1987). Cognitive semantics contributes to this project by bringing to light the linguistic evidence for embodied cognition.

References

Allan, Keith
    1995 The anthropocentricity of the English word(s) *back. Cognitive Linguistics* 6: 11–31.
Brugman, Claudia
    1983 The use of body-part terms as locatives in Chalcatongo Mixtec. In: Alice Schlichter, Wallace L. Chafe, and Leanne Hinton (eds.), *Survey of California and Other Indian Languages* 4, 235–290. Berkeley: University of California.

Brugman, Claudia and Monica Macaulay
    1986   Interacting semantic systems: Mixtec expressions of location. In: Vassiliki Nikifori-
           dou (ed.), *Proceedings of the Twelfth Annual Meeting of the Berkeley Linguistics Soci-
           ety*, 315–327. Berkeley: Berekeley Linguistics Society.
Danesi, Marcel
    1993   *Vico, Metaphor, and the Origin of Language*. Bloomington, IN: Indiana University
           Press.
Gibbs, Raymond W.
    1994   *The Poetics of Mind: Figurative Thought, Language, and Understanding*. Cambridge:
           Cambridge University Press.
Goossens, Louis
    1995   Metaphtonymy: The interaction of metaphor and metonymy in figurative expres-
           sions for linguistic action. In: Louis Goossens, et al., 159–174.
Goossens, Louis, Paul Pauwels, Brygida Rudzka-Ostyn, Anne-Marie Simon-Vandenbergen, and
    Johan Vanparys
    1995   *By Word of Mouth: Metaphor, Metonymy and Linguistic Action in a Cognitive Perspec-
           tive*. Amsterdam: John Benjamins.
Heine, Bernd
    1995   Conceptual grammaticalization and prediction. In: John R. Taylor and Robert E.
           MacLaury (eds.), *Language and the Cognitive Construal of the World*, 119–135. Ber-
           lin: Mouton de Gruyter.
Hollenbach, Barbara E.
    1995   Semantic and syntactic extensions of body-part terms in Mixtecan: the case of "face"
           and "foot". *International Journal of American Linguistics* 61: 168–190.
Johnson, Mark
    1987   *The Body in the Mind: The Bodily Basis of Meaning, Imagination, and Reason*. Chica-
           go: University of Chicago Press.
Kövecses, Zoltán and Péter Szabó
    1996   Idioms: A view from cognitive semantics. *Applied Linguistics* 17: 326–355.
Kövecses, Zoltán and Günter Radden
    1998   Metonymy: Developing a cognitive linguistic view. *Cognitive Linguistics* 9: 37–77.
Lakoff, George
    1987   *Women, Fire, and Dangerous Things: What Categories Reveal about the Mind*. Chi-
           cago: University of Chicago Press.
Lakoff, George and Mark Johnson
    1980   *Metaphors We Live By*. Chicago: University of Chicago Press.
    1999   *Philosophy in the Flesh: The Embodied Mind and Its Challenge to Western Thought*.
           New York: Basic Books.
Langacker, Ronald W.
    1987   Foundations of Cognitive Grammar: Theoretical Prerequisites. Vol. 1. Stanford, CA:
           Stanford University Press.
Levinson, Stephen
    1994   Vision, shape, and linguistic description: Tzeltal body-part terminology and object
           description. *Linguistics* 32: 791–855.
Lü, Shuxiang and Ding Shengshu (gen. eds.)
    1980   *Xiandai Hanyu Cidian* [Modern Chinese Dictionary]. Beijing: The Commercial
           Press.

1989 *Xiandai Hanyu Cidian Bubian* [Modern Chinese Dictionary Supplement]. Beijing: The Commercial Press.

MacLaury, Robert E.

1989 Zapotec body-part locatives: Prototypes and metaphoric extensions. *International Journal of American Linguistics* 55: 119–154.

Matsumoto, Yo

1999 On the extension of body-part nouns to object-part nouns and spatial adpositions. In: Barbara Fox, Dan Jurafsky, and Laura Michaelis (eds.), *Cognition and Function in Language,* 15–28. Stanford: CSLI Publications.

McNeill, David

1992 *Hand and Mind: What Gestures Reveal about Thought.* Chicago: University of Chicago Press.

Pauwels, Paul and Anne-Marie Simon-Vandenbergen

1995 Body parts in linguistic action: Underlying schemata and value judgements. In: Louis Goossens, et al., 35–69.

Shapiro, Kenneth Joel

1985 *Bodily Reflective Modes: A Phenomenological Method for Psychology.* Durham, NC: Duke University Press.

Sheets-Johnstone, Maxine

1990 *The Roots of Thinking.* Philadelphia: Temple University Press.

1992 (ed.) *Giving the Body Its Due.* Albany, NY: State University of New York Press.

Svorou, Soteria

1994 *The Grammar of Space.* Amsterdam: John Benjamins.

Sweetser, Eve E.

1990 *From Etymology to Pragmatics: Metaphorical and Cultural Aspects of Semantic Structure.* Cambridge: Cambridge University Press.

Turner, Mark

1991 *Reading Minds: The Study of English in the Age of Cognitive Science.* Princeton, NJ: Princeton University Press.

Ukosakul, Margaret

2003 Conceptual metaphors motivating the use of Thai 'face'. In: Eugene H. Casad and Gary B. Palmer (eds.), *Cognitive Linguistics and Non-Indo-European Languages,* 275–303. Berlin: Mouton de Gruyter.

Vico, Giambattista

1968 *The New Science of Giambattista Vico.* Revised translation of the third edition [1744] by Thomas Goddard Bergin and Max Harold Fisch. Ithaca, NY: Cornell University Press.

Walsh, Michael

1994 Body parts in Murrinh-Patha: Incorporation, grammar and metaphor. In: Hilary Chapell and William McGregor (eds.), *The Grammar of Inalienability: A Typological Perspective on Body Part Terms and the Part-whole Relation,* 327–380. Berlin: Mouton de Gruyter.

Wei, Dongya (gen. ed.)

1995 *Han Ying Cidian* [A Chinese-English Dictionary] (revised ed.). Beijing: Foreign Language Teaching and Research Press.

Wu, Guanghua (gen. ed.)
　　1993　*Han Ying Da Cidian* [Chinese-English Dictionary] (vols. 1 and 2). Shanghai: Shanghai Jiao Tong University Press.
Yu, Ning
　　1995　Metaphorical expressions of anger and happiness in English and Chinese. *Metaphor and Symbolic Activity* 10: 59–92.
　　1998　*The Contemporary Theory of Metaphor: A Perspective from Chinese.* Amsterdam: John Benjamins.
　　2000　Figurative uses of *finger* and *palm* in Chinese and English. *Metaphor and Symbol* 15: 159–175.
　　2001　What does our face mean to us? *Pragmatics and Cognition* 9: 1–36.

CHAPTER 6

Figurative uses of *finger* and *palm* in Chinese and English

This paper studies two Chinese body-part terms *zhi* 'finger' and *zhang* 'palm' as they are used in compounds and idioms to express abstract concepts. Primarily, *zhi* 'finger' is used to express intention, aim, guidance and direction whereas *zhang* 'palm' is used to refer to power and control. The metaphoric and metonymic expressions involved are based on two common acts with hands: pointing with the index finger and holding in the palm of the hand. A comparison between Chinese and English data reveals two differences. First, the conceptual metaphor CONTROL IS HOLDING IN THE PALM OF THE HAND is not richly manifested in English, although it is in Chinese. Second, the conceptual metaphor THE FINGER IS THE DOER is well manifested in English, but it is not realized in Chinese. These differences consist in the choice of a subpart (palm or finger) over the part (hand) as a result of cultural preferences. They reside, however, in a larger context of common grounding of meaning in bodily experiences.

1. Introduction

Metaphoric and metonymic uses of body-part terminology have attracted considerable attention from scholars concerned with human language. For instance, it has been widely documented that body-part terms are used to describe or characterize object parts and locative relationships across languages (e.g., Allan, 1995; Brugman, 1983; Brugman & Macaulay, 1986; Heine, 1995; Levison, 1994; MacLaury, 1989; Matsumoto, 1999; Svorou, 1994; Walsh, 1994). Body-part terms are also found to denote temporal and logical relationships (e.g., Hollenbach, 1995) and linguistic actions (e.g., Goossens, 1995; Pauwels & Simon-Vandenbergen, 1995). Lakoff and Johnson (e.g., 1980, 1999) stress the role of the body in linguistic expressions, and contend these expressions reflect and influence our thought in many ways.

This study is part of a larger project on metaphoric and metonymic use of Chinese body-part terminology (see also Yu, 1995, 1998). In particular, it is a follow-up of my earlier study of the Chinese body-part term 手 *shou* 'hand' (Yu, 2003), and focuses on 指 *zhi* 'finger' and 掌 *zhang* 'palm.' When we do things with our hands, we generally do them with our fingers and palms. When we hold things,

Table 1. The body-part terms for subparts of the hand in Chinese and English

Chinese	(shou) zhi (hand) finger	(shou) zhang (hand) palm	shou bei hand back
English	finger (of the hand)	palm (of the hand)	back of the hand

we generally hold them in our palm, with the help of our fingers. Table 1 offers Chinese and English terms for these parts, and shows the order of the modifiers. Surely reflecting the relative salience of the parts, there is no special term in Chinese or English for the back of the hand. The word 背 *bei* 'back' in Chinese and *back* in English primarily refer to the rear surface of the body between shoulders and hips. When they refer to the subpart, the "outer surface," of the hand, they have to be modified to make it clear.

There is more linguistic evidence showing that the finger and the palm occupy a more central position in our bodily experiences than the back of the hand. In Chinese, *zhi* 'finger' and *zhang* 'palm' have derived through metonymy and metaphor a number of abstract meanings. The former can mean "point at/to"; "point out, indicate, demonstrate, show"; "refer to, direct at"; "depend, rely, or count on" and so forth. The latter, in its more abstract senses, means "control" and "be in charge of." Although the Chinese compounds and idioms containing finger or palm cover a broad range of abstract meanings, they are likely grounded in two common acts: pointing with one's (index) finger and holding in the palm of one's hand.

2. The finger that points

In this section, I provide examples that suggest the majority of the Chinese compounds and idioms involving *zhi* 'finger' are likely consonant with the following two pairs of metonymy and metaphor.

(1)　a.　THE POINTING FINGER STANDS FOR INTENTION OR TARGET
　　　b.　INTENTION OR TARGET IS WHAT THE FINGER POINTS TO

(2)　a.　THE POINTING FINGER STANDS FOR GUIDANCE OR DIRECTION
　　　b.　TO GUIDE OR DIRECT IS TO POINT WITH THE FINGER

As is obvious, the two pairs are rooted in the act of pointing. We point for various purposes – identifying a target or giving directions, for instance. I first illustrate with examples realizing (1a) and (1b). But before I proceed, a word about data collection and presentation. In collecting the Chinese data I used the following popular dictionaries in China: Lü and Ding (1980, 1989, 1996), Wang (1992), Wei (1995), and G. Wu (1993), and J. Wu (1981). In the lexical examples, the parentheses contain glosses. In the glosses of sentential examples, PRT is particle and MOD is modifier marker.

In (3a) the aim or intention is "the goal or destination to which the finger points." In (3b) the main idea or gist is "the main or important point at which the finger points." It is the intention of a speaker or writer who tries to "reach an aim" or "hit a target" in a discourse or text. But before anything else, he or she first points to it and identifies it.

(3)　a.　指归　*zhi-gui* (pointing finger-goal/destination) 'aim; intention'
　　　b.　指要　*zhi-yao* (pointing finger-main/important point) 'main idea; gist'

The metaphorical connection of finger pointing and the meaning of intention is also found in the idioms in (4), where the person says something but means something else. The real intended target of the remarks is what the finger is pointing to.

(4)　a.　指鸡骂狗　*zhi-ji ma-gou* (finger pointing-chicken curse-dog) 'point at the chicken and curse the dog; abuse one over the shoulder of another; scold a person indirectly'
　　　b.　指桑骂槐　*zhi-sang ma-huai* (finger pointing-mulberry curse-locust) 'point at the mulberry and abuse the locust; point at one but abuse another'
　　　c.　指东说西　*zhi-dong shuo-xi* (finger pointing-east talk-west) 'point to the east and talk west; make a concealed/roundabout reference to something; make insinuations'
　　　d.　指黑道白　*zhi-hei dao-bai* (finger pointing-black talk-white) 'point to black and say it's white'

The examples in (5) illustrate the connection between finger pointing and (identification of) a target. Example (5a), the compound meaning "accuse" or "charge," shows that when one accuses another, the accuser's finger also points at the accused. Example (5b) evokes the image that the witness points at the defendant when testifying against him or her. The compound can also mean "confess," especially also identifying other suspects. Identification is what (5c) is about, again rooted in the image of finger pointing. Examples (5d–f) all refer to verbal attacks, with which fingers pointed at the target are associated. Example (5') gives two sentential examples.

(5)　a.　指控　*zhi-kong* (finger pointing-accuse) 'accuse; charge'
　　　b.　指供　*zhi-gong* (finger pointing-testify/confess) 'testify; confess'
　　　c.　指认　*zhi-ren* (finger pointing-recognize/confirm) 'point out and confirm; identify'

d. 指斥   *zhi-chi* (finger pointing-scold) 'reprove; reprimand; denounce'

e. 指责   *zhi-ze* (finger pointing-reproach) 'charge; censure; criticize; find fault with'

f. 指摘   *zhi-zhai* (finger pointing-blame) 'pick faults and criticize; censure; blame'

(5') a. 有人指控他纳贿。

   Youren   zhi-kong   ta   na-hui.
   someone finger pointing-accuse him accept-bribes
   'Someone accused him of taking bribes.'

   b. 大家指责他玩忽职守。

   Dajia   zhi-ze   ta   wanhu zhishou.
   everybody finger pointing-reproach him neglect duty
   'Everybody criticized him for neglect of duty.'

The idioms in (6) provide further exemplification. When a thousand people (i.e. everybody) point fingers at one, then the person is the target of universal condemnation, as in (6a). In (6b) and (6c) finger pointing is again connected with censure and criticism.

(6) a. 千夫所指   *qian-fu suo-zhi* (one thousand-people PRT-finger pointing) 'face a thousand accusing fingers; be universally condemned; be condemned by the public'

   b. 指指戳戳   *zhi-zhi chuo-chuo* ([finger] point-point jab-jab) 'comment unfavorably; censure'

   c. 指手划脚   *zhi-shou hua-jiao* ([finger] point-hand throw-foot) 'make indiscreet remarks or criticisms; find/pick fault with'

Although finger pointing identifies the target of criticism, its function is not limited to this. The compounds in (7) exemplify a different kind of target identification, (7') illustrating how they are used in sentences. These examples show that you point to people or things – that is, to identify them – on whom or which you count, rely, or depend for whatever reasons.

(7) a. 指望   *zhi-wang* (finger pointing-expect) 'look to; count on; prospect; hope'

   b. 指靠   *zhi-kao* (finger pointing-rely on) 'depend on (for ones' livelihood); look to (for help); count on'

   c. 指仗   *zhi-zhang* (finger pointing-depend on) '(*dial.*) count on; rely on'

(7')   a.   我不指望他帮忙。
       Wo bu zhi-wang   ta   bangmang.
       I   not finger pointing-expect him help
       'I don't count on him for help.'

     b.   这件事我们就指靠你了。
       Zhejian shi   women jiu   zhi-kao   ni   le.
       this   matter we   then finger pointing-rely on you PRT
       'We'll count on you for this.'

     c.   这里农民的一年生计就指仗地里的收成。
       Zheli nongmin de   yi-nian shengji   jiu
       here peasants MOD   one-year livelihood all
       zhi-zhang   di   li   de   shoucheng.
       finger pointing-depend on field in MOD crop
       'The whole year's livelihood of the peasants here all depends on the
       crop in the field.'

Example (8) demonstrates still another kind of target identification, as illustrated
by (8'). They show that appointment, assignment, designation, and instigation also
involve finger pointing. As in (8'a) and (8'b), you point at people when you appoint them to a certain position or assign them to a certain task. Example (8'c)
shows that instigators point their fingers when instigating.

  (8)   a.   指定   *zhi-ding* (finger pointing-decide) 'appoint; assign; designate'
      b.   指派   *zhi-pai* (finger pointing-dispatch) 'appoint; name; designate'
      c.   指使   *zhi-shi* (finger pointing-send) 'instigate; incite; put someone
                    up to something'

  (8')   a.   政府将指定谈判代表。
       Zhengfu   jiang zhi-ding   tanpan
       government will   finger pointing-decide negotiations
       daibiao.
       representatives
       'The government will appoint representatives to the negotiations.'

     b.   该国已指派代表出席会议。
       Gai guo   yi   zhi-pai   daibiao chuxi
       this nation already finger pointing-dispatch delegates attend
       huiyi.
       conference
       'This nation already named its delegates to the conference.'

c. 一定有人幕后指使他做坏事。

Yiding   you   ren   mu-hou   zhi-shi
definitely there-is someone scene-behind finger pointing-send
ta   zuo huai-shi.
him do   bad-things
'There must be someone behind the scene who instigates him to do evil.'

Now, I turn to examples that contribute to (2a) and (2b), namely THE POINTING FINGER STANDS FOR GUIDANCE OR DIRECTION and TO GUIDE OR DIRECT IS TO POINT WITH A FINGER. These examples are in effect related to the previous ones in that finger pointing here also helps to identify something, broadly understood as a target. The overall image is that a superior is guiding or directing an inferior by means of finger pointing.

The compounds in (9) are both verbs and nouns. Example (9a) refers to certain actions and people who perform those actions. Examples (9b) and (9c) refer to some linguistic actions and contents of those actions. The abstract senses here have their bodily roots.

(9) a. 指挥 *zhi-hui* (finger pointing-wave) 'command; direct; conduct; commander; director; conductor'

b. 指令 *zhi-ling* (finger pointing-order) 'instruct; order; direct; directive; command'

c. 指示 *zhi-shi* (finger pointing-show) 'indicate; point out; instruct; directive; instruction; indication'

The compounds in (10) all have senses related to guiding, directing, supervising, or advising, exemplified by (10'). In (10a) finger pointing is associated with advice giving or demonstration. As in (10b), people "point out" things with their finger. When things are "out," they are easier to "see," or rather, to understand, since UNDERSTANDING IS SEEING according to the MIND AS BODY metaphor (Sweetser 1990). Things are easier to "see" when they are "brought out to light" rather than "hidden in the dark." The literal meaning of (10c) is "to point something out to light" so that it is easier to "see." In (10d) and (10e) when people lead or guide others, they point to the direction in which they are heading. As in (10f), people poke or pluck things with their fingers to "turn them right." In (10g) people point out where things are not straight to "straighten them up." Examples (10h) and (10i) show that teaching and instructing also involve finger pointing: Teachers or instructors point to direct students' attention.

(10) a. 指点 *zhi-dian* (finger pointing-point) 'give pointers, advice, directions; show how; gossip about someone's faults; find fault with'

b. 指出 *zhi-chu* (finger pointing-out) 'point out; lay/put one's finger on; state briefly; show clearly; advise; indicate; pinpoint'

c. 指明 *zhi-ming* (finger pointing-light/bright) 'show clearly; demonstrate; point out'

d. 指引 *zhi-yin* (finger pointing-lead) 'point the way; guide; show'

e. 指导 *zhi-dao* (finger pointing-guide) 'guide; direct; supervise; advise; coach'

f. 指拨 *zhi-bo* (finger pointing-pluck/poke) 'give pointers, advice; show how; coach'

g. 指正 *zhi-zheng* (finger pointing-straight/right) 'point out mistakes so that they can be corrected; make a comment or criticism'

h. 指教 *zhi-jiao* (finger pointing-teach) 'give advice or comments'

i. 指授 *zhi-shou* (finger pointing-instruct) 'instruct'

(10') a. 经他一指点，我就全明白了。

Jing ta yi zhi-dian,   wo jiu quan
after he once finger pointing-point I   then completely
mingbai   le.
understand PRT

'A few pointers from him made it all clear to me.'

b. 他果真指出了我的弱点。

Ta guozhen zhi-chu   le wode ruo-dian.
he indeed   finger pointing-out PRT my   weak-point

'He indeed laid his fingers on my weak spot.'

c. 她指明了两者之间的差别。

Ta zhi-ming   le liangzhe zhijian   de   chabie.
she finger pointing-light PRT two   between MOD difference

'She showed clearly the difference between the two.'

d. 教师正在指导学生做试验。

Jiaoshi zhengzai zhi-dao   xuesheng zuo shiyan.
teacher PRT   finger pointing-guide students do experiment

'The teacher was supervising his students in doing the experiment.'

Clearly, Chinese compounds and idioms containing *zhi* 'finger' are often rooted in the act of pointing. Another act is counting on our fingers. We often bend our fingers when doing so. Therefore, *qu-zhi* (bend-fingers) can mean "count" in a metonymic or metaphoric sense. If a number can be counted on one's fingers, it should not be a very large one.

(11) a. 屈指   *qu-zhi* (bend-finger) 'count on one's fingers'
   b. 屈指可数 *qu-zhi ke-shu* (bend-finger can-count) 'can be counted on one's fingers; very few'
   c. 莫可指数 *mo-ke zhi-shu* (not-can finger-count) 'beyond counting on one's fingers; innumerable'
   d. 指不胜屈 *zhi bu sheng qu* (finger not able bend) 'too many to be counted on the fingers; a great many; countless; innumerable'

Some other Chinese compounds and idioms containing *zhi* 'finger' refer to snapping one's fingers. They usually denote brief times (12a and 12b), time passing quickly (12c and 12d), or easy tasks that take little time (12e and 12f).

(12) a. 弹指   *tan-zhi* (snap-fingers) 'snap of fingers; (of time) quickly pass; a short moment'
   b. 弹指之间 *tan-zhi zhi-jian* (snap-fingers during-time) 'during the snapping of the fingers; in a flash; in a twinkling of an eye; in an instant'
   c. 弹指光阴 *tan-zhi guangyin* (snap-fingers time) 'time zipping by'
   d. 弹指数载 *tan-zhi shu-zai* (snap-fingers several-years) 'several years passed as rapidly as the snap of a finger; time passes swiftly as an arrow'
   e. 弹指可待 *tan-zhi ke-dai* (snap-fingers can-expect) 'can be accomplished during the snapping of the fingers; can be accomplished in a very brief space of time'
   f. 弹指可得 *tan-zhi ke-de* (snap-fingers can-get) 'can get it with a flick of the fingers'

In short, a study of the Chinese compounds and idioms containing *zhi* 'finger' reveals that many make reference to pointing. However, bending the fingers to count and snapping the fingers also play a role in the formation of some compounds and idioms.

3. The palm that holds

In this section, I will show that the term for palm in Chinese, *zhang*, has developed the meanings of "hold in one's hand," "control," and "be in charge of." Most of the Chinese compounds and idioms containing *zhang* 'palm' seem to be consonant with the following pair of metonymy and metaphor:

(13) a. THE PALM STANDS FOR CONTROL
      b. CONTROL IS HOLDING IN THE PALM OF ONE'S HAND

Consider the following four compounds:

(14) a. 掌心   *zhang-xin* (palm-center) 'the center/hollow of the palm; con-
                trol; influence'
      b. 掌控   *zhang-kong* (palm-control) 'control'
      c. 魔掌   *mo-zhang* (devil-palm) '(*derogatory*) devil's clutches; evil hands'
      d. 掌握   *zhang-wo* (palm-hold) 'have in hand; take in one's control;
                grasp; master; know well'

Examples (14a–c) are nominal compounds meaning "control." Example (14d) is a
commonly used verbal compound. In (15) are some of the collocations with its
objects. As can be seen, nothing expressed by the objects of the verb *zhang-wo*,
"techniques," "foreign language," "new developments," "military power," "situation," and "the sense of propriety," is something you can really hold physically. But
the abstraction is rooted in holding in the palm of the hand.

(15) a. 掌握技术   *zhang-wo jishu* (palm-hold techniques) 'master
                    techniques'
      b. 掌握一门外语 *zhang-wo yimen wai-yu* (palm-hold a foreign lan-
                    guage) 'have a good command of a foreign language'
      c. 掌握新情况   *zhang-wo xin qingkuang* (palm-hold new state of af-
                    fairs) 'keep abreast of new developments'
      d. 掌握军权   *zhang-wo jun-quan* (palm-hold military-power)
                    'hold the military power'
      e. 掌握局势   *zhang-wo jushi* (palm-hold the situation) 'have the situ-
                    ation well in hand; have the situation under control'
      f. 掌握分寸   *zhang-wo fencun* (palm-hold sense-of-propriety)
                    'handle appropriately; act or speak properly; exer-
                    cise sound judgment'

In the following compounds, *zhang* 'palm' is used as a verb, followed by an object.
It means "hold something in hand" or, rather, "be in charge of."

(16) a. 掌勺   *zhang-shaor* (palm holding-ladle) 'be the chef'
      b. 掌锅   *zhang-guo* (palm holding-wok) 'be the chef'
      c. 掌灶   *zhang-zao* (palm holding-kitchen range) 'be the chef'
      d. 掌柜   *zhang-gui* (palm holding-counter) 'manager (of a shop);
                shopkeeper'
      e. 掌舵   *zhang-duo* (palm holding-helm) 'be at the helm; operate the
                rudder'

Examples (16a–c) all refer to the chef. The chef in a Chinese restaurant is the person who holds a ladle and a wok when doing the cooking. The sense of "hold in hand," however, has extended to mean "be in charge of." This is apparent in (16c), because the chef does not hold the kitchen range in hand at all. Instead, he is just in charge of cooking done over the range. Example (16d) refers to the person in charge over the counter in a shop. Example (16e) denotes the function of a helmsman who steers a ship. Metaphorically, it can refer to what the leader of a nation does to lead the country in a particular direction of development.

The fact that in Chinese the palm of the hand is closely associated with the abstract concepts of power and control is better illustrated by (17). The seal is the symbol of power. People who hold the seal in hand are in power, as in (17a). By the same token, people who hold power are in power, as in (17b). The verb in (17c) suggests that people who hold affairs are in charge of these affairs. The verbs in (17d–f) all carry similar conceptions, as illustrated by (17').

(17) a. 掌印   *zhang-yin* (palm holding-seal) 'keep the seal; be in power'
b. 掌权   *zhang-quan* (palm holding-power) 'be in power; wield power; exercise control'
c. 掌事   *zhang-shi* (palm holding-affair) 'be in charge of; administer'
d. 掌管   *zhang-guan* (palm holding-administer) 'be in charge of; administer'
e. 主掌   *zhu-zhang* (manage-palm holding) 'be in charge of; manage'
f. 执掌   *zhi-zhang* (direct-palm holding) 'be in charge of; direct'

(17') a. 他掌管一项工程。
     Ta zhang-guan   *yixiang gongcheng.*
     he palm holding-administer a   project
     'He takes charge of a project.'

b. 他主掌财务。
     Ta zhu-zhang   *cai-wu.*
     she manage-palm holding financial-affairs
     'She is in charge of financial affairs.'

All the examples containing *zhang* 'palm' discussed so far involve holding in the palm of the hand. Other acts are reflected in the following idioms.

(18) a. 摩拳擦掌   *mo-quan ca-zhang* (rub-fist wipe-palm) 'rub one's fists and wipe one's palms; to be eager to start on a task; be itching for a fight'
b. 易如反掌   *yi ru fan-zhang* (easy as flipping over-palm) 'can be done as easily as flipping over one's palm'

c. 反掌可得   *fan-zhang ke-de* (flip over-palm can-get) 'can get as easily as turning one's hand over'
d. 掌上观纹   *zhang-shang guan-wen* (palm-on see-lines) 'as easy and convenient as looking at the lines of the palm of one's own hand; effortless'
e. 孤掌难鸣   *gu-zhang nan-ming* (single-palm difficult-make a sound) 'a single palm cannot clap; one can hardly do much single-handed; it's hard to succeed without support; alone and helpless'

As in (18a), when people are eager to do something, they tend to rub their fists and palms due to the itch they feel in their hands. The idiom based on this act expresses anxiety to start on a task. We know that it is easy and effortless to flip over our hand. In (18b) and (18c) this act becomes a metaphor for something easy to do or to get. In (18d) doing something easy is said to be the same as looking at the lines on the palm of one's hand. We know that it takes two palms to clap. Example (18e) makes use of this knowledge to express the helpless situation of getting no support when needed.

4. *Finger* and *palm* in English

The previous two sections show that Chinese compounds and idioms with *zhi* 'finger' and *zhang* 'palm' are primarily grounded in the acts of pointing and holding. English may differ from Chinese in two respects at least, one to do with the palm, the other with the finger.

First, metaphors consonant with CONTROL IS HOLDING IN THE PALM OF ONE'S HAND are not as common in English as in Chinese. For instance, one can find in English dictionaries the following idioms containing *palm*:

(19)   a. *cross somebody's palm* ('bribe somebody')
       b. *grease/oil the palm of somebody* ('bribe somebody')
       c. *have an itching/itchy palm* ('want money so greatly that one is willing to take it as a payment for doing unjust favors')
       d. *hold/have... in the palm of one's hand* ('have complete control over...')

Of these only (19d) represents CONTROL IS HOLDING IN THE PALM OF ONE'S HAND, whereas the remaining ones have to do with "giving or accepting bribes." On the other hand, as already seen in Section 3, the Chinese compounds consonant with the same metaphor are numerous.

The second difference between Chinese and English pertains to the finger. Again, instances consonant with INTENTION OR TARGET IS WHAT THE FINGER POINTS TO and TO GUIDE OR DIRECT IS TO POINT WITH A FINGER are not as common in English as in Chinese. Particularly, it seems that in English only TARGET IS WHAT THE FINGER POINTS TO is realized linguistically. For instance,

(20) a. *put the finger on* ('tell the police about [a criminal]; inform against; identify as victim')
      b. *put one's finger on* ('point with precision to [cause of trouble]; find; show [cause of trouble]')
      c. *point a/the/one's finger at* ('criticize; censure; scold')
      d. *shake/wag a/one's finger at* ('censure; scold; point out')
      e. *give somebody the finger* ('insult; mistreat')

On the other hand, a group of English idioms containing "finger" contributes to different meanings from what *zhi* 'finger' does in Chinese. In Chinese, as demonstrated in Section 2, *zhi* 'finger' occurs in the compounds mainly expressing these meanings: "point at/to"; "point out, indicate, demonstrate, show"; "refer to, direct at"; "depend/rely/count on," and so forth. In contrast, the finger in English is frequently conceptualized as the actual "doer" of things. The examples in English include those in (21). If one is doing something or participates in something, one's fingers must be IN the matter, as in (21a–d), or one's fingers should function and make contact with the matter, as in (21e–l).

(21) a. *get one's fingers into something* ('participate in something')
      b. *have a finger in something* ('take part in something; play a role in something')
      c. *have one's finger in the pie* ('concern oneself with or be connected with the matter, especially officiously')
      d. *have/stick a finger in every pie* ('have a part in everything that is going on; concern oneself with or be connected with many matters, especially in an unwelcome way')
      e. *keep fingers on something* ('take care of or handle something')
      f. *get one's fingers burnt* ('suffer after a foolish act or mistake; suffer for meddling or rashness')
      g. *one's fingers itch to do something* ('one is longing or anxious to do something')
      h. *do something without lifting one's finger* ('do something with least effort')
      i. *do something with a wet finger* ('do something with little effort')
      j. *get/pull/take one's fingers out* ('begin work in earnest; hurry up')
      k. *work one's fingers to the bone* ('work very hard')
      l. *one's fingers are (all) thumbs* ('one is clumsy')

These two differences between Chinese and English, as outlined earlier, should perhaps be viewed from a broader perspective. We may need to take into account the hand, of which the finger and the palm are subparts. In English, although the metaphor CONTROL IS HOLDING IN THE PALM OF ONE'S HAND is likely not as richly expressed at the linguistic level as in Chinese, CONTROL IS HOLDING IN THE HAND is expressed richly in the form of idioms (see Kövecses & Szabó, 1996; Yu, 2003). The examples include the following sentences.

(22) a. *He's got the matter in hand.*
 b. *We have the situation well in hand.*
 c. *His life was in my hand.*
 d. *The meeting is getting out of hand.*
 e. *We fell into enemy hands.*
 f. *I suffered at his hands.*
 g. *I'll soon have him eating out of my hand!*
 h. *You shouldn't force my hand!*
 i. *I'll give you a free hand.*
 j. *The cabinet approved last week strengthened his hand for the difficult tasks ahead.*

Besides, both verbal and nominal uses of such English words as *hold*, *grasp*, and *grip* in the sense of "control/possession" may also imply the use of the hand to hold, to grasp, or to grip, as the following examples demonstrate: *He tried to hold his temper, He's got a good hold of his subject, Grasp your chances while you can, He is in the grasp of a wicked man, The people regained power from the grasp of the dictator, An anarchic fervor gripped the campus, He kept a firm grip on his children, Don't get into the grip of moneylenders, Teachers should loosen their grip on the curriculum, She felt herself in the grip of sadness she could not understand.* That is, the body part related to the concept of control in English is primarily the hand, rather than its subpart, the palm. In Chinese, on the other hand, the concept of control is associated with both the palm (see Section 3 above) and the hand (Yu, 2003).

Also, most of the compounds and idioms containing *zhi* 'finger' in Chinese involve pointing. In English, however, the same act grounds relatively few expressions of this kind, as exemplified by (20). On the other hand, fingers in English are more "actual doers" of things, as illustrated by (21). This is certainly not the case with Chinese. Comparable examples can be hardly found in the language. If the finger is not conceptualized as the "actual doer" of things in Chinese, then what is? It is interesting to note that the Chinese body-part term *shou* 'hand' is doing the same job as "finger" in English. For instance, in English a thief's "fingers are sticky" whereas in Chinese a thief's "hands are sticky". In English one's "fingers itch" when anxious to do something while in Chinese one's "hands itch" under the same circumstances. In English, if one is said to have done something "without lifting a finger", that means the person has done it with ease. In Chinese, if something is done with ease, it is done "with one's hands drooping." Also, it is "sticking one's fingers into something" in English while it is "sticking one's hands into something" in Chinese. See Yu (2003) for further examples.

Thus, the two differences between Chinese and English can be summarized as choice of a subpart (finger or palm) over the part (hand). If so, the two cases may simply be the result of cultural preferences (Kövecses and Radden, 1998; Yu, 1995). The following idioms from Chinese and English further illustrate the point.

(23) a. 了如指掌
          liao   ru   zhi   zhang
          know like finger palm
          'know like the fingers and palms of one's hands; know very well'
     b. *know like the back of one's hand* ('know very well')
     c. *know like the palm of one's hand* ('know very well')

These idioms all mean "know very well," but the body parts involved are somewhat different between the two languages: the finger and palm of the hand in Chinese and the back and palm of the hand in English. The difference is one of preference conventionalized in a culture and language. On the other hand, the commonality between these two languages is also obvious, that is, both languages have chosen the body part of hand rather than, say, foot. The choice is not so difficult to account for: Physically, our hands are closer to our eyes than our feet; and experientially, our hands perform far more functions than our feet in daily life. So, there is a common bodily basis for these conventionalized phrases across the languages.

The body-part term "finger" in English also occurs in a few other idioms, as cited here:

(24) a. *can be counted on the fingers* ('few; not many')
     b. *let slip through one's fingers* ('lose hold of; miss opportunity of')
     c. *twist/wind somebody around one's (little) finger* ('persuade somebody without difficulty; dominate somebody completely')
     d. *cross one's fingers; keep one's fingers crossed* ('wish for good luck or success')

Example (24a) is based on a common experience with fingers – people tend to count with the help of their fingers. This idiom has a couple of comparable examples in Chinese as in (11), of which (11b) is a close equivalent. Example (24b) does not have an equivalent idiom in Chinese, but its word-for-word translation in Chinese is still an apt metaphor. In an English-Chinese dictionary (Lu, 1993), for instance, (24b) is given the following Chinese definitions:

(25)   a.   听任 … 从指缝间溜掉
            tingren... cong zhi   feng   jian   liudiao
            let...   from finger chink between slip
            'let slip through chinks between fingers; let slip through one's fingers'
        b.   错过(机会等)
            cuoguo (jihui   deng)
            miss   (opportunity etc.)

Of these two the first is a literal translation of the original, but it makes good sense in Chinese. Things tend to slip through our fingers if our hand does not hold them tight enough. This experience helps us conceptualize abstract notions of control and possession, which both figure in (24b). The same experience also helps us make sense of the manner of spending money. In Chinese, for instance, there are following two compounds:

(26)   a.   手紧   *shou-jin* (hand-tight) 'closefisted; tightfisted'
        b.   手松   *shou-song* (hand-loose) 'open-handed; free-handed; free with one's money'

Those who are unwilling to spend have their "hands tight" so that money will not slip through their fingers. Those who are happy to spend have their "hands loose," and money will slip through their fingers fast.

Example (24c) seems to be a less transparent idiom than (24a) and (24b), but still it is apparent that "to twist" physically is a metaphor for "manipulation" in an abstract sense. Example (24d) describes a culture-specific bodily act – cross one's fingers as one wishes for good luck or success. This practice does not exist in the traditional Chinese culture, and the idiom has no equivalent in the Chinese language either. The Chinese definition for (24d) in the English-Chinese dictionary (Lu, 1993) is an explanatory one to this effect: "crook the middle and index fingers together in wish for good luck or success." In sum, the degree of universality and relativity of the idioms varies, just as the degree of universality and relativity of the bodily experiences in which the idioms are grounded varies.

5.   Conclusion

In this article I have studied the Chinese compounds and idioms that contain the body-part terms of *zhi* 'finger' and *zhang* 'palm'. It is found that most of such compounds and idioms are rooted respectively in two common acts: pointing with one's (index) finger and holding in the palm of one's hand. A comparison of data in Chinese and English reveals two differences between these two languages. First, the metaphor CONTROL IS HOLDING IN THE PALM OF THE HAND is not richly manifested at the linguistic level in English, although it is in Chinese. Second, the metaphor THE FINGER IS THE DOER is well manifested in English, but it is not realized in Chinese. Despite these differences it is shown that they are grounded in the universal bodily experiences with the hand. The demonstrated differences should be viewed as cultural variations in the choice of a body part (the hand) over its subparts (the palm and the finger). In the first case, English holds CONTROL IS HOLDING IN THE HAND, instead of CONTROL IS HOLDING IN THE PALM OF THE HAND, as its primary metaphor. In the second case, the Chinese counterpart of the English THE FINGER IS THE DOER is THE HAND IS THE DOER. In both cases, commonality resides in the grounding of metaphor and metonymy in the common bodily experiences, whereas the difference lies in the choice of a body part versus its subpart. Overall, relativity, in this regard, exists in the larger context of universality.

It is worth noting that the Chinese compounds discussed here are very different from the idioms. They are just everyday homely words, constituting the core of the Chinese lexicon. They are not metaphoric or metonymic in the traditional sense of the terms. Individual Chinese speakers use them because they have no other choices to express the same ideas. However, these compounds are metaphoric and metonymic in the sense of Lakoff and Johnson (1980, 1999) because they involve mappings from the bodily to the abstract.

From a comparative perspective, this study has revealed both commonalities and differences in metaphoric and metonymic uses of finger and palm between Chinese and English. The commonalities are grounded in the common bodily experiences, specifically in the acts of pointing and holding, which are universal among all human beings. On the other hand, cross-cultural variations are also obvious. In particular, I have observed the following differences. First, the body-part term is used to express a certain concept in one language but not the other, even though the act in which the metaphor or metonymy is grounded is a universal experience. For instance, "finger" occurs in such Chinese compounds as meaning "direct," "depend," "accuse" and so forth, but their English equivalents often do not involve this body-part term. Second, the use of a body-part term is explicit in one language but implicit in the other. For example, in English *point out* implies the use of (index) finger, but its Chinese equivalent *zhi-chu* (finger pointing-out) 'point out' makes an explicit use of the body part. Third, if a bodily act is not universal but specific to a culture, then the metaphoric or metonymic expression based on it should be language-specific as well. The English idiom *cross one's fingers* or *keep one's fingers crossed* is a telling example, with no equivalent in Chinese. Finally, a major difference this study has highlighted is in the choice of a body part (hand) in one language and its subpart (finger or palm) in the other. Although the human body plays an important role in human meaning and understanding in the mode of metaphor and metonymy, this role is tinted by specific cultures. For that matter, metaphoric and metonymic uses of body-part terminology may have much in common across languages because they reflect universal experiences with our body, but we also expect cross-linguistic differences as a reflection of cultural differences. Only through comparative study in a systematic fashion can we map potential human universals and cultural differences accurately.

References

Allan, K. (1995). The anthropocentricity of the English word(s) *back. Cognitive Linguistics, 6,* 11–31.

Brugman, C. (1983). The use of body-part terms as locatives in Chalcatongo Mixtec. *Survey of California and other Indian languages, Report No. 4* (pp. 235–290). Berkeley: University of California.

Brugman, C., & Macaulay, M. (1986). Interacting semantic systems: Mixtec expressions of location. *Proceedings of the Twelfth Annual Meeting of the Berkeley Linguistics Society* (pp. 315–327). Berkeley: Berkeley Linguistics Society.

Goossens, L. (1995) Metaphtonymy: The interaction of metaphor and metonymy in figurative expressions for linguistic action. In L. Goossens, P. Pauwels, B. Rudzka-Ostyn, A. Simon-Vandenbergen, & J. Vanparys *By word of mouth: Metaphor, metonymy and linguistic action in a cognitive perspective* (pp. 159–174). Amsterdam: John Benjamins.

Heine, B. 1995. Conceptual grammaticalization and prediction. In J. R. Taylor & R. E. MacLaury (Eds.). *Language and the cognitive construal of the world* (pp. 119–135). Berlin: Mouton de Gruyter.

Hollenbach, B. E. (1995) Semantic and syntactic extensions of body-part terms in Mixtecan: The case of "face" and "foot." *International Journal of American Linguistics, 61,* 168–190.

Kövecses, Z., & Szabó, P. (1996). Idioms: A view from cognitive semantics. *Applied Linguistics, 17,* 326–355.

Kövecses, Z., & Radden, G. (1998). Metonymy: Developing a cognitive linguistic view. *Cognitive Linguistics, 9,* 37–77.

Lakoff, G., & Johnson, M. (1980). *Metaphors we live by.* Chicago: University of Chicago Press.

Lakoff, G., & Johnson, M. (1999). *Philosophy in the flesh: The embodied mind and its challenge to western thought.* New York: Basic Books.

Levinson, S. (1994) Vision, shape, and linguistic description: Tzeltal body-part terminology and object description. *Linguistics, 32,* 791–855.

Lu, G. (Gen. Ed.). (1993). *Yin-Han da cidian* [The English-Chinese dictionary (Unabridged)]. Shanghai: Shanghai Translation Press.

Lü, S., & Ding, S. (Gen. Eds.). (1980). *Xiandai Hanyu cidian* [Modern Chinese dictionary]. Beijing: The Commercial Press.

Lü, S., & Ding, S. (Gen. Eds.). (1989). *Xiandai Hanyu cidian bubian* [Modern Chinese Dictionary Supplement]. Beijing: The Commercial Press.

Lü, S., & Ding, S. (Gen. Eds.). (1996). *Xiandai Hanyu cidian* [Modern Chinese Dictionary] (revised ed.). Beijing: The Commercial Press.

MacLaury, R. E. (1989). Zapotec body-part locatives: Prototypes and metaphoric extensions. *International Journal of American Linguistics, 55,* 119–154.

Matsumoto, Y. (1999). On the extension of body-part nouns to object-part nouns and spatial adpositions. In B. Fox, D. Jurafsky, & L. Michaelis (Eds.), *Cognition and function in language* (pp. 15–28). Stanford: CSLI Publications.

Pauwels, P., & Simon-Vandenbergen, A. (1995). Body parts in linguistic action: Underlying schemata and value judgements. In L. Goossens, P. Pauwels, B. Rudzka-Ostyn, A. Simon-Vandenbergen, & J. Vanparys *By word of mouth: Metaphor, metonymy and linguistic action in a cognitive perspective* (pp. 35–69). Amsterdam: John Benjamins.

Svorou, S. (1994). *The grammar of space*. Amsterdam: John Benjamins.

Sweetser, E. E. (1990). *From etymology to pragmatics: Metaphorical and cultural aspects of semantic structure*. Cambridge: Cambridge University Press.

Walsh, M. (1994). Body parts in Murrinh-Patha: Incorporation, grammar and metaphor. In H. Chapell & W. McGregor (Eds.), *The grammar of inalienability: A typological perspective on body part terms and the part-whole relation* (pp. 327–380). Berlin: Mouton de Gruyter.

Wang, T. (Gen. Ed.). (1992). *Xin xiandai Hanyu cidian* [A new dictionary of modern Chinese language]. Haikou, China: Hainan Press.

Wei, D. (Gen. Ed.) (1995). *Han Ying cidian* [A Chinese-English dictionary] (revised ed.). Beijing: Foreign Language Teaching and Research Press.

Wu, G. (Gen. Ed.) (1993). *Han Ying da cidian, Vols. 1 & 2* [Chinese-English dictionary]. Shanghai: Shanghai Jiao Tong University Press.

Wu, J. (Gen. Ed.). (1981). *Han Ying cidian* [A Chinese-English dictionary]. Beijing: The Commercial Press.

Yu, N. (1995). Metaphorical expressions of anger and happiness in English and Chinese. *Metaphor and Symbolic Activity, 10*, 59–92.

Yu, N. (1998). *The contemporary theory of metaphor: A perspective from Chinese*. Amsterdam: John Benjamins.

Yu, N. (2003). The bodily dimension of meaning in Chinese: What do we do and mean with "hands"? In E. H. Casad and G. B. Palmer (eds.), *Cognitive linguistics and non-Indo-European languages* (pp. 337–362). Berlin: Mouton de Gruyter.

CHAPTER 7

What does our face mean to us?

This study is a semantic analysis of metonymic and metaphoric expressions involving body-part terms for the face in Chinese. These expressions are discussed regarding four perceived roles of face, namely, as highlight of appearance and look, as indicator of emotion and character, as focus of interaction and relationship, and as locus of dignity and prestige. It is argued that the figurative extensions are based on some biological facts about our face: it is the most distinctive part on the interactive side of our body capable of revealing our inner states. Referring to English the study shows that the terms for the face in both languages have developed figurative meanings along similar routes with similar stops. It also shows that the concepts of "face and facework", admittedly ubiquitous in all cultures, are manifested more richly in Chinese than in English – a reflection of cultural differences in values attached to those concepts. Finally, a hypothetical "Triangle Model" is proposed to account for the relationship between language, culture, body, and cognition.

1. Introduction

Our face is one of the most important parts of our body. Its importance is determined fundamentally by the kind of body we have and how it functions. Specifically, the face is the body part that is most distinctive of a person. It is on the interactive side, the front, of our body. Whenever we want to interact with somebody or something, our face turns to the person or thing. Conversely, we turn our face away, leaving the person or thing behind. The face is really the focus of human interaction. It conveys or betrays our intentions and states of mind. Consciously or unconsciously, it shows our emotions and feelings. Thus, our face is the most important identity mark of who we are, both physically and socially. The human face has, for two decades, captivated research interests in multidisciplinary science including psychology, clinical case studies, neuroscience, and computer science (Stevenage 2000). In social and behavioral sciences, for much longer, the concept of face has been an important theoretical construct and research subject for various disciplines such as sociology, anthropology, linguistics, communication as well as psychology (Tracy 1990).

In this study I make a semantic analysis of what our face means to us in our language. In particular, I study metonymic and metaphoric extensions in the form of compounds and idioms containing the lexical items denoting the face in Chinese. I also refer to English for comparison. The English word *face* has two basic counterparts in modern Chinese: 脸 *lian* 'face' and 面 *mian* 'face', the other derivatives including 脸面 *lianmian*, 脸孔 *liankong*, 面孔 *miankong*, 颜面 *yanmian*, all denoting the face. Besides, 面子 *mianzi*, derived from *mian* 'face', means "outer part of something" and "face" in abstract senses, but not "face" as part of our body. In the next four sections I examine how *lian* 'face' and *mian* 'face' derive their metonymic and metaphoric extensions based on the role of face as part of our body. These four sections bear the headings "Face as highlight of appearance and look", "Face as indicator of emotion and character", "Face as focus of interaction and relationship", and "Face as locus of dignity and prestige". I should note at the outset that, while I treat them as four separate topics, they are in essence closely linked to one another in intricate ways. Over the four sections, we will follow two parallel tracks: one extending from the biological to the social face, and the other from the metonymic to the metaphoric face.

The central claims of this study are that the peculiar nature of our face actually shapes our metonymic and metaphoric understanding of certain abstract concepts and that what our face means to us really emerges from what our face does for us. I hope that my study will shed some light on the philosophical aspect of human meaning and understanding by highlighting their bodily basis that, until recently, had been largely overlooked (see Johnson 1987; Lakoff 1987; Lakoff and Johnson 1980, 1999). In conclusion I will propose a hypothetical "Triangle Model" to account for the complicated relationship between language, culture, body, and cognition.

2. Face as highlight of appearance and look

A very common metonymy, richly manifested in language, is THE FACE STANDS FOR THE PERSON. The bodily basis for this metonymy is that the face, with eyes, nose and mouth on its front and ears to its sides, is the most distinctive part of a person. For that reason we identify or remember people primarily by their face. Picture IDs show people's face. One thing that stands out in our memory of people is their face. For instance, we refer to old or new members of a group as "old or new faces", as in (1).[1]

---

1.   All the Chinese data presented in this study were collected from the following popular dictionaries: Lü and Ding (1980, 1989, 1996), Wang (1992), Wei (1995), and Wu (1993). The only exceptions are a couple of sentential examples (i.e. 4, 8'a, and 20) that were collected from actual discourse in published sources. In the lexical examples, the parentheses contain glosses. In the glosses of sentential examples, PRT = particle, and MOD = modifier marker.

(1) a. 老面孔 *lao miankong* 'old face (i.e. old member)'
     b. 新面孔 *xin miankong* 'new face (i.e. new comer)'

As the face-for-person metonymy is extended to objects and abstract things via metaphor, we then refer to the most important surface (often the front) of something and the outward appearance or apparent state of something (abstract) as "the face". For example,

(2) a. 门面 *men-mian* (door-face) 'face, facade, front (e.g. of a shop)'
     b. 门脸 *men-lian* (door-face) 'face, facade, front (e.g. of a shop)'

There is little doubt that the metaphor here derives from the kind of body we have: the face is the most distinctive body part that is on our interactive side or front. Further illustrating the metaphoric extension are idioms below:

(3) a. 面目一新 *mian-mu yi-xin* (face-eyes entirely-new) 'take on an entirely new look; present a completely new appearance'
     b. 面目全非 *mian-mu quan-fei* (face-eyes all-different) 'lose one's identity; a complete change; all looks wrong or different; be changed or distorted beyond recognition'
     c. 改头换面 *gai-tou huan-mian* (change-head switch-face) 'change the appearance but not the essence; dish up the same old stuff in a new form; sell old wine in a new bottle'
     d. 人面兽心 *ren-mian shou-xin* (human-face beast-heart) 'the face of a man but the heart of a beast; a beast in human form'
     e. 革面洗心 *ge-mian xi-xin* (change-face wash-heart) 'flay the face and wash the heart; turn over a new leaf; thoroughly reform oneself; redeem oneself by a thorough change'

In Chinese, as in (3a) and (3b), the compound *mian-mu* 'face-eyes' means "appearance" or "look" in general. More often than not it refers to the appearance or look of things rather than humans, giving rise to a metaphorical extension. While the face represents the appearance of something as a whole, it represents the appearance only, not the essence. The change of the face as well as the head (3c) does not change the essence, which is represented by the heart (3d). A thorough change requires that one "change his face and wash his heart" (3e). In the sentence below *lao miankong* 'old face' of (1a) refers to the characteristic playing style or "appearance" of a soccer team.

(4)   该队一改攻弱守强的老面孔，主场以四比一大胜客队。
       Gai dui yi   gai   gong-ruo   shou-qiang   de   lao
       this team completely changed offense-weak defense-strong MOD old
       miankong, zhu chang yi si   bi yi   da-sheng ke   dui.
       face   home field by four to one rout   visiting team
       'This team completely changed its old face of weak offense and strong de-
       fense, routing the visiting team four to zero on its home field.'

In sum, the metonymic and metaphoric extensions discussed in this section seem
to have derived from the following biological facts about the body part of face:

(5)   a.   Face is the most distinctive part of a person. (part for whole).
       b.   Face is on the interactive side, the front, of a person. (interactive side;
            front)
       c.   Face is an external body part of a person. (surface vs. essence)

In fact (5a) and (5b) presuppose (5c). When in combination with the metaphor of
personification, these facts can explain all the examples in this section. Thus, we
refer to people by their most distinctive part (5a for 1). After personification, the
front of a shop, which is the most distinctive side of the structure, is the "face" (5a
and 5b for 2). The "face" is the most distinctive external part of a person or thing
(with personification) and, therefore, its change will lead to the change of appearance or look (i.e. identity) of the person or thing (5a and 5c for 3 and 4), but not
the essence (3c).

3.   Face as indicator of emotion and character

The face is the most distinctive part of a person because it has on it features such
as eyes, brows, nose, mouth that importantly characterize a person. With those
features, the face displays one's emotion and suggests one's character, as the Chinese idiom goes:

(6)   面如其心   *mian-ru-qi-xin* (face-like-one's-heart) 'One's face reveals one's
            heart.'

For instance, we smile when happy, and we cry when sad. The reactions to emotions all show on our face. The link between facial expressions and emotions is an
important research topic in psychology (e.g., Ekman and Rosenberg 1997; Russell
and Fernández-Dols 1997). More recently the interest has also extended into linguistics (e.g., Wierzbicka 1993, 1999, 2000). The relationship between the face and
character of a person is far less studied in real life, but intuitively perceived in

artistic works. For instance, a movie director will select actors and actresses with particular faces that "match" particular characters. Writers' depictions of characters to some extent depends on how they portray their faces. An extreme example is Beijing operas where actors and actresses have to paint stereotypical makeup on their face determined by the characters they play.

In Chinese there is a large number of compounds and idioms that describe people's emotions or states of mind in terms of what happens on their face. Expressions of this kind are metonymic in nature: FACIAL DISPLAYS STAND FOR EMOTIONS OR STATES OF MIND (see also Yu 1995, 1998, 2002). That is, whatever is said about the face actually points to the mental state of the person. The idioms in (7) contain *lian* 'face' and *mian* 'face'.[2]

(7) a. 脸堆笑容 *lian-dui-xiao-rong* (face-pile up-smiling-expression) 'one's face wreathed with smiles; be all smiles with happiness'

   b. 脸红耳赤 *lian-hong-er-chi* (face-red ears-red) 'become red in the face; flush with anger'

   c. 脸如黄蜡 *lian-ru-huang-la* (face-like-yellow-wax) 'one's face turned waxen with fright; become waxen yellow in the face with fright'

   d. 脸不改色 *lian-bu-gai-se* (face-not-change-color) 'keep one's countenance; not show the slightest fear'

   e. 脸色阴沉 *lian-se-yin-chen* (face-color-overcast-heavy) 'look sullen; look unhappy'

   f. 脸涨绯红 *lian-zhang-fei-hong* (face-swell-red-red) 'flush with embarrassment'

   g. 面带愁色 *mian-dai-chou-se* (face-bring-sad-color) 'wearing a sad/anxious expression; with a troubled countenance'

   h. 面露不安 *mian-lu-bu-an* (face-show-not-peace) 'show an anxious/disturbed expression'

   i. 面有愠色 *mian-you-yun-se* (face-has-irritated-color) 'look irritated, disgruntled, or angry'

---

2. While I use English words of emotions and other abstract concepts in the glosses and translations of Chinese examples and within the text, I am aware of the fact that categorizations and lexicons of emotions and other abstract concepts can be different to varying degrees across languages and cultures. That is the primary motivation behind the Natural Semantic Metalanguage (NSM) for cross-linguistic analysis (see, e.g., Wierzbicka 1992, 1999). So, such English words as *anger, shame, dignity, prestige* and so on should not be interpreted as exact equivalents to the Chinese originals or as culture-independent analytical tools.

Note that (7a–f) do not include any emotion words, but their usage is convention-alized with certain emotions. For instance, both (7b) and (7f) refer to redness in the face, but the former is associated with anger and the latter with embarrass-ment. On the other hand, Examples (7g–i) contain emotion words, thus specifying the emotions as expressed on the face. In (8) are compounds with *lian* 'face' indi-cating people's emotions or states of mind.

(8) a. 脸热   *lian-re* (face-hot) 'feel ashamed'
     b. 脸红   *lian-hong* (face-red) 'blush with shame or embarrassment'
     c. 红脸   *hong-lian* (redden-face) 'blush (for being shy); blush with an-ger; get angry'
     d. 绷脸   *beng-lian* (stretch-face) 'pull a long face; look serious or dis-pleased'
     e. 板脸   *ban-lian* (harden-face) 'straighten one's face; put on a stern expression'
     f. 冷脸   *leng-lian* (cold-face) 'cold face; severe expression'
     g. 好脸   *hao-lian* (good-face) 'a smiling face'
     h. 傻脸   *sha-lian* (stupid-face) 'find or feel oneself stupid or silly; dis-graceful; lose face'
     i. 上脸   *shang-lian* (up to-face) 'blush for drinking wine; grow dizzy with success or praise'

People's face will "feel hot" (8a), burning with shame. Their face will also "turn red" (8b), blushing with shame or embarrassment. However, *hong-lian* (redden-face) in (8c) means "blush for being shy or with anger". Unhappy or displeased, people have muscles on their face tight, resulting in a "stretched face" (8d). In (8e) *ban* is originally a noun meaning "board (e.g., of metal)". In this case it is a verb meaning "harden (the face like a board)". One's face appears to be a "cold face" (8f) when "stretched" and "hardened". A "good face" (8g) is usually a reflection of a good mood. If people find themselves stupid, say, for having done something stupid, they are likely to have a "stupid face" (8h). Originally meaning "blush for drinking wine", (8i) has come to mean, by extension, "being too complacent with success or praise". Being over complacent is similar to being intoxicated. In (8') below are sentential examples of (8b) and (8d). It is worth mentioning that in (8'a) the per-son is not really "holding others' thigh asking for favor". It is a metaphor describing the "cringing" attitude in bodily terms.

(8')   a.   他抱着人家的大腿要照顾，应该感到脸红。

            Ta bao-zhe   renjiade datui yao   zhaogu, yinggai gandao

            he hold-PRT others' thigh ask-for favor   should feel

            lian-hong.

            face-red

            'Holding others' thigh asking for favor, he should feel ashamed.'

       b.   他绷着脸不说话。

            Ta beng-zhe-lian   bu   shuo hua.

            he stretch-PRT-face not say   words

            'He kept a straight face and remained speechless.'

I would like to mention here that there is a close tie between emotion and character. If people tend to have a certain emotion, then it is part of their character. But the connection between face and character is not so obvious. It seems that this fact is also reflected in the Chinese language. There are fewer examples of this kind.

(9)   a.   脸急   *lian-ji* (face-impatient) 'irritable; irascible'

       b.   面善   *mian-shan* (face-kind) 'look kind in the face; affable; amiable'

       c.   铁面无私   *tie-mian wu-si* (iron-face no-self) 'disinterested'

If a person tends to be irritable or irascible, it is all shown on his or her face: the "face looks impatient" (9a). Thus it reveals something about the person's character. In (9b) those who "look kind in the face" are believed to be "affable and amiable" in character. As in (9c), disinterested people (especially, officials, judges, referees, etc.) have an "iron face" and are "selfless". They seek no personal interest. To do so they need to have an "iron face", which is hard and does not show any emotions. More importantly, as next section will show, the face is the focus of interpersonal interaction and relationship. With an "iron face" one can be firm facing bad people and rejecting their lures or threats. Thus, the metaphoric "face" is associated with the strong character of disinterestedness. Related to (9b) Chinese compounds involving face seem to concentrate on a single aspect of character – the degree of sensibility to shyness or shame, as shown by (10).

(10)   a.   皮脸   *pi-lian* (leather-face) '(*dial.*) naughty; shameless'

       b.   老脸   *lao-lian* (old-face) 'thick-skinned; brazen-faced'

       c.   厚脸（皮）   *hou-lian*(pi) (thick-face[skin]) 'thick-skinned; brazen; cheeky; shameless'

       d.   脸（皮）厚   *lian(pi)-hou* (face[skin]-thick) 'thick-skinned; shameless'

       e.   脸薄   *lian-bao* (face-thin) 'thin-skinned; shy; sensitive'

       f.   脸嫩   *lian-nen* (face-tender) 'bashful; shy'

       g.   面嫩   *mian-nen* (face-tender) 'shy; bashful; sensitive; timid'

h.	面软	*mian-ruan* (face-soft) 'thin-skinned; shy; sensitive'
i.	脸软	*lian-ruan* (face-soft) 'soft-hearted; good-natured; disinclined to hurt others' feelings; having too much consideration for others' feelings or sensibilities'
j.	脸硬	*lian-ying* (face-hard) 'not easily persuaded to give in; not easily swayed by emotions; not sparing anyone's sensibilities'

Apparently, the degree of sensibility to shyness or shame varies with "quality" of face: the tougher the face is, the less likely it will be affected by shyness or shame. Leather is a kind of material that has extraordinary resistance to damage. So, a person with a "leather face" (10a) does not have to worry about it being damaged by shame: he is "shameless". The "older" the face is, the harder it grows and the more it is resistant to damage (10b). Examples in (10c) and (10d) have similar meanings based on the metaphorical conceptualization that thicker faces are less prone to damage. The opposite is also true, as illustrated by (10e). Examples (10f) and (10g) show that people whose "faces are tender" are shy and bashful. While (10h) and (10i) both literally mean that one's "face is soft", the person in (10h) is inclined to save his own face whereas the one in (10i) is likely to save other people's face. In (10j) "face hard" is an antonym to both (10h) and (10i). People with their "face hard" are not easily swayed by feelings and, for that reason, will not spare other people's sensibilities. Illustrating (10g) and (10i) are the following two sentences, where timid or soft-hearted people are said to have "tender or soft faces".

(10')   a.   他和生人谈话简直像小孩子一样面嫩。
        Ta he   shengren tanhua jianzhi xian xiao   haizi yiyang
        he with strangers talk   really   like   small child same
        mian-nen.
        face-tender
        'He shows an almost childlike timidity in talking with strangers.'

        b.   他太脸软，总是不好意思拒绝别人的要求。
        Ta tai   lian-ruan, zongshi buhaoyisi   jujue   bierende yaoqiu.
        he too face-soft   always   find-it-difficult reject others'   demands
        'He's too soft-hearted, always finding it difficult to reject others' demands.'

It is apparent that the compounds in (10) reflect our metaphorical understanding of an inclination to shyness and shame. It is not true in real life: a thin-faced person may not be more sensitive to shyness or shame than a thick-faced person, and a soft-hearted person does not necessarily have a soft face.

It should also be pointed out that real life is not a Beijing opera where faces and characters usually match. Judging people's character by their face is not always reliable. This again is reflected in the language. For instance,

(11) a. 脸软心善   *lian-ruan xin-shan* (face-soft heart-kind) 'be shy and kind; kind-hearted'

b. 面善心慈   *mian-shan xin-ci* (face-kind heart-kind) 'affable and kind-hearted'

c. 面善心恶   *mian-shan xin-e* (face-kind heart-wicked) 'a kind face but a wicked heart'

d. 面善心诈   *mian-shan xin-zha* (face-kind heart-cheat) 'have an honest appearance but be actually full of cunning and deceit'

In the first two idioms "kind-hearted" people also have "soft and kind faces". But in the last two "kind faces" are really deceptive, covering the true character of evil. The face is after all an external body part. It can only stand for people's outward appearance, in contrast to the heart that represents their inner state. When the face and the heart match, the former is an open window into the latter, as (11a) and (11b) suggest. When the face and the heart do not match, the former covers up the latter like a window shut up, as illustrated by (11c) and (11d) as well as (3d).

In this section, the compounds and idioms involving *lian* 'face' and *mian* 'face' are based on two functions of the face:

(12) a. Face displays emotion.

b. Face suggests character.

As the verbs suggest, the link between face and emotion is closer than that between face and character. These two functions are interrelated. If a person's face tends to display a certain emotion, the inclination to this emotion becomes part of the person's character. Conversely, people with a certain character tend to display certain emotions on their face. In Chinese there is a large number of compounds and idioms that refer to emotions by describing facial displays or gestures, and included in (7) and (8) are just some examples. Conventional expressions such as these are based on actual facial reactions to emotions. In that sense, they are originally metonymic in character. Once conventionalized, however, they are also used metaphorically regardless of emotional symptoms on the face (Yu 2002). As I have noted, there are not many compounds and idioms that make an explicit reference to the connection between face and character. Primarily, they concentrate on people's inclination to shyness and shame, as in (10). The difference in this particular aspect of character is conceptualized metaphorically as degree to which the face can resist the impact of shyness or shame. This depends on the toughness and thickness of the face. The tougher the material of the face is, the more resistant it is. Also, materials being equal, the thicker the face is, the stronger it is. Apparently, shyness and shame as emotions are conceptualized as forces. Hence, the metaphors are SHYNESS IS FORCE and SHAME IS FORCE. Of the two, the latter is a much stronger force than the former. The two metaphors fall into the master metaphor: EMOTION IS FORCE (Kövecses 2000). Although the metaphors of emotions as forces are imaginative in nature, they have an experiential basis in our body: emotions such as shyness and shame bring about immediate physical changes and reactions on our face. That is why people tend to "hide their face" when embarrassed or ashamed.

4.   Face as focus of interaction and relationship

Since the face is our most distinctive body part on our interactive side, it is naturally the focus of attention in interpersonal interaction. It then becomes the focus of relationship as it is formed between interacting people. Face in this sense is both physical and social. The social aspect of face is an important research topic in social science. Studies of "face and facework" started decades ago (e.g., Goffman 1959, 1967; Ho 1976; Hu 1944), and have generated impressive results (e.g., Brown and Levinson 1987; Cody and McLaughlin 1990; Friedman and Tucker 1990; Hwang 1987; Lee-Wong 2000; Ng 1990; Pan 2000; Ting-Toomey 1988, 1994a; Tracy 1990).[3]

The importance of face as focus of human interaction and relationship is richly reflected in the Chinese lexicon. First look at (13).

(13)   a.   谋面   *mou-mian* (seek-face) 'meet; meet each other; get acquainted with each other'

　　 b.   见面   *jian-mian* (see-face) 'meet; see; contact'

---

3.   According to Ting-Toomey (1994b: 5), "face and facework are two ubiquitous concepts that are tied closely to everyday social and personal interactions". Face "entails the presentation of a civilized front to another individual within the webs of interconnected relationships in particular culture" (p. 1), and "is a claimed sense of self-respect or self-dignity in an interactive situation" (p. 3). Facework involves "the verbal and nonverbal negotiation aspects of face maintenance, face claim, and face expectation" (p. 3), and "the enactment of face strategies" (p.1) "to diffuse, manage, enhance, or downgrade self and/or other's face" (p.3). As characterized by Tracy (1990: 210), "Face is a social phenomenon ... created through the communicative moves of interactants. Whereas face references the socially situated identities people claim or attribute to others, facework references the communicative strategies that are the enactment, support, or challenge of those situated identities". Admittedly, face and facework are universal concerns, but conceptions of face and rules and criteria governing face behavior are shaped by cultural variability (see, e.g., Chang and Holt 1994; Ho 1976, 1994; Morisaki and Gudykunst 1994; Ting-Toomey 1988, 1994b; Tracy 1990).

    c.   出面   *chu-mian* (turn out-face) 'act in one's own capacity or on be-half of an organization; appear personally; come forward'

    d.   露面   *lou-mian* (show-face) 'show one's face; make or put in an ap-pearance; appear or reappear on public occasions'

    e.   会面   *hui-mian* (get together-face) 'meet; come together'

    f.   碰面   *peng-mian* (bump-face) 'meet'

    g.   当面   *dang-mian* (to-face) 'to sb.'s face; in sb.'s presence; face to face'

    h.   面对面 *mian-dui-mian* (face-to-face) 'face to face'

    i.   面熟   *mian-shu* (face-familiar) 'look familiar'

    j.   面生   *mian-sheng* (face-strange) 'look unfamiliar'

As in these examples, when we meet or see someone, we say that we "seek or see the person's face" (13a and 13b). When someone does something in person or on behalf of others, or shows up on a certain occasion, we say that he "turns out his face" (13c) or "shows his face" (13d). If we get together for meetings, we "get our faces together" (13e), or even "bump our faces" (13f). It is often desirable that interpersonal matters can be handled "face to face" (13g and 13h). People looking familiar or unfamiliar are "faces familiar or unfamiliar" to us (13i and 13j), since we remember them primarily by their faces. Sentences in (13') illustrate (13c) and (13f). It is noteworthy that, while in (13'a) *chu-mian* (turn out-face) is metonymic in character, the same in (13'b) is metaphorical when applied to things like organizations.

(13') a. 部长亲自出面向大使们说明情况。

        Buzhang qinzi   chu-mian   xiang dashimen   shuoming
        minister in-person turn out-face to   ambassadors explain
        qingkuang.
        situation
        'The minister personally explained the matter to the ambassadors.'

    b. 双方由民间团体出面商谈贸易。

        Shuang fang you minjian   tuanti   chu-mian
        both   sides by non-governmental organizations turn out-face
        shangtan maoyi.
        negotiate trade
        'Trade talks are to be held by non-governmental organizations of both sides.'

    c. 明天我们还是在这儿碰面。

        Mingtian women hai   zai zher peng-mian.
        tomorrow we   again at here bump-face
        'Let's meet (lit. bump our faces) here again tomorrow.'

While the face is the focus of human interaction, it is conceptualized as embodying interpersonal relationship. Intentionally or not, people convey their feelings about other people through their facial expressions. The face has thus become a sign of interpersonal relationship. A "warm" or "cold" facial expression may as well reflect a "warm" or "cold" interpersonal relationship. The compounds and idioms in (14) illustrate the metonymic or metaphoric connections between face and interpersonal relationship.

(14) a. 变脸 *bian-lian* (change-face) 'suddenly turn hostile'
      b. 甩脸 *shuai-lianzi* (fling-face) '(*dial.*) pull a long face (to show one's unhappiness)'
      c. 抹脸 *ma-lian* (wipe-face) 'be strict with sb. all of a sudden; straighten one's face; put on a stern expression'
      d. 翻脸 *fan-lian* (turn-face) 'fall out; suddenly turn hostile'
      e. 翻脸不认人 *fan-lian bu ren ren* (turn-face not recognize person) 'deny or turn against a friend; pretend not to know old friends; turn one's back on old associates'
      f. 翻脸无情 *fan-lian wu-qing* (turn-face no-affection) 'turn against sb.; turn against a friend and show him/her no mercy'

In (14a) "suddenly turn hostile" is literally "change face". Sometimes just "change face" is still not enough to show one's displeasure or anger; people can also "fling their face" (14b) to draw attention to their feeling. Also, one's face changes with the act of "wiping" it (14c), like in a magic show. When breaking up with someone, you "flip your face over or turn it away" (14d), which refers to a falling-out in bodily terms. In (14e) and (14f) are two idioms containing (14d). The examples in (14') illustrate (14a) and (14d).

(14') a. 他跟我变脸了。我哪儿得罪他了？
          Ta gen wo bian-lian   le. Wo nar   dezui ta   le?
          he with me change-face PRT I   where offend him PRT
          'He turned (lit. changed his face) on me. What did I do to offend him?'
      b. 他俩从来没有翻过脸。
          Talia   conglai meiyou fan-guo-lian.
          they-two ever   haven't turn-PRT-face
          'The two of them have never quarreled (lit. flipped over their faces).'

Since the face is a sign, indexical or iconic, of interpersonal relationship, if you want to maintain a relationship, you need to keep the face. If, on the other hand, you do not want to maintain the relationship, you no longer need to keep up the face. You can simply "pull down the face" (15a). Or, you can just "rip it off" (15b), by "scratching" (15c) or "tearing" it (15d). However, those who still care about the relationship may find themselves "unable to pull down the face" (15e). In all these examples, face is really metaphoric, very much like a mask. It is put on, pulled down, or even torn off, for the purpose of marking a particular relationship. The importance of face as a mask kept up to maintain a relationship is further illustrated by idioms in (15f) and (15g). They characterize two kinds of relationship that are maintained only on the surface. Again, the face contrasts the heart as they represent, respectively, one's outside and inside. The idiom in (15h) describes people who are "double-faced" and good at "double-dealing". Of the two faces they have, at least one is fake, that is, a mask put on to be deceptive.

(15) a. 拉下脸 *la-xia-lian* (pull-down-face) 'pull a long face; put on a stern expression; not spare sb.'s sensibilities'

   b. 破脸 *po-lian* (rip-face) 'turn against (an acquaintance or associate); fall out'

   c. 抓破脸 *zhua-po-lian* (scratch-rip-face) 'scratch each other's face; quarrel openly'

   d. 撕破脸 *si-po-lian* (tear-rip-face) 'rip the face; put aside all considerations of face; not spare one's sensibilities; come to an open break in friendship with sb.'

   e. 拉不下脸 *la-bu-xia-lian* (pull-unable-down-face) 'be afraid of hurting one's feelings'

   f. 面和心不和 *mian-he xin-bu-he* (face-harmonious heart-not-harmonious) 'remain friendly in appearance but estranged at heart; be friends only on the surface'

   g. 面从心违 *mian-cong xin-wei* (face-follow heart-oppose) 'comply in appearance but oppose in heart'

   h. 两面三刀 *liang-mian san-dao* (two-face three-knife) 'two-faced; double-dealing; double cross'

It is interesting to note that the observations here of face as mask in human interaction and relationship conform to Goffman's (1959, 1974) role theory in terms of a theatrical metaphor, according to which human communication is action on a metaphorical stage playing out roles in interaction with one another.

Those who really care about interpersonal relationship are usually very sensitive about preserving other people's face as well as their own. That is, they always "take face into consideration" (16a) and "take care to preserve it" (16b). They often "talk face" (16c), and are likely "hindered by face" (16d) so as not to "contradict or hurt others' face" (16e and 16f). Because they "preserve and buy others' face" (16g and 16h), others will consider them as having a "satisfying or sufficing face" (16i). According to the Chinese concept of face, as these expressions show, face is relational and reciprocal in nature: people need to show regard to others' face as well as to their own (Ho 1976, 1994). Therefore, it is both a blessing and a burden (Chang and Holt 1994).

(16)　a.　顾面子　　　*gu-mianzi* (take into consideration-face) 'save (sb's) face; keep up appearances; spare sb's feelings'

　　　b.　顾全面子　　*guquan-mianzi* (take care to preserve-face) 'save sb's face; spare sb's sensibilities'

　　　c.　讲面子　　　*jiang-mianzi* (talk-face) 'take face into consideration; care about sb's sensibilities; have consideration for one's face'

　　　d.　碍面子　　　*ai-mianzi* (hindered by-face) 'just to spare sb's feelings; be afraid of hurting sb's feelings.

　　　e.　驳面子　　　*bo-mianzi* (contradict-face) 'not spare sb's sensibilities; not show due respect for sb's feelings'

　　　f.　伤面子　　　*shang-mianzi* (hurt/injure-face) 'hurt face; hurt sb's feelings'

　　　g.　留面子　　　*liu-mianzi* (preserve-face) 'save sb's face (so as not to embarrass him)'

　　　h.　买面子　　　*mai-mianzi* (buy-face) 'have regard for sb's face; defer to sb.'

　　　i.　够面子　　　*gou-mianzi* (satisfy/suffice-face) 'gain enough recognition of one's face; have favorable responses to one's request as mark of such recognition'

(16')　a.　碍着他爸爸的面子，我不好说什么。
Ai　　　zhe ta babade mianzi, wo buhao　　shuo shenme.
hindered by　his father's face　I　couldn't say　anything
'I didn't say anything for fear of hurting his father's feelings (lit. because I was hindered by his father's face).'

　　　b.　不是我不买你的面子，实在这事不好办。
Bu shi wo bu　mai nide mianzi, shizai zhe shi　buhao ban.
not that I　not buy your face　really this matter can't-be done
'I'd be happy to defer to your wishes, but there's really nothing I can do about it (lit. It's not that I don't buy your face, but this matter really can't be done).'

As shown in the translations in (16'), face has to do with people's feelings and sensibilities. To keep a good relationship people would consider and save others' face, that is, to spare their sensibilities and not to hurt their feelings.

Just as the English word *face* can be used as a verb, so is *mian* 'face' in Chinese. For instance, an old-fashioned punishment applied by parents or teachers to their children or students is called 面壁 *mian bi* 'face the wall'. Extending the verb to a house, for instance, we say that the house 面南坐北 *mian-nan zuo-bei* (face-south sit-north), meaning that it "faces south (and against north)". Apparently, the verbal use is derived from the fact that our face is on the interactive side of our body. In (17) below the three verbal compounds all mean "to face" roughly but have different connotations or implications, as shown by their translations. Examples in (17') illustrate their use in sentences.

(17) a. 面临 *mian-lin* (face-near) 'be faced with; be confronted with; be up against'
    b. 面对 *mian-dui* (face-to) 'face; confront'
    c. 面向 *mian-xiang* (face-toward) 'turn one's face to; turn in the direction of; face; be geared up to the needs of; cater to'

(17') a. 我们面临一场严重的危机。
       Women mian-lin   yichang yanzhong de   weiji.
       we   be-faced-with a   serious MOD crisis
       'We are faced with a serious crisis.'
    b. 你必须面对现实。
       Ni bixu mian-du xianshi.
       you must face-to   reality
       'You must face reality.'
    c. 教育应该面向四个现代化。
       Jiaoyu   yinggai mian-xiang sige xiandaihua.
       education should face-toward four modernizations
       'Education should cater to (or meet) the needs of four modernizations.'

When forced to confront or willing to interact with things or people, we emphasize the fact that our face is oriented against or toward them. When we say that one "faces" crises or reality (17'a and 17'b), we are talking about the abstract in bodily terms. This is more obvious in (17'c) where a nonhuman subject like education does not really have a face.

To summarize, the conception of face as focus of interaction and relationship follows directly our knowledge of the face as part of our body. As listed in (5), the face is the most distinctive part that is on the interactive side of our body. This biological fact about the structure of our body is the basis for the metonymic uses of *mian* 'face' in (13) and (17). In (13) people in interaction focus on each other's face. In (17) they always orient their face to the person or thing they are to interact with. Of course, as in (17'c), interaction between abstract things can be understood in metaphoric terms of human interaction.

When people interact with each other, they form a particular relationship between them. The focus of human interaction, the face, then becomes the focus of human relationship by metaphorical projection. Whereas the face as focus of human interaction is basically physical, the face as focus of human relationship becomes more social. The social face serves as a semiotic sign that marks a particular relationship. Any change of the sign marks a change of the relationship, as in (14). Any damage of the sign marks a damage of the relationship, as in (15). Those who care about the relationship always try to preserve the sign that marks it, as in (16). Apparently, the social face as a semiotic sign is metaphorical in nature, but the metaphor is grounded in the structure of our body. The face can serve as a semiotic sign for interpersonal relationship because of a combination of its biological facts and functions listed in (5) and (12). In addition, the face, with facial gestures, also plays a function of conveying one's intentions. We add this function to (12) to get (18).

(18) a. Face displays emotion.
      b. Face suggests character.
      c. Face conveys intention.

My point is that the social aspects and functions of the face are based on its biological facts and functions. This point will be further evidenced in the next section.

5. Face as locus for dignity and prestige

Dignity and prestige are important factors in interaction and relationship between people or organizations. As weights that determine the balance or imbalance of such interaction and relationship, they are evaluated as the perceived amount of respect claimed or given, that is, how much respect people claim for themselves or obtain from other people. In one sense, people's success in interaction and relationship with others is determined by the amount of dignity and prestige they win. They will gain "weight" with more dignity and prestige and vice versa. What is interesting is that, as the focus of human interaction and relationship, the face is also the locus for dignity and prestige by metaphorical projection. In this sense, face is social, defining one's location in the social system (Ho 1976) or corresponding to one's position in the relational hierarchy (Chang and Holt 1994).

The examples in (19) pertain to dignity or perceived amount of respect one claims for oneself, understood and expressed in metaphorical terms related to the face.

(19) a. 丢脸   diu-lian (lose-face) 'lose face; be disgraced'
      b. 抛脸   pao-lian (toss-face) '(dial.) lose face'
      c. 抢脸   qiang-lian (scrape-face) 'get bruised in the face; lose face; make a fool of oneself'
      d. 扫脸   sao-lian (sweep-face) 'lose face'

e. 保全面子 *baoquan-mianzi* (keep intact-face) 'save face; keep up appearances'
f. 整脸儿 *zheng-lianr* (whole-face) 'face-saving'
g. 舍脸 *she-lian* (sacrifice-face) '(do sth.) at the sacrifice of dignity'
h. 没脸 *mei-lian* (no-face) 'feel ashamed; feel embarrassed'
i. 没脸见人 *mei-lian-jian-ren* (no-face-see-people) 'be too ashamed or embarrassed to face anyone'
j. 有脸 *you-lian* (have-face) 'have the face or cheek (to do sth.)'
k. 要脸/面子 *yao-lian/mianzi* (want-face) 'be keen on face-saving; care much about one's reputation'
l. 爱面子 *ai-mianzi* (love-face) 'be concerned about face-saving; be sensitive about one's reputation'
m. 不要脸 *bu-yao-lian* (not-want-face) 'have no sense of shame; shameless'

If people "lose their face" (19a), they also lose their dignity. To "toss face" in (19b) lays a little more emphasis on one's own responsibility for the loss of face. In (19c) people's dignity is damaged when their face is "scraped". In (19d) people's "face is swept" away and their dignity is gone with it. That is why people think it important to "keep their face intact" (19e) from any damage, so that they can have "whole faces" (19f). Sometimes, however, people have no choice but to "sacrifice their face" (19g) and dignity in order to achieve some purpose. This, of course, is regarded as a shame. If people have lost their face for some reason, they then "have no face" (19h) and can no longer "face other people" (19i). Example (19j) is often used in a rhetorical question for people who are supposed to have no composure or courage to do something. Those who are really concerned about losing face "want or love their face" (19k and 19l). On the other hand, those who have no sense of shame or are shameless do not care about losing face, because they do "not want their face" (19m) in the first place. The sentences in (19') exemplify (19g) and (19j) while (20) further illustrates the relation between face and dignity.

(19') a. 出于无奈，他只好舍脸向人借钱。
Chuyu wunai,   ta zhihao   she-lian   xiang ren
out-of no-choice he is-forced sacrifice-face from others
jie   qian.
borrow money
'With no option left, he was forced to borrow money from others at the sacrifice of his dignity (lit. his face).'

b. 我骂过他，怎么有脸去求他？

Wo ma   guo ta,   zenme   you-lian qu qiu   ta?

I   curse PRT him how-could have-face go ask-a-favor-of him

'I once insulted him. How could I have the face to ask a favor of him?'

(20) 交往应以尊严为前提，我们不能拿热脸去贴人家的冷屁股。

Jiaowang ying   yi   zunyan wei qianti,   women bu-neng na

contact   should have dignity as   precondition we   cannot take

re   lian qu tie   renjiade leng pigu.

warm face to touch others' cold ass

'The contacts should have dignity as a precondition, and we cannot take our warm face to touch their cold ass.'

In (20) the loss of dignity, the taste of humiliation, and the sense of shame are described metaphorically in bodily terms. They stem from the sharp contrast in attitude: "face" versus "ass" and "warm" versus "cold".

In the next group of examples the face is pertinent to prestige or perceived amount of respect obtained from other people. Those who have prestige command respect from other people. In (21a) and (21b) the expressions that literally mean "have face" in Chinese actually mean "have prestige", "command respect", or "enjoy due respect". Note that (21a) is exactly the same as (19j), but *liàn* 'face' in (21a) means "prestige" and the same in (19j) means "effrontery" or "composure". The face is part of the head, the most important external body part. So in (21c) and (21d) prestigious, famous, and respected people are said to be "people with heads and faces". As many abstract concepts are understood spatially, the spatial metaphor also extends into the use of face to refer to prestige. Thus, people whose "faces are big" (21e and 21f) have much more prestige than people whose "faces are small" (21g and 21h). In (21i) *bo-mian* (thin-face) is used modestly or humbly to request some attention or respect from other people. The examples in (21') exemplify (21c), (21g), and (21i).

(21) a. 有脸   *you-lian* (have-face) 'have prestige; command respect; have the face or cheek'

b. 有面子   *you-mianzi* (have-face) 'enjoy due respect'

c. 有头有脸 *you-tou you-lian* (have-head have-face) 'have prestige; command respect'

d. 有头脸   *you-tou-lian* (have-head-face) 'have prestige; command respect'

e. 脸大   *lian-da* (face-big/large) 'have (much) prestige; command (much) respect'

f. 面子大   *mianzi-da* (face-big/large) 'have (much) prestige; command (much) respect'

g. 脸小   *lian-xiao* (face-small) 'have little or no prestige; be nobody'

h. 面子小   *mianzi-xiao* (face-small) 'have little or no prestige; be nobody'

i. 薄面   *bo-mian* (thin-face) 'for my sake; humble respect'

(21') a. 他们都是有头有脸的社会名流。

Tamen dou shi you-tou-you-lian   de   shehui-mingliu.

they   all   are   have-head-have-face   MOD   noted-public-figures

'They are all noted public figures with much prestige.'

b. 我知道我的脸小，说话也不顶用。

Wo zhidao wode lian-xiao,   shuohua   ye   bu-dingyong.

I   know   my   face-small   words   still   not-useful

'I know I'm just a nobody (lit. have a small face); my words carry no weight.'

c. 看在我的薄面上，原谅他这一次。

Kan zai wode bo-mian   shang, yuanliang ta   zhe yici.

look at   my   thin-face   on   forgive   him   this time

'Looking at my humble face (i.e. for my sake), forgive him this time.'

As in (21'a), the celebrities are people who "have head and face", that is, people who have much prestige and command much respect. In (21'b) and (21'c) the degree of prestige is conceptualized spatially as dimensions of face. Little wonder it is argued that one's face, as social image, is measurable in terms of how much face one claims from others and how much face people give the person (Ho 1994). If, as is said, one's face "is a function of perceived social position and prestige within one's social network" (Hwang 1987: 961), that "position" should be capable of quantification.

The concept of prestige always goes with honor, regard, favor, and attention. All these are important elements that form a good interactive relationship. Look at (22).

(22) a. 争脸   *zheng-lian* (vie for-face) 'try to win credit or honor'

b. 争面子   *zheng-mianzi* (vie for-face) 'try to win credit or honor'

c. 给脸   *gei-lian* (give-face) 'do sb. a favor; save sb.'s face (so as not to embarrass)'

d. 给面子   *gei-mianzi* (give-face) 'do sb. a favor; save sb.'s face (so as not to embarrass)'

e. 赏脸   *shang-lian* (grant-face) '(used when requesting sb. to accept one's request, invitation, or presence) honor me with your presence; favor me with'

f. 赏面子   *shang-mianzi* (grant-face) 'accept sth. in order to do sb. honor'

g. 露脸   *lou-lian* (show-face) 'look good as a result of receiving honor or praise; do sth. that brings honor or glory; become known (by doing sth.); be successful'

h. 作脸   *zuo-lian* (compose-face) '(*dial.*) win honor or glory; try to make a good showing'

i. 得脸   *de-lian* (obtain-face) 'find favor with sb.; gain favor from sb.; become known (by doing sth.); be successful; shine'

j. 讨脸   *tao-lian* (beg for-face) 'curry favor with sb.; ingratiate oneself with; fawn on; toady to; please others'

Those who try to win credit or honor for themselves are said to "vie for face" (22a and 22b). Face can be "given" (22c and 22d) or "granted" (22e and 22f) to someone as much as honor can. One's face is "shown" (22g) with greater publicity and better known as the person wins more success, honor, or fame. To win honor, glory, and success means to "create or compose a face" (22h). In (22i) and (22j), specifically, face is also a metaphor for favor, but favor can be seen as a special kind of honor that adds to one's prestige. So, as people find or gain favor from others, they "obtain face" (22i) from them. This compound also means that people gain more prestige as they "shine" with success. If some people curry favor with or fawn on someone, they are actually "begging for face" from that person. Sentences in (22') demonstrate (22c), (22e), and (22i).

(22') a. 董事长来打了一个照面，也算是给脸了。

    Dongshizhang lai   dale   yige zhaomian, ye suan shi gei-lian
    president   come put-in a   appearance so count as give-face
    le.
    PRT
    'As a favor, the president put in a brief appearance (lit. The president put in a brief appearance, which counted as giving face).'

b. 我想请你吃晚饭，你肯不肯赏脸？

    Wo xiang qing ni chi wanfan, ni ken-bu-ken   shang-lian?
    I   want invite you eat dinner you willing-or-not grant-face
    'I'd like to invite you to dinner. May I have the honor (lit. Are you willing to grant me the face)?'

c. 在兄弟几个中间，他是最得脸的一个。

    Zai xiongdi jige   zhongjian, ta shi zui de-lian   de   yige.
    at   brothers several among   he is most obtain-face MOD one
    'Among the several brothers, he is the one most in favor (lit. he is the one who obtains most face).'

As seen from the compounds and examples, "face carries both affective and social cognitive implications", and it is related to concepts that "involve both affective reactions and social cognitive judgments" (Ting-Toomey 1994b: 3–4).

This section has shown that face is really conceptualized as the locus for dignity and prestige. Face as locus for dignity is illustrated by (19). The loss of face results in loss of dignity. Those who care about dignity will try to save their face. Those who do not care about their face have no dignity or are shameless. The conceptualization of face as locus for dignity is built on our understanding of face as highlight of people's appearance, as indicator of their emotion, and as focus of their interaction, discussed in the previous sections. In short, the face, more than any other part of the body, demonstrates one's status of dignity. Closely related to dignity is prestige, which also has face as its locus, as shown by (21). It is expressed in spatial terms as dimensions of face (cf. 10). Dignity and prestige are based on respect, both self-respect and respect from others. But prestige, more than dignity, depends on respect from other people. This again highlights the face as focus of interaction and relationship. In human relationship, one's respect (or disrespect) to another is focused on that person's face, as well as shown on one's own face. Naturally, the face becomes the locus for the respect and prestige one enjoys. Two related concepts are honor and favor. Embodied in face as much as dignity and prestige, honor and favor are treated as commodities and transferred among people in their interaction and relationship, as exemplified by (22).

6. *Face* in English: A comparative perspective

In the last four sections I demonstrated the metonymic and metaphoric extensions of the body-part terms denoting the face in Chinese. It is shown that these extensions are in fact based on some biological facts and functions of the face as part of our body. If there is indeed a bodily basis for such figurative meaning and understanding, we should find similar extensions in other languages. That is, the phenomenon should be widespread, if not universal. In this section, I turn to English for a comparative perspective.[4] I do not, however, intend to present a thorough analysis here. But "flat" as it is, I hope that it will serve as a mirror that provides a comparative view of potential cross-linguistic similarities and differences.

---

4. The English data presented in this section are collected from the following sources: *Cambridge International Dictionary of Idioms* (Cambridge: Cambridge University Press, 1998), *Webster's Third New International Dictionary, Webster's New Collegiate Dictionary, Longman Dictionary of Contemporary English,* and an English-Chinese dictionary (Lu 1993).

A striking finding that emerged in the comparison is that English and Chinese share many of the metonymic and metaphoric conceptions of the face. In English the body-part term *face* has semantic extensions similar to those of its Chinese counterparts. First, the metonymy THE FACE STANDS FOR THE PERSON is widely scattered in daily English. It is common, for instance, to refer to a new member as *a new face*, as opposed to *an old face* for an old member. The following are some sentential examples.

(23)   a.   *I don't know how he dares show his face in this pub after how he behaved the other night!*
       b.   *He has become a familiar face in Washington, D.C.*
       c.   *He put some new faces in the Cabinet.*
       d.   *He'd always wanted to star in action movies but his face just didn't fit.*
       e.   *Crowds of faceless people pour into the city each day.*

In (23a–c) the face as highlight of a person stands for the whole person. In (23d) the face stands for personality and character as well as appearance of the person. The people in (23e) are said to be "faceless" because their identity and character, and possibly their appearance also, are not clear. Both (23d) and (23e) involve metaphorical mapping.

(24)   a.   *Now it's done, we have to put a good face on it.*
       b.   *Though he was obviously distressed, he put the best face he could on the matter.*
       c.   *On the face of it, the trip seems quite cheap, but there could be extra expenses we don't know about yet.*
       d.   *The whole village presented a face of placid contentment.*
       e.   *His report put a new face on the matter.*

As in (23), the face can stand for the physical appearance of a person. This metonymy then extends via metaphor to people's behavior or manner, or to things that may be abstract in nature and have no physical appearances, as in (24). In (24a) and (24b), the face can be interpreted as either the highlight of one's outward appearance of behavior and manner, or as apparent state of the matter. If it is the former, the face suggests one's state of mind and conveys one's intention. If it is the latter, the word *face* means an aspect, a state, or a condition of something abstract that may not be visible at all. This is certainly the case with (24c–e).

(25)   a.   *"I hate pepperoni pizza!" he said, making a face.*
       b.   *She pulled a long face.*
       c.   *George came in with a face as long as a fiddle and said it was raining again.*
       d.   *He argued until he was blue in the face.*

e. *Her face was a picture when I told her the news.*

f. *He laughed on the other (or wrong) side of his face.*

g. *He always keeps a straight face.*

Just as in Chinese, the link between facial expression and emotion or character is also reflected in English. Phrases such as "a stern face", "an angry face", "a happy face", and "a smiling face" indicate people's emotional states. In the sentences of (25), the reference to the face suggests the person's current emotion or his personality. Example (25c) is an extension of (25b), and both indicate a sad or unhappy emotion. In (25d) the facial color of "blue" is conventionally associated with anger, and in (25e) "the picture" on the face refers to one's surprise or anger. In (25f) the face has "two sides". If people "laugh on the wrong side of their face", their emotion drops from happiness to sadness. In (25g) the face that is habitually "straight" suggests an aspect of the person's personality.

(26) a. *I'd prefer to sort this problem out face to face rather than over the phone.*

    b. *I don't know how you can look her in the face after what you've done.*

    c. *Everyone refers to him as "Junior" but no one would dare call him that to his face.*

    d. *He slapped me in the face.*

    e. *One of the managers is always in my face.*

    f. *Just get out of my face and leave me alone!*

    g. *Each time I make a suggestion she just throws it back in my face and says I don't understand.*

    h. *How could he be so two-faced?*

    i. *He has a two-faced political attitude.*

    j. *The government's attempts at reform have blown up in its face, with demonstrations taking place all over the country.*

In English, the word *face* is very often used in idioms indicating human interaction, especially confrontation, as shown in (26). These examples also show that the face is the focus of interpersonal interaction and relationship. In (26a–c) it is the physical face that is referred to, whereas the attack on the face in (26d) can be physical, verbal, or some other abstract kind of engagement. The face in (26e–h) is metonymic or metaphoric. In (26h), for instance, the compound adjective *two-faced* characterizes the person who is a "double-dealer" in human interaction and relationship. In (26i) the metaphorical mapping transfers the epithet *two-faced* from the person to his political attitude. In the last example (26j), the government is confronted with demonstrations all over the country. Here human bodily experience has extended into the domain of social interaction and confrontation. In (27) below human beings face, or are faced with, abstract things, or abstract things face each other. The uses of *face* in these examples are derived through metaphor from actual bodily interaction between human beings.

(27) a. *It was only after I started working for the charity that I came face to face with poverty.*
b. *Despite fierce competition from rival companies, they've set their face against price cuts.*
c. *How could he win in the face of such united opposition?*
d. *Starvation seemed to stare them in the face.*
e. *It's pop music that's sexy, colorful and in your face.*
f. *These recommendations fly in the face of previous advice on safe limits for alcohol consumption.*

In (28) below the word *face* is used as a verb to mean, either alone or in combination with an adverb particle, "overcome", "carry through", "accept", or "meet", which all imply certain kind of interaction in which one's face is oriented toward whoever or whatever one interacts with.

(28) a. *He faced down the critics of his policy.*
b. *He knew he was in the wrong, but was determined to face it out.*
c. *She faced up to her responsibilities.*
d. *He's squandered his money and now he's got to face the music.*

In a metaphorical sense, the English word *face* has the meaning of "effrontery", "composure", or "confidence", as illustrated in (29a) and (29b) below. Apparently, the metaphor here stems from the understanding that one's effrontery, composure, and confidence are all shown on one's face. Also metaphorically, the word *face* is extended to refer to dignity and prestige, as in Examples (29c–g). In this sense, as discussed in the previous section, face as locus of dignity and prestige is an entity that can be "lost" or "saved", and that is measurable with its dimensions.

(29) a. *How could anyone have the face to ask such a question?*
b. *He maintained a firm face in spite of adversity.*
c. *He refused to admit he made a mistake because he didn't want to lose face.*
d. *Are the ministers involved more interested in saving face than telling the truth?*
e. *Face is sometimes a major consideration in diplomatic negotiations.*
f. *She gained great face with the extraordinary performance.*
g. *He's a man of considerable face in the local community.*

It seems that English and Chinese bear much similarity in the metonymic and metaphoric extensions of their body-part nouns referring to the face. In English, as shown in (23) and (24), the face is conceptualized as highlight of a person or matter to stand for the whole. The fact that the face indicates one's emotion and character reveals itself in (25). Furthermore, the face is the focus of human and nonhuman interaction and relationship, as shown in (26–28). Finally, the face in English also serves as locus for dignity, prestige, and related concepts, as demonstrated by (29).

Having presented data from Chinese and English, I now discuss the similarities and differences between the two. For the purpose of comparison, Table 1 provides a checklist of relevant senses discussed above under English *face* and Chinese *lian* 'face' and *mian* 'face'. As the table shows, the English word *face* possesses all the listed meanings. On the Chinese side, *mian* possesses all eight, and *lian* five of the eight, excluding (4) and the last two verbal senses. This table, of course, is just a rough outline rather than a complete picture. It only indicates presence versus absence in a particular cell, but not whether it is a strong or weak presence. For instance, at definition 3 "front, upper, outer, or most important surface of something", the Chinese *mian* has a much stronger presence than *lian*. But the difference is not reflected in the table, with both marked with a "+" sign. Also, the table does not consider the internal difference between, for instance, "front surface" and "upper surface" in definition 3, but lumps them together as a single category in a single definition.

Despite its nature of a rough outline, the table still demonstrates a high degree of similarity between English and Chinese at a certain level of abstraction. The nouns that refer to the face have developed their figurative senses via metonymy and metaphor along similar routes with similar stops. The question to ask is: What underlying principle is responsible for such high degree of similarity across languages and cultures? The answer is our body. Disregarding all the differences in details, humans across races have similar bodies with similar structures. In this study I have suggested that the metonymic and metaphoric conceptions and expressions are built on some facts and functions of the face as part of our body. These are listed in (5) and (18) and repeated here as (31).

Table 1. Senses associated with the body part of face in English and Chinese

	English	Chinese	
Relevant senses associated with the body part of face	*face*	*lian*	*mian*
1. front of head from forehead to chin	+	+	+
2. a look on the face as expressing emotion, character, etc.	+	+	+
3. front, upper, outer, or most important surface of something	+	+	+
4. outward appearance or aspect; apparent state or condition	+		+
5. composure; courage; confidence; effrontery	+	+	+
6. dignity; prestige	+	+	+
7. have or turn the face or front towards or in a certain direction	+		+
8. meet confidently or defiantly; not shrink from; stand fronting	+		+

(31) a. Face is the most distinctive part of a person.
      b. Face is on the interactive side, the front, of a person.
      c. Face is an external body part of a person.
      d. Face displays emotion.
      e. Face suggests character.
      f. Face conveys intention.

Here is a case of embodiment of human meaning. The kind of body we have and how it functions influence and shape what and how we mean (see also Yu 2000, 2003). In both languages the extensions are structured by metonymy and metaphor, which in turn are grounded in common bodily experiences. So the common bodily experiences account for the parallel meaning extensions between them. At this point, I want to emphasize that the similarity under discussion exists at a level of abstraction. When it comes down to the more concrete level of specific linguistic expressions, the differences are also obvious, in contrast to their similarities.

As already shown, the metonymic and metaphoric senses, namely (2–8) in Table 1, are manifested linguistically in both Chinese and English. Some conventionalized expressions are even closely equivalent across the languages. Listed below are some examples. The parentheses on the left side of the Chinese examples contain their original numbers in Sections 2 through 5.

	Chinese	English
(1a)	*lao miankong* (old face)	old face
(8d)	*beng-lian* (stretch-face)	pull a long face
(8e)	*ban-lian* (harden-face)	straighten one's face
(13d)	*lou-mian* (show-face)	show one's face
(13g)	*dang-mian* (to-face)	to one's face
(13h)	*mian-dui-mian* (face-to-face)	face to face
(15h)	*liang-mian* (two-face)	two-faced
(19a)	*diu-lian* (lose-face)	lose face
(19e)	*baoquan-mianzi* (keep intact-face)	save face
(19j)	*you-lian* (have-face)	have the face/cheek

While the above pairs of examples are parallel across the linguistic boundary, the overall amount of data are not so symmetric on both sides under comparison. Chinese seems to have much more conventionalized expressions, in the form of compounds and idioms, involving the body-part terms for the face. This difference seems to be proportionate to the fact that there are several Chinese body-part terms corresponding to the English word *face*, as mentioned in the introductory section of this paper. Specifically, this difference has various facets. First, some English expressions have multiple Chinese counterparts used in different contexts with different emphases. For instance, the English idiom *lose face* corresponds to several Chinese compounds: (19a) *diu-lian* (lose-face), (19b) *pao-lian* (toss-face), (19c) *qiang-lian* (scrape-face), and (19d) *sao-lian* (sweep-face). Here, the last three Chinese examples elaborate on the first one (19a) by conflating the semantic component of manner in them. Incidentally, according to *The Concise Oxford Dictionary* (New Edition), English *lose face* is a translation from Chinese *diu-lian* 'lose face'. The next example shows a different kind of elaboration. The English idiom *save face* basically means "save one's own dignity or self-respect". Equivalent to this meaning Chinese has (19e) *baoquan-mianzi* (keep intact-face), that is, "to save one's own face". Related to this Chinese also has compounds such as (16a) *gu-mianzi* (consider-face), (19k) *yao-mianzi* (want-face) and (19l) *ai-mianzi* (love-face) referring to people who are "keen on saving their face". Furthermore, the elaboration also takes a different direction to "saving other people's face". Therefore, in Chinese there are compounds like (16b) *guquan-mianzi* (take care to preserve-face), (16c) *jiang-mianzi* (talk-face), (16d) *ai-mianzi* (hindered by-face), (16g) *liu-mianzi* (preserve-face), (16h) *mai-mianzi* (buy-face), (22c) *gei-lian* (give-face) and (22d) *gei-mianzi* (give-face). These examples show that it is important to save not only one's own face, but also others' face. Face-saving is more reciprocal in Chinese.

The quantitative difference between Chinese and English also arises from the fact that in some English expressions face is implied while their Chinese counterparts make an explicit reference to it. For instance, English *blush* and *flush* are semantically equivalent to (8b) *lian-hong* (face-red) or (8c) *hong-lian* (redden-face) in Chinese. Having conflated the semantic component of location, the English words mean "become red *in the face*". Also, English *thin-skinned* and *thick-skinned* roughly correspond to (10e) *lian-bao* (face-thin) and (10d) *lian-hou* (face-thick) or (10c) *hou-lian* (thick-face) in Chinese. It can be assumed that the "skin" in the English compounds refer to the "skin of the face" that is most visibly affected by emotions or feelings.

It is worth mentioning here that the other Chinese compounds in (10), which all elaborate on the "quality" of the face in one way or another, demonstrate still another facet of the difference. For many Chinese compounds and idioms with *lian* or *mian,* their English equivalents make no reference to face at all. Examples of this kind abound, such as those in (14), (15), (21), and (22). In (14) and (15) one's face can be "changed", "flung", "flipped over", "pulled down", or "ripped off" in interpersonal interaction and confrontation. In (21) and (22) faces of prestige, honor, favor and so on are conceptualized as entities that can be "vied for" or "passed around".

These are the major facets that constitute the difference between Chinese and English: Chinese is richer than English with conventional expressions involving the body part of face. Here is an apparent reason for it. The concept of face, that is, social face, is Chinese in origin (e.g., Ho 1976; Hu 1944; Morisaki and Gudykunst 1994), and "is central to Chinese construal of their social life" (Chang and Holt 1994: 97). According to Lin Yutang, a famous Chinese scholar, face is "the most delicate standard by which Chinese social intercourse is regulated" (from Ho 1976: 867). That is to say, Chinese culture attaches special importance to face, as further illustrated by the following proverbial sayings:

(32) a. 人活面子树活皮。
      Ren   huo mianzi shu   huo pi.
      humans live face   trees live bark
      'Humans live for their face whereas trees live for their bark.'

   b. 打人不要打脸，揭人不要揭短。
      Da ren   buyao da lian, jie   ren   buyao jie
      hit people don't hit face expose people don't   expose
      duan.
      shortcomings
      'Don't hit people on the face, and don't catch people on the raw.'

The first proverb says "Save your face, because it's all the purpose of your life". The second one says "Spare others' sensibilities and save their face". If Chinese culture attaches special values to face, it then should not be surprising to find these values richly lexicalized in the Chinese language. It is a linguistic manifestation of the complex and dynamic character of the culture-specific Chinese concept of face.

While in English there are not as many conventionalized expressions containing *face*, it does not mean that the concept of face is of little or no significance in English-speaking cultures. In fact, face and facework are acceptedly ubiquitous concepts across cultures, although conceptions of face and rules and criteria governing facework are shaped by cultural variability (e.g., Chang and Holt 1994; Ho 1976, 1994; Hu 1944; Hwang 1987; Morisaki and Gudykunst 1994; Ting-Toomey 1988, 1994b; Tracy 1990). At the linguistic level, in fact, many English idioms containing *face* do not have equivalents in Chinese. These include, for instance, *one's face is a picture, get out of one's face, set one's face against, fly in the face of,* and *face the music,* contained in the examples in this section. To me, a nonnative speaker of English, these idioms vary in their degrees of opacity or transparency. For example, *get out of one's face* and *set one's face against* are transparent and vivid to me because, I believe, they are rooted in common bodily and psychological experiences. On the other hand, *face the music* is not so transparent to me, but its opacity lies in *the music* rather than *face*.

At this point, I want to cite another example that may shed some light on the relationship between linguistic differences and the common bodily basis for meaning and understanding. As in the English-Chinese dictionary (Lu 1993) that I use, given below in (33a) and (33d) are two phrasal examples for the verbal idiom *face up to* under the entry *face*.

(33) a. *face up to one's responsibilities*
   b. *jianyi-de   cheng-dan   ziji-de zhize*
   c. determinedly accept-shoulder self's   responsibilities
   d. *force sb. to face up to that problem*
   e. *poshi mouren zheng-shi   nage wenti*
   f. force sb.   straight-see that   problem

As can be seen, through the glosses in (33c) and (33f), the Chinese translations in (33b) and (33e) do not involve the body part of face, as their English originals do. However, it is apparent that the Chinese translations still involve bodily projection that is metaphorical in character. In (33b) one "accepts and shoulders the responsibilities" while in (33e) the person is forced to "look squarely at the problem". Moreover, in the bodily projection of (33e) the involvement of face is implied: one has to "face" the problem in order to "look at it squarely". In sum, there is a common bodily basis for meaning and understanding something abstract, but the bodily projection varies with regard to the actual body part projected. In English it is the face in both cases, whereas in Chinese it is the shoulder in one and the eyes and, indirectly, the face in the other. So the linguistic differences here still have a common root in the bodily basis.

Finally, I would like to draw attention to the following expressions and collocations that are not usually found in everyday English. These are key and frequent phrases in the English scholarly literature on face and facework:

(34) a. face expectation, face negotiation, face violation, face moderation, self-face protection, other-face violation
   b. positive face, negative face
   c. face claims, face wants, face strategies, face relations
   d. face need, face concern, face maintenance, face behavior, face threat, face respect, hierarchical face system
   e. face-honoring, face-compensating, face-giving, face-withdrawing, face-disregarding, face-enhancing, face-downgrading, face-threatening, face-saving
   f. protect self-face, preserve other-face, defend self-face, confront other-face, manage face, diffuse face

These phrases are used in an academic context to expound ubiquitous concepts and phenomena of face and facework. It is a good example illustrating the point that the lack of a set of linguistic labels in a language does not necessarily negate the existence of corresponding concepts in the culture (Chang and Holt 1994). Language can always make adjustment to meet the needs that arise.

In this section, I laid out data from English consisting of conventionalized expressions structured by metonymy and metaphor. It is shown that, similar to its Chinese counterparts, the English word *face* has also developed related senses motivated by metonymy and metaphor grounded in bodily roles of the face. The commonality in the phenomenon of polysemy, however, exists at a level of abstraction. When it comes down to the level of specific conventionalized expressions, English and Chinese display obvious differences as well as some similarities. Chinese is richer with such expressions, which, I suggest, constitute the linguistic manifestation of special values attached to the Chinese conceptions of face and facework.

7. Conclusion

To put my study presented above in perspective, I propose a "Triangle Model" for the relationship between language, culture, body, and cognition, of which my semantic study of face has brought out a good example. The model is represented schematically by the diagram in Figure 1.

This triangle-shaped diagram is interpreted as follows. A stands for the bodily basis, which consists of our basic knowledge about the structure and function of our body. Line BC represents the level of language, with the distance between B and C representing the difference between two languages. By the same token, line DE represents the level of culture (including environment), with the distance between D and E representing the difference between two cultures. The distance between D and E is a variable, depending on how different or similar the two cultures are. The cultural distance between D and E affects the corresponding linguistic distance between B and C. No matter how far apart D and E may be, they always come down, respectively through B and C, and meet at A. That is, cultures and languages are all wired to the very essence of humanness – the human body, more so with languages than cultures as represented by the different distances. Thus, line AF has a double function. First, it sets the boundary between the two languages and cultures. Second, it also represents the commonality between these two languages and cultures, arising from the common structure and function of human body. What this means is that, however different two languages and cultures may be, they should always have a shared dimension that extends from point A to point F. It is impossible for them to be separated because they are all tied together by their humanness that exists in the common human body. Outlined above is the relationship between language, culture, and body while cognition is the totality of the relationships between all the points and all the lines in Figure 1.

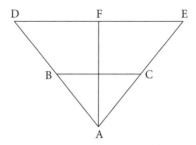

Figure 1. Triangle Model for relationship between language, culture, body, and cognition

The above model is proposed as a generalized model for the relationship between language, culture, body, and cognition. It can indeed illuminate the study of the face-related expressions and concepts I have presented in this paper. The metonymic and metaphoric senses shared by English and Chinese, as listed in Table 1, have emerged from A, namely the bodily basis. They have extended their way more or less in parallel along line AF. The specific linguistic expressions I have discussed, however, are distributed along line BC. Some of those expressions are distributed symmetrically on both sides of line AF, resulting in close equivalents between the two languages. But most of them are distributed asymmetrically across line AF, influenced simultaneously by one force from the bodily pole A and by two separate forces from the cultural poles D and E. The actual location of a particular linguistic expression is determined by the ratio between the forces from the bodily pole and the cultural pole. With a greater force from the bodily pole, for instance, the expression will be drawn toward line AF. A stronger pull from the cultural pole, on the other hand, will draw it toward point B or C.

The social concepts of face and facework that I have mentioned, however, stay on the level of culture represented by line DE. When I said that they are "ubiquitous", I meant that their existence is widespread, if not universal, across cultures. However, their actual conceptions in different cultures can be very different, as far apart as represented by the distance between D and E. Again, no matter how far apart or how close together these conceptions may be, they can be traced back down, through language, to the universal bodily basis, the routes being represented by lines AD, AE, and AF. As a matter of fact, the social concepts of face and facework are very different between English and Chinese, as I have already pointed out, but in this paper I have laid special emphasis on point A and the lines connected to it from D, E, and F. I have especially focused on the smaller triangle ABC. The reason is simple: this smaller triangle is what has been largely overlooked in the field of linguistics.

The critical role of the body in human meaning and understanding was noted a long time ago, for instance, by Vico (1968 [1744]), who suggested that human beings tend to turn to their own body for the understanding of things around them. The bodily basis for meaning and understanding, however, had not received much attention until the rise of the cognitive sciences. Cognitive linguistics has made a special contribution in this regard by bringing into the foreground the linguistic evidence for the connection between human body and meaning (e.g. Johnson 1987; Lakoff 1987; Lakoff and Johnson 1980, 1999).

Finally a word about what linguistics can do to contribute to the study of face, both physical and social. So far studies in linguistics have concentrated on a fruitful pragmatic approach, in line with politeness theory, to linguistic principles and strategies for constructing politeness speech in various languages and cultures (e.g., Brown and Levinson 1987; Lee-Wong 2000; Pan 2000). A more recent exciting development in linguistics has expanded its territory to semantic studies of the links between human facial expressions and emotions across languages and cultures (Wierzbicka 1993, 1999, 2000). Another thing linguists can do, as I have just started to do with this study, is to make a triple jump. The first step is to make systematic studies of body-part terms for the face and their involvement in metonymic and metaphoric expressions. The second is to find out if and to what extent these linguistic expressions are grounded in our bodily experiences. The third is to compare and contrast the results across linguistic and cultural boundaries in order to map out cognitive universals and cultural differences between them. Such an attempt is obviously collective and collaborative in nature. Once achieved, it should be able to help unveil the ties between our physical and social faces in particular, and between language, culture, body, and cognition in general.

References

Brown, P. and Levinson, S.C. 1987. *Politeness: Some Universals in Language Usage*. Cambridge: Cambridge University Press.

Chang, H. and Holt, G.R. 1994. "A Chinese perspective on face as inter-relational concern". In S. Ting-Toomey (ed.), 95–132.

Cody, M.J. and McLaughlin, M.L. 1990. "Interpersonal accounting". In H. Giles and W. P. Robinson (eds), 227–255.

Ekman, P. and Rosenberg, E.L. (eds). 1997. *What the Face Reveals*. New York: Oxford University Press.

Friedman, H.S. and Tucker, J.S. 1990. "Language and deception". In H. Giles and W.P. Robinson (eds), 257–270.

Giles, H. and Robinson, W.P. (eds). 1990. *Handbook of Language and Social Psychology*. Chichester, England: John Wiley & Sons.

Goffman, E. 1959. *The Presentation of Self in Everyday Life*. Garden City, NY: Doubleday.

Goffman, E. 1967. *Interaction Ritual: Essays on Face-to-Face Behavior.* Garden City, NY: Doubleday.

Goffman, E. 1974. *Frame Analysis: An Essay on the Organization of Experience.* Cambridge, MA: Harvard University Press.

Ho, D.Y. 1976. "On the concept of face". *American Journal of Sociology* 81(4): 867–884.

Ho, D.Y. 1994. "Face dynamics: From conceptualization to measurement". In S. Ting-Toomey (ed.), 269–286.

Hu, H.C. 1944. "The Chinese concepts of 'face'". *American Anthropologist* 46: 45–64.

Hwang, K. 1987. "Face and favor: The Chinese power game". *American Journal of Sociology* 92(4): 944–974.

Johnson, M. 1987. *The Body in the Mind: The Bodily Basis of Meaning, Imagination, and Reason.* Chicago: University of Chicago Press.

Kövecses, Z. 2000. *Metaphor and Emotion: Language, Culture, and Body in Human Feeling.* Cambridge: Cambridge University Press.

Lakoff, G. 1987. *Women, Fire, and Dangerous Things: What Categories Reveal about the Mind.* Chicago: University of Chicago Press.

Lakoff, G. and Johnson, M. 1980. *Metaphors We Live By.* Chicago: University of Chicago Press.

Lakoff, G. and Johnson, M. 1999. *Philosophy in the Flesh: The Embodied Mind and Its Challenge to Western Thought.* New York: Basic Books.

Lee-Wong, S.M. 2000. *Politeness and Face in Chinese Culture.* New York: Peter Lang.

Lu, G. (ed.). 1993. *Ying-Han Da Cidian* [The English-Chinese Dictionary (Unabridged)]. Shanghai: Shanghai Translation Press.

Lü, S. and Ding, S. (eds). 1980. *Xiandai Hanyu Cidian* [Modern Chinese Dictionary]. Beijing: The Commercial Press.

Lü, S. and Ding, S. (eds). 1989. *Xiandai Hanyu Cidian Bubian* [Modern Chinese Dictionary Supplement]. Beijing: The Commercial Press.

Lü, S. and Ding, S. (eds). 1996. *Xiandai Hanyu Cidian* [Modern Chinese Dictionary] (revised ed.). Beijing: The Commercial Press.

Morisaki, S. and Gudykunst, W.B. 1994. "Face in Japan and the United States". In S. Ting-Toomey (ed.), 47–93.

Ng, S.H. 1990. "Language and control". In H. Giles and W.P. Robinson (eds), 271–285.

Pan, Y. 2000. *Politeness in Chinese Face-to-Face Interaction.* Stamford, CT: Ablex.

Russell, J.A. and Fernández-Dols, J.M. (eds). 1997. *The Psychology of Facial Expression.* Cambridge: Cambridge University Press.

Stevenage, S.V. 2000. "Giving each other a helping hand: Introduction to the special issue on facial information processing". *Pragmatics and Cognition* 8(1): 1–7.

Ting-Toomey, S. 1988. "Intercultural conflict styles: A face-negotiation theory". In Y.Y. Kim and W.B. Gudykunst (eds), *Theories in Intercultural Communication.* Newbury Park, CA: Sage, 213–235.

Ting-Toomey, S. (ed.). 1994a. *The Challenge of Facework: Cross-Cultural and Interpersonal Issues.* Albany: State University of New York Press.

Ting-Toomey, S. 1994b. "Face and facework: An introduction". In S. Ting-Toomey (ed.), 1–14.

Tracy, K. 1990. "The many faces of facework". In H. Giles and W.P. Robinson (eds), 209–226.

Vico, G. 1968 [1744]. *The New Science of Giambattista Vico.* Revised translation of the third edition by T.G. Bergin and M.H. Fisch. Ithaca, NY: Cornell University Press.

Wang, T. (ed.). 1992. *Xin Xiandai Hanyu Cidian* [A New Dictionary of Modern Chinese Language]. Haikou, China: Hainan Press.

Wei, D. (ed.). 1995. *Han Ying Cidian* [A Chinese-English Dictionary] (revised ed.). Beijing: Foreign Language Teaching and Research Press.

Wierzbicka, A. 1992. *Semantics, Culture, and Cognition: Universal Human Concepts in Culture-Specific Configurations*. New York: Oxford University Press.

Wierzbicka, A. 1993. "Reading human faces: Emotion components and universal semantics". *Pragmatics and Cognition* 1(1): 1–23.

Wierzbicka, A. 1999. *Emotions across Languages and Cultures: Diversity and Universals*. Cambridge: Cambridge University Press.

Wierzbicka, A. 2000. "The semantics of human facial expressions". *Pragmatics and Cognition* 8(1): 147–183.

Wu, G. (ed.). 1993. *Han Ying Da Cidian* [Chinese-English Dictionary], *Vols. 1 & 2*. Shanghai: Shanghai Jiao Tong University Press.

Yu, N. 1995. "Metaphorical expressions of anger and happiness in English and Chinese". *Metaphor and Symbolic Activity* 10(2): 59–92.

Yu, N. 1998. *The Contemporary Theory of Metaphor: A Perspective from Chinese*. Amsterdam: John Benjamins.

Yu, N. 2000. "Figurative uses of *finger* and *palm* in Chinese and English". *Metaphor and Symbol* 15(3): 159–175.

Yu, N. 2002. "Body and emotion: Body parts in Chinese expression of emotion". *Pragmatics and Cognition* 10(1/2): 341–367.

Yu, N. 2003. "The bodily dimension of meaning in Chinese: What do we do and mean with 'hands'?". In E.H. Casad and G.B. Palmer (eds), *Cognitive Linguistics and Non-Indo-European Languages*. Berlin: Mouton de Gruyter, 337–362.

CHAPTER 8

The eyes for sight and mind

This is a study of metonymic and metaphoric expressions containing body-part terms for the eye(s) in Chinese. It also discusses similar expressions in English in order to provide a cross-linguistic perspective. It is found that Chinese and English share the conceptual metonymy PERCEPTUAL ORGAN STANDS FOR PERCEPTION and the conceptual metaphors SEEING IS TOUCHING and THINKING, KNOWING, or UNDERSTANDING IS SEEING. At the level of linguistic instantiation, however, there are both similarities and differences between the two languages. These similarities and differences take three major forms: (1) similar expressions with similar meanings, (2) similar expressions with different meanings, and (3) different expressions with similar meanings. It is shown that, despite the fact that imagination is involved in these metonymic and metaphoric expressions, they seem to have experiential roots in common bodily experiences as they arise from the interaction between culture and body.

1. Introduction

In this study, I attempt to analyze the metaphoric and metonymic nature of the Chinese compounds and idioms that contain the body-part terms for 'eye(s)' from a cognitive linguistic perspective (Barcelona, 2000a; Dirven and Pörings, 2002; Gibbs and Steen, 1999; Johnson, 1987; Lakoff, 1987; Lakoff and Johnson, 1980, 1999; Panther and Radden, 1999). According to cognitive linguistics, metaphor and metonymy are cognitive mechanisms that give rise to conceptual projection. Metaphor involves conceptual mappings across different experiential domains; the target domain is understood in terms of the source domain. For metonymy, on the other hand, conceptual mappings take place across different subdomains within the same common, or superordinate, experiential domain so that the source domain mentally activates the target domain (Barcelona, 2000b). In actuality, however, "the distinction between metaphor and metonymy is scalar, rather than discrete: they seem to be points on a continuum of mapping processes" (Barcelona, 2000b: 16), and they are often mingled together in complicated interaction and combination. It has been noted that metonymy may be a more fundamental cognitive phenomenon than metaphor (Panther and Radden, 1999) and, in many cases, metaphor may be motivated by metonymy (Barcelona, 2000c).[1] At the linguistic level, metaphor and metonymy are main motivating forces behind much of semantic evolution and extension.

In Chinese, the two basic body-part terms for the eyes are 眼 *yan* 'eye(s)' and 目 *mu* 'eye(s)', the latter being a more formal counterpart of the former. Besides, the disyllabic word 眼睛 *yanjing*, which literally means 'eye(s) and eyeball(s)', is also commonly used for 'eye(s)' in modern Chinese. I believe that the large number of compounds and idioms involving 'eye(s)' in the Chinese lexicon reflect the importance of our eyes as organs of sight in particular, and of cognition in general.

As the Chinese old sayings go:

(1) a. 百闻不如一见。
         Bai   wen   bu-ru   yi   jian.
         hundred hearing not-as-good-as one seeing
         'It is better to see once than to hear a hundred times.'

     b. 眼见为实，耳闻为虚。
         Yan-jian   wei shi,   er-wen   wei xu.
         eyes-seeing is solid ears-hearing is   void
         'What one sees is real whereas what one hears may not.'

Both of these sayings stress the belief that seeing for oneself is better than hearing from others. They highlight the importance of our eyes as our organ of vision in getting to know the world in which we live. With our eyes we see and read. Seeing and reading are important channels through which we expand the territory of our knowledge and cognition. As indicated by the sayings, our eyes, i.e. vision, are more important than our ears, i.e. hearing, although they both are our essential organs of perception.

The eyes are important not only for what they do, but also for how they look. They are the important physical features that constitute people's identity. While the face is the most distinctive part of a person, both physically and socially (Yu, 2001), its focus is really where the eyes are, paralleled by the brows (Yu, 2002). In Chinese, the eyes and brows are paired together both conceptually and linguistically as highlights of the face, the latter as a whole being the barometer of emotions

---

1.   In cognitive linguistics, while metaphor is well defined, metonymy has given rise to some controversy in terms of how it works. For current issues and recent developments in cognitive linguistic studies of metaphor and metonymy, see Barcelona (2000a), Dirven and Pörings (2002), Gibbs and Steen (1999), and Panther and Radden (1999).

and states of mind (Yu, 2001, 2002). The compounds in (2), illustrated in (3), serve as good exemplification.[2]

(2) a. 眉眼 *mei-yan* (brow-eye) 'appearance; looks'
     b. 眉目 *mei-mu* (brow-eye) 'features; looks; logic (of writing); sequence of ideas; prospect of a solution; sign of a positive outcome'
     c. 面目 *mian-mu* (face-eye) 'face; features; look; appearance (of things); self-respect; honor; sense of shame; face (as dignity)'

(3) a. 小姑娘眉眼长得很俊。
         Xiao guniang mei-yan zhang de   hen jun.
         little girl   brow-eye look COM very pretty
         'The little girl is very pretty.'

     b. 计划有了眉目。
         Jihua you le   mei-mu.
         plan have PRT brow-eye
         'The plan is beginning to take shape.'

     c. 他政治面目不清。
         Ta zhengzhi mian-mu bu qing.
         he political face-eye not clear
         'He is of dubious political background.'

Apparently, the compounds in (2) have developed their metonymic and metaphoric meanings to various extents. Underlying these semantic extensions are some conceptual metonymies and metaphors, such as THE PART STANDS FOR THE WHOLE and THE MIND IS A BODY. Thus, brows and eyes are such important features of the human face that they together stand for the whole face or looks (2a and 2b). Furthermore, (2b) is also mapped metaphorically onto an abstract domain to refer to the 'face' of abstract things. If people's brows and eyes are pretty, they are 'good-looking' as a whole (3a). If things, concrete or abstract, start to show their 'brows and eyes', then they have already gained a 'face' and taken 'shape' (3b). Similarly, 'face and eyes' in (2c) are so important that they can stand for the whole look of a person. As in (3c), they also refer to the abstract look, say, 'political appearance', of a person.[3]

---

2. In collecting Chinese and English data I used the following sources: Lü and Ding, 1980, 1989, 1996; Wei, 1995; Wen, 1996; Wu, 1993; Lakoff, 1993b; Worrall, 1975; *Cambridge International Dictionary of Idioms* (Cambridge University Press, 1998); *The Concise Oxford Dictionary* (New edition, Oxford University Press, 1976); and *Longman Dictionary of Contemporary English* (Longman, 1978). For glossing purposes, MOD = modifier marker, COM = complement marker, and PRT = particle, used in a broad sense.

3. Readers are referred to Yu (2001) for a detailed discussion of 'face' as self-respect, honor, sense of shame, dignity, and so on.

The importance of the eyes in what we do and who we are is certainly reflected in the Chinese language. In this study, which is part of my recent attempt to investigate the role of the body in human meaning and understanding (see, also, Yu, 2000, 2001, 2002, 2003a, 2003b, 2003c, 2003d), I examine how Chinese compounds and idioms involving the body-part terms for 'eyes' have derived their metonymic and metaphoric meanings based on the role of the eyes as part of our body. In Section 2, I discuss the Chinese way of talking about 'seeing with the eyes'. In Section 3, I discuss how 'seeing with the eyes' is mapped onto thinking, knowing, understanding, and other mental activities. In Section 4, I discuss English idioms with *eye(s)*. In Section 5, I take a comparative perspective on similarities and differences between the two languages. Section 6 presents the conclusion.

2.   The eyes for sight in Chinese

In Chinese, seeing with one's eyes is often talked about in terms of a ray of 'light' traveling from the eyes to the target (Yu, 2003d). Underlying the linguistic expressions is the common image schema, SOURCE-PATH-GOAL, upon which several conceptual metaphors operate, including EYES ARE LIGHT SOURCES and SEEING IS REACHING OUT AND TOUCHING. That is, seeing involves 'spatial movement' and 'physical contact', the contact between the traveling 'eye light' or, sometimes, even the eyes themselves and the target. For instance,

(4)   a.   目光   *mu-guang* (eye-light) 'eye; sight; vision; view; gaze; look'
     b.   眼光   *yan-guang* (eye-light) 'eye; sight; foresight; insight; vision'
     c.   目击   *mu-ji* (eye-hit) 'see with one's own eyes; witness'
     d.   目击者   *mu-ji zhe* (eye-hit person) 'eyewitness; witness'

As in (4a) and (4b), the eyes are 'light sources' that can extend a ray of 'light' to the target. Thus, seeing with one's own eyes literally means 'one's eye hits the target' (4c), and an eyewitness is 'a person whose eye has hit the target' (4d). In other words, seeing takes place when one's eye 'reaches' the target. Example (5) contains two sentences illustrating (4a) and (4b).

(5)   a.   两人的目光碰到了一起。
     Liang ren-de   mu-guang peng-dao yiqi.
     two   persons' eye-light bump   together
     'The two persons' eyes met (lit. Their eye lights bumped each other).'

b. 她的眼光锐利，什么事情都瞒不过她
Tade yan-guang ruili,　　　shenme　shiqing dou
her　eye-light　sharp-pointed　whatever　things　all
man-bu-guo　　　ta.
unable-hide-from　her
'You can hide nothing from her sharp eyes.'

Example (5a) shows that when two persons' eyes meet, their 'eye lights' actually 'bump into' each other in the air. The 'eye light' that moves in space has force; it has a sharp point, as it were, that can penetrate like a dagger. In Chinese, as in (5b), the 'eye light' is often modified or predicated by such adjectives as 锐利 *ruili*, 犀利 *xili* and 锋锐 *fengrui*, which all primarily mean 'sharp-pointed' or 'sharp-edged' and are associated with weapons like daggers and swords. So, the use of these adjectives is metaphorical in that they cause the 'eye light' to acquire properties of metal weapons. Note that in (5b) the 'eye light' itself is also subject to a metaphoric interpretation in which the person actually gets to 'know', rather than sees with her own eyes, all the things happening around her (I will come back to this point in Section 3). In fact, the BODY PART FOR PERSON metonymy is also at work in the instance.

The compounds in (6) all describe various ways of seeing or viewing. They manifest the metonymy PERCEPTUAL ORGAN STANDS FOR PERCEPTION. At the same time, they seem to be metaphorical, too, since they suggest that seeing is 'reaching out and touching'.

(6)　a.　过目　*guo-mu* (pass-eye) 'look over so as to check or approve; read quickly through'
　　b.　举目　*ju-mu* (raise-eye) 'raise one's eyes (to look into the distance)'
　　c.　极目　*ji-mu* (reach the utmost point-eye) 'look as far as the eye can see'
　　d.　穷目　*qiong-mu* (reach the limit-eye) 'look as far as the eye can see'
　　e.　纵目　*zong-mu* (release-eye) 'look as far as one's eyes can see'
　　f.　骋目　*cheng-mu* (give free rein to-eye) 'look as far as the eye can see; look into the distance'
　　g.　放眼　*fang-yan* (let go/set free-eye) 'take a broad view; scan widely'
　　h.　着眼　*zhuo-yan* (put to-eye) 'see/view from the angle of; have sth. in mind'

When people look over or read through something, that something 'passes their eye light' (6a), just as in 'scanning'. As people look into the distance, they 'raise their eyes' so that 'the eye light will travel farther' (6b). To look as far as the eye can see means that one makes 'the eye light reach the utmost point or limit' (6c and 6d). To do this, one needs to 'let the eye light go as far as it can' (6e, 6f, and 6g).

Example (6h) is usually used in a metaphorical sense. When you 'put your eye (light) to something', you actually set a 'viewpoint' that shapes your 'view' of the whole situation. Example (7) is a saying that makes use of this metaphor.

(7)   大处着眼，小处着手。
      Da-chu   zhuo-yan, xiao-chu   zhuo-shou.
      large-place put to-eye small-place put to-hand
      'Keep the general goal in sight (or bear larger interests in mind) while tak-
      ing hold of the daily tasks (lit. Put one's eyes to large things, and put one's
      hands to small things).'

That is, one should 'think big' and 'act small'. Only when you 'see' the general goal and 'handle' the ordinary tasks day in and day out can you actually succeed. Here the verb *zhuo* 'put to' suggests actual contact between the 'eyes' and the 'hands' on one side, and the 'big things' and 'small things' on the other, but this 'contact' should be interpreted metonymically or even metaphorically. Metonymically, we have, here, PERCEPTUAL ORGAN FOR PERCEPTION (or EYES FOR SEEING) and IN-STRUMENTALITY FOR ACTIVITY (or HANDS FOR DOING). In reality, however, this saying may simply describe a situation in which people 'keep the general goal in mind while working on the daily tasks'. That is, they do not see their goal with their eyes at all, and they do not necessarily work with their hands. In that case, the use of words *yan* 'eye(s)' and *shou* 'hand(s)' is metaphorical in this saying.

The compounds in (6) all describe a person who sees in a certain manner. There are also many compounds involving 'eyes' that describe the target that in one way or another attracts people's attention. In this case, the metaphor is CAUSING TO SEE IS CATCHING THE EYE (LIGHT), in addition to the metonymy PERCEPTUAL ORGAN STANDS FOR PERCEPTION. The compounds in (8) are some examples.

(8)   a.   惹眼   *re-yan* (invite/provoke-eye) 'conspicuous; showy'
      b.   招眼   *zhao-yan* (beckon-eye) 'eye-catching'
      c.   触眼   *chu-yan* (touch-eye) 'eye-catching; striking; conspicuous'
      d.   打眼   *da-yan* (beat-eye) 'catch the eye; attract attention'
      e.   扎眼   *zha-yan* (prick-eye) 'dazzling; offending to the eye; loud; of-
                   fensively conspicuous'
      f.   刺眼   *ci-mu* (thorn/stab-eye) 'dazzling; offending to the eye'
      g.   夺目   *duo-mu* (seize-eye) 'catch the eye; dazzle the eyes; be striking
                   to the eye'
      h.   掠目   *lüe-mu* (brush past-eye) 'sweep past one's eye'

In these compounds, the target seems to be animate and have force of its own. It 'attracts' one's attention by contact with one's 'eye light' or eyes themselves. Thus, it can 'invite' or 'provoke' the eyes (8a), 'beckon' to the eyes (8b), 'touch' or 'beat' the eyes (8c and 8d), 'prick', 'thorn' or 'stab' the eyes (8e and 8f), or even 'seize' the eyes (8g). Example (8h) is different in that it describes a situation in which the target 'sweeps in and out of one's eyesight' very quickly. The eyesight, however, is the range of one's 'eye light'. In these examples, seeing takes place when the target 'comes into one's sight' or 'catches one's eye'. Either way, there is 'physical contact' involved.

In this section, we have seen how Chinese, using the compounds and idioms containing 'eye(s)', describes seeing with one's eyes. The conceptual metonymy involved is PERCEPTUAL ORGAN STANDS FOR PERCEPTION. Moreover, seeing is also described metaphorically in terms of 'touching', that is, as contact between the eye (light) and the target. The underlying conceptual metaphor is SEEING IS TOUCH-ING. The eyes can send the 'eye light' to the target. Conversely, the target can catch the 'eye light' or even contact the eyes directly. Of course, the distance the 'eye light' can travel is limited. The limits constitute one's eyesight.

3.   The eyes for mind in Chinese

The metonymic and metaphoric use of the body-part terms for 'eyes' has been found in various domains in Chinese. For instance, it has been found in the domain of time (see Yu, 1998, 1999), as exemplified by the following words:

(9)   a.   眼/目前   *yan/mu-qian* (eye-front) 'at the moment; at present; now'
      b.   眼看   *yan-kan* (eye-see) 'soon; in a moment'
      c.   转眼   *zhuan-yan* (turn-eye) 'in the twinkling of an eye; in an instant; in a flash'
      d.   眨眼   *zha-yan* (blink-eye) 'very short time; wink; twinkle'

Note that in Chinese, as well as in English, the future is 'ahead of us' whereas the past is 'behind us' (see, e.g., Lakoff, 1990, 1993a; Yu, 1998, 1999). Thus, what is 'right before our eyes' is 'now' in time (9a), and what our eyes 'see right before us' is 'soon' to happen (9b). In these two examples, the spatial is mapped onto the temporal, and the physical onto the abstract, so they are metaphoric. Examples (9c) and (9d) are based on our bodily experience with our eyes: rolling or blinking our eyes takes just an instant of time. They are metaphoric with an apparent metonymic basis.

In this section, I focus on the compounds and idioms involving 'eye(s)' that do not describe seeing per se, but states or activities of the mind. In the previous section, there was a predominant pair of conceptual mappings: the first one is metonymic, and the second is metaphoric, namely, PERCEPTUAL ORGAN STANDS FOR PERCEPTION and SEEING IS TOUCHING. In both of these cases, seeing is the target domain, with mappings from more concrete source domains (the eyes and touching). The examples to be considered in this section retain that pair of conceptual metonymy and metaphor and extend them to a new predominant metaphor, MENTAL FUNCTION (thinking, knowing, and understanding) IS PERCEPTUAL EXPERIENCE (seeing), on which my discussion will concentrate.

As illustrated by the following saying, our eyes, as organ of sight, are connected to our heart and mind:

(10) 眼睛是心灵的窗户。
　　　Yanjing shi xinling-de chuanghu.
　　　eyes are heart/mind's window
　　　'One's eyes are the windows into one's heart/mind.'

One's mental states and activities include emotions and feelings. In Chinese, there are a large number of compounds and idioms involving 'eye(s)' for the description of emotions because the eyes, paired with brows, are conceived of as most expressive of emotions. In what follows, however, I will not include those compounds and idioms because I have dealt with them elsewhere (see Yu, 1995, 1998, 2002). Instead, I will concentrate on the description of mental states and activities other than emotions and feelings. The linguistic instances, in one way or another, all manifest the conceptual metaphor THINKING, KNOWING, or UNDERSTANDING IS SEEING, which can be seen as a subversion of the central metaphor THE MIND IS A BODY (see, e.g., Fortescue, 2001; Jäkel, 1995; Johnson, 1992; Lakoff and Johnson, 1999; Radden, 1996; Sweetser, 1990; Turner, 1991; Yu, 2003d). As will be seen shortly, THINKING, KNOWING, or UNDERSTANDING IS SEEING entails two related mappings, MENTAL CAPABILITY IS EYESIGHT and MENTAL CAPACITY IS EYESHOT.

In the previous section, I showed that the Chinese talk about seeing in terms of 'eye light' sent from the eyes to the target. The 'eye light' is also mapped onto the domain of mental states and activities, as exemplified by (11).

(11) a. 他有政治眼光。
　　　　 Ta you zhengzhi yan-guang.
　　　　 he has political eye-light
　　　　 'He has political foresight.'

　　　b. 他开始用新的眼光来观察周围事物。
　　　　 Ta kaishi yong xin-de yan-guang lai guancha zhouwei shiwu.
　　　　 he begin use new eye-light to observe around things
　　　　 'He began to view everything around him in a different light (lit. a new eye light).'

c. 我们应该用长远的眼光看长期的发展趋势。
Women yinggai yong chang-yuan de   yan-guang kan
we   should use   long-far MOD eye-light see
chang-qi   de   fazhan   qushi.
long-term MOD developmental trend
'We should take a long-range vision (lit. use a long-far eye light) to
view the long-term developmental trend.'

In (11a), the person has the mental ability to predict and perhaps influence, for
instance, the outcome of a current political situation. In (11b), the person now
thinks and understands things around him differently, with a newly adopted outlook or perspective, which is 'eye light' in the Chinese original. In the English
translation, 'eye light' is rendered as 'light', which of course affects the result of
'viewing' or 'seeing' as well. Example (11c) contains metaphorical mappings from
the spatial to the temporal domain and from the physical to the mental domain, as
is also reflected in the English translation. As we take a 'long-range vision', we 'see
far into the future'.

The idioms in (12) further illustrate the metaphorical sense of 'eye light'. The
farther one's 'eye light' can extend, the better one's mental vision is.

(12) a. 目光远大   *mu-guang yuan-da* (eye-light far-large) 'far-sighted; far-
                    seeing'
      b. 目光短浅   *mu-guang duan-qian* (eye-light short-shallow) 'short-
                    sighted'
      c. 目光如炬   *mu-guang ru-ju* (eye-light like-torch) 'eyes blazing like
                    torches – looking ahead with wisdom; far-sighted'
      d. 目光如豆   *mu-guang ru-dou* (eye-light like-bean) 'vision as narrow
                    as a bean – of narrow vision; short-sighted'

Note that these idioms really refer to one's mental capability rather than to physical
eyesight. If someone's 'eye light' is 'far and large', this person has great wisdom and
predictive power. On the other hand, if someone's 'eye light' is 'short and shallow',
this person lacks intellectual wisdom and can only 'see what lies right in front of the
eyes'. The contrast between mental 'farsightedness' and 'shortsightedness' is brought
out by the simile added to the metaphor in (12c) and (12d). A torch is something
that helps people see farther in the dark. When one's 'eye light', like a torch, travels
farther in the dark, the seeing person is one of vision and wisdom. If one's 'eye light'
is as tiny as a bean, it will not help the person 'see' in the dark, and the person is one
of narrow vision and little wisdom. In other words, one's mental capacity depends
on how 'bright' one's eyes are, as further illustrated by the idioms in (13).

(13) a. 眼明心亮   *yan-ming xin-liang* (eye-bright heart-light) 'see and think clearly; be sharp-eyed and clear-headed'

    b. 心明眼亮   *xin-ming yan-liang* (heart-bright eye-light) 'see and think clearly; be sharp-eyed and clear-headed; be able to see everything clearly and correctly; be clear-minded and clear-sighted'

Examples (13a) and (13b) are synonymous. They emphasize the parallel relation between 'seeing' and 'thinking'. If one 'sees' clearly, one also 'thinks' clearly. If one is 'clear-minded', one is 'sharp-eyed' as well. As we can see, 'brightness' of the eyes is really important: 'brighter' eyes are 'sharper' in vision. This is also illustrated by the idiomatic expressions in (14).

(14) a. 明眼人   *mimg-yan ren* (bright-eye person) 'a person with a discerning eye; a person of good sense'

    b. 擦亮眼睛   *ca-liang yanjing* (rub-shining eye) 'remove the scales from one's eyes; keep one's eyes shined/polished; sharpen one's vigilance'

    c. 拭目以待   *shi-mu yi-dai* (wipe-eye to-wait) 'rub one's eyes and wait; wait and see; wait expectantly (for sth. to happen); wait for the result anxiously'

    d. 刮目相看   *gua-mu xiang-kan* (scrape-eye PRT-see) 'look at sb. with new eyes; treat sb. with increased respect; regard sb. with special esteem'

(15) a. 我们要擦亮眼睛识破他们的阴谋。

Women yao   ca-liang   yanjing shipo   tamen-de yinmou.
we   should   rub-shine eyes   see-through their   schemes
'We should sharpen our vigilance and guard against their schemes (lit. We should rub and shine our eyes so as to see through their schemes).'

    b. 古人云，"士别三日便当刮目相看。"

Gu   ren   yun, "Shi   bie   san   ri   bian   dang
ancient people say   scholar away three days should be
gua-mu   xiang-kan".
scrape-eye PRT-seen
'The ancients say, "A scholar who has been away three days must be looked at with new eyes."'

As in (14a), a 'bright-eyed person' in Chinese is a person of good sense. (14b–d) all evoke the same image, that is, people have to 'polish' or 'shine' their eyes in order to 'see' better. Thus, they need to 'shine their eyes by rubbing them' to sharpen their vigilance (14b). When they anxiously 'wait and see', they 'wipe their eyes' to 'polish' them (14c). In (14d), the eyes are 'polished' by 'scraping' them. This is what happens when people 'look at someone with new eyes' or treat someone with increased respect. Example (15) provides sentential examples of (14b) and (14d). Example (15b) is a classic saying, which emphasizes the fact that a scholar can learn a lot and, therefore, 'take on a new look' in just three days. A 'new look' beyond recognition must be 'seen with new (scraped) eyes'.

As we know from our bodily experiences with the eyes, we can see when our eyes are open, and cannot when they are closed. We tend to open our eyes widely when we are alert. We tend to turn our eyes away from the person with whom we have fallen out. If our eyes are blocked by something, we cannot see even if our eyes are open. If our eyes are blind, we of course can see nothing. All this is reflected in the metaphorical use of metonymy-based compounds and idioms involving 'eye(s)', as in (16).

(16) a. 开眼   *kai-yan* (open-eye) 'open one's eyes; widen one's view (or horizons); open one's mental horizon; broaden one's mind'
      b. 闭目塞听 *bi-mu se-ting* (close-eye stop-hearing [by plugging one's ears]) 'shut one's eyes and stop one's ears – cut oneself off from reality; turn a blind eye and a deaf ear to'
      c. 瞪眼   *deng-yan* (stare-eye) 'open one's eyes wide; stare; glare'
      d. 反目   *fan-mu* (reverse-eye) 'fall out; have a falling-out'
      e. 障眼法   *zhang-yan fa* (block-eye method) 'cover-up; camouflage; throw dust in people's eyes; a deceptive trick; means of camouflaging; a method to deflect suspicion from oneself'
      f. 盲目   *mang-mu* (blind-eye) 'blind; blindly'
      g. 瞎眼   *xia-yan* (blind-eye) 'blind'

Apparently, various metonymies, such as CAUSE FOR EFFECT, PRECONDITION FOR RESULT, MANNER FOR ATTITUDE, are operating in these examples, but our central interest here is in the conceptual metaphor: THINKING, KNOWING, or UNDERSTANDING IS SEEING or, more generally, MENTAL FUNCTION IS PERCEPTION.

In (17a) a sentential example is provided for (16a). In this sentence, 'open one's eyes' really means 'widen one's horizon of knowledge'. Example (17b) is somewhat different: here, the person's 'eyes open widely' at the sight of money. That is, he is greedy. In (17c), 'with one's eyes open' means 'with full awareness' while 'with one's eyes shut' suggests 'willingness and readiness (to accept the bad consequences)'.

(17) a. 这个展览会真叫人开眼。
          Zhege zhanlanhui zhen jiao   ren   kai-yan.
          this   exhibition   really make people open-eye
          'The exhibition is a real eye-opener.'

b. 他这个人见钱眼开。

Ta zhege ren   jian-qian   yan-kai.

he this   person see-money eye-open

'He's such a person who is wide-eyed at the sight of money (i.e. greedy).'

c. 我睁眼做，合眼受。

Wo zheng   yan zuo, he   yan shou.

I   opening   eyes do   shutting eyes accept

'I did (it) with my eyes open, and I will accept (it, or its consequence) with my eyes shut (i.e. be willing and prepared to accept its consequence).'

The idiomatic saying in (18a) below is related to (16b). Each human being has two eyes. If a person 'opens one eye' and 'closes the other', then this person is pretending not to 'see' something that he actually 'sees'. People sometimes don't want to see something bad, because 'what is out of sight is out of mind' (18b).

(18) a. 睁一只眼，闭一只眼

zheng yizhi yan, bi   yizhi yan

open one eye close one eye

'turn a blind eye to sth.; close one's eyes to sth.; wink at sth.'

b. 眼不见，心不烦

yan bu jian, xin   bu fan

eyes not see   heart not worry

'what the eye doesn't see the heart doesn't worry about – out of sight, out of mind'

The sentence in (19a) illustrates (16c). When people work on something with 'staring eyes', they take it seriously and deal with it with no reservation. The people in (19a) dare to work on management with their 'eyes staring'. The 'staring eyes' in this case is originally associated metonymically with people's attitude toward their work, but is now used metaphorically, regardless of the metonymic link between manner and attitude, to describe their mental state of being bold and brave. Examples (19b) and (19c) respectively exemplify (16f) and (16g). Apparently, they are about people's mental 'blindness' rather than their inability to see physically.

(19) a. 我们敢于瞪起眼来抓管理。

Women gan yu deng-qi-yan-lai zhua   guanli.

we   dare to staring-eyes   work-on management

'We dare to work on management with our eyes staring (i.e. boldly, bravely).'

b. 他盲目乐观。
   Ta mang-mu leguan.
   he blind-eye optimistic
   'He is unrealistically (lit. blindly) optimistic.'

c. 我真瞎了眼，把他当作好人了。
   Wo zhen xia-le-yan, ba-ta-dangzuo hao ren le.
   I really blind-PRT-eye take-him-for good person PRT
   'I was so blind as to take him for a gentleman.'

In real life, blind people cannot see; in metaphor, however, it is possible that seeing people still cannot 'see', as illustrated by the idioms in (20).

(20) a. 目无法纪   *mu-wu-faji* (eye-not have-law and discipline) 'act in utter disregard of law and discipline; flout law and discipline'

b. 目中无人   *mu-zhong wu-ren* (eye-inside no-people) 'consider everyone beneath one's notice; be supercilious; be overweening'

c. 目空一切   *mu-kong-yiqie* (eye-void of-all) 'consider everybody and everything beneath one's notice; be supercilious'

d. 有眼不识泰山   *you-yan-bu-shi-Taishan* (have-eye-not-recognize-Mount Tai) 'have eyes but not see Mount Tai; entertain an angel unawares'

In (20a–c), when the idioms say that law and discipline, people, and things do not exist 'inside one's eye', it actually means that they do not exist inside this person's mind. That is, the person either disregards or ignores them, mentally. In (20d), Mount Tai is a well-known mountain in China, and is taken as a symbol of great weight or import. Those who do 'not see Mount Tai with their eyes' do not recognize the great importance of someone or something.

In contrast, those who have extraordinary mental capability and wisdom are often said to 'have a unique eye', distinguished from all others, as the idioms in (21) say.

(21) a. 别具只眼   *bie-ju zhi-yan* (distinctively-have one-eye) 'be able to see what others cannot; penetrating eye that sees things others cannot see; have an original view/opinion'

b. 独具慧眼   *du-ju hui-yan* (uniquely-have intelligent-eye) 'have exceptional insight; discern what others don't; have mental discernment or perception'

In addition, one's distinctive use of eyes can represent one's attitude toward someone or something. However, the MANNER FOR ATTITUDE metonymy is often used metaphorically regardless of its experiential basis. For instance,

(22) a. 另眼相看   *ling-yan xiang-kan* (different-eye PRT-see) 'regard (or look up to) sb. with special respect; give sb. special treatment; view sb. in a new, more favorable light; see sb. in a new light; treat sb. with special consideration'

     b. 冷眼相看   *leng-yan xiang-kan* (cold-eye PRT-see) 'look coldly upon; look at coldly; look unfavorably upon; look with a cold eye; give sb. the cold eye'

     c. 冷眼相待   *leng-yan xiang-dai* (cold-eye PRT-treat) 'snub sb.; give sb. the cold shoulder; turn the cold shoulder on sb.; give sb. the frozen mitt'

     d. 冷眼旁观   *leng-yan pang-guan* (cold-eye side-look on) 'look coldly from the sidelines at; look on as a disinterested bystander; look on indifferently or unconcerned; stand aloof and look on with cold indifference; take a detached point of view'

Example (22a) is somewhat related to (14d) above. A different attitude is manifested in a different eye look. Examples (22b–d) all involve 'cold eye(s)', which means either 'cool detachment' or 'cold shoulder' in attitude. It is worth noting that 热眼 *re-yan* (hot-eye) is not a lexicalized item in Chinese. Yet, 热心 *re-xin* (hot-heart) means 'enthusiastic' or 'warmhearted' (cf. 23c). Chinese does have 眼热 *yan-re* (eye-hot) as a lexical item, meaning 'cast covetous eyes at sth.', 'eye sth. covetously', or 'be envious' (see, also, Yu 2002).

Finally, (23) provides a group of idioms that involve 'eye(s)' and another body part. The metaphorical nature of these idioms is obvious.

(23) a. 眼大心肥   *yan-da xin-fei* (eye-big heart-fat) 'be proud and arrogant'

     b. 眼高心傲   *yan-gao xin-ao* (eye-high heart-haughty) 'be proud and haughty'

     c. 冷眼热心   *leng-yan re-xin* (cold-eye hot-heart) 'outward indifference but inward fervency; affected indifference'

     d. 明目张胆   *ming-mu zhang-dan* (bright-eye stretched-gallbladder) 'brazenly; flagrantly'

     e. 眼高手低   *yan-gao shou-di* (eye-high hand-low) 'have high standards but little ability; have great ambition but little talent; have sharp eyes in criticizing others but clumsy hands in doing things oneself'

Examples (23a) and (23b) once again stress the close relationship between the 'eyes' and the 'heart' (cf. 13a and 13b). 'Big-eyed' and 'fat-hearted' people are proud and arrogant (23a). Their eyes are so 'big' and their heart is so 'fat' that others appear very 'small' in their eye or heart. It is interesting to note that in English people who think too highly of their own importance have a 'big head' whereas those who are 'big-hearted' are generous people. In (23b), proud and haughty people have 'high eyes' and a 'haughty heart'. Apparently, people with their eyes 'high' either 'look down upon' or 'look over' other people. Example (23c) describes a situation in which the person has 'cold eyes' but a 'hot heart' (cf. 22b–d), and the outward and the inward do not match. In (23d), the internal organ involved is the gallbladder, which is responsible for one's courage, according to the theory of internal organs in Chinese medicine (Chen, 1989; Wang et al., 1997). The idiom is derogatory in meaning nowadays. Those who have their 'eyes bright' (i.e. eyes glaring) and 'gallbladder stretched' are brazen and flagrant. The 'glaring eyes' refers to a mental attitude, and a 'stretched gallbladder' has a larger capacity of (negative) 'courage' (see, also, Yu, 1995, 2002, 2003a).

The last example, (23e), coordinates 'eyes' with 'hands'. As already mentioned, 'high eyes' are associated with pride and haughtiness (cf. 23b). This accords with the metaphorical conceptualization that what is perceived as superior is 'higher' in space, and vice versa. The hands are our most important external body parts with which we do things (see Yu, 2000, 2003c). The idiom as a whole describes people whose ability does not match their wishes, or who are too critical of others' ability while they themselves are not capable at all. The division of labor for the eyes and hands as parts of our body is such that our eyes set goals and our hands act to achieve those goals. While we can 'aim high' with our eyes, our aim may be too high for us to 'reach' with our hands. What (23e) implies is that people should be realistic and tolerant. It is interesting, for our purpose, to note that the abstract concepts are expressed via metaphor that is bodily based and derived from metonymy.

In this section, I have presented data from Chinese evidencing that some mental states and activities are expressed in metonymic and metaphoric terms of how one's eyes behave and see. Metonymy describes the physical conditions of the eyes that accompany, or 'go along with', certain states and activities of the mind so that the description of the former suggests or activates the latter (THE PHYSICAL FOR THE MENTAL). Based on metonymy, metaphor goes further and refers to certain states and activities of the mind in terms of physical conditions of the eyes that do not really fit, or 'come along' (THE MENTAL AS THE PHYSICAL). Via metaphor, for instance, physical eyesight is mapped onto mental capability, and physical eyeshot is mapped onto mental capacity. The metonymies and metaphors discussed here (which are intertwined with each other) seem to result from the role our eyes play as part of our body. As 'windows' into our mind, our eyes 'show' what we think. As organs of sight, they are major channels of cognition through which we get to know and understand the world: what we see and how we see it, largely determine our knowledge and cognition of the world. In short, the metaphor (THE MENTAL AS THE PHYSICAL) is based on the metonymy (THE PHYSICAL FOR THE MENTAL), and the metonymy is rooted in common bodily experience.

4. The eyes for sight and mind in English

Lakoff (1993b) has discussed metaphors for perception in English. The general metaphor is PERCEPTION IS CONTACT BETWEEN PERCEIVER AND PERCEIVED, with two special cases: PERCEIVING IS TOUCHING and PERCEPTION IS RECEPTION. With respect to seeing, the more specific metaphor is SEEING IS TOUCHING. The use of the body-part term *eye(s)* in some cases, however, can be seen as involving the metonymy EYES STAND FOR SEEING (or PERCEPTUAL ORGAN STANDS FOR PERCEPTION) that works in interaction and combination with the metaphor. First look at (24):

(24) a. *My eyes picked out every detail of the pattern.*
　　　b. *I've loved him ever since I first laid/set eyes on him.*
　　　c. *I can't take my eyes off her.*
　　　d. *His eyes are glued to the TV.*
　　　e. *Would you mind casting your eye over my essay and giving me your comments?*
　　　f. *They made eye contact.*
　　　g. *The dress in the window caught her eye when she passed the store.*

While each of the above examples presents a unique way of interaction between the perceiver, his or her eye(s), and the perceived, they all suggest physical contact of some kind between one's eye(s) and the target. The idiomatic collocations in (25) provide further exemplification. These expressions, which all mean that the target is 'eye-catching', make the target animate, so as to 'come into contact with one's eye(s)'.

(25) a. *take sb.'s eye*
　　　b. *jump to the eye(s)*
　　　c. *leap to the eye*
　　　d. *strike the eye*
　　　e. *hit sb. in the eye*

What is more interesting is that the metaphor THINKING, KNOWING, or UNDERSTANDING IS SEEING is richly manifested in English, just as it is in Chinese. This is reflected in the metonymic and metaphoric nature of the English idioms containing the body-part term *eye(s)*.

(26) a. *She is nothing but a slave in her husband's eyes.*
b. *It's just a gleam in my eye.*
c. *He cast a professional economist's eye over the problem.*
d. *The scientists at the meeting all cast a skeptical eye on that theory.*

In (26a), the idiom *in one's eyes* means 'in one's opinion' or 'in one's mind', since how one 'sees' determines how one 'thinks'. In (26b), *gleam in one's eye* refers to 'a hazy idea in one's mind' given that the eyes are 'windows' into the mind. In (26c), the person 'views' the problem from the 'perspective' of a professional economist. The 'eye' is 'tinted' by the special knowledge and mentality of a person with professional training in economics. The 'eye' in (26d), however, stands for the scientists' mental attitude toward the theory. Again, the way they 'look at' the theory reflects how they think about it. All these examples are special cases of THINKING, KNOWING, or UNDERSTANDING IS SEEING.

As can be seen, there is a close relationship between 'sight' and 'mind'. A particular way of thinking, knowing, and understanding often derives from a particular way of seeing. Metonymy usually alludes to physical aspects associated with certain mental processes (THE PHYSICAL FOR THE MENTAL), whereas metaphor maps the physical onto the abstract domain of mental states and activities (THE MENTAL AS THE PHYSICAL). They are often tightly intertwined.

(27) a. *There were lots of dresses to choose from, but none of them really caught my eye.*
b. *I've got my eye on a really nice sofa – I just hope we can afford it.*
c. *He only has eyes for his beautiful wife.*
d. *She has an eye for detail.*
e. *All eyes are on the Prime Minister to see how he will respond to the challenge to his leadership.*
f. *With an eye to the upcoming election the President has hired a new speech-writer.*

Note that the phrase *to catch one's eye* in (27a) is slightly different from the same one in (24g). It adds mental dimensions of 'liking' and 'interest' to the meaning of 'being seen and noticed' in the previous case. So does the *eye* in (27b), which suggests a 'desire to possess' on the part of the perceiver. Example (27c) expresses a man's mental state, in which he is only interested in, and attracted to, his wife. Example (27d) is about a particular quality of a person, namely, her close attention to detail. Both (27e) and (27f) have to do with attention, too, but they differ in the degree of abstraction. In (27e) it is possible for people to 'watch' the Prime Minister in both physical and abstract senses, but the 'upcoming election' in (27f) is an event that cannot be 'seen' until it is 'here'. These examples manifest the conceptual metaphors LIKING IS SEEING and PAYING ATTENTION IS SEEING. It is worth noting that both of these metaphors have a metonymic basis constructed from our bodily experience: our eye tends to be oriented toward what we like and where our attention is.

When people close their eyes for some reason, they cannot see. On the other hand, when their eyes are opened, they are able to see things they cannot see when their eyes are closed. Our bodily experiences with the eyes provide an experiential grounding for metaphors in language. In other words, these metaphors are motivated by, or based on, metonymy. For instance,

(28) a. *You can't just shut your eyes to your problems and hope they'll go away.*
      b. *The president turned a blind eye to corruption within his administration.*
      c. *I'll close my eyes to your mistake this time, my boy, but don't let it happen again.*
      d. *It was a mistake, and I did it with my eyes shut.*
      e. *He's finally opened his eyes to what has been going on behind his back.*
      f. *The way he deceived me opened my eyes to his true character.*
      g. *Living in an Indian village was a real eye-opener for all of us.*
      h. *It was difficult to succeed in the acting profession but I went into it with my eyes open.*

The expressions in (28a–d) are all based on the bodily image of closing one's eyes, while those in (28e–h) find their bodily roots in opening one's eyes. The underlying metaphors are PAYING ATTENTIONS IS SEEING and THINKING, KNOWING, or UNDERSTANDING IS SEEING, as well as their corresponding forms in negation.

Sometimes it is not enough to 'see with open eyes', and one has to do more in order to 'see' better, as shown by the following English idioms.

(29) a. *keep one's eyes open*
      b. *keep one's eyes polished*
      c. *keep one's eyes peeled*
      e. *keep one's eyes skinned*

All these idioms mean 'keep a sharp look-out' or 'watch very carefully for something'. To watch carefully, of course, one has to 'keep one's eyes open', but that may not be enough. One can also make one's eyes 'shine' by 'polishing', 'peeling', or 'skinning' them (cf. 14b–d). Remember that EYES ARE LIGHT SOURCES (as in Chinese). More 'shining' eyes shed more 'light' and therefore 'see' better.

The examples in (30) below contain some more metaphorical expressions with *eye(s)*.

(30) a. *We see eye to eye on most important issues.*
      b. *Anyone can see with half an eye that you're in love with her.*
      c. *He tried to throw dust in my eyes, but I knew he was lying.*

People in complete agreement with each other 'see each other in the eye' (30a). If something can be seen without using one's full visual power, it must be obvious (30b). If people have dust in their eyes, they of course cannot see well (30c). What happens with examples like these is that the bodily experiences are mapped metaphorically onto more abstract concepts, such as agreement, obviousness, and deception. The metaphor, with its concrete experiential basis, helps us better understand those more abstract concepts.

5.   A comparative view

Having presented data from both Chinese and English involving the body part 'eye(s)', I would like to touch upon some similarities and differences between these two languages. First, it seems that both Chinese and English share the conceptual metonymy PERCEPTUAL ORGAN STANDS FOR PERCEPTION, or EYES FOR SEEING, and the conceptual metaphor SEEING IS TOUCHING. That is, in both languages seeing is described in terms of the eye(s) and their physical contact with the target. For instance, both Chinese and English have a special case of SEEING IS TOUCHING, in which the target is animate in a metaphorical sense and 'acts' in a certain manner to 'catch' one's eye. The examples in (8) for Chinese and those in (25) for English display a certain level of semantic similarity between the two languages.

While Chinese and English have the same conceptual metaphor SEEING IS TOUCHING, a difference seems to exist in the way the conceptual metaphor is manifested in each language. Lakoff (1993b) argues that in English the eyes are often understood as 'limbs' that can 'reach out' and 'touch' the target they see (see, e.g., 24a). On the other hand, in Chinese, as I have observed and discussed in Section 2, seeing is generally understood as the eyes sending out 'eye light' that 'touches' the target they see. My observation, nevertheless, does not exclude the possibility that the eyes-as-limbs metaphor is somehow dormant in Chinese; it may be activated in novel metaphorical expressions. In a similar vein, the metaphor SEEING IS CONTACT BETWEEN THE EYE LIGHT AND THE TARGET may also exist in English. I assume that the English word *eye* in its singular form, when meaning 'power of seeing', may be conceptualized as a beam of light extending from the eyes to the target. In fact, this conceptualization is sometimes manifested visually in Western cartoons and science fiction movies.

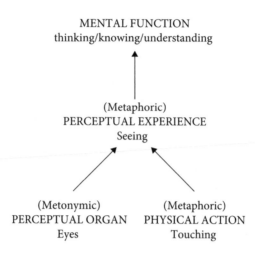

Figure 1. Metonymic and metaphoric mappings shared by Chinese and English

A second commonality between Chinese and English is that both languages share the conceptual metaphor THINKING, KNOWING, or UNDERSTANDING IS SEEING. Under this metaphor, the body-part terms for the eyes are used metaphorically to describe mental states and activities. The metaphorical expressions seem to be rooted in some common bodily experiences with the eyes. For instance, one has to open one's eyes to 'see', and one cannot 'see' with closed or blind eyes.

In sum, both Chinese and English share the metonymic and metaphoric mappings that can be presented schematically as in Figure 1. At the lower level, there are two mappings onto the same target domain, the perceptual experience of seeing. One is a metonymic mapping from the perceptual organ of eyes; the other is a metaphoric mapping from the physical action of touching. At the upper level, the perceptual experience of seeing now serves as the source domain, and is metaphorically mapped onto the mental function of thinking, knowing, or understanding, the target domain. These mappings, metonymic and metaphoric, show how 'lower' bodily experiences work their way up to help conceptualize 'higher' mental experiences, or how the more abstract is understood in terms of the more concrete.

While Chinese and English share the general conceptual mappings of metonymy and metaphor, at the linguistic level, however, there are both symmetrical and asymmetrical correspondences in the two languages. The correspondences in expression and meaning across the language boundary may take three major forms: (1) similar expressions with similar meanings, (2) similar expressions with different meanings, and (3) different expressions with similar meanings. Let me illustrate these forms with some examples. Consider the following pair.

(31) a. *I can do it with my eyes shut.*
    b. 那我闭着眼睛都能做。
      Na wo bi-zhe yanjing dou neng zuo.
      that I   closed eyes   still can do
      'I can do that with my eyes shut.'

This is an example of similar expressions with similar meanings, that is, one knows something very well and can do it 'with great ease'. The match seems to be parallel in both form and meaning. The English idiom *with one's eyes shut*, however, has a different meaning, 'without full awareness' (see 28d), that is not matched by the Chinese expression. This means that the match between the two expressions is still partial. For another example, let me refer back to (28h) for English and (17c) for Chinese. In both of these examples, 'with one's eyes open' roughly means 'knowing about all the problems there could be with something that one wants to do'. However, in the second half of (17c), 'with one's eyes shut' does not mean either 'without full awareness' or 'with great ease', but means something like 'disregarding, and ready for, the consequence'. In fact, there may not be many full matches parallel in both form and meaning across languages. For instance, in both Chinese and English people can 'shine' their eyes in order to 'see' better, but in English the eyes are 'polished', 'peeled', or 'skinned' (see 29 above) whereas in Chinese they are 'rubbed', 'wiped', or 'scraped' (see 14 above). Yet, the overall image and the metaphorical reasoning behind the expressions are quite similar. Expressions of this kind are imaginative in nature, but they are still experientially grounded in the very nature of our eyes as organ of sight. They can mean what they mean because we have the kind of eyes we have.

Now, let us look at an example of similar expressions with different meanings. In both Chinese and English, the image of having eyes in the back of one's head is used, but with different meanings based on different kinds of reasoning.

(32) a. *Parents of young children have to have eyes in the back of their heads.*
    b. 你眼睛长到后脑勺上啦？
      Ni yanjing zhang dao hou-nao-shao   shang la?
      you eyes   grow to back-of-the-head on   PRT
      'Do you have your eyes grown on the back of your head?'

In the English sentence, if people 'have eyes in the back of their heads', they 'know everything that is happening around them' thanks to their having 'extra eyes', on both sides of their heads. In contrast, in the Chinese sentence, 'having one's eyes grown on the back of one's head' means 'having one's (two) eyes in a wrong place', and the consequence is that one 'cannot see what one is supposed to see'. Remember that our face, on which our eyes should grow, is on the 'interactive side' of our body (see Yu, 2001 for a detailed discussion). The eyes in the back of one's head are on the 'wrong' side. It is worth mentioning here that (32b) is an idiomatic Chinese expression, often cast in the form of a rhetorical question and used to blame someone. Relevant to the above contrast is the following Chinese sentence taken from actual discourse:

(33) 人嘛，都是有前眼没后眼的。
      Ren   ma, dou shi you qian yan mei   hou yan de.
      humans PRT all   PRT have front eyes don't-have back eyes PRT
      'It is human to have only front eyes, not back eyes.'

This sentence emphasizes humans' limitation in thinking, knowing, and understanding by referring metaphorically to the structure of their bodies. Humans can only have a 'one-sided view' at a time, although it might be desirable to be able to 'see' both front and back at the same time, as in (32a).

A good example of different expressions with similar meanings is found in (18a) for Chinese and (28b) and (28c) for English. In Chinese, when pretending not to notice something bad or allowing the person who did it to go 'unnoticed' or unpunished, people would 'have one eye open and the other eye closed'. 'With one eye open', they have actually 'seen' what is going on. 'With the other eye closed', they pretend not to 'see' it. On the other hand, in English people simply 'turn a blind eye' or 'close their eyes' to the bad thing they do not want to deal with. That is, they do not want to, or pretend not to, see something they have already seen. Here, different bodily images (with one eye open and the other eye closed vs. with both eyes closed or 'blind') contribute to a common metaphor, PAYING ATTENTION IS SEEING, in both languages.

At this point, it is interesting to mention another English example in contrast with the Chinese Example (18a). When talking about his experience of watching the soccer games of the World Cup in Japan and Korea live on TV during his usual sleeping hours (late night and early morning), an American said, "I watched those games with one eye open and the other eye closed". In this case, the expression 'with one eye open and the other eye closed' describes his 'suffering entertainment' in the experience. Obviously, it differs in meaning from the similar Chinese expression in (18a).

The examples mentioned above merely illustrate how two languages can be similar or different in their match-ups between expression and meaning. But these are just surface linguistic phenomena and, no matter how similar or different, they are governed by their underlying conceptual metaphors, such as THINKING, KNOWING, or UNDERSTANDING IS SEEING and PAYING ATTENTION IS SEEING, which, shared by both languages, are grounded in our common bodily experiences with our eyes as the most important organ of perception and cognition. At the same time, while human beings all have similar bodies that function in similar ways, cultures may attach different values to, and make different interpretations of, certain parts of the body and certain aspects of the bodily experience (see, also, Yu, 2000, 2001, 2002, 2003a, 2003c, 2003d). That is how and why, in different languages, different bodily images may converge to the same metaphorical import, and the same bodily image may diverge into different metaphorical interpretations.

In summary, there is a broad range of common bodily experiences that serve as the breeding ground for conceptual metonymies and metaphors beneath their linguistic manifestations. In each language, however, only a portion of it is cultivated, as determined by cultural preferences. The existence of uncultivated areas accounts for the phenomenon in which a particular metonymic or metaphoric expression in one language is readily understandable in another even though it has no equivalent in that language. It should be pointed out that the stress on common bodily experiences as breeding ground for metonymy and metaphor does not deny the fact that there are metonymies and metaphors that fall outside its boundaries. It can be hypothesized, however, that those originating outside are culture-specific and, for that matter, may be more opaque in comprehension, especially to speakers of other languages.

6. Conclusion

In talking about the 'turn toward the body' in contemporary scholarship in the human sciences, Csordas (1994: 1) says:

> Much has been written about the body in recent years. Beginning in the early 1970s, and with increased energy in the late 1980s, the body has assumed a lively presence on the anthropological scene, and on the stage of interdisciplinary cultural studies. Feminist theory, literary criticism, history, comparative religion, philosophy, sociology, and psychology are all implicated in the move toward the body.

Notably, the list of disciplines mentioned does not include linguistics. Linguistics may have made a slower turn in this intellectual move. However, in the field of linguistics during the past two decades, a branch known as cognitive linguistics has been leading in this turn. In cognitive linguistics, a central concern is the role of the body, and its interaction with culture, in human meaning and understanding. According to cognitive linguistics, our embodiment in and with the physical and cultural worlds sets out the contours of what is meaningful to us and determines the ways of our understanding (Johnson 1987, 1999). From the cognitive perspective, metonymy describes the bodily 'that is', whereas metaphor describes the bodily 'that might have been'. That is why cognitive linguistics postulates a metonymic basis for metaphor (see, e.g., Barcelona, 2000a, 2000b, 2000c; Dervin and Pörings, 2002; Panther and Radden, 1999).

In this study, I have discussed the metonymic and metaphoric nature of Chinese compounds and idioms involving body-part terms for 'eye(s)'. I have also adopted a cross-linguistic perspective, taking into account English idioms containing *eye(s)*. I have found that the two languages share the conceptual metonymy PERCEPTUAL ORGAN STANDS FOR PERCEPTION, and the conceptual metaphors SEEING IS TOUCHING, THINKING, KNOWING, or UNDERSTANDING IS SEEING, and PAYING ATTENTION IS SEEING. At the level of linguistic instantiation, there are both similarities and differences in the metonymic and metaphoric expressions between Chinese and English. Whether similar or different, these expressions seem to have an experiential grounding in our common bodily experiences with the eyes. Apparently, human imagination is involved in the use of metonymy and metaphor investigated here, but this imagination seems to be rooted in the basic structure of our body, and in the division of labor for our body parts. Very often, metonymy and metaphor emerge in the interaction between body and culture. While the body is a potentially universal source domain for metonymies and metaphors that structure abstract concepts, cultural models set up specific perspectives from which certain aspects of bodily experience or certain parts of the body are viewed as especially salient and meaningful in the understanding of those abstract concepts (see Gibbs 1999; Yu, 2000, 2001, 2002, 2003a, c). Systematic studies of linguistic data should be able to shed light on how this happens, and cross-linguistic studies of metonymies and metaphors may reveal cultural differences and potential universals in human cognition.

References

Barcelona, Antonio (Ed.), 2000a. Metaphor and Metonymy at the Crossroads: A Cognitive Perspective. Mouton de Gruyter, Berlin.

Barcelona, Antonio, 2000b. Introduction: the cognitive theory of metaphor and metonymy. In: Barcelona, Antonio (Ed.), pp. 1–28.

Barcelona, Antonio, 2000c. On the plausibility of claiming a metonymic motivation for conceptual metaphor. In: Barcelona, Antonio (Ed.), pp. 31–58.

Chen, Zelin, 1989. Zang xiang [Theory of internal organs]. In: Jin, Wentao (Ed.), Jiating Yixue Quanshu [Family Medicine]. Shanghai Science and Technology Press, Shanghai, pp. 1003–1012.

Csordas, Thomas J., 1994. Introduction: the body as representation and being-in-the-world. In: Csordas, Thomas. J. (Ed.), Embodiment and Experience: The Existential Ground of Culture and Self. Cambridge University Press, Cambridge, pp. 1–24.

Dirven, René, Pörings, Ralf (Eds.), 2002. Metaphor and Metonymy in Comparison and Contrast. Mouton de Gruyter, Berlin.

Fortescue, Michael, 2001. Thoughts about thought. Cognitive Linguistics 12, 15–45.

Gibbs, Raymond W., 1999. Taking metaphor out of our heads and putting it into the cultural world. In: Gibbs, Raymond. W., Steen, Gerard. J. (Eds.), pp. 145–166.

Gibbs, Raymond W., Steen, Gerard J. (Eds.), 1999. Metaphor in Cognitive Linguistics. John Benjamins, Amsterdam.

Jäkel, Olaf, 1995. The metaphorical conception of mind: "Mental activity is manipulation". In: Taylor, John R., MacLaury, Robert E. (Eds.), Language and the Cognitive Construal of the World. Mouton de Gruyter, Berlin, pp. 197–229.

Johnson, Mark, 1987. The Body in the Mind: The Bodily Basis of Meaning, Imagination, and Reason. University of Chicago Press, Chicago.

Johnson, Mark, 1992. Philosophical implications of cognitive semantics. Cognitive Linguistics 3, 345–366.

Johnson, Mark, 1999. Embodied reason. In: Weiss, Gail, Haber, Honi F. (Eds.), Perspectives on Embodiment: The Intersections of Nature and Culture. Routledge, New York, pp. 81–102.

Lakoff, George, 1987. Women, Fire, and Dangerous Things: What Categories Reveal about the Mind. University of Chicago Press, Chicago.

Lakoff, George, 1990. The Invariance Hypothesis: Is abstract reason based on image-shemas? Cognitive Linguistics 1, 53–62.

Lakoff, George, 1993a. The contemporary theory of metaphor. In: Ortony, Andrew (Ed.), Metaphor and Thought (2nd ed.). Cambridge University Press, Cambridge, pp. 202–251.

Lakoff, George, 1993b. The metaphor system and its role in grammar. In: Beals, Katharine, Cooke, Gina, Kathman, David, Kita, Sotaro, McCullough, Karl-Erik, Testen, David (Eds.), What We Think, What We Mean, and How We Say It: Papers from the Parasession on the Correspondence of Conceptual, Semantic and Grammatical Representations. Chicago Linguistic Society, Chicago, pp. 217–241.

Lakoff, George, Johnson, Mark, 1980. Metaphors We Live By. University of Chicago Press, Chicago.

Lakoff, George, Johnson, Mark, 1999. Philosophy in the Flesh: The Embodied Mind and Its Challenge to Western Thought. Basic Books, New York.

Lü, Shuxiang, Ding, Shengshu (Eds.), 1980. Xiandai Hanyu Cidian [Modern Chinese Dictionary]. The Commercial Press, Beijing.

Lü, Shuxiang, Ding, Shengshu (Eds.), 1989. Xiandai Hanyu Cidian Bubian [Modern Chinese Dictionary Supplement]. The Commercial Press, Beijing.

Lü, Shuxiang, Ding, Shengshu (Eds.), 1996. Xiandai Hanyu Cidian [Modern Chinese Dictionary] (Revised Ed.). The Commercial Press, Beijing.

Panther, Klaus-Uwe, Radden, Günter (Eds.), 1999. Metonymy in Language and Thought. John Benjamins, Amsterdam.

Radden, Günter, 1996. Motion metaphorized: the case of *coming* and *going*. In: Casad, Eugene H. (Ed.), Cognitive Linguistics in the Redwoods: The Expansion of a New Paradigm in Linguistics. Mouton de Gruyter, Berlin, pp. 423–458.

Sweetser, Eve E., 1990. From Etymology to Pragmatics: Metaphorical and Cultural Aspects of Semantic Structure. Cambridge University Press, Cambridge.

Turner, Mark, 1991. Reading Minds: The Study of English in the Age of Cognitive Science. Princeton University Press, Princeton, NJ.

Wang, Qi, Luo, Xijia, Li, Yun, Liu, Yanjiao, 1997. Zhongyi Zangxiang Xue [Theory of Internal Organs in Chinese Medicine]. People's Health Press, Beijing.

Wei, Dongya (Ed.), 1995. Han Ying Cidian [A Chinese-English Dictionary] (Revised Ed.). Foreign Language Teaching and Research Press, Beijing.

Wen, Duanzheng (Ed.), 1996. Hanyu Changyongyu Cidian [A Dictionary of Chinese Idioms]. Shanghai Dictionary Press, Shanghai.

Worrall, A. J., 1975. English Idioms for Foreign Students. Longman, London.

Wu, Guanghua (Ed.), 1993. Han Ying Da Cidian [Chinese-English Dictionary] (Vols. 1 & 2). Shanghai Jiao Tong University Press, Shanghai.

Yu, Ning, 1995. Metaphorical expressions of anger and happiness in English and Chinese. Metaphor and Symbolic Activity 10, 59–92.

Yu, Ning, 1998. The Contemporary Theory of Metaphor: A Perspective from Chinese. John Benjamins, Amsterdam.

Yu, Ning, 1999. Spatial conceptualization of time in Chinese. In: Hiraga, Masako K., Sinha, Chris, Wilcox, Sherman (Eds.), Cultural, Psychological and Typological Issues in Cognitive Linguistics. John Benjamins, Amsterdam, pp. 69–84.

Yu, Ning, 2000. Figurative uses of *finger* and *palm* in Chinese and English. Metaphor and Symbol 15, 159–175.

Yu, Ning, 2001. What does our face mean to us? Pragmatics and Cognition 9, 1–36.

Yu, Ning, 2002. Body and emotion: body parts in Chinese expression of emotion. In: Enfield, N. J., Wierzbicka, Anna (Eds.), the special issue on "The Body in Description of Emotion: Cross-linguistic Studies". Pragmatics and Cognition 10, 341–367.

Yu, Ning, 2003a. Metaphor, body, and culture: the Chinese understanding of *gallbladder* and *courage*. Metaphor and Symbol 18, 13–31.

Yu, Ning, 2003b. Synesthetic metaphor: a cognitive perspective. Journal of Literary Semantics 32, 19–34.

Yu, Ning, 2003c. The bodily dimension of meaning in Chinese: what do we do and mean with "hands"? In: Casad, Eugene H., Palmer, Gary B. (Eds.), Cognitive Linguistics and Non-Indo-European Languages. Mouton de Gruyter, Berlin, pp. 337–362.

Yu, Ning, 2003d. Chinese metaphors of thinking. Cognitive Linguistics 14, 141–165.

CHAPTER 9

Speech organs and linguistic activity and function

This paper studies the Chinese cultural model for speech and language based on the metonymic chain from speech organ to language as proposed by Radden (2004): speech organ → speaking → speech → language. It attempts a systematic analysis of Chinese terms for such speech organs as tongue (*she*), teeth (*chi*), lips (*chun*) and mouth (*zui* and *kou*) as are used metonymically and metaphorically in conventionalized linguistic expressions referring to more abstract linguistic action and function. The study therefore focuses on three metonymies, SPEECH ORGAN FOR SPEAKING, SPEECH ORGAN FOR SPEECH, and SPEECH ORGAN FOR LANGUAGE. It is found that the first two metonymies, i.e. SPEECH ORGAN FOR SPEAKING and SPEECH ORGAN FOR SPEECH, are richly manifested in a large number of conventionalized expressions, but SPEECH ORGAN FOR LANGUAGE, which has been widely attested across languages (Radden, 2004), is not realized lexically in Chinese. What is particularly interesting, however, is the finding that in Chinese, while SPEECH ORGAN FOR LANGUAGE is not manifested in its lexicon, it is nevertheless realized in its ideographic writing system as components of the characters. That is, the Chinese characters representing "language" and "speech" all contain the "mouth" radical in them. This finding provides an interesting and telling example of how the general cognitive principle of embodiment can be realized in and embraced by a culture-specific environment.

1. Introduction

Cognitive science asserts that the human mind is embodied (Lakoff & Johnson, 1999), and the embodiment premise states that people's subjective, felt experiences of their bodies in action provide part of the fundamental grounding for language and thought (Gibbs, 2006). Studying linguistic data from numerous languages (dozens of them) over the world, Radden (2004) investigates "a naïve view" or "a folk model" of language based on the metonymic chain from speech organ to language: speech organ → speaking → speech → language. This metonymic chain, which is motivated by cognitive principles governing the selection of preferred metonymic vehicles (Radden & Kövecses, 1999) and which operates within the conceptual frame of "language", is expressed in conceptual formula as SPEECH ORGAN FOR SPEAKING, SPEAKING FOR SPEECH, and SPEECH FOR LANGUAGE. These conceptual metonymies are respectively specific instantiations of more general conceptual metonymies INSTRUMENT FOR ACTION, ACTION FOR RESULT, and SPECIFIC FOR GENERIC. They are often elaborated by metaphor in intricate ways resulting in what is called "metaphtonymy" (Goossens, 2002).[1] As a process of conceptual and semantic extension, the metonymic chain illustrates how the conception of a crucial human cognitive function is rooted in the human body and bodily experience.

The metonymic shifts along the metonymic chain, however, can skip one or more intermediate links. As a rule, therefore, the word for "language" is synchronically related to, or historically derived from, a more basic sense belonging to one of the three domains: (i) articulation and speech organs, (ii) linguistic action, and (iii) basic linguistic units (Radden, 2004, p. 543). In certain languages, for instance, the term for "word", which denotes a linguistic unit, can mean "language", or be part of a derived word or compound that means "language", i.e. SPEECH FOR LANGUAGE. In many other languages, the word for "language" derives from a word meaning "speak", "say", or "tell", i.e. SPEAKING FOR LANGUAGE. Skipping the intermediate links along the metonymic chain also results in a metonymy widely attested across world languages, i.e. SPEECH ORGAN FOR LANGUAGE. For example, the term for "tongue" is also used for "language" in virtually all Indo-European languages, and this is true for many non-Indo-European languages as well (pp. 554–555).

The folk understanding of language and linguistic behavior, which is rooted in embodied experience and has a physiological basis, focuses especially on the salient articulators: the tongue, the teeth, the lips, and the mouth. Radden (2004) expresses the need for systematic studies across languages in order to assess the possibly universal status of this folk model of language and to map out cross-linguistic differences that are likely to occur with respect to conventionalized implicatures invited by the metonymies.

---

1.   Over the past two decades, Cognitive Linguistics has published an enormous number of studies on the crucial role of metaphor and metonymy in human language and thought: See, e.g., Barcelona (2000a), Dirven and Pörings (2002), Forceville (1996), Forceville and Urios-Aparisi (in press), Gibbs (1994), Gibbs and Steen (1999), Goatly (2007), Johnson (1987); Kövecses (2000, 2002, 2005, 2006), Lakoff (1987), Lakoff and Johnson (1999), Lakoff and Núñez (2000), Panther and Radden (1999a), Panther and Thornburg (2003), Ruiz de Mendoza Ibáñez and Otal Campo (2002), Steen (2007), Yu (1998). Readers are referred particularly to Gibbs (2008) for a recent state-of-the-art collection of multidisciplinary studies on metaphor and thought. In the past decade, Cognitive Linguistics has especially emphasized the interaction between metonymy and metaphor, which after all form a continuum with no clear distinction between them in the middle (Barcelon, 2000b). It is claimed that metonymy is a more fundamental cognitive phenomenon than metaphor (Panther & Radden, 1999b) and, very often, metaphor is motivated by metonymy (e.g., Barcelona, 2000c; Niemeier, 2000; Panther, 2006; Radden, 2000).

Following Radden (2004), this paper studies the cultural model for speech and language as is manifested in the Chinese language. It attempts a systematic analysis of Chinese terms for such speech organs as tongue (*she*), teeth (*chi*), lips (*chun*) and mouth (*zui* and *kou*) as are used metonymically and metaphorically in conventionalized linguistic expressions, including compounds and idioms, which refer to more abstract linguistic action and function. The study intends to document how speech organ terms extend their meanings along the metonymic chain as proposed by Radden (2004), and how metonymic extension interacts with metaphoric projection along such semantic transfers in Chinese. It attempts to demonstrate the extent to which Chinese conforms to the metonymic chain and displays its cultural characteristics. It is shown that while the metonymy SPEECH ORGAN FOR LANGUAGE is not realized lexically in Chinese, it is realized in its ideographic writing system in the form of Chinese characters. Thus, the study presents a striking case of the general cognitive principle of embodiment embraced in a culture-specific context, or what cognitive linguists call "socioculturally situated embodiment" (Ziemke et al., 2007; Frank et al., 2008; Sharifian et al., 2008; see, also, Maalej, 2004, 2007, 2008).

2. Speech organ terms in Chinese

In Chinese, the characters that represent the speech organs of a human being are as follows:

(1) a. 口 *kou* 'mouth'
    b. 嘴 *zui* 'mouth'
    c. 唇 *chun* 'lip (or lips)'
    d. 牙 *ya* 'tooth (or teeth)'
    e. 齿 *chi* 'tooth (or teeth)'
    f. 舌 *she* 'tongue'
    g. 喉 *hou* 'throat'

The words and the characters that represent them in (1a) and (1b) both mean "mouth". They are of equally common use in present-day Chinese although they are sometimes found in different collocations or contexts. In terms of characters in the writing system, however, 口 *kou* (1a) is more basic than 嘴 *zui* (1b) because it is also one of the basic radicals, i.e. components of characters, found in many of the Chinese characters semantically related to the mouth as their semantic component, e.g. in 嘴 *zui* 'mouth' (1b), 舌 *she* 'tongue' (1f), and 喉 *hou* 'throat' (1g) above, and many others, such as 吃 *chi* 'eat', 喝 *he* 'drink', 唱 *chang* 'sing', and 叫 *jiao* 'shout'.

The speech organ terms in (1) are not equally productive in their metonymic and metaphoric extension along the metonymic chain under discussion. In fact, among them *ya* 'tooth' (1d) and *hou* 'throat' (1g) are found, it seems, in very few conventionalized expressions, such as the following two compounds that are results of metonymic and metaphoric extension.

(2)   a.   磨牙 *mo-ya* (grind-teeth) '*dial.* indulge in idle talk; argue pointlessly'
      b.   喉舌 *hou-she* (throat-tongue) 'mouthpiece'

Here, (2a) refers originally to people grinding their teeth in sleep, but metaphorically to their "indulging in idle talk" or "arguing pointlessly". The metaphor, however, is based on a metonymy SPEECH ORGAN FOR SPEAKING. Example (2b) is a compound word consisting of *hou* 'throat' and *she* 'tongue', i.e. the combination of two speech organ terms. While the word can refer to the speech organ in general, it is usually used figuratively to refer to the "tool or person that speaks representing others". Thus, for instance, the spokesperson of the White House can be called 白宫"喉舌", which literally means "the White House's 'Throat and Tongue'". Also, in China, newspapers are often called 人民的喉舌, i.e. "people's throat and tongue", which means they represent people's voices or views.

Because their metonymic and metaphoric use in terms of the metonymic chain is very limited, *ya* 'tooth' and *hou* 'throat' will be excluded from my discussion unless they occur together with the remaining speech organ terms.

3.   Analysis of the data for the metonymic chain

In present-day Chinese, compound words, which mostly consist of two constituents (represented by two characters), make up the vast majority of its lexical items. In this study, one of the two elements is a speech organ term, which can take the first or the second position. When the speech organ term takes the first position, it very often combines with a verbal or adjectival constituent, and the compound takes up the subject-predicate construction (S-P). When the speech organ term occupies the second position, it can be preceded by a verbal or adjectival element, the internal relationship between the two constituents being, respectively, verb-object (V-O) or adjective-noun (A-N). Occasionally, however, two speech organ terms can combine to form a noun-noun (N-N) construction too. Chinese idiomatic phrases, or *chengyu* (成语) 'set phrases', are usually composed of four constituents (i.e., four characters in writing). Quite often, they are two compounds in juxtaposition. In this case, they sometimes involve two body-part terms or, more specifically, speech organ terms.

Before I move on to analyze the data manifesting the metonymic chain, I first point out that a kind of examples that is not directly related to the chain is however relevant to our discussion too. Look at the following group:

(3) a. 大嘴 *da-zui* (big-mouth) 'one given to loud offensive talk; one who has a loose tongue; one who shoots one's mouth off'

      b. 快嘴 *kuai-zui* (fast/quick-mouth) 'one who readily voices his thoughts; one who is quick to articulate his ideas; a straight person; one who has a loose tongue'

      c. 利口 *li-kou* (sharp-mouth) 'a glib tongue'

      d. 恶口 *e-kou* (evil-mouth) 'an abusive tongue; a foul tongue; a wicked tongue'

      e. 长舌 *chang-she* (long-tongue) 'a long tongue – a gossipy person; gossip-monger'

      f. 舌头 *she-tou* (tongue-SUF) 'tongue; an enemy soldier captured for the purpose of extracting information'

All these compounds instantiate the conceptual metonymy SPEECH ORGAN FOR PERSON or, more generally, PART FOR WHOLE, which are traditionally known as cases of synecdoche. Obviously, when a speech organ term is used in the metonymy BODY PART FOR PERSON, it differs from some of the other body part terms that serve the same purpose. In Chinese, for instance, the following body part terms are often found as standing metonymically for the whole person, but they have different emphases or highlight different abstract qualities of the person in serving this function:

(4) Different emphases of the BODY PART FOR PERSON metonymy

      a. 心 *xin* 'heart' → cognition and the inner self (Yu, 2007a, 2007b, 2008, 2009)

      b. 胆 *dan* 'gallbladder' → courage (Yu, 2003a)

      c. 脸 *lian* 'face'

            面 *mian* 'face' → social identity and the outer self (Yu, 2001)

      d. 手 *shou* 'hand' → skill and capability of doing things (Yu, 2003b)

Now, when such speech organ terms as *zui* or *kou* 'mouth' and *she* 'tongue' are used metonymically to stand for the whole person, they emphasize the person's characteristics of speaking or talking, as illustrated by the compounds in (3), or the person's function as a speaker, as found in the example where the Spokesperson of the White House is referred to as the "First Mouth of the White House" (白宫第一嘴), and well-known talk show hosts are referred to as "famous/name mouths" (名嘴).

Having discussed some cases of the SPEECH ORGAN FOR PERSON metonymy and how it differs from other cases of BODY PART FOR PERSON, I now turn to the data that contribute to the metonymic chain under investigation. I will do this in the next two subsections: 3.1 focuses on the mouth, which in Chinese is represented by two words or characters, *kou* and *zui* 'mouth'; 3.2 deals with *chun* 'lip/lips', *chi* 'tooth/teeth', and *she* 'tongue'.

3.1   The mouth in conventionalized expressions

The Chinese language is very rich with compounds and set phrases that contain either *kou* 'mouth' or *zui* 'mouth' for the purpose of morphological construction and semantic extension. Some of them are related to the semantic category of eating (e.g., 口福、口感、口味、口腹之欲、清口、适口、爽口、忌口、胃口、倒胃口、众口难调、嘴馋、馋嘴、忌嘴、贪嘴、偷嘴、缺嘴), but the vast majority are found in the semantic category of speaking along the metonymic chain under discussion.

I first discuss the compounds that instantiate the SPEECH ORGAN FOR SPEAKING metonymy.

(5) a. 动口   *dong-kou* (move-mouth) 'talk; speak'
   b. 开口   *kai-kou* (open-mouth) 'open one's mouth; start to talk'
   c. 张口   *zhang-kou* (open-mouth) 'open one's mouth to say sth.; ask for a favor'
   d. 启口   *qi-kou* (open-mouth) 'open one's mouth; start to talk about sth.'
   e. 出口   *chu-kou* (exit-mouth) 'speak; utter'
   f. 闭口   *bi-kou* (shut-mouth) 'keep one's mouth shut; refuse to express one's opinions'
   g. 住口   *zhu-kou* (stop-mouth) 'shut up; stop talking'
   h. 动嘴   *dong-zui* (move-mouth) 'talk; speak'
   i. 张嘴   *zhang-zui* (open-mouth) 'open one's mouth to say sth.; ask for a favor'
   j. 住嘴   *zhu-zui* (stop-mouth) 'stop talking'

In this group of examples, as we can see, the term *kou* or *zui* 'mouth' is preceded by a verb that means "move", "open", "close", "exit", or "stop", whereas the compounds so formed all mean "talk or not talk" or "start or stop talking" in some fashion. Apparently, in some compounds *kou* and *zui* are interchangeable (i.e. in a, c, and g vs. h, i, and j respectively), but this is not always the case. In some cases, a particular constituent can only combine with one but not the other (e.g., in b, d, and e, only *kou* but not *zui* is possible). Occasionally, a particular constituent can combine with both but the results do not have exactly the same meaning.

(6) a. 缄口   *jian-kou* (seal-mouth) 'keep one's mouth shut; hold one's tongue; say nothing'

   b. 绝口   *jue-kou* (sever-mouth) 'stop talking; keep one's mouth shut'

   c. 钳口   *qian-kou* (clamp-mouth) 'force sb. into silence; prevent sb. from talking; shut up; keep silent'

   d. 灭口   *mie-kou* (extinguish-mouth) 'do away with a witness or accomplice'

   e. 堵嘴   *du-zui* (block up-mouth) 'gag sb.; silence sb.'

   f. 松口   *song-kou* (loosen-mouth) 'relax one's bite and release what is held; be less unyielding; soften; relent'

   g. 松嘴   *song-zui* (loosen-mouth) '*inf.* relax one's bite and release what is held; be less unyielding; soften; relent'

The compounds in (6) have to do with "keeping silent oneself" or "silencing others". The compound in (6c), which literally means to "grip or clamp one's mouth with pliers or pincers", means "force oneself or others into silence". The one in (6d) usually means "silence a witness by killing him" or "kill someone to prevent him from disclosing a secret". Both (6f) and (6g) have the same meaning, with the latter less formal than the former, and evoke the same image where one's mouth has relaxed from being tightly shut into a release (of a promise or permission).

(7) a. 斗口   *dou-kou* (fight-mouth) 'quarrel; bicker; squabble'

   b. 斗嘴   *dou-zui* (fight-mouth) 'quarrel; bicker; squabble; banter'

   c. 争嘴   *zheng-zui* (contend/vie-mouth) 'quarrel; bicker; vie for more food'

   d. 吵嘴   *chao-zui* (quarrel-mouth) 'quarrel; bicker'

   e. 闹嘴   *nao-zui* (make noises/stir up trouble-mouth) 'quarrel; bicker'

   f. 拌嘴   *ban-zui* (mix-mouth) 'bicker; squabble; quarrel'

   g. 嚷嘴   *rang-zui* (yell-mouth) '*dial.* quarrel; bicker'

The examples in (7) belong to the semantic domain of quarreling. As we can see, arguing is "fighting", "contending", "quarreling", "making noises", "mixing", and "yelling", all with one's mouth. That is, arguing or quarreling is "fighting a mouth battle" (打嘴仗). Given in the following are some more relevant examples:

(8) a. 破口   *po-kou* (break-mouth) 'shout (abuse); let loose (a torrent of abuse)'

   b. 还口   *huan-kou* (return-mouth) 'answer back; retort'

   c. 回口   *hui-kou* (return/go back-mouth) '*dial.* answer back; retort'

   d. 还嘴   *huan-zui* (return-mouth) '*inf.* answer or talk back; retort'

   e. 回嘴   *hui-zui* (return/go back-mouth) 'answer or talk back; retort'

f. 顶嘴   *ding-zui* (push up/retort-mouth) '*inf.* reply defiantly (usu. to one's elder or superior; answer back; talk back'

g. 犟嘴   *jiang-zui* (obstinate/stubborn-mouth) 'reply defiantly; answer or talk back'

h. 强嘴   *jiang-zui* (stubborn/unyielding-mouth) 'reply defiantly; answer or talk back'

The image evoked by (8a) is that a person's mouth "cracks" to let out "a torrent of abuse or curses". The compounds in (8b–e) all mean "to hit back" in "a verbal battle". Instead of hitting back with their fists, people "hit back with their mouths" in such a battle. The compound in (8f) evokes the image of one pushing up with one's head. Conceptualized in spatial terms, younger or junior people have a lower status than that of their elders or superiors. Thus, when they "talk back" in a verbal battle against their seniors and superiors, they not only "stand up to" them, but also "push their heads against" them.

(9) a. 夸口   *kua-kou* (exaggerate/boast-mouth) 'boast; brag; talk big'

b. 夸嘴   *kua-zui* (exaggerate/boast-mouth) '*inf.* boast; brag; talk big'

c. 说嘴   *shuo-zui* (talk-mouth) 'brag; boast; *dial.* argue; quarrel'

d. 失口   *shi-kou* (lose-mouth) 'make a slip of the tongue'

e. 走口   *zou-kou* (go-mouth) '*dial.* make a slip of the tongue; let slip an inadvertent remark'

f. 走嘴   *zou-zui* (go-mouth) 'make a slip of the tongue; let slip an inadvertent remark'

g. 漏嘴   *lou-zui* (leak-mouth) 'let slip a remark; make a slip of the tongue'

h. 改口   *gai-kou* (change-mouth) 'withdraw or modify one's previous remark; correct oneself'

i. 改嘴   *gai-zui* (change-mouth) 'withdraw or modify one's previous remark'

Found in (9) are some compounds that fall into three categories: bragging (9a–c), making a slip of the tongue (9d–g), and correcting oneself (9h, i). As can be seen, people who "make a slip of the tongue" would "lose their mouths" (9d), "let go their mouths" (9e, f), or have "a leaking mouth" (9g), and those who "withdraw or modify their previous remark" would actually "change their mouths" (9h, i).

The compounds given below indicate various manners of talking or reading aloud.

(10) a. 插口   *cha-kou* (insert-mouth) 'interrupt; chip in'

b. 插嘴   *cha-zui* (insert-mouth) 'interrupt; chip in'

c. 抢嘴   *qiang-zui* (rush/rob-mouth) 'try to get the first word in; try to be heard above the rest'

    d. 随口   *sui-kou* (follow-mouth) 'speak thoughtlessly or casually; blurt out whatever comes into one's head'

    e. 信口   *xin-kou* (trust/at random-mouth) 'speak thoughtlessly or casually

    f. 拗口   *ao-kou* (disobey/defy-mouth) 'be hard to pronounce; be awkward reading'

    g. 绕嘴   *rao-zui* (wind-mouth) 'not be smooth; be difficult to articulate'

    h. 咬嘴   *yao-zui* (bite-mouth) 'be difficult to articulate; be awkward-sounding'

    i. 上口   *shang-kou* (go up to-mouth) 'be able to read aloud fluently; be suitable for reading aloud'

    j. 顺口   *shun-kou* (obey/go with-mouth) 'read smoothly; say off-handedly'

    k. 顺嘴   *shun-zui* (obey/go with-mouth) 'read smoothly; say off-handedly'

The compounds in (10a) and (10b) both mean "interrupt", and to do so one "inserts one's mouth" into the flow of discourse. When people try to be heard above the rest, they "rush their mouths" (10c). People speaking thoughtlessly or casually "follow or trust their mouths" (10d, e.). The compounds in (10f–k) show that things hard to pronounce, articulate, or read aloud "disobey", "defy", "wind" or "bite" the mouth whereas in the opposite case they "obey" or "go with" the mouth. Also, when people speak offhandedly, they "go with their mouths" rather than their heart/mind (10j, k).

(11) a. 卖嘴   *mai-zui* (sell-mouth) 'show off verbal skill; indulge in clever talk'

      b. 磨嘴   *mo-zui* (grind/rub-mouth) '*dial.* jabber; do a lot of talking; indulge in idle talk; argue pointlessly'

      c. 碍口   *ai-kou* (hinder-mouth) 'be too embarrassing to mention'

      d. 借口   *jie-kou* (borrow-mouth) 'use as an excuse or pretext; excuse or pretext'

      e. 矢口   *shi-kou* (vow-mouth) 'state categorically; insist emphatically; assert positively'

      f. 交口   *jiao-kou* (exchange/cross-mouth) 'with one voice; converse; talk'

      g. 吐口   *tu-kou* (throw up-mouth) 'tell truth; put forward a claim; make a demand'

As in (11), people showing off their verbal skill by indulging in clever talk are trying to "sell their mouths" (11a). Indulging in idle talk or arguing pointlessly is to "grind the mouth" (11b). Things too embarrassing to mention actually "hinder the mouth" (11c). To use something as an excuse is to "borrow a mouth" and an excuse is a "borrowed mouth" (11d).

In all the compounds discussed above, the first constituent is a verbal element whereas the ones in (12) below have an adjectival element as their first constituent and they have an adjective-noun construction.

(12)   a.   多嘴   *duo-zui* (many-mouth) 'speak out of turn; shoot off one's mouth'
     b.   油嘴   *you-zui* (oily/greasy-mouth) 'glib; a glib talker'
     c.   贫嘴   *pin-zui* (nagging-mouth) 'garrulous; loquacious'
     d.   满口   *man-kou* (full-mouth) '(speak) unreservedly or profusely; be full of'
     e.   苦口   *ku-kou* (bitter-mouth) '(admonish) in earnest'
     f.   羞口   *xiu-kou* (shy-mouth) 'find it difficult to bring the matter up'
     g.   极口   *ji-kou* (extreme-mouth) '(praise) in highest terms'
     h.   亲口   *qin-kou* (personal-mouth) '(say sth.) personally'

Thus, for instance, a person who speaks out of turn has too "many mouths" whereas a glib talker has a "greasy mouth".

While all the compounds discussed so far have the speech organ term, *kou* or *zui* 'mouth' as their second constituent, preceded by a verbal or adjectival element, the ones given below have the speech organ term as their first element.

(13)   a.   口称   *kou-cheng* (mouth-call/claim) 'claim to be; profess'
     b.   口吃   *kou-chi* (mouth-eat) 'stutter; stammer'
     c.   口角   *kou-jue* (mouth-contend/wrestle) 'quarrel; bicker; wrangle'
     d.   口才   *kou-cai* (mouth-talent) 'eloquence'
     e.   口气   *kou-qi* (mouth-air/breath) 'manner of speaking; what is actually meant'
     f.   口风   *kou-feng* (mouth-wind) 'one's intention or view as revealed in what one says'
     g.   口实   *kou-shi* (mouth-seed) 'a cause for gossip'
     h.   口过   *kou-guo* (mouth-mistake) 'make a slip of the tongue'
     i.   口误   *kou-wu* (mouth-error) 'make a slip of the tongue; a slip of the tongue; an oral slip'
     j.   口语   *kou-yu* (mouth-language) 'spoken language'

Those in (13) have either a noun-verb or a noun-noun construction. For instance, if one claims something, one's "mouth claims" it (13a), and the spoken language is the "mouth language" (13j).

In the many compounds in (14) below, the speech organ term for "mouth", while taking the first position, combines with an adjective that follows it.

(14) a. 口快 *kou-kuai* (mouth-fast) 'outspoken; plainspoken; thoughtless in speech; quick with one's tongue'

 b. 口惠 *kou-hui* (mouth-favor) 'lip service; empty promise'

 c. 口紧 *kou-jin* (mouth-tight) 'closemouthed; tight-lipped'

 d. 嘴快 *zui-kuai* (mouth-fast) 'have a loose tongue'

 e. 嘴损 *zui-sun* (mouth-damaging/cutting) '*dial.* sharp-tongued; sarcastic'

 f. 嘴稳 *zui-wen* (mouth-stable) 'able to keep a secret; discreet in speech'

 g. 嘴直 *zui-zhi* (mouth-straight) 'outspoken; plainspoken'

 h. 嘴尖 *zui-jian* (mouth-pointed) 'sharp-tongued; cutting in speech; be choosy about what one eats'

 i. 嘴冷 *zui-leng* (mouth-cold) '*dial.* blunt'

 j. 嘴贫 *zui-pin* (mouth-nagging) 'loquacious; garrulous'

 k. 嘴碎 *zui-sui* (mouth-fragmented) 'loquacious; garrulous'

 l. 嘴笨 *zui-ben* (mouth-stupid) 'inarticulate; clumsy of speech'

 m. 嘴刁 *zui-diao* (mouth-tricky) '*dial.* talk cunningly and craftily; be choosy with food'

 n. 嘴乖 *zui-guai* (mouth-well-behaved) '(of children) clever and pleasant when speaking to elders'

 o. 嘴甜 *zui-tian* (mouth-sweet) 'ingratiating in speech; smooth-tongued; honey-mouthed'

For instance, an outspoken and plainspoken person has a "fast" (14a) or "straight" (14g) mouth; a loose-tongued person also has a "fast" mouth (14d) while a sharp-tongued person has a "pointed" mouth (14h); a loquacious or garrulous person has a "nagging" (14j) or "fragmented" (14k) mouth.

(15) a. 嘴勤 *zui-qin* (mouth-diligent) 'fond of talking; chatty'

 b. 嘴懒 *zui-lan* (mouth-lazy) 'not inclined to talk much'

 c. 嘴松 *zui-song* (mouth-loose) 'have a loose tongue'

 d. 嘴紧 *zui-jin* (mouth-tight) 'tight-lipped; closemouthed'

 e. 嘴敞 *zui-chang* (mouth-open wide) '*dial.* have a loose tongue'

 f. 嘴严 *zui-yan* (mouth-shut tight) 'tight-lipped; closemouthed'

 g. 嘴软 *zui-ruan* (mouth-soft) 'afraid to speak out'

 h 嘴硬 *zui-ying* (mouth-hard) 'stubborn and reluctant to admit mistakes or defeats'

As shown in (15), there are pairs of compounds where the two adjectives following the speech organ terms are antonyms. However, the two compounds with antonymous adjectives are not necessarily antonyms (e.g. 15g and 15h).

A prominent characteristic of the Chinese language is that it contains a great number of set phrases or idiomatic expressions or collocations. Very often, these idioms consist of four characters. Listed below are the ones that contain *kou* or *zui* 'mouth'. Because there are so many of them, I will do nothing more than just listing them.

(16) a. 开口闭口   *kai-kou bi-kou* (open-mouth close-mouth) 'every time one opens one's mouth; whenever one speaks'

    b. 难以开口   *nan-yi kai-kou* (difficult-to open-mouth) 'find it difficult to bring the matter up'

    c. 闭口不谈   *bi-kou bu-tan* (shut-mouth not-talk) 'refuse to say anything about'

    d. 闭口无言   *bi-kou wu-yan* (shut-mouth no-speech) 'remain silent; be tongue-tied'

    e. 三缄其口   *san-jian qi-kou* (three-seal one's-mouth) 'with one's lips sealed'

    f. 破口大骂   *po-kou da-ma* (break-mouth big-curse) 'shout abuse; let loose a torrent of abuse'

    g. 顺口搭音   *shun-kou da-yin* (go with-mouth throw in-sound) 'echo what others say; chime in with others'

    h. 交口称赞   *jiao-kou chengzan* (cross-mouth praise) 'unanimously praise'

    i. 信口开河   *xin-kou kai-he* (at will-mouth open-river) 'talk irresponsibly; wag one's tongue too freely; talk at random'

    j. 出口成章   *chu-kou cheng-zhang* (exit-mouth become-essay) 'words flow from the mouth as from the pen of a master'

    k. 出口伤人   *chu-kou shang-ren* (exit-mouth hurt-people) 'say things that will hurt others' feelings; speak bitingly'

    l. 杀人灭口   *sha-ren mie-kou* (kill-people extinguish-mouth) 'silence a witness by killing him; kill sb. to prevent him from disclosing a secret'

    m. 空口无凭   *kong-kou wu-ping* (empty-mouth no-guarantee) 'a mere verbal statement is no guarantee'

    n. 祸从口出   *huo cong kou chu* (disaster from mouth come out) 'trouble comes out of the mouth (i.e. from a loose tongue)'

    o. 恶口伤人   *e-kou shang-ren* (evil-mouth hurt-people) 'hurt people with one's abusive tongue'

    p. 血口喷人   *xue-kou pen-ren* (bloody-mouth spurt-people) 'make unfounded and malicious attacks upon sb.; venomously slander'

q. 金口玉言   *jin-kou yu-yan* (gold-mouth jade-words) 'precious words; utterances that carry great weight'

r. 口若悬河   *kou-rou xuan-he* (mouth-like hanging-river) 'let loose a flood of eloquence; be eloquent; speak volubly'

s. 口口声声   *kou-kou sheng-sheng* (mouth-mouth voice-voice) 'say again and again; keep on saying'

t. 口角春风   *kou-jiao chun-feng* (mouth-corner spring-wind) 'make favorable remarks about sb.; put in a good word for sb.'

u. 口角生风   *kou-jiao sheng-feng* (mouth-corner produce-wind) 'speak fluently'

v. 口诛笔伐   *kou-zhu bi-fa* (mouth-punish pen-attack) 'condemn both in speech and writing'

w. 如出一口   *ru chu yi kou* (like coming out of one mouth) 'as if from one mouth; unanimously'

x. 嘴不关风   *zui bu guan feng* (mouth not enclose wind) 'shoot one's mouth off; have a loose tongue'

y. 嘴不干净   *zui bu ganjing* (mouth not clean) 'use dirty language'

z. 嘴不饶人   *zui bu rao ren* (mouth not forgive people) 'fond of making sarcastic remarks'

In (17) below are idiomatic expressions consisting of three characters:

(17) a. 碎嘴子   *sui-zui-zi* (fragmented-mouth-SUF) 'chatter; jabber; prate; a garrulous person; chatterbox'

b. 支嘴儿   *zhi-zui-er* (pay-mouth-SUF) '*dial.* give advice; suggest ideas; make suggestions'

c. 嘴把式   *zui-bashi* (mouth-master) '*dial.* a person given to idle talk'

d. 耍贫嘴   *shua pin-zui* (play nagging-mouth) 'be garrulous'

e. 打嘴仗   *da zui-zhang* (wage mouth-battle) '*inf.* argue; quarrel'

f. 婆婆嘴   *popo-zui* (old woman's mouth) 'a nagging tongue; a garrulous person'

As can be seen, many such idioms actually contain the compounds discussed above. In this sense, we can see these idioms as constructed from expansion and elaboration on those compounds.

As show in (18), such idiomatic expressions or collocations may contain another body part term, suggesting the relationship of this body part with the mouth under certain circumstances.

(18) a. 杜口裹足   *du-kou guo-zu* (shut out-mouth bind-feet) 'speechless and motionless with fear'

b. 口蜜腹剑   *kou-mi fu-jian* (mouth-honey belly-sword) 'honey-mouthed and dagger-hearted; honey on one's lips and murder in one's heart; hypocritical and malignant'

c. 目瞪口呆   *mu-deng kou-dai* (eyes-stare mouth-dumb) 'gaping; dumbstruck'

d. 嘴闭眼明   *zui-bi yan-ming* (mouth-shut eye-bright) 'keep the mouth shut and the eyes open'

e. 利嘴花牙   *li-zui hua-ya* (sharp-mouth flowery-teeth) 'have a ready tongue; saponaceous'

f. 拙嘴笨腮   *zhuo-zui ben-sai* (clumsy-mouth stupid-cheek) 'clumsy-tongued; inarticulate'

g. 嘴硬骨软   *zui-ying gu-ruan* (mouth-hard bone-soft) 'talk tough but act soft'

h. 嘴软骨硬   *zui-ruan gu-ying* (mouth-soft bone-hard) 'talk soft but act tough'

Other than the mouth, the body parts included in these idioms are feet, belly, eyes, teeth, cheeks, and bones. However, such partnership is found most common between the mouth and the heart, as the following examples show.

(19) a. 锦心绣口   *jin-xin xiu-kou* (splendid-heart beautiful-mouth) 'elegant thought and flowery speech'

b. 苦口婆心   *ku-kou po-xin* (bitter-mouth old woman-heart) '(admonish) earnestly and maternally'

c. 心直口快   *xin-zhi kou-kuai* (heart-straight mouth-fast) 'frank and outspoken; straightforward and plainspoken'

d. 嘴快心直   *zui-kuai xin-zhi* (mouth-fast heart-straight) 'be outspoken and frank; straightforward and sincere'

e. 有口无心   *you-kou wu-xin* (have-mouth not have-heart) 'be sharp-tongued but not malicious'

f. 有嘴无心   *you-zui wu-xin* (have-mouth not have-heart) 'be sharp-tongued but not malicious'

g. 心服口服   *xin-fu kou-fu* (mouth-convinced heart-convinced) 'to be genuinely convinced'

h. 口心如一   *kou-xin ru-yi* (mouth-heart like-one) 'what one says is indeed what one thinks; one means what one says'

i. 口凶心软   *kou-xiong xin-ruan* (mouth-fierce heart-soft) 'one's bark is worse than one's bit'

j. 嘴硬心软   *zui-ying xin-ruan* (mouth-hard heart-soft) 'firm in speech but soft in heart'

   k. 口是心非   *kou-shi xin-fei* (mouth-yes heart-no) 'say yes and mean no; say one thing and mean another'

   l. 口甜心辣   *kou-tian xin-la* (mouth-sweet heart-peppery) 'honey on the lips and viciousness in the heart'

   m. 嘴甜心辣   *zui-tian xin-la* (mouth-sweet heart-peppery) 'a cruel heart under the cover of sugar-coated words; sweet words and a bitter heart'

   n. 佛口蛇心   *fu-kou she-xin* (Buddha-mouth snake-heart) 'honeyed words but evil intent'

This is because the Chinese *xin* 'heart' is culturally conceptualized as the central faculty of cognition, which is the agent of thinking, as well as feeling, and as the seat of both mental and emotional lives, where feelings and thoughts are stored (Yu, 2007a, 2007b, 2008, 2009). The idiomatic phrases highlight either the unity or the difference between people's words and thoughts.

3.2 The lips, teeth, and tongue in conventionalized expressions

In Chinese, there is no doubt that the vast majority of the conventionalized expressions manifesting the metonymic chain under discussion contain the speech organ term for "mouth". The mouth, however, has its own parts, notably the lips, the teeth, and the tongue, which also participate in the metonymic chain, as exemplified by the compounds in (20).

(20) a. 启唇   *qi-chun* (open-lips) 'open one's mouth; start to talk about sth.'

       b. 启齿   *qi-chi* (open-teeth) 'open one's mouth; start to talk about sth.'

       c. 挂齿   *gua-chi* (hang on-teeth) 'mention'

       d. 不齿   *bu-chi* (not-teeth/mention) 'not worth mentioning; despise'

       e. 齿及   *chi-ji* (teeth-reach) 'mention; touch upon'

       f. 齿冷   *chi-leng* (teeth-cold) '*form.* laugh sb. to scorn'

       g. 饶舌   *rao-she* (rich-tongue) 'too talkative; garrulous; say more than is proper; shoot off one's mouth'

       h. 卖舌   *mai-she* (sell-tongue) 'make sensational statements for the sake of publicity'

       i. 结舌   *jie-she* (tie/knot-tongue) 'be tongue-tied; be at a loss for words'

       j. 嚼舌   *jiao-she* (chew-tongue) 'wag one's tongue; chatter; gossip; argue meaninglessly; squabble'

       k. 鼓舌   *gu-she* (beat-tongue) 'wag the tongue (esp. in honeyed talk)'

       l. 学舌   *xue-she* (learn-tongue) 'mechanically repeat other people's words; *inf.* wag one's tongue spreading hearsay'

m. 舌耕　*she-geng* (tongue-plow) '*form.* make a living by teaching'
n. 舌战　*she-zhan* (tongue-battle/war) 'have a verbal battle with; argue heatedly with; a hot dispute; a verbal battle'

As we can see, starting to talk is "opening the lips or teeth" (20a, b). To mention something is to "hang it on the teeth" (20c). In (20e), to mention or touch upon something is one's "teeth reach" it. As in (20g), a talkative or garrulous person has a "rich tongue". Making sensational statements for the sake of publicity is "selling one's tongue" (20h; cf. 11a). As in (20j), to gossip or argue meaningless is to "chew one's tongue". Interestingly, a formal way of saying that someone makes a living by teaching is to say that this person have his "tongue plow" (20m). Notably, a writer does "pen-plowing" (i.e. 笔耕*bi-geng* [pen-plow] 'live by one's pen; make a living by writing'). The figurative use of the verb *geng* 'plow' reflects the values of a traditionally agrarian culture, where a peasant makes a living by plowing the land.

(21)　a.　反唇相讥　*fan-chun xiang-ji* (reverse-lips PRT-redicule) 'answer back sarcastically'
　　　b.　嘴唇油滑　*zuichun you-hua* (lips greasy-slippery) 'eloquent in speech; with one's tongue in one's cheek'
　　　c.　难以启齿　*nan-yi qi-chi* (difficult-to open-teeth) '(find it) difficult to talk about sth.'
　　　d.　不便启齿　*bu-bian qi-chi* (not-convenient open teeth) '(find it) inconvenient to talk about sth.'
　　　e.　何足挂齿　*he-zu gua-chi* (why-sufficient hang on-teeth) 'not worth mentioning'
　　　f.　不足挂齿　*bu-zu gua-chi* (not-sufficient hang on-teeth) 'not worth mentioning'
　　　g.　不足齿数　*bu-zu chi-shu* (not-sufficient teeth-count) 'not worth mentioning'
　　　h.　伶牙俐齿　*ling-ya li-chi* (clever-teeth smart-teeth) 'have the gift of the gab; have a glib tongue; have a ready tongue'

The above are some idiomatic phrases or collocations that contain *chun* 'lip' and *chi* 'tooth'. Note that *chun* 'lip' is also called *zuichun*, as in (21c), which literally means "mouth lip". *Zuichun* 'lip' has an informal variant, given in (22a).

(22)　a.　嘴皮子　*zui-pizi* (mouth-skins) '*inf. derog.* lips (of a glib talker); ability to talk'
　　　b.　磨嘴皮子　*mo zui-pizi* (grind mouth-skins) '*dial.* jabber; do a lot of talking; indulge in idle talk; argue pointlessly'
　　　c.　费嘴皮子　*fei zui-pizi* (cost mouth-skins) 'talk nonsense; waste one's breath'

    d. 耍嘴皮子   *shua zui-pizi* (play with mouth-skins) 'talk glibly; be a slick talker; mere empty talk; lip service'

As shown in (22a), the lips are also called the "mouth skins", which however is informal and, quite often, derogatory, referring to a glib talker's lips, for instance. The idiomatic collocations in (22b–d) illustrate this point.

(23) **a.** 烂舌头   *lan she-tou* (rotten tongue-SUF) '*inf.* be fond of gossip; gossip; scandalmonger'

     b. 烂舌根   *lan she-gen* (rotten tongue-root) 'same as above'

     c. 嚼舌头   *jiao she-tou* (chew-tongue-SUF/head) 'wag one's tongue; chatter; gossip; argue meaninglessly; squabble'

     d. 嚼舌根   *jiao she-gen* (chew-tongue-root) 'wag one's tongue; chatter; gossip; argue meaninglessly; squabble'

     e. 磨舌头   *mo she-tou* (grind tongue-SUF) '*dial.* indulge in idle talk; argue pointlessly'

The idiomatic expressions in (23) contain the speech organ term for "tongue". In (23a, c, e), the term for the tongue literally means "tongue head", but *tou* 'head' here is grammaticalized into a suffix, so *she-tou* (tongue-head) simply means "tongue". In (23b) and (23d), *gen* 'root' is not grammaticalized, so *she-gen* means "the root of the tongue".

(24) **a.** 口舌   *kou-she* (mouth-tongue) 'dispute or misunderstanding caused by gossip; talking round'

     b. 口齿   *kou-chi* (mouth-teeth) 'enunciation; ability to speak'

     c. 唇舌   *chun-she* (lip-tongue) 'words; argument'

The three examples in (24) show that speech organ terms can combine to form compounds encoding the concepts related to speaking and speech, as illustrated by the following conventionalized expressions:

(25) **a.** 口舌意气   *kou-she yiqi* (mouth-tongue personal feelings) 'get involved in a verbal dispute to let out one's personal feelings'

     b. 口舌是非   *kou-she shi-fei* (mouth-tongue right-wrong) 'disputes and quarrels'

     c. 口齿清楚   *kou-chi qingchu* (mouth-teeth clear) 'have clear enunciation'

     d. 口齿伶俐   *kou-chi lingli* (mouth-teeth clever) 'be fluent and eloquent'

     e. 斗口齿   *dou kou-chi* (fight with mouth-teeth) 'squabble; bicker; banter'

f. 费唇舌 *fei chun-she* (cost lip-tongue) 'take a lot of talking or ex-
        plaining'
g. 白费唇舌 *bai-fei chun-she* (in vain-cost lip-tongue) 'waste one's
        breath'

Apart from forming compounds, as in the examples above, pairs of speech organ
terms are also found in idiomatic phrases, as in the examples below.

(26) a. 摇唇鼓舌 *yao-chun gu-she* (shake-lips beat-tongue) 'flap one's lips
            and beat one's tongue – wag one's tongue; engage in
            loose talk (to stir up trouble)'
      b. 唇枪舌剑 *chun-qiang she-jian* (lip-spear tongue-sword) 'cross ver-
            bal swords; engage in a battle of words'
      c. 唇焦舌敝 *chun-jiao she-bi* (lips-scorched tongue-worn out) 'talk
            till one's tongue and lips are parched; wear oneself out in
            pleading, expostulating, etc.'

In the set phrases above the two speech organ terms juxtaposed are *chun* 'lip' and
she 'tongue'. However, it is *kou* or *zui* 'mouth' and *she* 'tongue' that most frequently
found in such set phrases.

(27) a. 张口结舌 *zhang-kou jie-she* (open-mouth tie-tongue) 'be agape
            and tongue-tied; be at a loss for words'
      b. 钳口结舌 *qian-kou jie-she* (clamp-mouth tie-tongue) 'keep one's
            mouth shut; hold one's tongue'
      c. 轻口薄舌 *qing-kou bo-she* (light-mouth thin-tongue) 'have a caus-
            tic and sharp tongue'
      d. 笨口拙舌 *ben-kou zhuo-she* (stupid-mouth clumsy-tongue) 'awk-
            ward in speech; slow of speech; inarticulate'
      e. 赤口毒舌 *chi-kou du-she* (red-mouth poisonous-tongue) 'venom-
            ous tongue; vile language'
      f. 尖嘴薄舌 *jian-zui bo-she* (pointed-mouth thin-tongue) 'have a
            caustic and flippant tongue'
      g. 轻嘴薄舌 *qing-zui bo-she* (light-mouth thin-tongue) 'have a caus-
            tic and sharp tongue'
      h. 多嘴多舌 *duo-zui duo-she* (many-mouth many-tongue) 'gossipy
            and meddlesome; long-tongued'
      i. 贫嘴薄舌 *pin-zui bo-she* (nagging-mouth thin-tongue) 'be garru-
            lous and sharp-tongued'
      j. 七嘴八舌 *qi-zui ba-she* (seven-mouth eight-tongue) 'with every-
            body trying to get a word in; all talking at once'

k. 甜嘴蜜舌 *tian-zui mi-she* (sweet-mouth honey-tongue) 'speaking honeyed words; honey-mouthed'

l. 拙嘴笨舌 *zhuo-zui ben-she* (clumsy-mouth stupid-tongue) 'clumsy-tongued; inarticulate'

m. 油嘴滑舌 *you-zui hua-she* (greasy-mouth slippery-tongue) 'glib-tongued'

n. 利嘴巧舌 *li-zui qiao-she* (sharp-mouth skilful tongue) 'have the gift of the gab'

o. 利嘴毒舌 *li-zui du-she* (sharp-mouth poisonous-tongue) 'have a shrewd tongue; a sharp tongue'

p. 调嘴学舌 *tiao-zui xue-she* (adjust-mouth learn-tongue) 'tittle-tattle; gossip'

q. 嘴乖舌巧 *zui-guai she-qiao* (mouth-good tongue-skilful) 'be full of gibes and ready with one's tongue'

r. 嘴尖舌巧 *zui-jian she-qiao* (mouth-pointed tongue-skilful) 'gifted with a quick and sharp tongue'

s. 嘴尖舌快 *zui-jian she-kuai* (mouth-pointed tongue-fast) 'be fluent in speech'

t. 嘴尖舌酸 *zui-jian she-suan* (mouth-pointed tongue-sour) 'cutting in speech; sharp-tongued'

u. 嘴巧舌能 *zui-qiao she-neng* (mouth-skilful tongue-capable) 'clever and plausible in speech; gifted with a quick and sharp tongue; shine in conversation'

As we can see, many of these set phrases are constructed by using one or two existing compounds. Therefore, it can be said that set phrases are constructed from expansion and elaboration of more basic compounds.

4. Discussion

A few implications can be drawn from this study in the light of Radden (2004). According to the "naïve view" or "folk model" of language proposed by Radden (2004), languages generally observe the metonymic principle by which they make metonymic extension along the metonymic chain from speech organ to language: speech organ → speaking → speech → language. However, the metonymic shifts along the metonymic chain can skip one or more intermediate links, thus resulting in a metonymy widely attested across languages, SPEECH ORGAN FOR LANGUAGE.

My study has focused on the speech organ terms *kou* or *zui* 'mouth', *chun* 'lip', *chi* 'tooth', and *she* 'tongue' in Chinese with regard to their roles in contributing to the formation of the metonymic chain in Chinese. Specifically, I investigated the manifestation of these three conceptual metonymies: (a) SPEECH ORGAN FOR SPEAKING, (b) SPEECH ORGAN FOR SPEECH, and (c) SPEECH ORGAN FOR LANGUAGE. My first finding is that the first two metonymies SPEECH ORGAN FOR SPEAKING and SPEECH ORGAN FOR SPEECH are richly manifested in Chinese.

Among the large number of conventionalized expressions discussed, the majority instantiate SPEECH ORGAN FOR SPEAKING, which is, unsurprisingly, the first link of the metonymic chain. For instance, "open the mouth (开口、张口、张嘴)" means "start talking", "move the mouth (动口、动嘴)" means "talk", "shut the mouth (闭口)" means "keep silent" or "not talk about something", and "stop the mouth (住口、住嘴)" means "stop talking" or "shut up". Some of the conventionalized expressions, however, realize SPEECH ORGAN FOR SPEECH, which is a metonymic transfer that skipped over the intermediate link SPEAKING. For instance, "change the mouth (改口、改嘴)" means "withdraw or modify the previous remark", "insert the mouth (插嘴)" means "interrupt or chip in", i.e. "insert remarks into other people's remarks", and "the mouth sweet or tough (嘴甜、嘴硬)" means "what one says sounds sweet or tough". That is, one's speech organ, the mouth in these cases, stands metonymically for what one says: words, sentences, utterances, or remarks, which all fall into the category of speech.

While the conventionalized expressions all contribute to the manifestation of the underlying metonymic chain under discussion, it must be emphasized that metaphor also plays an important role in the construction of many of them. For instance, metaphor is involved in these expressions: "sell the mouth (卖嘴)" meaning "show off one's verbal skill or indulge in clever talk", "block the mouth (堵嘴)" meaning "keep somebody from talking or silence somebody", "grind the mouth (磨嘴)" meaning "indulge in idle talk or argue pointlessly", and "wind the mouth (绕嘴)" meaning "be difficult to articulate". Obviously, the use of the verbs in these cases is metaphorical. In a similar vein, in the expressions such as "the greasy mouth (油嘴)" meaning "glib", "the bitter mouth (苦口)" meaning "(admonish) in earnest", "the mouth pointed (嘴尖)" meaning "cutting in speech", "the mouth straight (嘴直)" meaning "outspoken", and "the mouth fragmented (嘴碎)" meaning "loquacious or garrulous", the use of the adjectives is also metaphorical. For the purpose of illustration, I provide a figure (Figure 1) below showing how metonymy and metaphor interact with each other to result in the compound word 磨嘴:

As shown in this figure, the compound involves two mappings: one is metonymic (i.e. mapping within the same conceptual frame or matrix domain), represented by an open-headed arrow line, and the other is metaphoric (i.e. mapping across two conceptual frames or domains), represented by a solid-headed arrow line. The figure (Figure 2) below illustrate the case of 嘴尖:

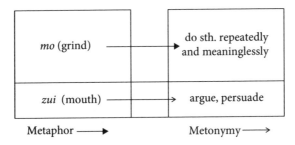

Figure 1. Interaction between metonymy and metaphor in *mo-zui* (grind-mouth) 'indulge in idle talk or argue pointlessly'

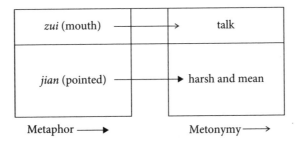

Figure 2. Interaction between metonymy and metaphor in *zui-jian* (mouth-pointed) 'cutting in speech'

Again, as we can see, this compound word involves two different mappings, metonymic and metaphoric. Since in both of the above cases, the mappings, metonymic or metaphoric, take place within the conceptual frame of speaking, we can refer to them as cases of "metaphor within metonymy" (Goossens, 2002).

What is interesting is my finding regarding the third conceptual metonymy SPEECH ORGAN FOR LANGUAGE, the metonymic transfer that has skipped the two intermediate links, SPEAKING and SPEECH. As Radden (2004) shows and points out, this metonymy has been widely attested across languages. It is, however, not manifested lexically in Chinese. None of the speech organ terms in Chinese, from "mouth" to "tongue", can really mean "language" in any context. For instance, *mother tongue* in English can only be translated into 母语*muyu*, i.e. "mother language", but not 母舌*mushe* (i.e. "mother tongue"); and 人口*renkou* (human-mouth) in Chinese does not mean "language", but means "population" (because population counts the number of "human mouths" that need feeding!). This finding seems to suggest that Chinese has fallen short of the metonymic chain widely attested across languages (Radden, 2004). What is particularly interesting, however, is the discovery that in Chinese, while SPEECH ORGAN FOR LANGUAGE is not manifested lexically, it is nevertheless realized in its ideographic writing system as components of the characters. Look at (28).

(28) a. 口   *kou* 'mouth'
      b. 舌   *she* 'tongue'
      c. 言   *yan* 'speech'
      d. 话   *hua* 'speech; oral language' (Traditional character: 話)
      e. 语   *yu* 'speech; language' (Traditional character: 語)
      f. 言语   *yanyu* 'speech" (Traditional characters: 言語)
      g. 语言   *yuyan* 'language' (Traditional characters: 語言)

In (28a) and (28b) are the Chinese words for "mouth" and "tongue" respectively. They both also serve as radicals, i.e. components of other characters. Thus, the Chinese characters for the words "speech" and "language", 言 *yan* (28c) and 语 *yu* (28e) respectively, both contain the "mouth" radical 口 *kou*. In contemporary Chinese, in fact, these two words combine to form a compound 言语 *yanyu* (28f), meaning "speech", and when its two constituents are reversed in order, the result is the compound word for "language" 语言 *yuyan* (28g). It is worth mentioning that in the traditional writing system, the semantic radical, known as the "speech" radical, on the left side of the character for "language" 语 *yu* (28e) is 言 *yan*, which itself contains a "mouth" radical 口 *kou* (28a), as in (28c). Besides, another word that is represented by the character 话 *hua* (28d) also means "speech", and it is composed of two constituents: on the left is the "speech" radical, which contains the "mouth" 口 *kou* in its traditional variant (言 *yan* as in 28c), and on the right is the radical 舌 *she* that means "tongue", which is also a character with the same meaning when used alone (28b). As we can see, the character for "tongue", i.e. 舌 *she*, also contains a "mouth" radical 口 *kou* in it. Therefore, it is clear that the Chinese characters meaning "speech" and "language" all contain the radical for "mouth" 口 *kou* and one of them meaning "speech" or "oral/spoken language" contains the radical for "tongue" 舌 *she*. Based on these facts, it can be concluded that in Chinese the metonymy SPEECH ORGAN FOR LANGUAGE is manifested in the ideographic writing system although it is not manifested lexically as in many other languages. This finding provides an interesting and telling example of how the general cognitive principle of embodiment can be realized in and embraced by a culture-specific environment.

The Chinese ideographic writing system is an important area where the manifestation of conceptual metonymies and metaphors can be studied in the Chinese language. For instance, in Yu (2007b, 2009), I argue that the heart is traditionally conceptualized as the central faculty of cognition in Chinese culture. Therefore, in the Chinese language, the word 心 *xin* that primarily denotes the heart organ may also refer to it as the "organ for thinking" and the "seat of thought and emotions".

This fact is displayed clearly in the unique ideographic writing system of Chinese. Thus, many Chinese characters for words related to thought and feelings contain the "heart" radical as their semantic component. Here are a few examples pertaining to thinking or thought: 思*si* 'think; consider; deliberate; think of; long for; thought; thinking', 想*xiang* 'think; ponder; think back; try to remember; recall; recollect; consider; miss', 虑*lü* 'consider; ponder; think over; concern; worry', and 念*nian* 'think of; miss; thought; idea'. The following are two common characters representing words for feeling: 感*gan* 'feel; sense; feeling' and情*qing* 'feeling; affection; sentiment; passion'. Note that the "heart" radical has two variants in the Chinese writing system. The canonical one, which looks the same as the word 心*xin* 'heart', often occurs at the bottom of a character, as in 思*si*, 想*xiang*, 虑*lü*, 念*nian*, and 感*gan*. The other one, usually called the "vertical heart radical", stands on the left side of a character, as in 情*qing*. Also, single-character words often combine with others to form so-called compound words in present-day Chinese. For instance, the preceding single-character words can form the following compounds: 思想*sixiang* 'thought; thinking; idea; ideology', 思虑*silü* 'consider; contemplate; deliberate', 思念*sinian* 'think of; long for; miss', 感情*ganqing* 'emotion; feeling; sentiment; affection', and 情感*qinggan* 'emotion; feeling'. As suggested by the ideographic characters and meanings of the words they encode, or the connection between form and meaning, the heart represents a person's intellectual and affective center and locus of mental and emotional life, and it is therefore traditionally regarded as the central faculty of cognition in Chinese culture (Yu, 2007a, b, 2008, 2009). From a linguistic point of view, these characters manifest a conceptual metonymy HEART FOR THOUGHT AND FEELINGS, or at the generic level CONTAINER FOR CONTAINED, since according to the Chinese cultural conceptualization, the heart is seat (or container) of both thought and feelings.

Here is another example that I have discussed elsewhere (Yu, 2009): the Chinese compound word 忖度*cunduo* 'speculate; conjecture; surmise', which is represented by two characters that have a spatial connotation. The first character is composed of the "heart" radical on its left and the character for "inch" on the right; the second character *duo* originally means "to measure",[2] and with a change in pronunciation (*du*) and tone (from the second to the fourth) it means "linear measure". Thus, by "face value", the mental activities of speculating, conjecturing and surmising something is to "measure it for its spatial dimensions". That is, SPECULATING, CONJECTURING, or SURMISING IS MEASURING. Interestingly, in a related compound 忖量*cunliang* 'think over; turn over in one's mind; conjecture; guess', the second character can mean "measure" when used as a verb (and "capacity", "volume", etc. when used as a noun); when its tone is changed (from the fourth

---

2. See *Hanyu Da Cidian* (*Grand Dictionary of Chinese Language*), p. 983.

to the second), it becomes a verb that again means "measure". In another related word 忖摸 *cunmo* 'reckon; estimate; conjecture', the second character means to "feel", "stroke" or "touch" with one's hand. The metaphorical mapping from bodily onto mental experience is very obvious. It is again interesting to note that, while the first character 忖 *cun* 'think over; ponder; speculate' contains the "heart" radical on its left, the second character of the compound 摸 *mo* 'feel; stroke; touch' contains the "hand" radical on its left side. Applying the metaphorical formula A IS B, we can say that the first character represents the target concept whereas the second represents the source concept. The metaphor so derived is THINKING OVER, PONDERING, or SPECULATING (IN ONE'S HEART) IS FEELING, STROKING, or TOUCHING (WITH ONE'S HANDS). That is, at the generic level, it is MENTAL FUNCTION IS MANUAL ACTION, or MIND IS BODY, a conceptual metaphor that summarizes the embodied nature of human cognition.

For this paper, I did not study the metonymic shifts along the metonymic chain SPEAKING FOR SPEECH and SPEECH FOR LANGUAGE since my focus is on the initial link, the speech organs. Let us look at the following list (with reference to Wei 1995):

(29) a. 说 *shuo* (i) speak; talk; explain (ii) theory; teachings; doctrine
   b. 讲 *jiang* (i) speak; say; tell; explain; interpret; discuss; negotiate (ii) lecture (e.g. 第一讲)
   c. 谈 *tan* (i) talk; chat; discuss (ii) what is said or talked about
   d. 话 *hua* (i) word; talk; oral language (e.g. 中国话) (ii) talk about; speak about
   e. 言 *yan* (i) speech; word; character (ii) say; talk; speak
   f. 语 *yu* (i) language; words; set phrase; proverb; saying (ii) speak; say

In (29a–c) are three verbs of speaking, as in (i), but they all have nominal meanings that fall into the category of speech, as in (ii). In other words, we can hypothesize that the nominal meanings of these verbs reflect the underlying metonymy SPEAKING FOR SPEECH. Of course it takes thorough diachronic studies to confirm the historical development of the senses of these words (i.e. to find out if they are instances of SPEAKING FOR SPEECH), but the synchronic link between their verbal and nominal senses are obvious.

The three words in (29d–f) are regarded as primarily nominal in present-day Chinese, as in (i). All three of them have verbal meanings as well, as in (ii), and their verbal senses can be traced back to ancient times when they might be even more common verbs of linguistic action back then than they are today. Again, the link between their verbal and nominal senses is there, but it takes diachronic studies to find out whether they represent cases of SPEAKING FOR SPEECH (i.e. ACTION

FOR RESULT). The word in (29f) is the only one in the list that can mean "language" in a complete sense (whereas 29d usually means "oral language" only), but it also possesses the meanings that fall into the categories of speech and speaking. We can hypothesize that the links are related to each other in a way that conforms to the metonymic chain: speaking → speech → language, but again it takes diachronic studies to confirm it.

In sum, my study as a whole is a case of "embodiment via body parts". It demonstrates that human meaning and understanding are indeed embodied. We can mean what we do and understand what we do because we have the kind of the body we do. If we had a different kind of body, with a different kind of structure, the way we understand the world and the way we use the language would be different accordingly. It is because human beings all have similar bodies with similar functions that the metonymic chain under discussion may have the possible potential of a universal value. Nonetheless, the body always exists in its cultural context, and the mind that is embodied is never free from the dynamic forces of culture. In my study, for instance, the rich manifestation of SPEECH ORGAN FOR SPEAKING and SPEECH ORGAN FOR SPEECH at the lexical level reveals a preference of the culture. Similarly, the manifestation of SPEECH ORGAN FOR LANGUAGE, not at the level of lexicon, but at the level of writing system, also displays a unique characteristic of Chinese language and culture.

5. Conclusion

In this paper I have reached the following conclusions for my study of the Chinese speech organ terms and their roles in the manifestation of the metonymic chain in the Chinese cultural model of language:

1. The metonymies SPEECH ORGAN FOR SPEAKING and SPEECH ORGAN FOR SPEECH are richly manifested by the conventionalized expressions in Chinese. The rich manifestation of the conceptual metonymies itself is the preference and characteristic of the culture.

2. In contrast, however, the metonymy SPEECH ORGAN FOR LANGUAGE is not realized at the level of lexicon, as in many other languages, but at the level of writing system in Chinese. This finding presents a striking example of how the general cognitive principle of embodiment can be realized in and embraced by a culture-specific environment – in this study, the ideographic writing system characteristic of Chinese culture and language.

3. Metaphor plays an important role in the construction of many of the conventionalized expressions that are primarily metonymic in character. This finding reinforces the argument of Cognitive Linguistics that metaphor is often

motivated by metonymy and therefore often has a metonymic basis (e.g., Barcelona, 2000c; Niemeier, 2000; Radden, 2000).

4. The findings of my study of certain metonymic links confirm the hypothesis of the metonymic chain (Radden, 2004).

5. The findings of my study, in general, support the claim for the embodied nature of human cognition (Gibbs, 2006; Johnson, 1987, 2007; Lakoff, 1987; Lakoff & Johnson, 1999), and embodiment situated in cultural contexts (Gibbs, 1999; Ziemke et al., 2007; Frank et al., 2008; Sharifian et al., 2008).

To conclude my study I also want to raise the following question for further research. That is, an initial look at the metonymies SPEAKING FOR SPEECH, SPEECH FOR LANGUAGE, and SPEAKING FOR LANGUAGE in Chinese seems to suggest that Chinese conforms to the hypothesized metonymic chain. Thorough diachronic studies are needed to confirm its validity.

References

Barcelona, A. (Ed.) (2000a). *Metaphor and metonymy at the crossroads: A cognitive perspective.* Berlin and New York: Mouton de Gruyter.

Barcelona, A. (2000b). Introduction: The cognitive theory of metaphor and metonymy. In A. Barcelona (Ed.), *Metaphor and metonymy at the crossroads: A cognitive perspective* (pp. 1–28). Berlin and New York: Mouton de Gruyter.

Barcelona, A. (2000c). On the plausibility of claiming a metonymic motivation for conceptual metaphor. In A. Barcelona (Ed.), *Metaphor and metonymy at the crossroads: A cognitive perspective* (pp. 31–58). Berlin and New York: Mouton de Gruyter.

Dirven, R. & Pörings, R. (Eds.) (2002). *Metaphor and metonymy in comparison and contrast.* Berlin and New York: Mouton de Gruyter.

Forceville, C. (1996). *Pictorial metaphor in advertising.* London and New York: Routledge.

Forceville, C. & Urios-Aparisi, E. (Eds.) (in press). *Multimodal metaphor.* Berlin and New York: Mouton de Gruyter.

Frank, R. M., Dirven, R., Ziemke, T. & Bernárdez, E. (Eds.) (2008). *Body, language and mind Vol. 2: Sociocultural situatedness.* Berlin and New York: Mouton de Gruyter.

Gibbs, R. W. (1994). *The poetics of mind: Figurative thought, language, and understanding.* Cambridge and New York: Cambridge University Press.

Gibbs, R. W. (1999). Taking metaphor out of our heads and putting it into the cultural world. In R. W. Gibbs & G. J. Steen (Eds.), *Metaphor in Cognitive Linguistics* (pp. 145–166). Amsterdam and Philadelphia: John Benjamins.

Gibbs, R. W. (2006). *Embodiment and cognitive science.* Cambridge: Cambridge University Press.

Gibbs, R. W. (2008) (Ed.). *The Cambridge handbook of metaphor and thought.* Cambridge and New York: Cambridge University Press.

Gibbs, R. W. & Steen, G. J. (Eds.) (1999). *Metaphor in cognitive linguistics.* Amsterdam and Philadelphia: John Benjamins.

Goatly, A. (2007). *Washing the brain: Metaphor and hidden ideology*. Amsterdam and Philadelphia: John Benjamins.

Goossens, L. (2002). Metaphtonymy: The interaction of metaphor and metonymy in expressions for linguistic action. In R. Dirven & R. Pörings (Eds.), *Metaphor and metonymy in comparison and contrast* (pp. 349–377). Berlin and New York: Mouton de Gruyter.

Johnson, M. (1987). *The Body in the mind: The bodily basis of meaning, imagination, and reason.* Chicago: University of Chicago Press.

Johnson, M. (2007). *The Meaning of the body: Aesthetics of human understanding.* Chicago: University of Chicago Press.

Kövecses, Z. (2000). *Metaphor and emotion: Language, culture, and body in human feeling.* Cambridge and New York: Cambridge University Press.

Kövecses, Z. (2002). *Metaphor: A practical introduction.* Oxford and New York: Oxford University Press.

Kövecses, Z. (2005). *Metaphor in culture: Universality and variation.* Cambridge and New York: Cambridge University Press.

Kövecses, Z. (2006). *Language, mind, and culture: A practical introduction.* Oxford and New York: Oxford University Press.

Lakoff, G. (1987). *Women, fire, and dangerous things: What categories reveal about the mind.* Chicago: University of Chicago Press.

Lakoff, G. & Johnson, M. (1999). *Philosophy in the flesh: The embodied mind and its challenge to Western thought.* New York: Basic Books.

Lakoff, G. & Núñez, R. (2000). *Where mathematics comes from: How the embodied mind brings mathematics into being.* New York: Basic Books.

Maalej, Z. (2004). Figurative language in anger expressions in Tunisian Arabic: An extended view of embodiment. *Metaphor and Symbol, 19*(1), 51–75.

Maalej, Z. (2007). The embodiment of fear expressions in Tunisian Arabic: Theoretical and practical implications. In F. Sharifian & G. B. Palmer (Eds.), *Applied cultural linguistics: Implications for second language learning and intercultural communication.* Amsterdam and Philadelphia: John Benjamins.

Maalej, Z. (2008). The heart and cultural embodiment in Tunisian Arabic. In R. Dirven, F. Sharifian, N. Yu & S. Niemeier (Eds.), *Culture, body, and language: Conceptualizations of internal body organs across languages and cultures* (pp. 395–428). Berlin: Mouton de Gruyter.

Niemeier, S. (2000). Straight from the heart – metonymic and metaphorical explorations. In A. Barcelona (Ed.), *Metaphor and metonymy at the crossroads: A cognitive perspective* (pp. 195–213). Berlin and New York: Mouton de Gruyter.

Panther, K. (2006). Metonymy as a usage event. In G. Kristiansen, M. Achard, R. Dirven & F. J. Ruiz de Mendoza Ibáñez (Eds.), *Cognitive linguistics: Current applications and future perspectives* (pp. 147–185). Berlin and New York: Mouton de Gruyter.

Panther, K. & Radden, G. (Eds.) (1999a). *Metonymy in language and thought.* Amsterdam and Philadelphia: John Benjamins.

Panther, K. & Radden, G. (1999b). Introduction. In K. Panther & G. Radden (Eds.), *Metonymy in language and thought* (pp. 1–14). Amsterdam and Philadelphia: John Benjamins.

Panther, K. & Thornburg, L. (Eds.) (2003). *Metonymy and pragmatic inferencing.* Amsterdam and Philadelphia: John Benjamins.

Radden, G. (2000). How metonymic are metaphors? In A. Barcelona (Ed.), *Metaphor and metonymy at the crossroads: A cognitive perspective* (pp. 93–108). Berlin and New York: Mouton de Gruyter.

Radden, G. (2004). The metonymic folk model of language. In B. Lewandowska-Tomaszczyk & A. Kwiatkowska (Eds.), *Imagery in language* (pp. 543–565). Bern: Peter Lang.

Radden, G. & Kövecses, Z. (1999). Towards a theory of metonymy. In K. Panther & G. Radden (Eds.). *Metonymy in language and thought* (pp. 17–59). Amsterdam and Philadelphia: John Benjamins.

Ruiz de Mendoza Ibáñez, F. J. & Otal Campo, J. L. (2002) *Metonymy, grammar, and communication*. Granada: Editorial Comares.

Sharifian, F., Dirven, R., Yu, N. & Niemeier, S. (2008) (Eds.), *Culture, body, and language: Conceptualizations of internal body organs across cultures and languages*. Berlin and New York: Mouton de Gruyter.

Steen, G. J. (2007). *Finding metaphor in grammar and usage*. Amsterdam and Philadelphia: John Benjamins.

Wei, D. (gen. ed.) (1995). *Han Ying cidian* [A Chinese-English dictionary] (Revised ed.). Beijing: Foreign Language Teaching and Research Press.

Yu, N. (1998). *The contemporary theory of metaphor: A perspective from Chinese*. Amsterdam and Philadelphia: John Benjamins.

Yu, N. (2001). What does our face mean to us? *Pragmatics and Cognition, 9*, 1–36.

Yu, N. (2003a). Metaphor, body, and culture: The Chinese understanding of *gallbladder* and *courage. Metaphor and Symbol, 18*, 13–31.

Yu, N. (2003b). The bodily dimension of meaning in Chinese: What do we do and mean with "hands"? In E. H. Casad & G. B. Palmer (Eds.), *Cognitive linguistics and non-Indo-European languages* (pp. 337–362). Berlin and New York: Mouton de Gruyter.

Yu, N. (2007a). Heart and cognition in ancient Chinese philosophy. *Journal of Cognition and Culture, 7*, 27–47.

Yu, N. (2007b). The Chinese conceptualizaiton of the heart and its cultural context: Implicaitons for second language learning. In F. Sharifian & G. B. Palmer (Eds.), *Applied cultural linguistics: Implications for second language learning and intercultural communication* (pp. 65–85). Amsterdam and Philadelphia: John Benjamins.

Yu, N. (2008). The Chinese heart as the central faculty of cognition. In F. Sharifian, R. Dirven, N. Yu & S. Niemeier (Eds.), *Culture, body, and language: Conceptualizations of internal body organs across languages and cultures* (pp. 131–168). Berlin and New York: Mouton de Gruyter.

Yu, N. (2009). *The Chinese HEART in a cognitive perspective: Culture, body, and language*. Berlin and New York: Mouton de Gruyter.

Ziemke, T., Zlatev, J. & Frank, R. M. (Eds.) (2007). *Body, language and mind Vol. 1: Embodiment*. Berlin and New York: Mouton de Gruyter.

Internal body organs in conceptualization

CHAPTER 10

Metaphor, body, and culture

The Chinese understanding
of *gallbladder* and *courage*

According to the theory of internal organs in traditional Chinese medicine, the gallbladder has the function of making judgments and decisions in mental processes and activities, and it also determines one's degree of courage. This culturally constructed medical characterization of the gallbladder forms the base of the cultural model for the concept of courage. In the core of this cultural model is a pair of conceptual metaphors: (a) GALLBLADDER IS CONTAINER OF COURAGE, and (b) COURAGE IS QI (GASEOUS VITAL ENERGY) IN GALLBLADDER, which are partly constitutive of the understanding of the gallbladder and courage in Chinese culture. A description and analysis of the data from the Chinese language show that numerous conventional expressions are systematically tied to each other and contributive to the underlying conceptual metaphors. The study presents a case in which an abstract concept (courage) is understood in part via a conceptual metaphor grounded in the body, but shaped by a culture-specific metaphorical understanding of an internal organ (gallbladder) inside the body. Although the human body is a potentially universal source domain for metaphors structuring abstract concepts, cultural models set up specific perspectives from which certain aspects of bodily experience or certain parts of the body are viewed as especially salient and meaningful in the understanding of those abstract concepts.

1. Introduction

Metaphor is an essential cognitive tool in that it structures many concepts, especially abstract ones, in our conceptual systems. Metaphorical mappings from source domains to target domains emerge largely from the interplay between body and culture. Our mind is embodied in the profound sense that the very structure of our thoughts comes from the nature of our body (Lakoff & Johnson, 1999). The cultural experience and knowledge we gain while submerged in our culture inevitably shape our worldview, making our mind enculturated. The interaction between common bodily experiences and varied cultural experiences determines the extent to which conceptual metaphors are universal, widespread, or culture-specific.

At the same time, the same basic embodied experiences, in which many conceptual metaphors are grounded, may be defined differently by different cultural beliefs and values (Gibbs, 1999). Also, our cultural models may be constructed metaphorically, thus framing our worldview metaphorically. As such, the relation between metaphor, body, and culture is extremely intricate, with all of them mingled together, and each of them penetrating the others, giving rise to a colorful spectrum of cognition.

In this article, I attempt to present a Chinese case of such intricate relation. In this case, an abstract concept, *courage*, is partly structured by a conceptual metaphor COURAGE IS QI (GASEOUS VITAL ENERGY) IN GALLBLADDER. The conceptual metaphor has the human body as its source domain, but the selection of this source domain depends on a culture-specific metaphorical understanding of an internal organ, the gallbladder, inside the body, namely GALLBLADDER IS CONTAINER OF COURAGE. Linguistic evidence suggests that both of these conceptual metaphors exist in the core of the Chinese cultural model for the concept of courage. Both of them can be traced down to their deeper roots in the theory of internal organs of traditional Chinese medicine that offers a unique perspective on the functions of the gallbladder.

2. Gallbladder and courage in Chinese culture

The gallbladder is one of the internal organs in our body. According to one encyclopedia, it is "a small, pear-shaped sac that stores bile, or gall, a yellowish brown or green fluid, secreted by the liver, that aids in the digestion of dietary fat" (Hartenstein, 1990, p.17). In another encyclopedia, it is said to be "a nonessential accessory digestive organ that is a reservoir in which bile is stored and concentrated between digestive periods" (Noback, 1992, p. 548). Because of its "nonessential" and "accessory" nature, the contraction of certain disease "may require the removal of the gallbladder" (Hartenstein, 1990, p. 17). These quotations represent the basic scientific understanding of what the gallbladder is, what it does, and what can be done in its treatment. However, the Chinese understanding of the gallbladder is more complicated. To illustrate the point, here is a real story about a Chinese scholar living and working in the United States who contracted a gallbladder disease. After diagnosing it, the doctor told him that he needed surgical treatment. Then, after the operation, the doctor told him that his gallbladder had been removed. At that, he and his wife were quite shocked and upset about the fact that the doctor had removed his gallbladder without letting them know in advance, although this surprise may have simply been caused by miscommunication, cross-cultural or not (i.e., when the doctor said that "surgical treatment" was needed, the removal of the gallbladder was actually meant, but not received as such by the Chinese couple). When their Chinese friends asked about her husband's gallbladder disease and its treatment, the wife said, with humor and sarcasm, "He," referring to her husband, "has now become 'a hero without gallbladder' (*wu-dan yingxiong*)." The friends, with shared cultural knowledge, fully understood what she meant by the remark.

Chinese culture attaches special importance to the gallbladder. This, for instance, is reflected in the following conventional expressions in (1). These expressions and those presented hereafter are collected from popular Chinese dictionaries (Lü & Ding, 1980, 1989, 1996; Wei, 1995; Wen, 1996; Wu, 1993) and actual discourse. In their glosses, I use *gall* for *gallbladder* for the purpose of simplicity. Furthermore, "MOD" stands for "modifier marker", and "PRT" for "particle" in a broad sense. In (1) the first example is a proverbial saying; the rest are idioms.

(1) a. 无胆之人事事难。
    Wu-dan   zhi   ren   shishi   nan.
    without-gall MOD people everything difficult
    'Everything appears difficult to people without gallbladder.'

  b. 浑身是胆   *hun-shen shi-dan* (whole-body is-gall) 'be every inch a hero; be the embodiment of valor'

  c. 七个头八个胆 *qige-tou bage-dan* (seven-heads eight-galls) 'extremely bold and not afraid of death'

  d. 孤胆英雄   *gu-dan yingxiong* (single-gall hero) 'a lone fighter'

  e. 群威群胆   *qun-wei qun-dan* (crowd-might crowd-gall) '(display) mass heroism and daring'

"Proverbs are generally regarded as repositories of folk wisdom" (White, 1987, p. 151). What folk wisdom does Example (1a) display while literally it says that "people without gallbladder" should find it difficult to do anything they face? The idioms in (1b–e) should provide some clues. In contrast to (1a), (1b) says that "the body of a hero is all gallbladder." As in (1c), those who are extremely bold and not afraid of death have "seven heads and eight gallbladders." While a lone fighter is called "a single-gall hero" (1d), many people who together display mass heroism and daring are said to be "a crowd of might and a crowd of gallbladders" (1e).

It may be apparent by now that the gallbladder in Chinese has to do with courage. Here, I am using the word *courage* in a very loose sense to cover a broad spectrum of meanings also represented by such words as *boldness, bravery, daring, pluck,* and *spunk*. I am aware that words of this kind could be language-specific and should be used with caution in analyzing one language using a different language (see, e.g., Goddard & Wierzbicka, 1994; Wierzbicka, 1992, 1999).

As in (1a), therefore, "people without gallbladder" actually refers to people without courage, and that is why they should find it difficult to do anything they face. Now it should also be clear why the Chinese scholar and his wife in the earlier story were upset about the "surgical treatment" that actually removed his gallbladder, for without his gallbladder, and courage, he was supposed to find it difficult to do anything he faces, as suggested by the proverb in (1a). Note that when the wife called her husband "a hero without gallbladder," she was coining a nonce expression based on (1d), that is, from "a single-gall hero" to "a no-gall hero." What kind of "hero" is a hero without gallbladder or, rather, courage? That is where the humor and irony lie.

The gallbladder has to do with one's courage in Chinese culture. As I have found earlier (Yu, 1995, 1998, 2002), in fact, a conceptual metaphor that is extensively manifested in the Chinese language is GALLBLADDER IS CONTAINER OF COURAGE. A closely linked one is COURAGE IS QI (GASEOUS VITAL ENERGY) IN GALLBLADDER. They are the two sides of one coin, with different focuses, and therefore different target domains.

In what follows, I attempt to outline the Chinese cultural model for, or culturally shared understanding of, "courage" conceptualized metaphorically in terms of the gallbladder. According to Quinn and Holland (1987, p. 4), "*Cultural models* are presupposed, taken-for-granted models of the world that are widely shared... by the members of a society and that play an enormous role in their understanding of that world and their behavior in it." With the cultural model in shape, it will not be surprising to see why there exist numerous conventional metaphorical expressions in the Chinese language that realize the underlying conceptual metaphors. I will proceed to show that this cultural model has its foundation in traditional Chinese medicine that shares many views of ancient Chinese philosophy such as Daoism (traditionally spelled as Taoism). I will then make a linguistic analysis of how this shared understanding and knowledge of the gallbladder in Chinese culture is reflected in the Chinese language as an important part of that culture.

3. Gallbladder in Chinese medicine

Traditional Chinese medicine is a mixture of folk and scientific medicine with a history of several thousand years. In this section, I present what Chinese medicine has to say about the gallbladder in its theory of internal organs (Chen, 1989; Wang et al., 1997). As will be clear shortly, the metaphor GALLBLADDER IS CONTAINER OF COURAGE actually reflects the folk beliefs regarding the functions of the gallbladder as an internal organ in our body.

In Chinese medicine, the internal organs in the human body are divided into two major classes. The five organs of primary importance are called 脏 *zang*: liver, heart, spleen, lung, and kidney. Each of them is matched with, and closely related to, an organ of secondary importance called 腑 *fu*: respectively, gallbladder, small intestine, stomach, large intestine, and bladder. An extra *fu* organ is called *san jiao* "the three visceral cavities housing the internal organs," supposed to be matched with *jingluo* "main and collateral channels, regarded as a network of passages, through which vital energy circulates and along which acupuncture points are distributed." According to the theory of *yin-yang*, all the *zang* organs belong to *yin*, whereas all the *fu* organs, the gallbladder included, belong to *yang*. According to the theory of five elements or five phases (*wood, fire, earth, metal,* and *water*), the gallbladder, paired with the liver, belongs to *wood*.

In the theory of internal organs, the gallbladder has two main functions. First, it stores and excretes bile, secreted by the liver, that aids in the digesting process operated by the stomach, spleen, and small intestine. The second perceived function of the gallbladder, which is probably unique to Chinese medicine, is that it has the capability and function of making judgments and decisions in the process of mental and psychological activities (Chen, 1989; Wang et al., 1997). As one ancient definition goes, "The gallbladder is the organ of justice, from which judgments and decisions emanate (胆者，中正之官，决断出焉。 *Dan zhe, zhongzheng zhi guan, jueduan chu yan.*)" (Wang et al., 1997, p. 750; the English translation here, and below, is my own). An interesting fact worth noting here is that the Chinese word *guan* can mean both "organ (as part of the body)" and "official or officer (as a governmental or military position)." Thus, the previous statement actually defines the gallbladder, an internal organ, as a righteous, unbiased, and selfless official, like a judge, that is likely to make right and resolute decisions. Even though the gallbladder is the "decision-making organ," it also determines one's personality in terms of boldness and timidity (Chen, 1989; Wang et al., 1997). In modern terms, these conceptions of the gallbladder can be interpreted "to mean that certain aspects of the nervous system are traditionally ascribed in Chinese medicine to the gallbladder" (Wiseman & Feng, 1998, p. 234).

According to the theory of internal organs, the gallbladder's decision-making function plays an important role in stabilizing one's emotional states and in maintaining the normal circulation of blood and the gaseous vital energy or life force of 气 *qi*. Those whose gallbladder *qi* is "strong" (壮 *zhuang*) are likely to be relatively calm in face of, say, adversity, danger or tragedy. Their troubled or upset state of mind is likely to return to normal more quickly. On the other hand, those whose gallbladder *qi* is "weak" (虚 *xu*) are more likely to experience emotional turmoil under the psychological impact of any negative stimulus. As a result, they are more likely to suffer from insomnia and have nightmares, for instance. It is believed that people's resistance to negative psychological impacts depends on the relative "strength" of their gallbladder *qi*. Those whose gallbladder *qi* is "solid" (实 *shi*) are bold; those whose gallbladder *qi* is "void" or "vacuous" (虚 *xu*) are timid. It is said, therefore, that one's gallbladder determines one's degree of courage (Wang et al., 1997).

In the theory of internal organs of Chinese medicine, the liver and the gallbladder are coupled together as a paired combination of *zang* and *fu*. While the liver, as one of the five *zang* organs, belongs to *yin*, the gallbladder belongs to *yang* as a *fu* organ; but both of them belong to the element of *wood*. The gallbladder is closely related to the liver in two senses. Physiologically, the gallbladder is attached to the liver, storing and excreting bile produced by the liver. The disease in one organ often affects the other. Psychologically, the gallbladder and the liver are also closely related to each other. Thus, "the liver is the organ of general, in charge of contemplation and deliberation, but it relies on the gallbladder for judgment and decision" (Wang et al., 1997, p. 750). So defined, the liver is the "strategy-planning general" whereas the gallbladder is the "decision-making official." "When the liver and the gallbladder complement each other, bravery is established" (Wang et al., 1997, p. 758).

In Chinese medicine, the heart and the gallbladder also hold a special relation between them. "The heart is the organ of emperor, ruling all psychological and mental activities" (Wang et al., 1997, p. 759). However, it is the gallbladder, the organ of justice, that makes judgments and decisions, guided by the heart. The disease of the gallbladder will affect the functions of the heart. For instance, if the gallbladder *qi* rises to trouble the heart, the patient will display unusual states of emotion. If the *qi* in both the heart and the gallbladder is "weak" or "vacuous" (*xu*), the patient may feel scared for no or any reason, and be laden with misgivings. If "the emperor (i.e. the heart) and the prime minister (i.e. the gallbladder) help each other, they will together promote vitality and preserve life" (Wang et al., 1997, p. 759).

In short, what is unique in traditional Chinese medicine is the view that the gallbladder is related to people's mental processes and personalities. It is worth noting that this view in the theory of internal organs is expressed as part of a metaphor system. In this system, the heart is the "emperor" or "monarch," the gallbladder is the "prime minister," "top advisor," or "judge," the liver is the "general," and so forth. Of course, this metaphor system is known basically within the community of Chinese medicine – the study of human body and its treatment – as part of its theory of internal organs. It metaphorizes the functions and relations of the internal organs and highlights their interrelationships as a unified system. The use of the metaphor reflects the influence of ancient Chinese philosophy, which advocates such ideas as "Man is an integral part of nature" (天人合一 *tian ren he yi*), and "There exists a correspondence between man and universe" (天人相应

tian ren xiang ying) (English translations adapted from Wu, 1993, p. 2504). Here *nature* and *universe,* both used to translate the Chinese word *tian* that primarily refers to the sky or heavens, should be interpreted as to mean "the external world," including the social and cultural structures, in which humans exist (see, e.g., Zhang & Rose, 2001, Ch. 4). Thus, for instance, the Daoists conceived of the human body as "a microcosm of the universe" (Zhang & Rose, 2001, p. 86). They "always tried to understand what was happening inside the body by comparing and contrasting it with what was happening outside in nature" (Chia & Chia, 1990, p. 14). To them, "The microcosm is a mirror image of the macrocosm," and "The universe within is the same as the universe without" (Chia & Chia, 1990, p. 15). Therefore, one can understand the entire universe by understanding one's own body and vice versa. According to these views, there exists a bridge that connects the body and the universe, and this bridge is built with metaphor.

However, what is especially interesting for my purpose in this study is the linguistic evidence that partially reflects the folk theory of the gallbladder in traditional Chinese medicine as outlined previoiusly. In the next section, I will lay out the linguistic data to show that the culturally constructed understanding of the roles of the gallbladder as an internal organ of our body has given rise to a unique highlight in the Chinese language.

4. *Gallbladder* in Chinese language

As related in the previous section, the gallbladder is believed, in traditional Chinese medicine, to govern decision making. The state of its *qi,* a gaseous vital energy or life force, whether "strong" or "weak," "solid" or "void/vacuous," determines the amount of courage one has. Note the state of the gallbladder in terms of *qi* is itself conceptualized and described metaphorically based on the image of a "pressurized container." When it is "strong" or "solid", there is much internal pressure of *qi* on the container. The opposite is true when the gallbladder is "weak," "vacuous" or "void" of *qi*. In the Chinese language, the gallbladder is also primarily related to courage, and the conceptual metaphors that can summarize the bulk of conventional linguistic expressions are GALLBLADDER IS CONTAINER OF COURAGE, and COURAGE IS QI IN GALLBLADDER. This pair of conceptual metaphors, based on the CONTAINER image schema, entails the following mappings or correspondences between the source and target domains:

Source domain		Target domain
physical container of courage	→	gallbladder
gaseous energy of *qi* in the container	→	courage
capacity of the container	→	amount of courage
degree of internal pressure of the container	→	degree of courage

In what follows I will analyze how these metaphors are manifested in the language. Let us first look at the following group of compounds.

(2) a. 胆子   *dan-zi* (gall-SUFFIX) 'courage; guts; nerve'
    b. 胆气   *dan-qi* (gall-*qi* [gaseous vital energy]) 'courage'
    c. 胆力   *dan-li* (gall-strength) 'courage and boldness'
    d. 胆量   *dan-liang* (gall-capacity) 'courage; guts; pluck; spunk'
    e. 胆魄   *dan-po* (gall-boldness) 'courage and boldness'
    f. 胆略   *dan-lüe* (gall-strategy) 'courage and resourcefulness; daring and resolution'
    g. 胆识   *dan-shi* (gall-discernment) 'courage and insight; superior judgment'
    h. 胆敢   *dan-gan* (gall-dare) 'dare; have the audacity to'

All these compounds contain *dan* 'gallbladder,' but are related to courage. As can be seen, courage is respectively connected to the gallbladder itself (2a), its gaseous vital energy (2b), its strength or internal pressure (2c), and its capacity (2d). In Examples (2e–g), the second morpheme X can be interpreted as either the content inside the gallbladder as a container, or the quality of the gallbladder as an official of justice. These compounds all suggest that the gallbladder has to do with right judgment and bold decision. Example (2h) is a verb meaning "dare (to do sth.)," but literally it means "the gallbladder dares." Given in (3), following, are sentential examples of (2d), (2f) and (2h).

(3) a. 他生来就有胆量。
       Ta shenglai jiu   you   dan-liang.
       he be-born then have gall-capacity
       'He has courage in his blood (lit. He was born with gallbladder-capacity).'
    b. 他胆略过人。
       Ta dan-lüe   guo   ren.
       he gall-strategy surpass people
       'He has unusual courage and resourcefulness.'

    c. 敌人胆敢来侵犯，就坚决消灭它。
        Diren dan-gan lai   qinfan, jiu   jianjue   xiaomie ta.
        enemy gall-dare come invade then resolutely wipe-out them
        'If the enemy dare to invade us, we'll resolutely wipe them out.'

As illustrated by (2d) and (3a), the "capacity" of one's gallbladder is equal to the amount of courage one has. When the internal pressure (i.e., the "strength") of *qi* is equal, the larger the gallbladder capacity is, the more courageous one is, as shown in the following compounds.

  (4) a. 胆大   *dan-da* (gall-big) 'bold; audacious'
        b. 大胆   *da-dan* (big-gall) 'bold; daring; audacious'
        c. 斗胆   *dou-dan* (*dou*[a measure container for a decaliter]-gall) 'make
            bold; venture; be of great courage; gall as big as a peck measure'

Because the gallbladder is the container of courage, those bold and brave people are believed to have "big gallbladders" (4a and 4b). As in (4c), *dou* is the measure container for a decaliter of dry grain in traditional Chinese culture. If some one's gallbladder is as big as a *dou*, this person must be very daring. The following sentences provide further illustration. When people do something boldly, they do it with their "gallbladder big" (5a and 5b). Example (5c) is a proverbial saying that looks dialectically at the relation between courage and scare, as well as between strength and pressure. In (5d), the compound *dou-dan*, that is, "with the gallbladder as big as a *dou*," is used adverbially to mean "boldly."

  (5) a. 好大的胆子！
        Hao da de   danzi!
        how big MOD gall
        'What a nerve! (lit. How big your gallbladder is!)'
        b. 你大着胆子去，不要怕。
        Ni da-zhe-danzi qu, bu-yao   pa.
        you big-PRT-gall go don't-be afraid
        'Go right ahead (lit. Go ahead with your gallbladder big) and don't be afraid.'
        c. 压大的力，吓大的胆。
        Ya-da   de li, xia-da   de dan.
        press-bigger MOD strength scare-bigger MOD gall
        'Strength grows under pressure, and courage grows out of scare (lit. Pressure makes strength bigger, and scare makes gall/courage bigger).'

d.　我斗胆说一句，这件事你做错了。
　　Wo dou-dan shuo yi ju,　　　zhe-jian shi　　ni
　　I　*dou*-gall say　one-sentence this-CL　thing　you
　　zuo cuo　　le.
　　did wrong PRT
　　'May I make bold to suggest (lit. suggest with my gallbladder as big as
　　a *dou*) that you were wrong to do so.'

Those appearing in (6), following, are idioms that contain (4a). As in (6a), if some
people's gallbladder is so big that it can "wrap their body," then they must be "audacious in the extreme." If their gallbladder can "wrap the sky" (6b), their boldness has
to be much bigger than the sky. Example (6d) involves two internal organs, the gallbladder and the heart. In Chinese, *xin-xi* (heart-thin) means "careful" or "scrupu-
lous." If one has "big gallbladder" but "thin heart," this person is bold but cautious.

(6)　a.　胆大包身　　*dan-da bao-shen* (gall-big wrap-body) 'courage appears
　　　　　　　　　　　to be bigger than body; audacious in the extreme'
　　b.　胆大包天　　*dan-da bao-tian* (gall-big wrap-sky) 'audacious in the
　　　　　　　　　　　extreme; heaven-daring'
　　c.　胆大妄为　　*dan-da wang-wei* (gall-big recklessly-behave) 'bold and
　　　　　　　　　　　reckless; daredevil'
　　d.　胆大心细　　*dan-da xin-xi* (gall-big heart-thin) 'bold but cautious;
　　　　　　　　　　　brave but not reckless; courageous and wise'

As the previous examples have demonstrated, the bigger gallbladder represents a
greater amount of courage. That is, the degree of courage depends on the size of
the gallbladder. This point is further illustrated by some related examples.

(7)　a.　明目张胆　　*ming-mu zhang-dan* (glaring-eye stretched-gall) 'bra-
　　　　　　　　　　　zenly; flagrantly'
　　b.　放胆　　　　*fang-dan* (let go/loosen-gall) 'act boldly and with confi-
　　　　　　　　　　　dence'
　　c.　事到万难须放胆。
　　　　Shi　　dao　　wan-nan　　　　　xu　　fang-dan.
　　　　things become ten thousand-difficult need let go-gall
　　　　'When things become extremely difficult, one needs to act boldly with
　　　　confidence (lit., let go or loosen up one's gall).'

The idiom in (7a) is derogatory in usage, describing those who do bad things "with
glaring eyes and stretched gallbladders." These people are brazen and flagrant, that
is, bold in a negative sense. Note that a "stretched" gallbladder is certainly bigger
in size than the same one that is in normal condition. The compound in (7b)

literally means "to release the gallbladder from any control or restraints" or "to set it free and loosen it up." Again, we can imagine that the gallbladder loosened up or set free of any restraints is bigger in size than the one that has contracted with pressure or restraints from outside. Example (7c) illustrates (7b) in a saying. Examples in (8) provide a different perspective.

(8)   a.   胆壮   *dan-zhuang* (gall-strong) 'bold; fearless; courageous'
      b.   壮胆   *zhuang-dan* (strengthen-gall) 'build up sb's courage; boost sb's
                  courage'
      c.   心亏胆不壮。
           Xin-kui   dan bu   zhuang.
           heart-lost gall not strong
           "If you feel guilty (lit. heart-lost), you won't be bold (lit. your gall won't
           be strong)."
      d.   你跟我一块儿去吧，起码可以壮壮我的胆。
           Ni   gen wo yikuair qu ba, qima   keyi zhuang-zhuang
           You with me together go PRT at-least can stengthen-a-bit
           wode dan.
           my   gall
           'Do come with me. You can at the very least build up my courage (lit.
           strengthen my gall a little bit).'

Here, (8a) and (8b) allude to the strength of the gallbladder: the stronger it is, the bolder one is. Remember that the gallbladder is the container of courage. When it is fully charged with courage, like a ball fully inflated, it is stronger as a whole. Once again, a stronger gallbladder, with more internal pressure, is expected to have a bigger size, as much as a balloon fully inflated. Examples (8c) and (8d) respectively illustrate (8a) and (8b). In Chinese, as in (8c), people who feel guilty of wrong doing have "lost their heart." As a result, their gallbladder will not be strong any more. Apparently, the "strength" and "capacity" images complement each other in the metaphorical conceptualization of the gallbladder as the container of courage. The capacity being equal, bigger strength (i.e., more internal pressure) means more courage. It is also true the other way around: the strength being equal, larger capacity contains more courage.

The amount of courage people have depends on the size or capacity of their gallbladder. As the previous examples have shown, people are courageous if they have a "big gallbladder." Conversely, as we may expect, those cowardly people have a "small gallbladder," as the following instances exemplify.

(9) a. 胆小   *dan-xiao* (gall-small) 'timid; cowardly'
  b. 胆小鬼   *dan-xiao gui* (gall-small devil) 'coward'
  c. 胆小难把将军做。
   Dan-xiao nan ba jiangjun zuo.
   gall-small difficult PRT general be
   'Being timid (lit. With the gall small), one cannot be a general.'

Example (9a) is illustrated by (9c), a proverbial saying. As we can see, being timid or cowardly literally means "having a small gallbladder," and a coward, in Chinese, is called a "gall-small devil" (9b).

 Of course, there are other words that describe people who are timid or fearful, but they also refer to the condition of the gallbladder, as illustrated in (10).

(10) a. 胆怯 *dan-qie* (gall-timid) 'timid; cowardly'
   b. 胆憷 *dan-chu* (gall-fear) 'fearful; timid; cowardly'
   c. 胆虚 *dan-xu* (gall-void) 'afraid; scared; timid'
   d. 胆寒 *dan-han* (gall-frigid) 'be terrified; be struck with terror; be overcome by fear'
   e. 落胆 *luo-dan* (drop/fall-gall) 'extremely scared'
   f. 丧胆 *sang-dan* (lose-gall) 'be terror-stricken; be smitten with fear'
   g. 闻风丧胆 *wen-feng sang-dan* (hear-wind lose-gall) 'become terror-stricken, panic-stricken, or terrified at the news'

As in (10a) and (10b), being timid, fearful, or cowardly is a symptom of the gallbladder. As in (10c), people are scared when their gallbladder is "void." A gallbladder "void" of any content is of course not "strong." It can be imagined that it is also smaller in size, just like a deflated ball or balloon. As I have studied and found elsewhere (Yu, 2002), in the Chinese language fear, as well as sadness, is cold related, in contrast to anger and anxiety, which are related to heat. So, as in (10d), when people are terrified, their gallbladder turns "frigid." It is expected that a "cold gallbladder" is smaller in size. In (10e) and (10f), the emotion of fear is so intense that it "snaps the base of the gallbladder" and "makes it drop off its stem" in a complete "loss." Example (10g) is an idiom containing (10f), which describes people so frightened that they "lose their gallbladder" when hearing the "wind" (i.e. what they perceive as bad news).

 Also as I have stated elsewhere (Yu, 2002), in the Chinese language the emotion of fear mainly affects two internal organs, the heart and the gallbladder. Besides, it also affects people's "soul." In (11), following, are some examples of how the heart and the gallbladder, and the soul and the gallbladder, are paired together in four-character idioms.

(11) a. 悬心吊胆   *xuan-xin diao-dan* (suspend-heart hang-gall) 'have one's heart in one's mouth; be on tenterhooks'

　　 b. 提心吊胆   *ti-xin diao-dan* (lift-heart hang-gall) 'have one's heart in one's mouth; be on tenterhooks'

　　 c. 胆战心惊   *dan-zhan xin-jing* (gall-tremble heart-startle) 'tremble with fear; be terror-stricken'

　　 d. 胆破心惊   *dan-po xin-jing* (gall-break heart-startle) 'be scared to death'

　　 e. 心胆俱裂   *xin-dan ju-lie* (heart-gall both-split) 'be so frightened that one's heart and gall burst; be frightened out of one's wits; be terror-stricken'

　　 f. 惊心掉胆   *jing-xin diao-dan* (shock-heart drop-gallbladder) 'be frightened out of one's wits'

　　 g. 亡魂丧胆   *wang-hun sang-dan* (dead-soul lost-gall) 'be scared out of one's wits; be half dead with fright'

　　 h. 胆裂魂飞   *dan-lie hun-fei* (gall-split soul-fly) 'be frightened out of one's wits'

In (11a) and (11b), fear "raises" the heart and the gallbladder and "hangs" them "up in the air," and "up in the air" is what one feels when one has a sense of insecurity. In (11c), fear "shakes" the gallbladder and makes it "tremble." In (11d–h), fear has "physically damaged" the gallbladder so that it is either "broken" (11d, 11e, and 11h) or completely "lost" (11f and 11g). Either way, the content inside, courage, is gone. Also, at the same time, the soul will either "die" (11g) or "desert the body" (11h), caused by intense fear. It is interesting to note that according to the theory of internal organs in traditional Chinese medicine, the emotion of fear/fright primarily affects the kidneys, which are paired with the bladder in the *zang* and *fu* combination, and have a strong connection with the heart and the gallbladder as well. However, the perceived connection between fear/fright and the kidneys in Chinese medicine has left little trace in the Chinese language. The term for the kidneys does not seem to be involved in any conventional expressions of metaphor or metonymy. This fact suggests that the language does not "mirror," but only "reflects," the medical theory.

　　In Chinese, idiomatic expressions also refer to animals' gallbladders while talking about human boldness or timidity, like in (12).

(12) a. 英雄虎胆   *yingxiong hu-dan* (heroes [have] tiger-gall) 'heroes as brave as tigers'

　　 b. 熊心豹胆   *xiong-xin bao-dan* (bear-heart leopard-gall) 'bear's heart and leopard's gall – fearlessness; tremendous courage; guts' c.　吃了豹子胆　*chi-le baozi-dan* (have-eaten leopard-gall) 'have eaten leopard's gall – be fearless'

    d.　鸡肠兔胆　*ji-chang tu-dan* (chicken-intestine rabbit-gall) 'chicken's intestine and rabbit's gall – narrow-minded and timid'

    e.　胆小如鼠　*dan-xiao ru-shu* (gall-small like-mouse) 'as timid as a mouse; chicken-hearted'

If some people have a gallbladder like that of a tiger or a leopard, they are as fearless as a tiger or leopard (12a and 12b). In case they "have eaten a leopard's gallbladder," it will make them as brave and courageous as a leopard (12c). In contrast, rabbits and mice, which are culturally understood as being timid, have their "gallbladders small," and people who have gallbladders like these animals' are of course very timid or cowardly.

In Chinese medicine, as related earlier, the liver and gallbladder form a pair of *zang* and *fu* combination, both categorized with the element of *wood*. "The liver is the general in charge of defending the body" (Chia & Chia, 1990, p. 47), while the gallbladder aids it with judgment and decision, like its "top advisor." They are very close to each other physically, and physiologically. Their close relation, as conceptualized in Chinese medicine, is reflected in the Chinese language by the use of idiomatic expressions.

(13) a.　肝胆　*gan-dan* (liver-gall) 'open-heartedness; sincerity; heroic spirit; courage'

    b.　肝胆过人　*gan-dan guo-ren* (liver-gall surpass-people) 'far surpass others in daring; unusually courageous'

    c.　肝胆俱裂　*gan-dan ju-lie* (liver-gall both-split) 'heart-broken or terror-stricken; overwhelmed by grief or terror'

    d.　摧肝裂胆　*cui-gan lie-dan* (destroy-liver split-gall) 'heart-broken; overwhelmed by grief'

    e.　肝胆相照　*gan-dan xiang-zhao* (liver-gall mutually-mirror) '(of friends) treat each other with all sincerity; be devoted to each other heart and soul'

    f.　披肝沥胆　*pi-gan li-dan* (open-liver sincere-gall) 'open one's heart; be open and sincere; be loyal and faithful'

    g.　忠肝义胆　*zhong-gan yi-dan* (loyal-liver righteous-gall) 'having good faith, virtue and patriotism'

Note that in all these expressions, the liver and gallbladder, which form a pair of *zang* and *fu* organs, are juxtaposed in a fixed order: the liver occurs before the gallbladder. This reflects the fact that the liver is of primary importance as a *zang* organ whereas the gallbladder, a *fu* organ, is of secondary importance. They together represent such virtues as sincerity, faith, devotion, loyalty, as well as courage, as is apparent in most examples in (13). As in (13e), the liver and gallbladder become the metaphor for good and close friendship built up on the basis of sincerity and devotion.

In addition to the liver, the only other organ that often co-occurs with the gallbladder in idiomatic expressions is the heart, which is the "ruler" of the body, mind, and spirit (Chia & Chia, 1990, p. 48). While the heart commands all psychological and mental activities, the gallbladder takes charge of some specific functions, such as making judgments and decisions, with its honorable character of being upright, selfless, impartial, and resolute (Wang et al., 1997). Above all, the gallbladder determines one's courage. In (11), we have already seen some idioms involving the heart and gallbladder. Those idioms describe one's state of mind when intense fear "shocks" one's heart and "shakes" or "damages" one's gallbladder. The examples in (14), following, are of a different kind.

(14) a. 心胆   *xin-dan* (heart-gall) 'will and courage'

      b. 琴心剑胆 *qin-xin jian-dan* (musical instrument-heart sword-gall) 'have the soul of a musician and the courage of a warrior; the sentiments of the lute and the spirit of the sword – a cultivated mind animated with a chivalrous spirit'

      c. 赤胆忠心 *chi-dan zhong-xin* (sincere-gall loyal-heart) 'utter devotion; whole-hearted dedication; ardent loyalty'

      d. 倾心吐胆 *qing-xin tu-dan* (pour out-heart throw up-gall) 'pour out one's heart; unburden one's heart; unbosom oneself; open one's heart wide and lay bare one's thoughts'

In (14a) the heart and gallbladder is the metaphor for "will and courage." In (14b), *qin* is a general term for certain musical instruments, such as all those with strings. The "musical instrument" and "sword" that modify the heart and gallbladder respectively consist of a case of metonymy inside metaphor. Those with "a heart of a musical instrument and a gallbladder of a sword" have "the soul of a musician and courage of a warrior." As in (14c), people with "sincere gallbladder and loyal heart" are most reliable. Finally, as in (14d), people can "unbosom themselves" by "pouring out their heart and throwing up their gallbladder" so that others can see them, and possibly their contents, and "seeing is understanding."

A survey of linguistic evidence shows that the compounds and idioms involving "gallbladder" in the Chinese language indeed reflect the folk beliefs about the gallbladder that have their roots in the theory of internal organs of traditional Chinese medicine. The conceptual metaphors that can summarize the bulk of data are GALLBLADDER IS CONTAINER OF COURAGE, and COURAGE IS QI IN GALLBLADDER. As the container, its "size" or "capacity" determines the amount of courage one has.

The bigger the gallbladder is, the more courage one has, whereas a small gallbladder represents lack of courage. The "strength" of the gallbladder, which suggests the internal pressure of *qi* on the container, also determines the degree of courage one has. The "stronger" the gallbladder is, the more courageous one is. On the other hand, if the gallbladder is "weak," then one lacks courage. A "void" or "vacuous" gallbladder is of course a "weak" one. Besides, a gallbladder "hanging in the air" rather than "standing on solid ground" certainly lacks "stability" and "strength." If, in any case, the gallbladder as container is physically "damaged" or completely "lost," the courage inside will be gone as well. As shown in the data, the other two internal organs that are affected with the gallbladder are the liver and heart.

5. Conclusion

In this study, I have attempted a linguistic description and analysis of the metaphorical expressions in Chinese that manifest the underlying conceptual metaphors GALLBLADDER IS CONTAINER OF COURAGE and COURAGE IS QI IN GALLBLADDER. This pair of metaphors partly structures the Chinese concept of courage and highlights the Chinese cultural understanding of the gallbladder. As has been shown, these conceptual metaphors can be traced down to their deeper roots in the theory of internal organs of Chinese medicine, which constitutes the base of the Chinese cultural model for courage, partly structured metaphorically in terms of the gallbladder. As a mixture of folk and scientific theory, traditional Chinese medicine claims that the gallbladder, the "organ/official of justice," is in charge of making judgments and decisions and determines one's degree of courage. It is worth noting that the conceptual metaphors GALLBLADDER IS CONTAINER OF COURAGE and COURAGE IS QI IN GALLBLADDER, as manifested by numerous linguistic metaphors, partially "reflects," but not exactly "mirrors," the underlying medical theory. Thus, it focuses on one aspect of it, the folk belief that the gallbladder determines one's degree of courage. Since the gallbladder is metaphorically conceptualized as "container" of courage, for instance, its "size" or "capacity" then becomes a crucial factor. Yet in the theory of internal organs, no mention is made about any direct relation between the physical size of the gallbladder and the amount of courage one has. The theory only claims that the relative "strength" of the vital energy of *qi* in the gallbladder, which determines the degree of the internal pressure, affects one's resistance to certain negative psychological impacts.

Apparently, the conceptual metaphors GALLBLADDER IS CONTAINER OF COURAGE and COURAGE IS QI IN GALLBLADDER are culture-specific, shaped in the folk beliefs about human internal organs of traditional Chinese medicine. It represents, to some extent, a culturally constructed and shared concept of courage, manifested in conventional metaphorical expressions in the form of proverbs, idioms, and compounds. These conceptual metaphors, as many others, may not be activated in individuals' minds as they actually produce and comprehend any particular one of the conventional metaphorical expressions cited in this study. Nevertheless, they are part of the "cultural sediment" in the collective memory, and deeply entrenched in the conceptual systems, of the people who speak the language, and are partly constitutive of their understanding of gallbladder and courage. That is why the Chinese couple in the story told earlier was more upset than grateful after the doctor cured the husband's gallbladder disease by removing his gallbladder without their actual knowledge in advance: A man without gallbladder, and courage by metaphorical extension, is supposed to be indecisive and irresolute, and that is certainly an undesirable quality of a man. Cognitive linguistics holds that conceptual metaphors are mostly unconscious, operating beneath the level of cognitive awareness as part of mechanisms of thought (Lakoff & Johnson, 1999). However, they are always there functioning, and are accessed on occasions where need arises, for instance, to guide one's reasoning and use of novel metaphorical expressions.

In sum, I would like to make the following hypothesis under a cross-cultural perspective. Any two different cultures may have different conceptions of courage, but to a great extent their concepts of courage also overlap each other, forming a common core shared by both cultures. For each culture, the part of the concept that does not overlap the common core defines its uniqueness and specificity. In the case of Chinese culture, this unique part of concept is tinted by the conceptual metaphors GALLBLADDER IS CONTAINER OF COURAGE and COURAGE IS QI IN GALL-BLADDER, which are manifested linguistically by numerous conventional expressions discussed in the previous section. The hypothesis here is probably applicable to cross-cultural description of other concepts as well, although each case may be materialized with a particular composition.

In the past two decades, cognitive linguistics has demonstrated that conceptual metaphors influence how people talk, think, feel, and reason in everyday life (e.g., Lakoff & Johnson, 1980, 1999; Gibbs, 1994; Gibbs & Steen, 1999; Barcelona, 2000; Kövecses, 2000). Many abstract concepts are inherently structured, to varying degrees, by metaphors arising from recurring embodied experience in the physical and cultural world. More generally, "all cognition is embodied in cultural situations" (Gibbs, 1999, p. 156), and it "is what happens when the body meets the world" (Gibbs, 1999, p. 153). Although the human body or, more abstractly, the body schema, is a potentially universal source domain for metaphors structuring abstract concepts, cultural models, which may be metaphorically constructed themselves, set up specific perspectives from which certain aspects of bodily experience or certain parts of the body are viewed as especially salient and meaningful in the understanding of those abstract concepts (Gibbs, 1999; Yu, 2000, 2001,

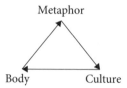

Figure 1. The "circular triangle" relationship between metaphor, body, and culture

2002, 2003). This study represents a case in which a conceptual metaphor is grounded in the body but shaped by a culture-specific metaphorical understanding of an internal organ inside the body. From a historical point of view, the internal organs, compared with the external body parts, must have been subject to greater cultural diversity in the understanding of how they work and relate to each other. In general, folk knowledge, diversified across cultural boundaries, precedes scientific knowledge and preoccupies general population's minds. Very often, folk knowledge is metaphorical. It is, therefore, important to study metaphor in the investigation of culture and cognition.

Finally, a summary of the relation between metaphor, body, and culture. It seems that the three of them form a "circular triangle" relation, as shown in Figure 1. That is, conceptual metaphors are usually derived from bodily experiences; cultural models, however, filter bodily experiences for specific target domains of conceptual metaphors; and cultural models themselves are very often structured by conceptual metaphors. As indicated by the direction of the arrows, any one element constraining the next one will affect the third one as well.

In short, without the body there would be no worldviews. However, the lenses of worldviews are "culturally colored" and "metaphorically framed." It is through such "glasses" that we cognize the world.

References

Barcelona, A. (Ed.). (2000). *Metaphor and metonymy at the crossroads: A cognitive perspective.* Berlin: Mouton de Gruyter.

Chen, Z. (1989). Zang xiang [Theory of internal organs]. In W. Jin (Ed.), *Jiating yixue quanshu* [Family medicine] (pp. 1003–1012). Shanghai: Shanghai Science and Technology Press.

Chia, M. T., & Chia, M. N. (1990). *Chi nei tsang: Internal organ chi massage.* Huntington, NY: Healing Tao Books.

Gibbs, R. (1994). *The poetics of mind: Figurative thought, language, and understanding.* New York: Cambridge University Press.

Gibbs, R. (1999). Taking metaphor out of our heads and putting it into the cultural world. In R. Gibbs & G. Steen (Eds.), *Metaphor in cognitive linguistics* (pp. 145–166). Amsterdam: John Benjamins.

Gibbs, R., & Steen, G. (Eds.). (1999). *Metaphor in cognitive linguistics*. Amsterdam: John Benjamins.

Goddard, C., & Wierzbicka, A. (Eds.). (1994). *Semantic and lexical universals: Theory and empirical findings*. Amsterdam: John Benjamins.

Hartenstein, R. (1990). Gallbladder. In *Academic American encyclopedia, Vol. 9* (p. 17). Danbury, CT: Grolier.

Kövecses, Z. (2000). *Metaphor and emotion: Language, culture, and body in human feeling*. New York: Cambridge University Press.

Lakoff, G., & Johnson, M. (1980). *Metaphors we live by*. Chicago: University of Chicago Press.

Lakoff, G., & Johnson, M. (1999). *Philosophy in the flesh: The embodied mind and its challenge to Western thought*. New York: Basic Books.

Lü, S., & Ding, S. (Eds.). (1980). *Xiandai Hanyu cidian* [Modern Chinese dictionary]. Beijing: Commercial Press.

Lü, S., & Ding, S. (Eds.). (1989). *Xiandai Hanyu cidian bubian* [Modern Chinese dictionary supplement]. Beijing: Commercial Press.

Lü, S., & Ding, S. (Eds.). (1996). *Xiandai Hanyu cidian* [Modern Chinese dictionary] (Rev. ed.). Beijing: Commercial Press.

Noback, C. (1992). Gallbladder. In *Collier's encyclopedia, Vol. 10* (pp. 548–549). New York: Macmillan Educational Co.

Quinn, N., & Holland, D. (1987). Culture and cognition. In D. Holland & N. Quinn (Eds.), *Cultural models in language and thought* (pp. 3–40). New York: Cambridge University Press.

Wang, Q., Luo, X., Li, Y., & Liu Y. (1997). *Zhongyi zangxiang xue* [Theory of internal organs in Chinese medicine]. Beijing: People's Health Press.

Wei, D. (Ed.). (1995). *Han Ying cidian* [A Chinese-English dictionary] (Rev. ed.). Beijing: Foreign Language Teaching and Research Press.

Wen, D. (Ed.). (1996). *Hanyu changyongyu cidian* [A dictionary of Chinese idioms]. Shanghai: Shanghai Dictionary Press.

White, G. (1987). Proverbs and cultural models: An American psychology of problem solving. In D. Holland & N. Quinn (Eds.), *Cultural models in language and thought* (pp. 151–172). New York: Cambridge University Press.

Wierzbicka, A. (1992). *Semantics, culture and cognition: Universal human concepts in culture-specific configurations*. New York: Oxford University Press.

Wierzbicka, A. (1999). *Emotions across languages and cultures: Diversity and universals*. Cambridge, UK: Cambridge University Press.

Wiseman, N., & Feng, Y. (1998). *A practical dictionary of Chinese medicine* (2nd ed.). Brookline, MA: Paradigm Publications.

Wu, G. (Ed.). (1993). *Han Ying da cidian* [Chinese-English dictionary], *Vols. 1 & 2*. Shanghai: Shanghai Jiao Tong University Press.

Yu, N. (1995). Metaphorical expressions of anger and happiness in English and Chinese. *Metaphor and Symbolic Activity, 10*, 59–92.

Yu, N. (1998). *The Contemporary theory of metaphor: A perspective from Chinese*. Amsterdam: John Benjamins.

Yu, N. (2000). Figurative uses of *finger* and *palm* in Chinese and English. *Metaphor and Symbol, 15*, 159–175.

Yu, N. (2001). What does our face mean to us? *Pragmatics and Cognition, 9,* 1–36.

Yu, N. (2002). Body and emotion: Body parts in Chinese expression of emotion. In N. Enfield & A. Wierzbicka (Eds.), the special issue on "The body in description of emotion: Cross-linguistic studies." *Pragmatics and Cognition, 10,* 341–367.

Yu, N. (2003). The bodily dimension of meaning in Chinese: What do we do and mean with "hands"? In E. Casad & G. Palmer (Eds.), *Cognitive linguistics and non-Indo-European languages* (pp. 337–362). Berlin: Mouton de Gruyter.

Zhang, Y. H., & Rose, K. (2001). *A brief history of qi.* Brookline, MA: Paradigm Publications.

CHAPTER 11

Heart and cognition in ancient Chinese philosophy

Following the theory of conceptual metaphor in cognitive linguistics, this paper studies a predominant conceptual metaphor in the understanding of the heart in ancient Chinese philosophy: THE HEART IS THE RULER OF THE BODY. The most important conceptual mapping of this metaphor consists in the perceived correspondence between the mental power of the heart and the political power of the ruler. The Chinese heart is traditionally regarded as the organ of thinking and reasoning, as well as feeling. As such, it is conceptualized as the central faculty of cognition. This cultural conceptualization differs fundamentally from the Western dualism that upholds the reason-emotion dichotomy, as represented by the binary contrast between mind and heart in particular, and mind and body in general. It is found that the HEART AS RULER metaphor has a mirror image, namely THE RULER IS THE HEART OF THE COUNTRY. The ruler as the "heart" of the country leads his nation while guided by his own heart as the "ruler" of his body. It is argued that the two-way metaphorical mappings are based on the overarching beliefs of ancient Chinese philosophy in the unity and correspondence between the microcosm of man and the macrocosm of universe. It is suggested that the conceptualization of the heart in ancient Chinese philosophy, which is basically metaphorical in nature, is still spread widely across Chinese culture today.

1. Introduction

From a cognitive linguistics perspective, this paper attempts to study a predominant conceptual metaphor in ancient Chinese philosophy: THE HEART IS THE RULER OF THE BODY. The target-domain concept here is an important one because the heart organ is regarded as the central faculty of cognition and the site of both affective and cognitive activities in ancient Chinese philosophy (Yu, 2007, 2008). It is conceptualized as the thinking and behavior guiding organ, as well as the organ that stores feelings and emotions. This "cultural conceptualization" (Sharifian, 2003) differs fundamentally from the dualism that dominated Western philosophical tradition for the last three hundred years. The Western dualism upholds the reason-emotion dichotomy: thoughts and ideas come from the mind, largely disembodied, whereas desires and emotions reside in the heart as part of the body (see, e.g., Damasio, 1994; Lakoff & Johnson, 1999). On the other hand, this "distinction between 'heart' and 'mind' in the Western sense does not exist in Chinese philosophy" (Lin, 2001, p. 202; see, also, Hansen, 1992). In other words, the "heart" and the "mind," in their Western senses, are conceptualized in ancient Chinese philosophy as being one, the 心 *xin* 'heart,' which houses thoughts and feelings, ideas and emotions. The Chinese heart is the core of affective and cognitive structure, conceived of as having the capacity for logical reasoning, rational understanding, moral will, intuitive imagination, and aesthetic feeling, unifying human will, desire, emotion, intuition, reason and thought. It is "a holistic-comprehensive structure in which all human faculties are unified and integrated" (Lin, 2001, p. 202). Little wonder that, by "taking into consideration both the affective and cognitive concerns that the concept of *xin* encompasses" (Chan, 2002b, p. 42), English literature on Chinese philosophy often glosses the Chinese term *xin* 'heart' as "heart-mind" or "heart/mind", as well as either "heart" or "mind" (e.g., Chan, 2002a; Hansen, 1992; Lee, 2005; Shun, 1997; Slingerland, 2003; Yearley, 1990).

The Chinese heart, as the locus of the "mind," is itself understood metaphorically. Among various metaphors found in the conceptualization of the heart in ancient philosophical texts, THE HEART IS THE RULER OF THE BODY is a predominant one. In what follows, after presenting the cognitive linguistic view of metaphor, I first survey the linguistic evidence from ancient Chinese philosophical texts that manifests and instantiates the conceptual metaphor THE HEART IS THE RULER OF THE BODY. I will then analyze the mappings of this conceptual metaphor and the cultural context of its formation.

2. Cognitive linguistic theory of conceptual metaphor

During the past two decades, cognitive sciences have seriously challenged the fundamental assumption that most of our thinking about the world is literal, directly corresponding to the external reality (see, e.g., Lakoff & Johnson, 1999). The results of cognitive linguistic studies show that human minds are embodied in the cultural world, and thinking and reasoning are largely metaphorical and imaginative, shaped by embodied and encultured experiences (e.g., Gibbs, 1994, 1999; Johnson, 1987; Lakoff, 1987; Lakoff & Johnson, 1980, 1999; Yu, 1995, 1998, 2003a, 2003b, 2004). It is argued that "all cognition is embodied in cultural situations" (Gibbs, 1999, p.156). As the *embodiment premise* states (Gibbs, 2003, p. 2):

> People's subjective, felt experience of their bodies in action provides part of the fundamental grounding for language and thought. Cognition is what occurs when the body engages the physical, cultural world and the environment. Human

language and thought emerge from recurring patterns of embodied activity that constrain ongoing intelligent behavior. We must not assume cognition to be purely internal, symbolic, computational, and disembodied, but seek out the gross and detailed ways that language and thought are inextricably shaped by embodied action.

According to the conceptual metaphor theory of cognitive linguistics, metaphor is not merely a figure of speech, but also a figure of thought, giving rise to understanding one conceptual domain in terms of another conceptual domain. Conceptual metaphors in people's conceptual systems influence a great deal how they think, understand, reason, and imagine in everyday life, and "many concepts, especially abstract ones, are structured and mentally represented in terms of metaphor" (Gibbs, 1999, p. 145).[1]

The cognitive linguistic theory of conceptual metaphor is a complex one, where metaphor is seen as involving a variety of components interacting with each other. These components include: (a) source and target domains, (b) experiential basis, (c) linguistic expressions, (d) mappings, entailments, and blends, and (e) cultural models (Kövecses, 2003, 2004, 2005). Specifically, conceptual metaphors, expressed in the formula A IS B, consist of a source and a target domain. The source is generally a more physical domain whereas the target a more abstract one. That is why conceptual metaphors are usually unidirectional, projecting elements from one domain to the other, but not the other way around. The choice of particular pairings of source and target domains is motivated by an experiential basis. Such pairings of sources and targets, primarily conceptual in nature, give rise to metaphorical linguistic expressions. There are basic conceptual correspondences or mappings between the source and target domains. Very often, however, additional mappings, called entailments or inferences, are also mapped from the source to the target domain. The connection of a source with a target domain can result in blends, that is, conceptual integrations that are new with respect to both the source and the target. Conceptual metaphors converge on, and often structure too, cultural models, which are, simultaneously cultural and cognitive, culturally specific mental representations of aspects of the world (Kövecses, 2003, 2004, 2005).

It is worth stressing that the experiential basis of conceptual metaphors is both bodily and cultural. Cognitive linguistics maintains that our minds are embodied in such a way that our conceptual systems draw largely upon the peculiarities of our bodies and the specifics of our physical and cultural environments (e.g., Gibbs,

---

1.　For cognitive linguistic studies of metaphor, metonymy, and figurative language in general, see, e.g., Barcelona (2000), Dirven & Pörings (2002), Gibbs (1994), Gibbs & Steen (1999), Johnson (1987), Kövecses (2000, 2002, 2005), Lakoff (1987, 1993), Lakoff & Johnson (1980, 1999), Lakoff & Turner (1989), Palmer (1996), Panther & Radden (1999), Sweetser (1990), and Turner (1991).

1994, 1999, 2003; Johnson, 1987, 1999; Lakoff, 1987, 1993; Lakoff & Johnson, 1980, 1999). In *Metaphors We Live By* (1980), Lakoff & Johnson argue that conceptual metaphors, which structure our conceptual systems to a significant extent, are not arbitrary, but grounded in our physical and cultural experience. While they emphasize the importance of "direct physical experience," or embodied experience, as part of the experiential basis of conceptual metaphors, they also point out that such experience (Lakoff & Johnson, 1980, p. 57):

> is never merely a matter of having a body of a certain sort; rather, *every* experience takes place within a vast background of cultural presuppositions. … Cultural assumptions, values, and attitudes are not a conceptual overlay which we may or may not place upon experience as we choose. It would be more correct to say that all experience is cultural through and through, that we experience our "world" in such a way that our culture is already present in the very experience itself.

When commenting on the relationship between physical (or bodily) and cultural experience as experiential bases for orientational or spatialization metaphors, Lakoff & Johnson (1980, p. 19) state:

> – Our physical and cultural experience provides many possible bases for spatialization metaphors. Which ones are chosen, and which ones are major, may vary from culture to culture.
> – It is hard to distinguish the physical from the cultural basis of a metaphor, since the choice of one physical basis from among many possible ones has to do with cultural coherence.

In arguing for the significance of cultural basis for metaphors, Gibbs (1999, p. 155) points out that "embodied metaphor arises not from within the body alone, and is then represented in the minds of individuals, but emerges from bodily interactions that are to a large extent defined by the cultural world," and the "bodily experiences that form the source domains for conceptual metaphors are themselves complex social and cultural constructions." Cultural models, "in shaping what people believe, how they act, and how they speak about the world and their own experiences," set up specific perspectives from which "aspects of embodied experience are viewed as particularly salient and meaningful in people's lives" (p. 154). That is, "social and cultural constructions of experience fundamentally shape embodied metaphor" (p. 155).

In summary, according to cognitive linguistic view, conceptual metaphors emerge from the interaction between body and culture: They are grounded in bodily experience, but shaped by cultural understanding.

In order to answer the question why some metaphors are widespread or even universal and others are culture-specific, the newer version of conceptual metaphor theory puts forth a "decomposition" account based on the distinction between two kinds of conceptual metaphors: *primary metaphors* and *complex metaphors* (see Grady, 1997a, 1997b, 1998; Grady et al., 1996; see, also, Kövecses, 2002, 2005; Lakoff & Johnson, 1999, 2003). In short, as argued, primary metaphors are derived directly from experiential correlations, or "conflations in everyday experience" that "pair subjective experience and judgment with sensorimotor experience" (Lakoff & Johnson, 1999, p. 49), whereas complex metaphors are combinations of primary metaphors and cultural beliefs and assumptions and, for that reason, tend to be culture-specific. As they suggest (Lakoff & Johnson, 2003, p. 257):

> Inevitably, many primary metaphors are universal because everybody has basically the same kinds of bodies and brains and lives in basically the same kinds of environments, so far as the features relevant to metaphor are concerned.
>
> The complex metaphors that are composed of primary metaphors and that make use of culturally based conceptual frames are another matter. Because they make use of cultural information, they may differ significantly from culture to culture.

For instance, Lakoff & Johnson (1999, pp. 60–61) suggest that the complex metaphor A PURPOSEFUL LIFE IS A JOURNEY is composed of the following cultural belief (reformulated here as two propositions) and two primary metaphors:

PEOPLE SHOULD HAVE PURPOSES IN LIFE
PEOPLE SHOULD ACT SO AS TO ACHIEVE THEIR PURPOSES
PURPOSES ARE DESTINATIONS
ACTIONS ARE MOTIONS

Whereas the two primary metaphors (PURPOSES ARE DESTINATIONS and ACTIONS ARE MOTIONS), based on common bodily experience, are likely to be universal, the complex metaphor (A PURPOSEFUL LIFE IS A JOURNEY) is not or less likely to be so. This is because its validity in a particular culture depends on this culture's holding the combination of the two propositions (PEOPLE SHOULD HAVE PURPOSES IN LIFE and PEOPLE SHOULD ACT SO AS TO ACHIEVE THEIR PURPOSES) and the two primary metaphors, as listed above.

Having presented the cognitive linguistic view of metaphor, I will proceed, in the following two sections, with a survey of the linguistic manifestation of the conceptual metaphor THE HEART IS THE RULER OF THE BODY in the texts of ancient Chinese philosophy, followed by an analysis in light of conceptual metaphor theory.

3.   Linguistic instantiation of the HEART AS RULER metaphor

In his recent monograph, Lee (2005, pp. 10–11) summarizes the significance of the concept of *xin* 'heart; mind' and how it distinguishes Chinese philosophy from Western philosophy as the following:

> The notion of *xin* is one of the most important concepts in the history of Chinese philosophy. Generally speaking, while much of Western philosophy can be said to hinge on the notion of a rational agent who can investigate the world and human-kind objectively, Chinese philosophy requires an agent who is able to carry out the self-transformative cultivation through which a human being can attain ideal personhood. Considering the overriding concern for self-cultivation in the major philosophical trends of Confucianism, Buddhism, and Daoism, it is not difficult to see the importance of the notion of *xin* for these religious and philosophical schools.

As Lee points out, for instance, "Although there is a great difference between Buddhism and neo-Confucianism in their understanding of the world and of the nature of successful living, they both give great weight to the notion of *xin* as an agent for self-cultivation" (p. 11).

There is no doubt that the Chinese concept of HEART lies at the core of Chinese thought. This is because the heart is traditionally believed to be the central faculty of cognition. Its importance in cognition can be seen in the following famous quotations from two representative figures of the "Learning of the Mind-and-Heart" (心学 *xinxue*), or literally the "Learning of Heart", a school of Neo-Confucianism lasting from the Song (960–1279) to the Ming (1368–1644) dynasty:[2]

(1)   a.   宇宙便是吾心，吾心即是宇宙。《陆九渊集・年谱》(Ji 1995, vol. 50, p. 2407)
       The universe is my heart, and my heart is the universe. *Collected Writings of Lu Jiuyuan: Chronological Life.*

   b.   人者，天地万物之心也；心者，天地万物之主也。《王阳明集・答季明德》(Ji 1995, vol. 54, p. 83)
       Man is the heart of Heaven and Earth and the ten thousand things; the heart is the master of Heaven and Earth and the ten thousand things. *Collected Writings of Wang Yangming: Reply to Ji Mingde.*

Apparently, the heart is the most important thing in the whole universe, to these two philosophers. In (1a), from Lu Jiuyuan (1139–1193), the heart is equated to the universe, thus highlighting the unity and correspondence between the

---

2.   The English translations, here and hereafter, are my own unless otherwise noted. For my translations, however, I referred to various versions of existing translations if such sources are available to me, and made modifications to varying degrees.

macrocosm and microcosm. In (1b), from Wang Shouren (1472–1529), also known as Wang Yangming, "Heaven and Earth and the ten thousand things," namely "Heaven and Earth and all things in between," is the literal translation of the Chinese phrase that can be interpreted as meaning, again, the "universe." The saying places man at the center of the universe and sees his heart as the core of that center. Regardless of what philosophical outlook these sayings manifest, the fact that the heart is regarded as the central faculty of cognition is obvious. The universe will make no sense to us without our heart functioning as the organ for thinking, knowing, and understanding.

In ancient Chinese philosophy, the heart is regarded as the organ of thinking and reasoning, as well as feeling. For instance, Mencius (c. 327–289 B.C.), the famous Confucian philosopher, distinguished the heart, the thinking organ, from the organs of ears and eyes, which do not think and which tend to be deceived by external things when in contact with them. He asserted that the function of the heart organ is to think, and a good sense of understanding and reasoning can only be obtained through thinking.

(2) 耳目之官不思，而蔽于物。物交物，则引之而已矣。心之官则思，思则得之，不思则不得也。《孟子 • 告子上》(Zheng et al., 1993, p. 418)

Such organs as ears and eyes do not think, so they tend to be deceived by external things. When in contact with external things, they are often led astray. The organ of heart is for thinking. If you think, you will get it; if you do not, then you will not get it. *Mencius: Gaozi*, Part I.

It is common sense that we should examine what we hear and scrutinize what we see. That is accomplished through our heart, as is further illustrated by the conversation, recorded in the *Kongcongzi*, between Confucius and his grandson, Zisi:

(3) 子思问于夫子曰：" 物有形类，事有真伪，必审之，奚由？" 子曰："由乎心，心之精神是谓圣，推数究理，不以物疑。"《孔丛子·记问》(Ji, 1995, vol. 49, p. 390)

Zisi asked Confucius, "Objects vary in shape and kind, and things may be true or false. Therefore, one has to examine them. But through what?" Confucius said, "Through the heart. The spirits of the heart are regarded as holy. Through inferring and reasoning, the heart studies the whys and wherefores of things, and will not be confused by them." *Kongcongzi: Recorded Questions.*

In Confucius' words, *jingshen* 'spirits' refers to the mental aspect of a person, which is close to the concept of "mind" as known in English, in contrast to the physical form, the body. The locus of that "mental half" is the heart. Through thinking and reasoning the heart can gain insights into things that are otherwise confusing. Thinking results in knowing and understanding. That is why Confucius referred to the mental aspect of a person as "holy."

It is because the heart is seen as the central faculty of cognition with superior mental power that it is conceptualized metaphorically as the ruler of the country. The body is under its command and control, as much as the whole country is under the command and control of its monarch or emperor. Thus, Xunzi (c. 313–238 B.C.), another famous Confucian philosopher, employed the HEART AS RULER metaphor when he argued that the heart is the ruler of the body and the master of the "spiritual light":

(4) 心者，形之君也，而神明之主也，出令而无所受令。《荀子·解蔽篇》(Ji, 1995, vol. 49, p. 362)
The heart is the ruler of the body and master of the spiritual light, who issues commands but does not receive commands. *Xunzi: Dispelling Blindness.*

In this sentence, the "spiritual light" again refers to the totality of mental aspects of a person. It is this "spiritual light" that enables people to "see." It is interesting to note that this MENTAL POWER IS LIGHT metaphor is but an entailment of the conceptual metaphor THINKING, KNOWING, or UNDERSTANDING IS SEEING. Similar metaphors are also seen in the following quote from the *Wenzi*, a classic Daoist text:

(5) 心者形之主也，神者心之宝也《文子·九守》(Ji, 1995, vol. 49, p. 82)
The heart is the master of the body, and the spirits are the treasures of the heart. *Wenzi: Nine Things to Be Preserved.*

That is, the heart, though part of the body, is unique in that it is also the master of the body. It is in this unique position because it "contains" all the "spirits-treasures." As the ruler, the heart has authority over other parts of the body. This kind of sovereign-subject relationship is further brought out by the following passage from the *Xunzi*:

(6) 耳目鼻口形能，各有接而不相能也，夫是之谓天官。心居中虚以治五官，夫是之谓天君。《荀子·天论篇》(Ji, 1995, vol. 49, p. 352)
Ears, eyes, nose, mouth, and body each have the capacity to provide sense contact, but their capacities are not interchangeable. They are called the heavenly officials/faculties. The heart dwells in the central cavity and governs the five officials/faculties, and hence it is called the heavenly ruler. *Xunzi: On Heaven.*

The heart takes the central position of the body both in the physical and metaphorical senses. It regulates and coordinates the functions of other parts of the body, and is in charge of all the sensorimotor experiences of a person. It is worth mentioning here that the Chinese word 官 *guan* means not only "organ" or "faculty", such as sense organs or faculties of eyes and ears, but also "official", "officer", or "office" that officials or officers hold. Therefore, *tianguan* 'heavenly organs/faculties' and *wuguan* 'five organs/faculties' in the above passage could be translated respectively as "heavenly officials" and "five officials", which would fit better into the HEART AS RULER metaphor.

As the ruler of the body, the heart is also conceptualized as the locus of a person's moral sense and moral character. When it is affected by selfish desires, it will lose its command of, and control over, other parts of the body. Thus,

(7)　夫心有欲者，物过而目不见，声至而耳不闻也。《管子·心术上》
　　　(Ji, 1995, vol. 49, p. 784)
　　　When the heart has desires, things passing across the eyes will not be seen, and sounds coming to the ears will not be heard. *Guanzi: Art of the Heart*, Part I.

The use of the HEART AS RULER metaphor in the *Guanzi* makes the point clearer:

(8)　心之在体，君之位也；九窍之有职，官之分也。心处其道，九窍循理；嗜欲充益，目不见色，耳不闻声。故曰：上离其道，下失其事。《管子·心术上》(Ji, 1995, vol. 49, p. 783)
　　　The heart holds the position of the monarch in the body. The functions of the nine apertures are the separate responsibilities of officials. If the heart follows the Way, the nine apertures will perform their functions properly. Should sensual desires occupy it to the full, the eyes will not see colors, nor will the ears hear sounds. Therefore, it is said, if the supreme one above departs from the Way, those below will lose their functions accordingly. *Guanzi: Art of the Heart*, Part I.

Here the "nine apertures" refers to the seven orifices of the sense organs in the head plus two in the lower body. As "officials," they each carry out their responsibilities under the command of the heart-monarch, which is supposed to follow the Way or Dao. When the monarch above, namely the heart, is filled with desires and, for that matter, departs the Way, the officials below, that is, the organs such as eyes and ears, will not be able to perform their functions properly.

The heart, as the ruler of the body, bears great moral responsibility as it makes moral judgments and issues authoritative commands. Look at the following passage from the *Shizi*.

(9)　然则令于天下而行，禁焉而止者，心也。故曰：心者，身之君也。天子以天下受令于心，心不当则天下祸；诸侯以国受令于心，心不

当则国亡；匹夫以身受令于心，心不当则身为戮矣。《尸子·贵言》(Ji, 1995, vol. 49, p. 1085)

Therefore, the heart is what issues, under Heaven, orders to be implemented or bans to be imposed. That is, as is said, the heart is the ruler of the body. The Son of Heaven receives commands from the heart on behalf of all under Heaven. If the heart is not right, then all under Heaven will suffer from disasters. Princes or dukes receive commands from the heart on behalf of their state. If the heart is not right, then their state will perish. Ordinary people receive commands from the heart on behalf of themselves (lit. bodies). If the heart is not right, then they themselves (lit. their bodies) will be punished. *Shizi: Valuable Words.*

As can be seen, all the people, up from the monarch, or the "Son of Heaven," down to commoners, rely on the heart, the command-issuing organ, for moral direction. There will be dire consequences if their hearts make wrong judgments. In short, ancient Chinese philosophy held that the heart is the core of cognitive system, governing one's mental activities and moral judgments and controlling one's perceptual and emotional experiences.

It is worth noting that, while the heart is understood as the ruler of a nation, the reverse is also true. That is, the ruler of a state or country is also understood as the heart of a person. In the *Wenzi*, for instance, a passage quotes Laozi as saying the following:

(10) 主者，国之心也。心治则百节皆安，心扰则百节皆乱。《文子·上德》(Ji, 1995, vol. 49, p. 91)

The sovereign is the heart of the state. When the heart is under control, all parts of the body are in order; when the heart is disturbed, all parts will be in disorder. *Wenzi: Upper Virtue.*

It is very important that the ruler be self-disciplined and under self-control. If not, the whole nation will be in trouble and disorder. The maintenance of the "upper virtue" (上德 *shangde*) should lead to the desirable governing situation in which "one starts singing and ten thousand will follow suit, like the body following the heart (*Heguanzi: Principle of Heaven*)" (一人唱而万人和，如体之从心《鹖冠子·天则》Ji, 1995, vol. 49, p. 118). Given below is another example of the RULER AS HEART metaphor from the *Guanzi*:

(11) 君之在国都也，若心之在身体也。道德定于上，则百姓化于下。戒心形于内，则容貌动于外矣。《管子·君臣下》(Ji, 1995, vol. 49, p. 777)

The monarch in the capital of the country is like the heart in the body. The ethics (lit. the Way and Virtue) are established above, and the masses will follow below. The heart of vigilance takes shape inside, and the looks will change outside. *Guanzi: Monarch and Subjects,* Part II.

It is crucial for the ruler to provide good moral leadership, for the masses will follow wherever their leader is going. If the ruler is on guard against immorality, the nation as a whole will display a difference. A good ruler should govern on morality. He should respect and trust his officials, who are to carry out his governance.

4. An analysis of the HEART AS RULER metaphor

As I have shown in the previous section, the conceived authoritative mental role assigned to the heart in ancient Chinese philosophy prompted a very popular conceptual metaphor of heart in terms of social structure and hierarchy:

THE HEART IS THE RULER OF THE BODY.

This metaphor emphasizes the perceived correspondences between the physiological system of the body and the social system of the country: The hart to a person is the same as the emperor, monarch, or sovereign to a country. It needs to be pointed out that this conceptual metaphor is a complex one that presumes the combination of the following more fundamental cultural understandings, both propositional and metaphorical:

THE HEART IS THE LOCUS OF THE MIND (a proposition)
A PERSON IS A SOCIETY (a metaphor)

Here the first is a proposition reflecting a cultural belief or assumption whereas the second is a metaphor, which in turn is combined from the following more primary metaphors:

PHYSIOLOGICAL SYSTEM IS SOCIAL SYSTEM
PHYSIOLOGICAL STRUCTURE IS SOCIAL STRUCTURE
PHYSIOLOGICAL FUNCTION/OPERATION IS SOCIAL FUNCTION/OPERATION

As we can see, the propositional component THE HEART IS THE LOCUS OF THE MIND, which reflects a cultural belief or assumption, makes the complex metaphor THE HEART IS THE RULER OF THE BODY quite culture-specific. Thus, this conceptual metaphor reflects the culturally-constructed and culturally-bound view of the mind-body relationship in ancient Chinese philosophy: While the mind controls the body, it is also (located in) a part of the body rather than being separated from it. So, it is indeed an "embodied" view of mind, in sharp contrast to, say, the Cartesian dualism in Western philosophical tradition, where the mind is "disembodied," seen as being severed from the body, with mental substance utterly different from physical substance (Damasio, 1994; Lakoff & Johnson, 1999). It is interesting to note that recent cognitive science advocates the slogan "to put the body back into the mind" (see, e.g., Johnson, 1987).[3]

To further analyze the conceptual metaphor under discussion, we can list the following mappings and entailments across its source and target domains:

THE HEART IS THE RULER OF THE BODY

Country	→	Body
Ruler (monarch, sovereign, emperor)	→	Heart
Central government/court	→	Central physiological system
Political power	→	Mental power
Administrative activities, processes, and states	→	Mental activities, processes, and states
Governmental officials	→	Bodily organs
Governmental functions, operations	→	Physiological functions, operations
Political situations of the country	→	Physiological conditions of the body

The key aspect of this metaphor is the mental power that distinguishes humans from lower animals. Humans are superior to the rest species of animals in that they are uniquely equipped with the mental power, the "mind," that enables them to think, know, understand, and reason. In ancient Chinese philosophy, and traditional Chinese medicine as well, this "mind" is accepted as being located in the heart.

Figure 1 is a schematic illustration of the metaphorical mappings from the ruler to the heart. In this figure, the horizontal lines indicate the direction of metaphorical mappings: the ruler is mapped onto the heart, the country onto the body, and political power onto mental power. The vertical lines represent the relationship of "possession," that is, the ruler possesses political power and the heart possesses mental power. As shown in the illustration, it is apparent that the conceptual metaphor is based on the center-peripheral (or figure-ground) image-schema. The heart is the center of the body just as the ruler is the center of the country. In addition, the political power of the ruler grounds his status as being the center of the country whereas the mental power of the heart grounds its status as being the center of the body. Thus, the key is the mapping from the political power of the

---

3.   Just to mention in passing that a theme session at the 9th International Cognitive Linguistics Conference (July 2005, Seoul, Korea), of which the present author is one of the three co-organizers, bears the theme topic "Looking for the Mind inside the Body."

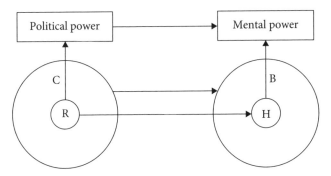

R = Ruler; C = Country; H = Heart; B = Body

Figure 1. Schematic illustration of the metaphorical mappings from Ruler to Heart

ruler to the mental power of the heart. It is this metaphorical projection that triggers off the mappings and entailments from the country to the body, from the ruler to the heart, and so forth.

It is interesting to note that the mental power of the heart itself is also understood metaphorically: MENTAL POWER IS (SPIRITUAL) LIGHT. This mental power is "spiritual" in that, although formless and intangible, it operates behind and above what is physical and obvious, as much as how supernatural spirits, deities, and divinities operate mysteriously in nature. This power is "light" in that it "enlightens" in a metaphorical sense derived from physical and bodily experience. Whereas light enables seeing, mental power enables thinking, knowing, understanding, and reasoning. Thus, the metaphorical mapping is but an entailment of the primary conceptual metaphor THINKING, KNOWING, or UNDERSTANDING IS SEEING, based on some conceptual associates in contrast between "darkness" and "light": obscurity, blockage, restriction, ignorance, and stupidity vs. enlightenment, penetration, expansion, knowledge, and wisdom. The reason why the heart is said to be the ruler of the body is that it is conceptualized as possessing the "supreme power" of the "spiritual light," with which it commands and governs other parts of the body.

As I have shown in the previous section, there exist in ancient Chinese philosophy two-way mappings between the heart and the ruler. That is, THE HEART IS THE RULER OF THE BODY, and THE RULER IS THE HEART OF THE COUNTRY. According to the theory of conceptual metaphor (e.g., Lakoff, 1993; Kövecses, 2002), however, metaphors mapping across conceptual domains are asymmetric, that is, such mappings are usually unidirectional, from one domain (the source) to another domain (the target), but not vice versa. The case under consideration is a culture-specific exception to that general principle.[4] Let us see how and why. As suggested earlier, the bi-directional mappings, namely THE HEART IS THE RULER OF THE BODY and THE RULER IS THE HEART OF THE COUNTRY, can be seen as instances of more general metaphors: A BODY/PERSON IS A SOCIETY/NATION and A SOCIETY/NATION IS A BODY/PERSON. Empirical studies of conceptual metaphors have shown that the human body, with its bodily experience, is a potentially universal source domain, whereas society is a common target domain (see, e.g., Kövecses, 2002, pp. 16–25). This means A SOCIETY/NATION IS A BODY/PERSON should be more widespread across cultures than A BODY/PERSON IS A SOCIETY/NATION. But why is the latter such an important metaphor in ancient Chinese philosophy (e.g, the heart as the monarch, and sense organs as officials)? This question brings us back to my earlier argument that this metaphor is the key to understanding the mind-body relationship in ancient Chinese philosophy: The heart as the locus of the mind is the "ruler" of the body. The embodied nature of this metaphor also lies in the biological fact that our heart organ, which pumps blood throughout our body to maintain its functioning, is the center of our physiological system.

It is interesting to note that in traditional Chinese medicine, which has borrowed a great deal from ancient Chinese philosophy, the metaphor A BODY/PERSON IS A SOCIETY/NATION is more extensively realized (Yu, 2008). In the *Yellow Emperor's Internal Classic* (《黄帝内经》), the earliest existent medical text in China, we find the following system of metaphors that manifest the BODY/PERSON AS SOCIETY/NATION metaphor:

(12) a. 心者，君主之官也，神明出焉。
The heart holds the office of monarch, whence the spiritual light emanates.

b. 肝者，将军之官，谋虑出焉。
The liver holds the office of general, whence strategies emanate.

c. 胆者，中正之官，决断出焉。
The gallbladder holds the office of justice, from which decision emanates.

d. 脾胃者，仓廪之官，五味出焉。
The spleen and stomach hold the office of the granaries, whence the five flavors emanate.

---

4. Other instances may include THE COMPUTER IS A BRAIN and THE BRAIN IS A COMPUTER, and ANGER IS A STORM and A STORM IS ANGER. See Kövecses (2002, pp. 24-25) for the discussion and the conclusion that conceptual metaphors are mostly unidirectional.

e. 肺者，相傅之官，治节出焉。
   The lung holds the office of assistant, whence management and regulation emanate.

f. 肾者，作强之官，伎巧出焉。
   The kidney holds the office of labor, whence agility emanates.

As already mentioned earlier, the "spiritual light" in (12a) is a metaphor for mental power. That is, the heart is the locus of the "mind," from which mental power comes. The reason why traditional Chinese medicine resorts to the systematic mappings in (12), from society or nation to the human body, is not so difficult to imagine. The purpose of medicine, especially traditional Chinese medicine, is to understand the functions of, and relations between, various parts of the body, and the relationship between mind and body, so as to cure any diseases, whereas the purpose of metaphor is to help people understand one thing in terms of another of a different kind. In traditional Chinese medicine, influenced by ancient Chinese philosophy, the mind is always "embodied," and it seeks to maintain the unity and harmony between mind and body.

As I have tried to explain above, the existence of the bi-directional mappings between HEART and RULER, and BODY and SOCIETY results from, and at the same time constitutes, the culture-specific understanding of the "mind," and its relationship with the body, of ancient Chinese philosophy in its historical context. In fact, these bi-directional mappings, as twin metaphors, converge on and constitute a more fundamental cultural model in Chinese cosmology, as is illustrated schematically in Figure 2. In this figure, there are two-way mappings between the ruler and the heart, the country and the body, and political power and mental power. These bi-directional mappings are possible and natural in the context of ancient Chinese philosophy and politics because the two sides, or domains, of the mappings are conceived of as parallel correspondences labeled as macrocosm and microcosm of each other. Thus, it is believed that one can try to understand the microcosm by comparing it with the macrocosm and vice versa. This belief is built on the foundation of the claim for the unity and correspondence between man and universe (天人合一 *tian ren he yi*; 天人相类 *tian ren xiang lei*), as an expression of the major tendency of humanism in ancient Chinese philosophy.

To illustrate the unity and correspondence between universe and man as perceived by the ancient Chinese, one example from the *Wenzi* should suffice:

(13) 老子曰：人受天地变化而生，…… 头圆法天，足方象地。天有四时、五行、九曜、三百六十日，人有四支、五藏、九窍、三百六十节；大有风雨寒暑，人有取与喜怒，胆为云，肺为气，脾为风，肾

为雨，肝为雷。人与天地相类，而心为之主；耳目者日月也，血气
者风雨也。《文子·九守》(Ji, 1995, vol. 49, p. 82)

Laozi said: Man is born in the change of heaven and earth, … his head is
round modeled on heaven; his feet are square just like earth. Nature has
four seasons, five elements, nine stars, and three hundred and sixty days;
man has four limbs, five zang organs, nine apertures, and three hundred
and sixty parts. Nature has winds and rains, and is affected by cold and
heat; man has likes and dislikes, and is affected by joy and anger.[5] The gall
bladder is the cloud, the lung the air, the spleen the wind, the kidney the
rain, and the liver the thunder. Man is similar to heaven and earth in kind,
and the heart is his master. His ears and eyes are the sun and moon, and
his blood and qi are rain and wind. *Wenzi: Nine Things to Be Preserved.*

As in this passage of a quotation from Laozi (c. 581–500 B.C.), the founder of Daoism, various correspondences, real or imaginary, are perceived between man and
nature. According to the Daoist conceptions, the heaven, which is yang, is round
whereas the earth, which is yin, is square.[6] Therefore, man has round head and
square feet (two rectangles), modeled on heaven and earth. The parallels then extend: nature has four seasons, and man has four limbs; nature has five elements or
phases (wood, fire, earth, metal, and water), and man has five zang organs (liver,
heart, spleen, lung, and kidney) that match the five elements accordingly; nature
has nine stars (九曜 *jiuyao* refers to the Big Dipper, consisting of seven stars, plus
two auxiliary ones [HYDCD, 2000, p. 114]), and man has nine apertures or orifices (seven in the head, plus two in the lower body); nature has 360 days for a year
(in the Chinese lunar calendar), and man has 360 parts for his body. Man's temperament varies and emotion changes, as much as nature's climate and weather. It
is noteworthy that the heart, which is one of the five zang organs, is singled out
separately as the "master" of the whole body.

---

5.   Two things in translation here need some explanation. First, the word 大 *da* in the original,
which means "big," "large," "great", "grand" etc. in modern Chinese, once has the sense of 天 *tian*
'sky, heaven, nature, universe' in old Chinese (HYDCD, 2000, p. 737). Second, in the original, 取
与 *quyu* means "accept and give" (HYDCD, 2000, p. 493). In general, people have things to gain
or lose. I translate the word into "likes and dislikes" in the specific context.

6.   The ancient Chinese conceptualized the earth as being square, under the vault of heaven
that is round.

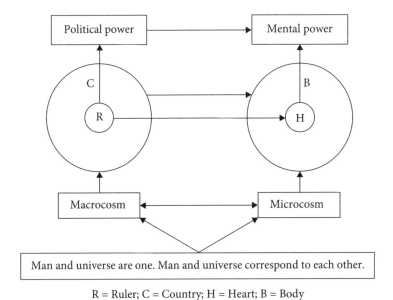

R = Ruler; C = Country; H = Heart; B = Body

Figure 2. Schematic illustration of the bi-directional mappings between Ruler and Heart

There are other "correspondences" observed between nature and man. For example, it is said that man has 12 major joints while nature has 12 months, man opens and closes his eyes and nature has days and nights, and so forth (see Cai, 2000, pp. 209–210). As Dong Zhongshu (179–104 B.C.), the representative Confucian in the Han dynasty (206 B.C.–A.D. 220), argued, "the essence of man is rooted in Heaven, which is also his great grandfather (人之为人，本于天，天亦人之曾祖父也《春秋繁露・为人者天》)" (from Cai, 2000, p. 209). Since "man is a replica of the universe (人副天数 *ren fu tianshu*)," they are fundamentally of the same kind (天人相类 *tian ren xiang lei*), and interact with each other (天人感应 *tian ren ganying*). Heaven created the ten thousand things (万物 *wanwu*) to raise man, whom it created to realize its own will. Heaven and man have the same physiological essence and moral nature. While Heaven's climate and weather changes affect man, man's behavior and mental activities evoke responses from Heaven, too (see Cai, 2000, pp. 206–212).

5. Conclusion

In conclusion, I have analyzed the conceptual metaphor THE HEART IS THE RULER OF THE BODY in ancient Chinese philosophy in light of cognitive linguistic view of metaphor. It is argued that the key mapping of this metaphor is based on the conceptual correspondences between the political power of the ruler and the perceived "mental power" of the heart. It is also found that the metaphor THE HEART IS THE RULER OF THE BODY has a mirror-image version: THE RULER IS THE HEART OF THE COUNTRY. The ruler (i.e. monarch, sovereign, king, or emperor) of the country or state is traditionally called the "Son of Heaven," and regarded as representing the will of heaven. While guided by his heart, the "ruler" of his body, he is also the "heart" of the country, leading the "body" of his nation. It is argued that the foundation of these mirror-image metaphors is the dominant worldview in ancient Chinese philosophy that holds that man and universe are a unified one and correspond to each other as microcosm and macrocosm of each other. These beliefs stand in sharp contrast with the Western philosophical beliefs in various binary contrasts such as those between mind and body, mind and heart, and subject and object.

It is worth mentioning that, although the HEART AS RULER metaphor is no longer richly manifested in modern Chinese discourse, it is still a predominant metaphor in the discourse of Chinese medicine today, which holds that the heart "rules" the body via the "spiritual light" it governs, that is, "The heart governs the spiritual light" (心主神明 *xin zhu shenming*). Nowadays, the relationship between the heart and the brain is still under debate in Chinese medicine (see Wang et al., 1997, pp. 180–182, 929–931). One view sees the brain as the house for mental activities, but the heart ultimately controls it through blood supply. A different view argues that the notion of "heart" in traditional Chinese medicine cannot be equated to the heart organ. Instead, it is a combination of heart and brain. These views can be summarized by the following statement:

(14) 神明之体藏于脑，神明之用发于心也。(Wang et al., 1997, p. 182)
The substance of the spiritual light is stored in the brain, whereas the application of the spiritual light arises from the heart.

That is, the brain stores the physiological substance of the "spiritual light", but the heart deploys and utilizes it. In short, Chinese medicine today still holds that the heart takes the dominant and central position in the body: it is still the "emperor" or "monarch" of the body.

Moreover, the heart as an internal organ is still regarded as the locus of the "mind" in the cultural conceptualization at large. Despite the fact that scientific findings have assigned the functions of thinking and feeling to the brain, the Chinese cultural model seems to retain, to a great degree, the cultural conceptualization of the heart as the seat of both feelings and thoughts, and this cultural conceptualization is richly manifested in the Chinese language today (Yu, 2003b, 2007, 2008). Sometimes, of course, there is only an indirect link between figurative expressions and culture, as the former could be merely reliquaries of the latter (Deignan, 2003). The metaphor THE HEART IS THE RULER OF THE BODY, however, seems to have survived the history of over two thousand years, and still lies in the foundation of the Chinese cultural model for the concept of the heart.

References

Barcelona, A. (Ed.). (2000). *Metaphor and metonymy at the crossroads: A cognitive perspective.* Berlin: Mouton de Gruyter.

Cai, D. (2000). *Zhongguo zhexue liuxingqu* [The pop music of Chinese philosophy]. Jinan, Shandong, China: Shandong People's Press.

Chan, A. K. L. (Ed.). (2002a). *Mencius: Contexts and interpretations.* Honolulu, HI: University of Hawaii Press.

Chan, A. K. L. (2002b). A matter of taste *qi* (vital energy) and the tending of the heart (*xin*) in Mencius 2A2. In A. K. L. Chan (Ed.), *Mencius: Contexts and Interpretations* (pp. 42–71). Honolulu, HI: University of Hawaii Press.

Damasio, A. R. (1994). *Descartes' error: Emotion, reason, and the human brain.* New York: Grosset/Putnam.

Deignan, A. (2003). Metaphorical expressions and culture: An indirect link. *Metaphor and Symbol, 18,* 255–271.

Dirven, R., & Pörings, R. (Eds). (2002). *Metaphor and metonymy in comparison and constrast.* Berlin: Mouton de Gruyter.

Gibbs, R. (1994). *The poetics of mind: Figurative thought, language, and understanding.* New York and Cambridge: Cambridge University Press.

Gibbs, R. (1999). Taking metaphor out of our heads and putting it into the cultural world. In R. Gibbs & G. Steen (Eds.), *Metaphor in cognitive linguistics* (pp. 145–166). Amsterdam: John Benjamins.

Gibbs, R. (2003). Embodied experience and linguistic meaning. *Brain and Language, 84,* 1–15.

Gibbs, R., & Steen, G. (Eds.). (1999). *Metaphor in cognitive linguistics.* Amsterdam: John Benjamins.

Grady, J. (1997a). Foundation of meaning: Primary metaphors and primary scenes. Ph.D. dissertation, University of California, Berkeley.

Grady, J. (1997b). THEORIES ARE BUILDINGS revisited. *Cognitive Linguistics, 8,* 267–290.

Grady, J. (1998). The conduit metaphor revisited: A reassessment of metaphors for communication. In J. Koenig (Ed.), *Discourse and cognition: Bridging the gap* (pp. 205–218). Stanford, CA: CSLI Publications.

Grady, J., Taub, S., & Morgan, P. (1996). Primitive and compound metaphors. In A. Goldberg (Ed.), *Conceptual structure, discourse and language* (pp. 177–187). Stanford, CA: CSLI Publicatoins.

Hansen, C. (1992). *A Daoist theory of Chinese thought: A philosophical interpretation.* Oxford: Oxford University Press.

HYDCD. (2000). *Hanyu da cidian* [Grand dictionary of Chinese language]. Shanghai: Grand Dictionary of Chinese Language Press.

Ji, X. (Gen. Ed.). (1995). *Chuanshi cangshu* 《传世藏书》 [Collection of classics over centuries], Vols. 49, 50, 54. Hainan, China: Hainan International Journalism Publishing Center.

Johnson, M. (1987). *The body in the mind: The bodily basis of meaning, imagination, and reason.* Chicago: University of Chicago Press.

Johnson, M. (1999). Embodied reason. In G. Weiss & H. Haber (Eds.), *Perspectives on embodiment: The intersections of nature and culture* (pp. 81–102). New York: Routledge.

Kövecses, Z. (2000). *Metaphor and emotion: Language, culture, and body in Human Feeling.* Cambridge and New York: Cambridge University Press.

Kövecses, Z. (2002). *Metaphor: A practical introduction.* Oxford: Oxford University Press.

Kövecses, Z. (2003). Language, figurative thought, and cross-cultural comparison. In F. Boers (Ed.), special issue on "Cross-Cultural Differences in Conceptual Metaphor: Applied Linguistics Perspective," *Metaphor and Symbol, 18,* 311–320.

Kövecses, Z. (2004). Introduction: Cultural variation in metaphor. In Z. Kövecses (Ed.), special issue on "Cultural Variation in Metaphor," *European Journal of English Studies, 8,* 263–274.

Kövecses, Z. (2005). *Metaphor in culture: Universality and variation.* Cambridge: Cambridge University Press.

Lakoff, G. (1987). *Women, fire, and dangerous things: What categories reveal about the mind.* Chicago: University of Chicago Press.

Lakoff, G. (1993). The contemporary theory of metaphor. In A. Ortony (Ed.), *Metaphor and thought* (2nd ed.) (pp. 202–251). Cambridge: Cambridge University Press.

Lakoff, G., & Johnson, M. (1980). *Metaphors we live by.* Chicago: University of Chicago Press.

Lakoff, G., & Johnson, M. (1999). *Philosophy in the flesh: The embodied mind and its challenge to Western thought.* New York: Basic Books.

Lakoff, G., & Johnson, M. (2003). Afterword, 2003. In G. Lakoff & M. Johnson, *Metaphors we live by* (pp. 243–276). Chicago: University of Chicago Press.

Lakoff, G., & Turner, M. (1989). *More than cool reason: A field guide to poetic metaphor.* Chicago: University of Chicago Press.

Lee, J. (2005). *Xunzi and early Chinese naturalism.* Albany, NY: State University of New York Press.

Lin, M. (2001). *Certainty as a social metaphor: The social and historical production of certainty in China and the West.* Westport, CT: Greenwood.

Palmer, G. (1996). *Toward a theory of cultural linguistics.* Austin, TX: University of Texas Press.

Panther, K., & Radden, G. (Eds.). (1999). *Metonymy in language and thought.* Amsterdam: John Benjamins.

Sharifian, F. (2003). On cultural conceptualizations. *Journal of Cognition and Culture, 3,* 187–207.

Shun, K. (1997). *Mencius and early Chinese thought.* Stanford, CA: Stanford University Press.

Slingerland, E. (2003). *Effortless action: Wu-wei as conceptual metaphor and spiritual ideal in early China.* Oxford: Oxford University Press.

Sweetser, E. E. (1990). *From etymology to pragmatics: Metaphorical and cultural aspects of semantic structure.* Cambridge: Cambridge University Press.

Turner, M. (1991). *Reading minds: The Study of English in the age of cognitive science.* Princeton, NJ: Princeton University Press.

Wang, Q., Luo, X., Li, Y., & Liu, Y. (1997). *Zhongyi zangxiang xue* [Theory of internal organs in Chinese medicine]. Beijing: People's Health Press.

Yearley, L. H. (1990). *Mencius and aquinas: Theories of virtue and conceptions of courage.* Albany, NY: State University of New York Press.

Yu, N. (1995). Metaphorical expressions of anger and happiness in English and Chinese. *Metaphor and Symbolic Activity, 10,* 59–92.

Yu, N. (1998). *The contemporary theory of metaphor: A perspective from Chinese*. Amsterdam: John Benjamins.

Yu, N. (2003a). Metaphor, body, and culture: The Chinese understanding of *gallbladder* and *courage*. *Metaphor and Symbol, 18*, 13–31.

Yu, N. (2003b). Chinese metaphors of thinking. In G. B. Palmer, C. Goddard, & P. Lee (Eds.), special issue on "Talking about Thinking across Languages." *Cognitive Linguistics, 14*, 141–165.

Yu, N. (2004). The eyes for sight and mind. *Journal of Pragmatics, 36*, 663–686.

Yu, N. (2007). The Chinese conceptualization of the heart and its cultural context: Implications for second language learning. In F. Sharifian & G. B. Palmer (Eds.), *Applied Cultural Linguistics: Implications for Second Language Learning and Intercultural Communication* (pp. 65–85). Amsterdam: John Benjamins.

Yu, N. (2008). The Chinese heart as the central faculty of cognition. In F. Sharifian, R. Dirven, N. Yu, & S. Niemeier (Eds.), *Culture, body, and language: Conceptualizations of internal body organs across cultures and languages* (pp. 131–168). Berlin: Mouton de Gruyter.

Zheng, X., Zhao, Z., Zhang, W., & Zhou, D. (1993). *Mengzi* [Mencius: A Chinese-English bilingual edition]. Trans. into modern Chinese by X. Zheng, and into English by Z. Zhao, W. Zhang, & D. Zhou. Shandong, China: Shandong Friendship Press.

CHAPTER 12

The Chinese conceptualization of the heart and its cultural context

Implications for second language learning

From the perspective of cultural linguistics, this study investigates (a) the Chinese conceptualization of the heart, based on a linguistic analysis, and (b) the cultural context for this conceptualization, based on a survey of ancient Chinese philosophy and traditional Chinese medicine. As found, the heart-mind dichotomy traditionally held by Western cultures does not exist in traditional Chinese culture, which regards the heart as the thinking and behavior guiding organ, as well as the organ that stores feelings and emotions. It then discusses the importance of studying cultural conceptualization, including conceptual metaphor, behind linguistic expression in the context of second language learning and teaching. Such study should facilitate the acquisition of conceptual fluency and metaphorical competence of the L2 learner.

1. Introduction

Cultural linguistics, with a broad interest in language and culture, maintains that language is a cultural form, and that conceptualizations underlying language and language use are largely formed or informed by cultural systems. It studies language in its social and cultural context, paying special attention to cultural schemas and cultural models that shape language evolution and govern language use (Palmer 1996, Sharifian 2002, 2003). Incorporating the major concerns of cultural linguistics, cognitive linguistics can gain a more balanced view of culture and body that should benefit its systematic study of language as a window into human cognition that is both embodied and enculturated.

Conceptualizations are distributed across the minds in a cultural group, representing cognition at the cultural level (Sharifian 2003). This paper studies the Chinese conceptualization of the heart, which represents a fundamental difference between Chinese and Western cultures. Western cultures maintain a binary contrast between the heart and the mind. The mind is the place for thoughts and ideas whereas the heart is the seat of emotions and feelings.[1] However, this distinction between the heart and the mind does not exist in traditional Chinese culture. The general conception of the heart in Chinese culture is reflected in the senses attached to the word *xin* (心) 'heart' in the Chinese language. Given in (1) is the translation (my own) of the first two senses listed under *xin* 'heart' in one of the most popular Chinese dictionaries (Lü and Ding 1996: 1397).

(1)   a.   the organ inside the body of human beings and other higher animals that gives impetus to the circulation of blood. The heart of a human being is in the center, a little to the left side, of the thoracic cavity, with the shape of a circular cone and the size of one's own fist. Inside the heart there are four cavities, of which the upper two are called atriums and the lower two called ventricles. The diastoles and systoles of the atriums and ventricles circulate blood to all parts of the body. The heart is also called "the heart organ".

   b.   usually also refers to the organ for thinking, and to thoughts, emotions, etc.

Obviously, (1a) is more of a scientific definition of the "physical heart" while (1b) represents more of a cultural conception of the "mental heart". According to a popular Chinese-English dictionary (Wei 1995), the word *xin* is given these two English senses supposed to be equivalent to (1a) and (1b): (a) "the heart"; and (b) "heart; mind". That is, the Chinese word *xin* 'heart' also includes what is described as "mind" in English.

The present study first investigates (a) the Chinese conceptualization of the heart, based on an analysis of linguistic evidence, and (b) the cultural context in which the Chinese conceptualization of the heart was born, based on a survey of ancient Chinese philosophy and traditional Chinese medicine. The emphasis is placed on the fact that the Chinese heart is conceptualized as the combination of "heart" and "mind" as they are understood in English. Finally, it discusses the importance of cultural conceptualization, including conceptual metaphor, in second language learning and teaching.

---

1.   This binary contrast was not so clear, however, in the Old and Middle English periods. According to the *Shorter Oxford English Dictionary on Historical Principles* (2002, 5th ed.), for instance, the English *heart* was regarded in those periods as the seat of both feeling and thought, where one's purpose, inclination, desire, courage, spirit, soul, disposition, temperament, etc. reside. It is very interesting that the heart conceptualized and characterized as such is very alike to the Chinese *xin* 'heart'. See, also, Wierzbicka (1992: Ch. 1) for discussions of such English concepts as *soul, mind,* and *heart,* as well as similar concepts in other languages.

2. Heart in the Chinese language

In the Chinese language, the word *xin* that primarily denotes the heart organ refers to it as the seat of thought and feeling, and by metonymy CONTAINER FOR CONTAINED it also refers to one's thoughts and feelings.

This section focuses on the conceptualization of the Chinese heart based on an analysis of linguistic evidence. As will be shown, the heart, while related to all emotional and mental states and processes, is often conceptualized as a container or a location, namely, the image-schemas of either three-dimensional or two-dimensional containment. For instance, Chinese has the following compound words referring to "heart", or more exactly "heart-mind", and related concepts:

(2) a. 心房   *xin-fang* (heart-house/room) 'heart; interior of heart'
   b. 心间   *xin-jian* (heart-room/inside) 'in the heart; at heart; in the mind'
   c. 心窝   *xin-wo* (heart-nest) 'heart; deep down in one's heart'
   d. 心田   *xin-tian* (heart-field) 'heart; intention'
   e. 心地   *xin-di* (heart-land) 'heart; mind; character; moral nature'

In (2a) and (2b) the heart is a "house" or "room", which is a special kind of container, a dwelling place for humans. In (2c) the heart is a "nest", the dwelling place for birds, for instance. As the following sentential examples show, the heart is indeed the "dwelling place" for thoughts and feelings. These and all the following sentential examples contain, in their word-by-word glosses, a few abbreviations: CL=classifier, DUR=duration, MOD=modifier, PER=perfective, and PRT=particle.

(3) a. 怡悦荡心房。
   Yiyue dang   ***xin-fang.***
   joy   wave (in) heart-house/room
   'Joy rippled in the heart.'
   b. 进城几年了，乡亲们的嘱托他一直记在心间。
   Jin   cheng ji   nian le, xiangqin-men   de
   enter city   several years PER fellow-villagers MOD
   *zhutuo ta yizhi   ji   zai **xin-jian.***
   advice he always remember in heart-room/inside
   'Having lived in the city for several years, he always bears in mind (lit. in the heart room or inside his heart) the fellow villagers' advice.'

c. 他第一次把掏心窝的话都和她说了。

*Ta diyi-ci   ba tao   **xin-wo**   de   hua   dou*
he first-time PRT scoop heart-nest MOD words all
he ta   shuo-le.
to her say-PER
'For the first time he told her all his innermost thoughts and feelings (lit. he said to her all the words scooped out of his heart-nest).'

Example (3a) evokes the image of the emotion of joy, conceptualized as a liquid, "rocking" gently inside the heart-house. While this example has to do with the emotion of happiness, the Chinese "heart" is actually linked to various emotions and is the most recurrent of all body parts in conventionalized emotion expressions (see Yu 2002: 358–359). This linguistic phenomenon, as will be shown in the next section, reflects the claim in Chinese philosophy and medicine that the heart, as master of the *zang-fu* organs, governs the "spiritual light" (i.e., thoughts and emotions). Example (3b) has to do with memory. When the advice is remembered, it is actually stored inside the "heart-room". In (3c), the words said are all "scooped out of the heart-nest": they express the "innermost thoughts and feelings".

As shown in the above examples, the heart is conceptualized as a "house" or "room", and this "house" or "room" actually has a "door" with a "threshold", which is the entrance of the innermost of the self.

(4) a. 心扉   *xin-fei* (heart-door leaf) 'the door of one's heart'
    b. 心坎   *xin-kan* (heart-threshold) 'the bottom of one's heart'

Houses and rooms have doors for people to get in and out. Our hearts also have doors for things to get in and out. When we want to accept certain things, we open the door of our heart to let them in. When we want to keep certain things out we lock our heart's door to prevent them from entering. By the same token, we can open or shut the door of our heart when we want to let the contents of our heart out or keep them in.

(5) a. 我愿意敞开自己的心扉，向她倾诉一切。

*Wo yuanyi chang-kai   ziji de   **xin-fei,**   xiang ta*
I   willing widely-open self MOD heart-door to   her
qing-su   yiqie.
pour-tell all
'I'm willing to open the door of my heart widely, and pour out everything (inside) to her.'

b. 字字句句都说到我心坎上。

*Zi-zi   ju-ju   dou shuo dao   wo **xin-kan***
each-word each-sentence all said reach my heart-threshold
shang.
on
'Each word struck a chord in my heart (lit. Each word said reached the threshold of my heart).'

In (5a) the speaker is willing and eager to "pour out" his thoughts and feelings that are stored inside his heart to someone he loves or trusts. To do that, he of course has to "open the door of his heart" first. When the door of the heart is widely open, one's innermost thoughts and feelings stored inside are free to come out. That is, the speaker is ready for a "heart-to-heart" talk. Example (5b) poses the image of reception, as opposed to that of production in (5a). This time the words someone has said are so appealing that they have found their way to the entrance of the listener's heart, its "threshold". The words that have struck the "threshold" of one's heart have "touched" the innermost of one's self. Interestingly, in Chinese, a common way of describing those people who are ignoring what others say, by choice or not, is to say that words have entered one of their ears and come out of the other one. And those who choose to ignore other people's words are said to have taken others' words as "wind past their ears" (*er-bian feng* 耳边风). In both of these cases, other people's words have never reached their heart.

As in (2d) and (2e) above, the heart is conceptualized as a two-dimensional location, either as "a plot of field" or "a stretch of land". The "heart-field", is apparently a SOIL metaphor that often appears in combination with, for instance, the PLANT and WATER metaphors, which together fall in the source domain of agriculture, as the examples in (6) illustrate.

(6) a. 我把环保种子播撒在他的心田里。

Wo ba huan-bao   zhongzi bosa   zai tade
I   PRT environment-protection seeds   sowed at   his
xin-tian   *li.*
heart-field in
'I sowed the environment-protection seeds in his heart (lit. heart-field).'

b. 有时她那短暂的微笑，真会令我的心田开出温暖的花朵呢！
   Youshi   ta   na   duanzan de   weixiao, zhen hui
   sometimes she that transient MOD smile   really would
   *ling   wode **xin-tian**   kai-chu   wennuan de   huaduo ne!*
   make my   heart-field bloom-with warm   MOD flowers PRT
   'Sometimes that transient smile of hers would really make my heart
   (lit. heart-field) bloom with warm flowers!'

c. 她那无助的感觉一波又一波地涌进我的心田。
   Ta   na   wu-zhu de   ganjue yi bo   you   yi bo
   she that no-help MOD feeling one wave again one wave
   *de   yong jin   wode **xin-tian**.*
   MOD surge into my   heart-field
   'That hopeless feeling of hers surged wave after wave into my heart (lit.
   heart-field).'

In (6a), ideas or thoughts are "seeds", and to communicate ideas or thoughts to
other people, or to educate them, is to "sow the seeds" into their "heart-field". The
seeds sowed into the field will grow, blossom, and bear fruits, and those fruits are
the "fruits" of earlier education. Thus, (6a) involves the following metaphorical
mappings and entailments:

Source		*Target*
Sower	→	Educator
Seeds	→	Ideas/thoughts
Sowing	→	Communicating
Field	→	Heart of the educated
Expected harvest	→	Expected result

At this point, the "harvest" is still expected as its realization will depend on many
other factors: the quality of the soil in the field, the climatic circumstances, contin-
ued cultivation, and so forth. Buddhism maintains that the heart stores the seeds
of good and evil that would grow under suitable circumstances, just like a field in
which both crops and weeds would grow. It is said that the Buddha taught the
disciples that the heart is a piece of land where you will get fruits in return for
whatever seeds you have sowed.

As in (6b), the heart is the seat of feelings or emotions. Happy and warm feelings are "flowers" grown out of the "heart-field". In Chinese, the idiom *xin-hua
nu-fang* 心花怒放 (heart-flowers wildly-blossom) is a common metaphorical expression for the emotion of happiness (see, also, Yu 1995). In this case, the cause
for the instant bloom of the "flowers", i.e. the "transient smile of hers", is the much-
needed "nourishment" (say, sunshine, water, fertilizer) for the plants.

Example (6c) describes the state of empathy, i.e., the sharing of one's feeling by another. Here, one person's feeling of helplessness is the "water" that "surges" into the "heart-field" of another person. It shows that true understanding and sympathy are established upon the connection of the two hearts through which feelings and thoughts in one person's heart can "flow" into that of another. This example involves the following metaphorical mappings and entailments:

Source		Target
Field	→	Heart
Water	→	Feeling
Way of water moving	→	Way of feeling experienced
Force of water	→	Strength of feeling
Water flowing from one field into another	→	Empathy

The metaphor here is structured by multiple image schemas, such as CONTAINERS, LINK, FORCE, and SOURCE-PATH-GOAL.

Here are some examples of the "heart-land" metaphor.

(7) a. "静"是心地最佳的风光。
   "Jing"   *shi* **xin-di**   *zui-jia de*
   "stillness/quiescence" is   heart-land('s) the-best MOD
   fengguang.
   scenery/landscape
   '"Quiescence" is the best scenery of the heart-land.'

   b. 现在最需要的是清净你的心地。
   Xianzai zui xuyao de shi qingjing nide **xin-di.**
   now   most needed MOD is cleanse your heart-land
   'Now what is needed most is to cleanse your heart (lit. heart-land).'

   c. 我以为只要自己心地清白，就可以避免肇害于人。
   Wo yiwei zhiyao ziji **xin-di** *qing-bai,*
   I   thought as.long.as self heart-land clear-white
   jiu keyi bimian zhao-hai yu ren.
   then can avoid do-harm to other-people
   'I thought as long as I maintained a clear and clean heart (lit. my heart-land remains clear and pure), I could avoid doing harm to others.'

The sentences in (7) exemplify (2e). As in (7a), a frame of mind (a peaceful and quiet mind) is the "landscape" or "scenery" of that "heart-land". This example reminds us of the traditional philosophical view that the heart should remain "still" or "quiescent" so that it can reflect the external reality accurately like still water or a mirror. The metaphor here contains the following mappings:

Source		Target
Land	→	Heart
Landscape	→	Mental state
Physical quiescence	→	Mental peace

Both (7b) and (7c) reflect the traditional view in ancient Chinese philosophy that the heart is the locus of morality and moral character. To be moral and ethical means "to have a pure and clean heart". They involve the following metaphorical mappings and entailments:

Source		Target
Land	→	Heart
Heart	→	Locus of morality and moral character
Being moral	→	Heart-land being clean and white
Being immoral	→	Heart-land being dirty and black
To become moral	→	To cleanse the heart-land

As shown by the above examples, the Chinese heart is locus for various mental states and activities. This observation is reinforced by the following group of compounds containing *xin* 'heart':

(8) a. 心思 *xin-si* (heart-think/thought) 'thought; idea; thinking; state of mind; mood'

    b. 心念 *xin-nian* (heart-think/idea) 'thought; idea; intention; thinking; state of mind; mood'

    c. 心愿 *xin-yuan* (heart-hope/wish/desire) 'cherished desire; aspiration; wish; dream'

    d. 心期 *xin-ji* (heart-expect) 'expectation; hope; wish; aspiration; intention; purpose; mood'

    e. 心得 *xin-de* (heart-obtain) 'what one has learned from work, study, etc.'

In (8a) and (8b), as we can see, when people think, their heart thinks, and thoughts, ideas, mood etc. are associated with the heart. People also hope, wish, desire, and expect with their heart (8c, d); desire, aspiration, hope, wish, expectation, and dream etc. come from the heart. Whatever one learns is also obtained by one's heart (8e). Given in (9) are some sentential examples:

(9)　a.　我猜不透他的心思。
　　　　Wo cai-bu-tou　　　　*tade **xin-si**.*
　　　　I　guess-not-penetrate　his　heart-thought
　　　　'I can't read his mind (lit. his heart-thought) / I can't figure out what's on his mind (lit. what's his heart-thought).'

　　b.　他的话说出了大家的心念。
　　　　*Tade hua　shuo chu le　dajia-de **xin-nian**.*
　　　　his　words　say　out PER everyone's heart-thought
　　　　'His words expressed (lit. brought out) everyone's thought.'

　　c.　这就了却了我的一桩心愿。
　　　　*Zhe jiu　liaoque-le wode yi-zhuang **xin-yuan**.*
　　　　this then　fulfill-PER my　one-CL　heart-wish
　　　　'This serves to fulfill a cherished desire (lit. a heart-wish/desire) of mine.'

　　d.　这符合人民的心愿。
　　　　*Zhe fuhe　　　renmin-de **xin-yuan**.*
　　　　this accord-with people's　heart-wish
　　　　'This accords with the aspirations (lit. heart-wishes) of the people.'

　　e.　我想谈谈学习这篇课文的心得。
　　　　Wo xiang tantan　　xuexi zhe-pian kewen de
　　　　I　want talk-about study this-CL　text　MOD
　　　　***xin-de**.*
　　　　heart-obtain
　　　　'I want to talk about what I have gained (lit. what my heart has obtained) from studying this text.'

As in (9a), "reading people's mind" is trying to figure out the thought in their heart. People may have a common thought that they each keep in their heart. The right articulation of that thought verbally will bring that thought out of their heart (9b). People all have desires and aspirations that they want to fulfill or satisfy, and these mental states and activities again originate in the heart: they are what the heart wishes for (9c, d). Learning is a process of receiving knowledge by the heart-container. What one has learned from study is the knowledge obtained by and stored in the heart (9e).

The above examples, all about mental activities, reflect the important difference across cultures: namely, in English, thinking is regarded as taking place in one's mind associated with one's head or brain, whereas in Chinese it is traditionally conceptualized as taking place in one's heart. As I have observed elsewhere (Yu 2003b), however, in modern Chinese, *tounao* 头脑 'head and brain' can also mean "mind". It is where one's thoughts and ideas are stored and one's thinking takes place, as illustrated by the examples in (10) (from Yu 2003b). Nevertheless, this usage is limited to modern Chinese in a relatively small scope. On the other hand, the bulk of conventionalized expressions, including compounds, idioms, and idiomatic sayings, demonstrate that the heart, rather than the brain, is the locus for the "mind" as understood in English (Yu 2003b).

(10)   a.   我们要有冷静的头脑。
       *Women yao   you lengjing de   **tou-nao**.*
       we   should have cool   MOD head-brain
       'We should have a cool head (or, be sober-minded).'

   b.   我们应该把头脑里的错误思想清除出去。
       *Women yinggai ba **tou-nao**   li de   cuowu sixiang*
       we   should PRT head-brain in MOD wrong ideas
       qingchu chuqu.
       clear   out
       'We should rid our minds of erroneous ideas.'

   c.   僵化思想束缚着一些人的头脑。
       *Jianghua sixiang shufu zhe yixie ren-de   **tou-nao**.*
       stiffened ideas   bind   DUR some people's head-brain
       'An ossified way of thinking shackles some people's minds. (lit. Stiffened ideas are binding some people's minds.)'

In this section, it has become clear, through analysis of linguistic evidence, that the Chinese heart is the combination of "heart" and "mind" in the Western sense. It is where emotions and thoughts are stored, processed, and manipulated. In the next section, I will cite evidence from ancient Chinese philosophy and traditional Chinese medicine to show that the linguistic evidence presented and analyzed in this section is actually embedded in its cultural context. Manifested linguistically, the conceptualization of the Chinese heart is indeed a phenomenon at the cultural level of cognition.

3.   Heart in ancient Chinese philosophy and traditional Chinese medicine

Western philosophical tradition upholds the reason-emotion dichotomy, contrasting "the reasoning faculty (the mind) with the irrational, base, physical desires and passions (the heart)", and to Western thinkers beliefs and ideas come from the mind whereas the heart is the seat of desires and emotions (Hansen 1992: 22). In ancient Chinese philosophy, however, the heart is "the site of both affective and cognitive activities" (Shun 1997: 48). In other words, the "heart" and the "mind", as known in English, are conceptualized as being one, the *xin* 'heart', which houses thoughts and feelings, ideas and emotions.

Importantly, the Chinese philosophical conception of the heart differs from the Western one in that the heart is a thinking and reasoning organ. In Chinese thought, the heart distinguishes between right and wrong, between good and bad, and thus guides action, conduct, and behavior (Hansen 1992). For instance, the famous ancient Confucian philosopher, Mencius, asserted that the function of the heart organ is to think, and a good sense of understanding and reasoning can only be obtained through thinking (心之官则思，思则得之，不思则不得也。《孟子・告子上》).

Clearly, the "distinction between 'heart' and 'mind' in the Western sense does not exist in Chinese philosophy" (Lin 2001: 202). That is why the Chinese term *xin* 'heart' is often glossed as "heart-mind" or "heart/mind", as well as either "heart" or "mind", in English literature on Chinese philosophy (e.g., Chan 2002a, Hansen 1992, Shun 1997, Slingerland 2003, Yearley 1990), by "taking into consideration both the affective and cognitive concerns that the concept of *xin* encompasses" (Chan 2002b: 42). As Hansen (1992: 20) points out, "The common translation of *xin* as *heart-mind* reflects the blending of belief and desire (thought and feeling, ideas and emotions) into a single complex dispositional potential".

As "the most valuable part of the self", the heart is conceptualized metaphorically as "the ruler of the other parts" (Slingerland 2003: 229). For instance, another famous Confucian philosopher, Xunzi, employed this HEART/MIND AS RULER metaphor (see Slingerland 2003: 230–231) when he argued that the heart is the ruler of the body and the master of the spiritual light, who issues commands but does not receive commands (心者，形之君也，而神明之主也，出令而无所受令。《荀子・解蔽篇》). While the Chinese heart is "the master of spiritual light", the "spirits", which refers to the totality of the mental aspect of a person, are "treasures" stored in the heart (心者形之主也，神者心之宝也《文子・九守》). Apparently, the Chinese heart is conceptualized as the locus of the mind, and as the thinking organ, a faculty given at birth. Thus, Guanzi, a Daoist statesman and philosopher, asserted that a baby in the mother's womb will take shape in five months, and be born in ten months: "After the birth, the eyes will see, the ears will hear, and the heart will think" (五月而成，十月而生。生而目视，耳听，心虑。《管子・水地》). It is taken for granted that humans are born with the heart to think, as much as with the eyes to see and the ears to hear.

In short, ancient Chinese philosophy held that the heart is the core of cognitive structure, conceived of as having the capacity for logical reasoning, rational understanding, moral will, intuitive imagination, and aesthetic feeling, unifying human will, desire, emotion, intuition, reason and thought. It is "part of a holistic-comprehensive structure in which all human faculties are unified and integrated" (Lin 2001: 202).

Traditional Chinese medicine is a mixture of folk and scientific medicine with a history of several thousand years. In the study of human body, it borrowed extensively from ancient Chinese philosophy, for instance, its theories of *yin-yang* and five-elements, which are aimed to explain the formation and operation of the universe. This is because traditional Chinese medicine shares the views of ancient Chinese philosophy that nature and human correspond to each other and they are a unified one.

In Chinese medicine, the internal organs of the human body are divided into two major classes. The five organs of primary importance are called *zang* (脏): liver, heart, spleen, lung, and kidney. Each of them is matched with, and closely related to, an organ of secondary importance called *fu* (腑): respectively, gallbladder, small intestine, stomach, large intestine, and bladder. An extra *fu* organ is called *san jiao* 'triple heater, i.e., the three visceral cavities housing the internal organs'. According to the theory of *yin-yang*, all the *zang* organs belong to *yin*, whereas all the *fu* organs belong to *yang*. According to the theory of five elements or five phases (wood, fire, earth, metal, and water), liver and gallbladder belong to wood, heart and small intestine belong to fire, spleen and stomach belong to earth, lung and large intestine belong to metal, and kidney and bladder belong to water.

In traditional Chinese medicine, while the heart is one of the eleven internal organs, its position among them is that of a "superior authority". "The heart is the grand master of the five *zang* and six *fu*, and the house of spirits" (心者，五脏六腑之大主也，精神之所舍也。《灵枢·邪客》). So the heart, the "central command" of all internal organs, coordinates their functions, and stores spirits, which include all mental activities and emotional states. That is why it has received much attention from those interested in the study of Chinese medicine (see, e.g., Claude Larre and Elisabeth Rochat de la Vallée 1991, 1992, 1995, 1996).

Traditional Chinese medicine uses a GOVERNMENT metaphor system to define the internal organs of the human body (see, also, Wang et al. 1997, Yu 2003a). According to this metaphor system, "the heart holds the office of monarch, whence the spiritual light emanates" (心者，君主之官也，神明出焉。《素问 · 灵兰秘典论》). So, it is the "master of the body" (心者，一身之主《医学入门 · 心脏》), as much as a king or emperor is the master of a nation. Functionally speaking, "the heart governs the spiritual light" (心主神明). Here, the "spiritual light" (*shen ming* 神明), also simply called the "spirits" (*shen* 神), refers to consciousness and mental vitality of a person. That is, as "the organ of emperor", the heart controls all mental activities and psychological states: carrying out thinking, storing memory, producing emotions, commanding will, governing perception, and evolving dreams (Wang et al. 1997: 181).

It is worth mentioning that, uniquely in traditional Chinese medicine, the five *zang* organs are all related to mental functions. This is because they produce and store essential elements of the body such as blood, qi, fluid, essence, which are taken as the physical basis for mental vitality. It is believed that the operations of the five *zang* organs result in mental activities. The spirits, which include all mental activities, are classified as five different types: *shen* (神), *hun* (魂), *po* (魄), *yi* (意), and *zhi* (志).[2] It is claimed that the five different types of spirits are stored separately in the five *zang* organs, but commanded all by the heart as the "grand master" of the five *zang* and six *fu*.

Also according to traditional Chinese medicine, the five *zang* organs produce five qi, which result in five emotions: anger (*nu* 怒), joy (*xi* 喜), anxiety or over-thinking (*si* 思), sorrow (*bei* 悲), and fear (*kong* 恐). They are each classified with a *zang* organ: anger with the liver, joy with the heart, anxiety with the spleen, sorrow with the lung, and fear with the kidney. While these emotions arise from the functions of their corresponding *zang* organs, their excessiveness will hurt each of them accordingly. For instance, sudden excessive joy can hurt the heart by making the spirit inside unsteady or dispersed so that the person can hardly concentrate on anything. However, because the heart is the "governor" of all psychological states and mental activities, it reacts to other emotions as well. Of all the internal organs, in fact, the heart is the most sensitive to emotional changes. This is because emotional changes, as is believed, originate in the heart but affect other *zang* organs depending on their kinds. Thus, for example, when anger stirs in the heart, it will affect the liver; when fear shakes in the heart, it will affect the kidney. As Zhang Jingyue in the Ming Dynasty argued:

> The heart is the master of the *zang-fu*, commanding soul and mood, and directing purpose and will. Therefore, when sorrow moves in the heart, the lung will respond, when overthinking moves in the heart, the spleen will respond, when anger moves in the heart, the liver will respond, and when fear moves in the heart, the kidney will respond. That is why the five emotions are operated only by the heart. … Wounds inflicted by emotions, although they each belong to one of the five *zang*, if their causes are traced, they all come from the heart.
> (心为脏腑之主，而总统魂魄，并赅意志，故忧动于心则肺应，思动于心则脾应，怒动于心则肝应，恐动于心则肾应，此所以五志唯心所使

---

2. The five types of mental activities (*wu shen* 五神) are collectively called the "spiritual light" (*shen ming* 神明), or simply as the "spirits" (*shen* 神). There are varying ways of translating them into English. They are rendered respectively as "spirit", "ethereal soul", "corporeal/animal soul", "intention/purpose", and "will" in one way, and as "spirit", "mood", "soul", "idea/reflection", and "will" in another.

也。…… 情志之伤，虽五脏各有所属，然求其所由则无不从心而发。 – 明代张景岳《类经》 From Wang et al. 1997: 87)

Apparently, traditional Chinese medicine also conceptualizes the heart as the "master" or "ruler" of the body, and as the locus of mental activity. It actually adopted the view from ancient Chinese philosophy (see Wang et al. 1997: 181). In the Ming and Qing dynasties, however, the functions of the brain as the organ for mental activities came to be recognized. Today, the relationship between the heart and the brain is still under debate in Chinese medicine (see Wang et al. 1997: 180–182, 929–931). One view sees the brain as the house for mental activities, but the heart ultimately controls it by transporting blood to it. A different view argues that the notion of "heart" in traditional Chinese medicine cannot be equated to the heart organ. Instead, it is a combination of heart and brain.

4.   Conceptual fluency and metaphorical competence in L2 context

Language reflects an underlying conceptual system constructed in its cultural context. The underlying conceptual system, which is metaphorical to a substantial degree, arises from the interplay of body and culture (Gibbs 1994, 1999, Lakoff and Johnson 1980, 1999). For instance, in Chinese, some of the words with the connotation of importance contain the body-part term referring to the heart:

(11)   a.   中心   zhong-xin (center-heart) 'center; heart; core; hub; key'
       b.   核心   he-xin (core-heart) 'core; nucleus; kernel; key'
       c.   重心   zhong-xin (weight-heart) 'center of gravity; heart; core; focus'

These compound words are formed on a combination of conceptual metaphors. Other than sharing the IMPORTANCE IS HEART metaphor, they are each based on another metaphor: IMPORTANCE IS CENTER/CENTRALITY for (11a), IMPORTANCE IS CORE (and the core, which is the center of a fruit, is important also because it has the potential for reproduction) for (11b), and IMPORTANCE IS WEIGHT for (11c). Note that most of the translated meanings given in English for (11) should be taken metaphorically too, as in English phrases such as *a central issue* (中心问题), *the core of leadership* (领导核心), *the kernel of a story* (故事的核心), *the heart of a matter* (问题的中心或重心), *a key figure* (核心人物), etc.

It is obvious that the IMPORTANCE IS HEART metaphor, by which the body-part term has extended to express the abstract concept of importance, has a bodily, experiential basis: the heart organ is the center of vital functions of the body. Nevertheless, it is the Chinese cultural model that has, in this case, highlighted this common bodily experience and interpreted it in such a way that makes explicit the connection between the bodily organ of heart and the abstract concept of importance. Such a connection is made by choice, not by necessity. In the English phrases listed above, for instance, only *the heart of a matter* contains a parallel bodily-based metaphor, whereas *the core of leadership* and *the kernel of a story* contain fruit metaphors. Even *the heart of a matter* has an alternate: *the core of a matter.* That is why conventionalized metaphorical expressions are said to be "culturally-loaded expressions" (Littlemore 2003: 273), and figurative language can serve as one of the main means for the transmission of cultural beliefs and attitudes (Charteris-Black 2003, Littlemore 2003).

What especially interests me here is the study of cultural conceptualization, including conceptual metaphor, behind linguistic expression in the context of second language learning and teaching, which has already attracted attention of many researchers (e.g., Achard and Niemeier 2004, Boers and Littlemore 2003, Cameron and Low 1999, Johnson and Rosano 1993, Ponterotto 1994, Pütz et al. 2001a, 2001b). One's first language, together with its underlying conceptual structure, is acquired *within* one's own cultural system, but the learning of a second language involves conceptual restructuring. That is, second language acquisition takes place in the process of transforming *into* a new cultural system. The ideal situation is where the acquired conceptual structure underlying the target language fits well into the new cultural system regardless of its difference from, or similarity to, one's own. This is, however, by no means easy.

As Danesi (1993, 1995, 1999) and Danesi and Mollica (1998) have suggested, second language learners often demonstrate a lack of "conceptual fluency" despite the fact that they may have achieved "verbal fluency". Their nonnativeness is usually betrayed by the way in which they "speak" with the formal structures of the target language but "think" in terms of their native conceptual system. In other words, they typically use target language words and structures as "carriers" of their own native language concepts (Danesi 1993, 1995). This problem, as Danesi (1995: 6–7) argues, lies in students' lack of "metaphorical competence" – parallel to grammatical competence and communicative or pragmatic competence – which "is closely linked to the ways in which a culture organizes its world conceptually" (see, also, Littlemore 2001). Very often, their typical "over-literalness" reveals their inadequate access to "the metaphorical structures inherent in the target language and culture" (Danesi 1995: 4). It is claimed that "to be conceptually fluent in a language is to know, in large part, how that language 'reflects' or encodes concepts on the basis of metaphorical reasoning", which "is by and large unconscious in native speakers" (Danesi 1995: 5). The programming of discourse in metaphorical ways is a basic property of native speaker competence. The studies reported show that, due to the absence of teaching metaphorical competence, the students "learned virtually no 'new ways' of thinking conceptually after three or four years of study in a classroom" (Danesi 1995: 12). It is therefore suggested that conceptual fluency should be an objective for second language teaching, through a curriculum based on "the notion that metaphor is the organizing principle of common discourse" (Danesi 1995: 3), and aimed at reducing "conceptual interferences" from both native and target conceptual systems (Danesi 1995: 16).

In a study of the extent to which typical classroom learners can comprehend second language metaphors at various stages of learning, Danesi (1993) found that their metaphorical competence was inadequate even at the level of comprehension (see, also, DeCunha 1993). "The reason for this is not that they are incapable of learning metaphor, but most likely that they have never been exposed in formal ways to the conceptual system of the target language" (Danesi 1993: 497). In another study of "metaphorical density" in second language writing, Danesi (1993: 496–497) found that the compositions of this kind show a high degree of "literalness" and the students "tended to use conceptual metaphors that were alike in both languages" (see, also, Feng 1997). That is, student-produced discourse texts seem to follow a native-language conceptual flow that is "clothed" in target language grammar and vocabulary. Danesi (1993: 498) concludes that "if the research on metaphor is any indication of the significance of metaphor to discourse, then there is no reason to believe that it will constitute an impossible task to translate the findings on metaphor into pedagogically usable insights and principles". Such a task starts with a proposed research question: To what extent do the conceptual domains of the native and target cultures overlap and contrast? In the contrastive analysis so involved, interlanguage studies attempt to find out what kinds of conceptual interferences come from the student's native conceptual system (interconceptual interference) and how much conceptual interference is generated by the target language itself (intraconceptual interference) (Danesi and Mollica 1998). In short, the central objective of "conceptual fluency theory", according to Danesi (1999: 16), "is to ensure that learners have access to the conceptual structures inherent in the target language and culture in a systematic, sequential, and integrated fashion with other areas of language learning". This theory underscores cultural variation and it views culture as being "built on metaphor, since conceptual metaphors coalesce into a system of meaning that holds together the entire network of associated meanings in the culture" (Danesi and Mollica 1998: 3).

In a *Metaphor and Symbol* special issue on "Cross-cultural Differences in Conceptual Metaphor: Applied Linguistics Perspectives" (Boers and Littlemore 2003), Boers (2003) points out that the general advantage of applying the notion of conceptual metaphor in the context of second language acquisition is that it offers motivation and coherence to whole clusters of figurative expressions that may otherwise appear to be arbitrary and unrelated. Without adapting the notion of conceptual metaphor, teachers can at best point out cross-linguistic differences at the level of individual expressions. Based on the studies reported in the articles (Low 2003, Deignan 2003, Littlemore 2003, Charteris-Black 2003) that appear in the same special issue, Boers (2003: 232) outlines three types of cross-cultural variation in metaphor usage:

> (a) differences with regard to the particular source-target mappings that have become conventional in the given cultures; (b) differences with regard to value-judgments associated with the source or target domains of shared mappings; and (c) differences with regard to the degree of pervasiveness of metaphor as such, as compared with other (rhetorical) figures.

Systematic comparison of conceptual metaphors along these lines may lead to a better understanding of cross-cultural differences and similarities, historically and/or currently, in conventional patterns of thought and conceptualization.[3] Boers (2003: 236), therefore, concludes:

> If language is an integral part of culture, and if culture is expressed (albeit indirectly) through metaphor, then it follows that cross-cultural communication would benefit substantially from a heightened metaphor awareness on the part of educators and language learners.

For instance, Boers (2000, 2004) demonstrates that conceptual metaphor awareness can help L2 learners expand and retain vocabulary. Csábi (2004) shows that the meaning structure of polysemous words is motivated by conceptual metaphor and conceptual metonymy and how making this motivation explicit to L2 learners can enhance their retention of the more peripheral senses of a polysemous lexical item. In a similar vein, Kövecses (2001) argues that such motivation always facilitates the learning of idioms in a L2 teaching context. Barcelona (2001) argues that the contrastive study of conceptual metaphors across languages should help L2 textbook writers and teachers in their selection and arrangements of the teaching materials.

---

3.   For the suggestion that metaphorical expressions are to some extent a cultural reliquary rather than a synchronic reflection of culture, see Deignan (2003). Although, as Deignan (2003: 270) points out quite correctly, many conventionalized figurative expressions may no longer be directly experienced by individual speakers, they allude to knowledge that is still shared as part of the "cultural repository"; thus, historical and systematic studies of figurative language are beneficial to the foreign language learner. For examples of comparative studies, see Barcelona (2001), Boers (2004), Charteris-Black (2002, 2003), Csábi (2004), Feng (1997), Johnson and Rosano (1993), Kövecses (2001), Yu (1995, 2000, 2003b, 2004). For a discussion of the issues involved in such studies, see Kövecses (2003).

As has been shown in the preceding two sections, the Chinese cultural model for the concept of heart includes some culturally constructed metaphors:

I. As a Physical Entity
   i. THE HEART IS A CONTAINER
   ii THE HEART IS A LOCATION
II. As a Part of the Body
   i. THE HEART IS THE RULER OF THE BODY
   ii. THE HEART IS THE MASTER OF THE INTERNAL ORGANS
III. As the Locus of Affective and Cognitive Activities
   i. THE HEART IS THE HOUSE OF ALL EMOTIONAL AND MENTAL PROCESSES
   ii. THE HEART IS THE HEADQUARTERS OF ALL EMOTIONAL AND MENTAL ACTIVITIES

These conceptual metaphors characterize the cultural schematization and categorization in the Chinese conceptualization of the heart. They are therefore partly constitutive of the Chinese cultural model for the concept of "heart". The identification of conceptual metaphors in specific languages, however, is just the first step of a series leading to their application to L2 teaching and learning. The next step comprises cross-linguistic and cross-cultural studies of thorough comparative and contrastive analysis (see, e.g., Sharifian et al., 2008). Only conceptual differences and similarities are carefully mapped out across languages and cultures can findings of such studies benefit L2 teaching and learning.

The cultural conceptualization of the heart, as discussed in this paper, is automatically distributed across the minds of native speakers of Chinese. In a second language acquisition context, however, conceptualizations that underlie and govern linguistic use are not automatically given, but have to be acquired in a process of negotiation and renegotiation. If the cultural conceptualization of the heart, including the conceptual metaphors listed above, is delineated clearly to L2 learners of Chinese, it would facilitate their learning and enable them to avoid misunderstanding in intercultural communication.

5. Conclusion

In this paper, I have first cited linguistic evidence showing that the semantic difference between the Chinese word *xin* and the English word *heart* actually reflects an important difference in the conceptualization of the heart between traditional Chinese and Western cultures. The heart-mind dichotomy traditionally held by Western cultures, in which the heart is taken as the seat of emotion and feeling whereas the mind is the place for thought and reason, does not exist in traditional

Chinese culture. In traditional Chinese culture, the heart is the locus of both affective and cognitive activities. Therefore, it is roughly equivalent to "heart" and "mind" conceptualized in English. As the linguistic analysis of compound words shows, the Chinese language evokes various images for the imagined mental functions of the heart: "heart-house", "heart-room", "heart-door", "heart-threshold", "heart-nest", "heart-field", and "heart-land". It also evokes various images that explicitly ascribe various mental functions to the heart: thus, the heart thinks, hopes, wishes, desires, memorizes, expects, learns, etc. Such linguistic imagery, which requires imagination for its interpretation, is a central concern of cultural linguistics. "Cultural linguistics is primarily concerned not with how people talk about some objective reality, but with how they talk about the world that they themselves imagine" (Palmer 1996: 36).

In this paper I have also studied the cultural context of the conceptualization of "heart" in philosophy and medicine. The study sheds much light on why the Chinese word *xin* 'heart' differs from the English word *heart* the way it does. In ancient Chinese philosophy, the heart is taken as the thinking and reasoning organ, and the "ruler" of the body. In traditional Chinese medicine, similarly, the heart is seen as the "ruler" of the body and the "grand master" of the internal organs, due to its perceived mental power. The metaphorical understanding of the heart, manifested linguistically in the Chinese language, is thus a cultural phenomenon, an instance of "cultural cognition" (Sharifian 2003: 188).

As language is embedded in culture (Palmer and Sharifian 2007), cultural context is the "physical environment" in which language acquisition takes place. However, first language acquisition and second language acquisition are very different. First language acquisition is "traveling by day", whereas second language acquisition is "traveling by night". That is, second language learners have to "feel their way in the dark". Introducing the cultural context to second language learners is to "set up street lights and road signs" for them so that they can "see" where they are going and "go faster".

References

Achard, M. and Niemeier, S. (eds.). 2004. *Cognitive Linguistics, Second Language Acquisition, and Foreign Language Teaching*. Berlin: Mouton de Gruyter.

Barcelona, A. 2001. "On the systematic contrastive analysis of conceptual metaphors: Case studies and proposed methodology". In *Applied Cognitive Linguistics II: Language Pedagogy*, M. Pütz, S. Niemeier and R. Dirven (eds.), 117–146. Berlin: Mouton de Gruyter.

Boers, F. 2000. "Metaphor awareness and vocabulary retention". *Applied Linguistics* 21: 553–571.

Boers, F. 2003. "Applied linguistics perspectives on cross-cultural variation in conceptual metaphor". *Metaphor and Symbol* 18: 231–238.

Boers, F. 2004. "Expanding learners' vocabulary through metaphor awareness: What expansion, what learners, what vocabulary?". In *Cognitive Linguistics, Second Language Acquisition, and Foreign Language Teaching*, M. Achard and S. Niemeier (eds.), 211–232. Berlin: Mouton de Gruyter.

Boers, F. and Littlemore, J. (eds.). 2003. Special issue on "Cross-cultural differences in conceptual metaphor: Applied linguistics perspectives". *Metaphor and Symbol* 18.

Cameron, L. and Low, G. 1999. *Researching and Applying Metaphor*. Cambridge: Cambridge University Press.

Chan, A.K.L. (ed.). 2002a. *Mencius: Contexts and Interpretations*. Honolulu, HI: University of Hawaii Press.

Chan, A.K.L. 2002b. "A matter of taste *qi* (vital energy) and the tending of the heart (*xin*) in Mencius 2A2". In *Mencius: Contexts and Interpretations*, A.K.L. Chan (ed.), 42–71. Honolulu, HI: University of Hawaii Press.

Charteris-Black, J. 2002. "Second language figurative proficiency: A comparative study of Malay and English". *Applied Linguistics* 23: 104–133.

Charteris-Black, J. 2003. "Speaking with forked tongue: A comparative study of metaphor and metonymy in English and Malay phraseology". *Metaphor and Symbol* 18: 289–310.

Csábi, S. 2004. "A cognitive linguistic view of polysemy in English and its implications for teaching". In *Cognitive Linguistics, Second Language Acquisition, and Foreign Language Teaching*, M. Achard and S. Niemeier (eds.), 233–256. Berlin: Mouton de Gruyter.

Danesi, M. 1993. "Metaphorical competence in second language acquisition and second language teaching: The neglected dimension". In *Language, Communication and Social Meaning*, J.E. Alatis (ed.), 489–500. Washington, DC: Georgetown University Press.

Danesi, M. 1995. "Learning and teaching languages: The role of 'conceptual fluency'". *International Journal of Applied Linguistics* 5: 3–20.

Danesi, M. 1999. "Expanding conceptual fluency theory for second language teaching". *Mosaic* 6(4): 16–21.

Danesi, M. and Mollica, A. 1998. "Conceptual fluency theory for second language teaching". *Mosaic* 5(2): 3–12.

DeCunha, D.S. 1993. Metaphor Comprehension and Second Language Acquisition. Ph.D. Dissertation. University of Toronto.

Deignan, A. 2003. "Metaphorical expressions and culture: An indirect link". *Metaphor and Symbol* 18: 255–271.

Dirven, R. 1985. "Metaphor and polysemy". In *La Polysémie: Exicographie et Cognition*, R. Jongen (ed.), 9–27. Louvain la Neuve: Cabay.

Feng, M. 1997. Metaphorical Thinking across Languages and Cultures: Its Implications for ESL/EFL Writing. Ph.D. Dissertation. State University of New York at Buffalo.

Gibbs, R.W. 1994. *The Poetics of Mind: Figurative Thought, Language, and Understanding*. Cambridge: Cambridge University Press.

Gibbs, R.W. 1999. "Taking metaphor out of our heads and putting it into the cultural world". In *Metaphor in Cognitive Linguistics*, R.W. Gibbs and G.J. Steen (eds.), 145–166. Amsterdam: John Benjamins.

Hansen, C. 1992. *A Daoist Theory of Chinese Thought: A Philosophical Interpretation*. Oxford: Oxford University Press.

Johnson, J. and Rosano, T. 1993. "Relation of cognitive style to metaphor interpretation and second language proficiency". *Applied Psycholinguistics* 14: 159–175.

Kövecses, Z. 2001. "A cognitive linguistic view of learning idioms in an FLT context". In *Applied Cognitive Linguistics II: Language Pedagogy*, M. Pütz, S. Niemeier and R. Dirven (eds.), 87–115. Berlin: Mouton de Gruyter.

Kövecses, Z. 2003. "Language, figurative thought, and cross-cultural comparison". *Metaphor and Symbol* 18: 311–320.

Lakoff, G. and Johnson, M. 1980. *Metaphors We Live By*. Chicago: University of Chicago Press.

Lakoff, G. and Johnson, M. 1999. *Philosophy in the Flesh: The Embodied Mind and Its Challenge to Western Thought*. New York: Basic Books.

Larre, C. and de la Vallée, E.R. 1991. *The Heart in Ling Shu Chapter 8*. Cambridge, UK: Monkey Press.

Larre, C. and de la Vallée, E.R. 1992. *Heart Master Triple Heater*. Cambridge, UK: Monkey Press.

Larre, C. and de la Vallée, E.R. 1995. *Rooted in Spirit: The Heart of Chinese Medicine*. New York: Station Hill Press.

Larre, C. and de la Vallée, E.R. 1996. *The Seven Emotions: Psychology and Health in Ancient China*. Cambridge, UK: Monkey Press.

Littlemore, J. 2001. "Metaphoric competence: A language learning strength of students with a holistic cognitive style?". *TESOL Quarterly* 35: 459–491.

Littlemore, J. 2003. "The effect of cultural background on metaphor interpretation". *Metaphor and Symbol* 18: 273–288.

Low, G. 2003. "Validating metaphoric models in applied linguistics". *Metaphor and Symbol* 18: 239–254.

Lü, S. and Ding, S. (eds.). 1996. *Xiandai Hanyu Cidian* [Modern Chinese Dictionary] (revised ed.). Beijing: The Commercial Press.

Palmer, G. 1996. *Toward a Theory of Cultural Linguistics*. Austin, TX: University of Texas Press.

Palmer, G.B. and Sharifian, F. 2007. "Applied cultural linguistics: An emerging paradigm". In *Applied Cultural Linguistics: Implications for Second Language Learning and Intercultural Communication*, F. Sharifian and G.B. Palmer (eds.), 1–14. Amsterdam: John Benjamins.

Ponterotto, D. 1994. "Metaphors we can learn by: How insights from cognitive linguistic research can improve the teaching/learning of figurative language". *Forum* 32(3): 2–7.

Pütz, M., Niemerier, S. and Dirven, R. 2001a. *Applied Cognitive Linguistics I: Theory and Language Acquisition*. Berlin: Mouton de Gruyter.

Pütz, M., Niemerier, S. and Dirven, R. 2001b. *Applied Cognitive Linguistics II: Language Pedagogy*. Berlin: Mouton de Gruyter.

Sharifian, F. 2002. Conceptual-Associative System in Aboriginal English: A Study of Aboriginal Children Attending Primary Schools in Metropolitan Perth. Ph.D. Dissertation. Edith Cowan University, Australia.

Sharifian, F. 2003. "On cultural conceptualizations". *Journal of Cognition and Culture* 3: 187–207.

Sharifian, F., Dirven, R., Yu, N. and Niemeier, S. (eds.). 2008. *Culture, Body, and Language: Conceptualizations of Internal Body Organs across Cultures and Languages*. Berlin: Mouton de Gruyter.

Shun, K. 1997. *Mencius and Early Chinese Thought*. Stanford, CA: Stanford University Press.

Slingerland, E. 2003. *Effortless Action: Wu-wei as Conceptual Metaphor and Spiritual Ideal in Early China*. Oxford: Oxford University Press.

Wang, Q., Luo, X., Li, Y. and Liu, Y. 1997. *Zhongyi Zangxiang Xue* [Theory of Internal Organs in Chinese Medicine]. Beijing: People's Health Press.

Wei, D. (ed.). 1995. *Han Ying Cidian* [A Chinese-English Dictionary] (revised ed.). Beijing: Foreign Language Teaching and Research Press.

Wierzbicka, A. 1992. *Semantics, Culture, and Cognition: Universal Human Concepts in Culture-Specific Configuration*. Oxford: Oxford University Press.

Wiseman, N. and Feng, Y. 1998. *A Practical Dictionary of Chinese Medicine* (2nd ed.). Brookline, MA: Paradigm Publications.

Yearley, L.H. 1990. *Mencius and Aquinas: Theories of Virtue and Conceptions of Courage*. Albany, NY: State University of New York Press.

Yu, N. 1995. "Metaphorical expressions of anger and happiness in English and Chinese". *Metaphor and Symbolic Activity* 10: 59–92.

Yu, N. 2000. "Figurative uses of *finger* and *palm* in Chinese and English". *Metaphor and Symbol* 15: 159–175.

Yu, N. 2002. "Body and emotion: Body parts in Chinese expression of emotion". In the special issue on "The Body in Description of Emotion: Cross-linguistic Studies", N.J. Enfield and A. Wierzbicka (eds.). *Pragmatics and Cognition* 10: 333–358.

Yu, N. 2003a. "Metaphor, body, and culture: The Chinese understanding of *gallbladder* and *courage*". *Metaphor and Symbol* 18: 13–31.

Yu, N. 2003b. "Chinese metaphors of thinking". In the special issue on "Talking about Thinking across Languages", G.B. Palmer, C. Goddard and P. Lee (eds.). *Cognitive Linguistics* 14: 141–165.

Yu, N. 2004. "The eyes for sight and mind". *Journal of Pragmatics* 36: 663–686.

Index